MW01130454

Magic Bean

CultureAmerica

Erika Doss

Philip J. Deloria

Series Editors

Karal Ann Marling

Editor Emerita

MAGIC BEAN
THE RISE OF SOY IN AMERICA

MATTHEW ROTH

UNIVERSITY PRESS OF KANSAS

Published by the University Press of Kansas (Lawrence, Kansas 66045), which was
organized by the Kansas Board of Regents and is operated and funded by Emporia
State University, Fort Hays State University, Kansas State University, Pittsburg
State University, the University of Kansas, and Wichita State University.

Library of Congress Cataloging-in-Publication Data

Names: Roth, Matthew (Matthew David), 1970– author.
Title: Magic bean : the rise of soy in America / Matthew Roth.
Description: Lawrence, Kansas : University Press of Kansas, [2018] | Series:
CultureAmerica | Includes bibliographical references and index.
Identifiers: LCCN 2018004671 | ISBN 9780700626335 (cloth : alk. paper) |
ISBN 9780700626342 (pbk. : alk. paper) | ISBN 9780700626359 (ebook)
Subjects: LCSH: Soybean—United States—History—20th century.
| Soyfoods—United States—History—20th century.
Classification: LCC SB205.S7 R68 2018 | DDC 633.3/40973—dc23.
LC record available at https://lccn.loc.gov/2018004671.

British Library Cataloguing-in-Publication Data is available.

Printed in the United States of America

10 9 8 7 6 5 4 3 2 1

The paper used in this publication is recycled and contains 30 percent
postconsumer waste. It is acid free and meets the minimum requirements of
the American National Standard for Permanence of Paper for Printed Library
Materials Z39.48-1992.

Contents

Illustrations

Acknowledgments

This project began many years ago with a conversation on a New York subway car with my friend and fellow Rutgers graduate student Eric Barry about when—historically speaking—tofu became a thing in the United States. As a vegetarian of twenty years at that point, and as somebody who had actually assisted in making tofu at an honest-to-god commune, I had only the vaguest of ideas. Neither did I know how the trajectory of tofu related to fake-meat products like textured vegetable protein, or TVP, which I had seen advertised years earlier in *Vegetarian Times*; or how these vegetarian incarnations of the soybean related to its other role in American life as a farm commodity that sustained our system of factory farming. How exactly had the soybean jumped the Pacific to lead such a strange double life?

Beginning in profound ignorance, I imagined that soybean history itself was not a thing, and that I was heading into terra incognita. This could not have been farther from the truth. I learned soon enough that many who worked with soybeans as a crop, or as an object of scientific investigation, developed a profound interest in their history. This includes William Morse, the USDA agronomist who shepherded the crop during its early years and whose 1923 *The Soybean* (with his boss, Charles Piper) remains an indispensable starting point. It includes genetic scientist Theodore Hymowitz, who has also carried out amazing archival research on the soybean's pre-twentieth-century presence in America. And it certainly includes William Shurtleff and Akiko Aoyagi, whose *The Book of Tofu* was a seminal hit in the 1970s. Since then, they have amassed an unparalleled archive on the soybean's history at the Soyinfo Center in Lafayette, California, much of which is freely available online at www.soyinfocenter.com. I owe an enormous debt to all of these historical investigations and am personally grateful for Shurtleff's generosity and support.

Research would of course be impossible without archives and academic libraries, and I would like to express my gratitude to the many dedicated staff members of the Rutgers University Library system, the National Agricultural Library in Beltsville, Maryland, and at a number of key archives: the Archives of the Chicago Board of Trade, Daley Library Special Collections, University of Illinois at Chicago; the National Agricultural Library Special Collections Department, which holds the records of the Dorsett-Morse Expedition; the Cornell University, Division of Rare and Manuscript Collections, where the Clive McCay Papers reside; the Department of Archives and Special Collections, Del E. Webb Memorial Library, Loma Linda University, which provided the manuscript autobiography of Harry Miller; the Bancroft Library, the University of California at Berkeley; the University of Illinois Archives; the New York Public Library Research Collections, which holds the papers of Dwayne Andreas's biographer; and the National Archives I and II, which hold records of Japanese American internment and the USDA Office of Forage-Crop Investigations, respectively. In addition, I would feel remiss not to acknowledge the people, whoever they are, who have scanned thousands of documents and newspapers into numerous online databases.

They say that a journey of a thousand miles begins with a single step, in this case that subway conversation so long ago. Sadly, it can feel that some journeys of a thousand miles do not truly count until the last step is taken over the finish line. A doctoral dissertation in history and the writing and completion of a book manuscript are two such journeys. I would not have gotten to the end of either without institutional support and the boundless patience of advisers, friends, and family. I am grateful to the Andrew W. Mellon Foundation for a Summer Small Grant and the honor of a Dissertation Completion Fellowship; the Rutgers Center for Historical Analysis and the Rutgers Center for Cultural Analysis for graduate fellowships; and the American Society for Environmental History, the Agricultural History Society, and the University of California at Berkeley for the opportunity to present chapters in progress to critical audiences. I am deeply grateful to my dissertation adviser, Jackson Lears, and my committee, which included Ann Fabian, Keith Wailoo, and Steven Stoll. My minor at Rutgers, in the History of Science, Technology, Environment, and Health, where I was ably advised by Paul Israel, has proven critical to this project. My editors at the University Press of Kansas have been remarkably understanding when it comes to deadlines. Finally, I cannot hope to adequately express my deep gratitude to my wife, Stephanie, for her love and support.

INTRODUCTION:
DESTINED TO SUCCEED?

Nobody actually knows how much American land in total was planted in soybeans in 1900, because nobody at the time was keeping track, but it was likely near zero. The earliest year for which there is any guess is 1907, when the area may have been around 50,000 acres, grown mostly for hay, scattered among the 300 million acres of American farmland, as compared to 45 million acres of wheat and 35 million acres of oats.[1] The US Census of Agriculture of 1909 was the first to list soybeans harvested for beans, documenting a total of 1,629 acres on 339 farms, most of them in North Carolina, which by then was supplying seeds for soybean hay to more northerly states where the cold winters forestalled the production of mature seeds.[2] In 2000, by contrast, soybeans were planted on upwards of 70 million acres, an area second only to that devoted to corn and which, in aggregate, was slightly larger than the state of New Mexico.[3] These acres produced 3 billion bushels of beans worth $12 billion to the farmers who grew them. Exports of soybeans and their two major derived products—oil and meal—brought in $7 billion, making them by far the nation's largest agricultural export. In a rare bit of good news for the US trade balance, much of this went to China, which in 1900 was the leading producer of soybeans, but which now came in fourth place. The United States, meanwhile, was now the world's leading producer of the crop, producing almost double that of the runner-up, Brazil.[4]

All told, the rise of the soybean was one of the most remarkable success stories of twentieth-century American agriculture, and, as with all success stories, the question arises: Was it destined to be or simply the result of some lucky breaks?

If destiny, it was a case of destiny much delayed. With the advent of regular ocean travel among all of the world's continents in the sixteenth century, explorers and those who followed them succeeded in "knitting together the seams of Pangaea," to use the environmental historian Alfred Crosby's evocative phrase. It would be centuries more before steam shipping, and then efficient diesel engines, would enable a truly global marketplace for even the bulkiest of goods, but the Age of Sail was quite effective at dispersing living things around the globe. Crop plants traveled inconspicuously as seeds or cuttings and then took root in foreign lands. Sugar and coffee made their way to the Americas and, as commodities shipped back across the ocean, bolstered empires and provided fuel for the Enlightenment and Industrial Revolution. Corn and potatoes appeared quietly in private gardens in Europe, then gradually spread as highly productive food sources for peasant farmers.[5] Hot peppers traveled to India, soon becoming an indispensable element of the native cuisine. Rice traveled to South Carolina from Africa, and the expertise to cultivate it arrived with African slaves.[6] Meanwhile, European wheat colonized the middle colonies of British America. Amid all of this global interchange, however, the soybean remained largely sequestered in Asia, despite the fact that soybeans could provide a bounty comparable to that of sugar or potatoes.

Its nearest wild ancestor, *Glycine ussuriensis*, native to the wet lowlands of northern and northeastern China, is a twining annual that grows among reeds at the edges of rivers and lakes. It is unprepossessing—with small trifoliate leaves, purple flowers, and seeds that are small and hard—and said to have no commercial use.[7] Its chief virtue, from the standpoint of agricultural potential, is that it is a legume, with nodules on its roots providing a nursery for symbiotic bacteria, which in return serve to "fix" nitrogen from the air in a chemical form readily assimilated by plants. Simply having legumes live and die on a farm field improves its fertility. Probably first domesticated successfully around the eleventh century B.C., with a logograph that honored its root nodules, the soybean provided a service to Chinese agriculture beyond soil fertility. Legumes, having fixed nitrogen, are able to channel it into an abundance of protein, filling a gap in diets lacking in milk or meat.[8] As researchers from the US Department of Agriculture (USDA) noted in

1917, soybeans could produce 294 pounds of usable protein per acre, more than twice the yield of peanuts (at 126 pounds).[9] Roughly fifty years later, the estimate would be revised upward to 376 kilograms per hectare (or 331 pounds per acre).[10] As William Shurtleff and Akiko Aoyagi would emphasize in their popular 1975 publication *Book of Tofu*, this was "twenty times as much usable protein as could be raised on an acre given over to grazing beef cattle."[11] And this is in addition to the substantial amount of vegetable oil soybeans also provide.

Part of the explanation for the delay in adoption is geographical. The latitudes of the soybean's heartlands in northern China and Manchuria, roughly 35 to 45 degrees north, are dominated in Europe by arid regions and the waters of the Mediterranean Sea. When the Hungarian botanist Friedrich Haberlandt encountered soybeans in the Asian exhibits of the 1873 Vienna Exposition, he began planting them experimentally throughout Central Europe, recognizing their value as a food for humans and livestock. His work inspired enthusiasm for the soybean in Europe, notably in Germany, which became a leader well into the twentieth century of technology to process the beans and make use of a wide array of derivatives. Yet, being too far north, Germany never succeeded in growing the crop to any great extent. It is not until, traveling west, one reaches North America that there are flat, well-watered plains at the right latitudes, stretching across half a continent. In retrospect, it is clear that this is where soybeans were destined to thrive—but not until the 1840s at the very earliest, when farmers were finally able to break the sod of the Midwest with John Deere's steel plow. Even then, however, the delay persisted.

This was in part a problem of infrastructure. There were in fact soybeans trickling into America, even before it was the United States. The earliest case was in 1765, when a former East India Company sailor, Samuel Bowen, planted what he called "pease or vetch" in Savannah, Georgia, and for a time successfully exported soy sauce to London.[12] In 1770, Benjamin Franklin sent "Chinese caravances" from London to his botanical contact in Philadelphia, John Bartram, noting "the universal use" in China "of a cheese made from them."[13] In 1851, the Illinois physician Benjamin Franklin Edwards (no relation to the founding father) improbably obtained "Japan peas" in San Francisco from Japanese castaways and passed them on to a member of the Illinois Horticultural Society who planted them in his garden. The resulting harvest in turn reached horticultural societies in Ohio, Massachusetts, and New York, as well as the US Commissioner of Patents, who was responsible for distributing new and promising seeds to farmers. By 1854, Japan peas had been sent to dozens of farmers throughout the United States and Canada, with the rural press acknowledging their potential value as chicken or hog feed.[14] In 1854, Commodore Matthew Perry's expedition sent further samples of Japan peas to the Patents office.[15]

Eventually, the establishment of land grant colleges and agricultural experiment stations following the Civil War would put importing soybean varieties—or "cultivars"—on a more systematic basis than the uncoordinated efforts of missionaries, sea captains, and diplomats. In 1879, two researchers at Rutgers College in New Jersey obtained Haberlandt beans while visiting Munich and Vienna.[16] In 1882, the North Carolina state chemist C. W. Dabney reported that soybeans had been planted by "a number of persons in different sections of the State," although the origins of the beans are unclear; local legend would later credit sea captains returning from Asia.[17] By the 1890s, experiment stations in both Massachusetts and Kansas were importing beans directly from Japan.[18] But to gather cultivars in sufficient quantity and diversity to establish the soybean as a viable American crop ended up requiring a program at the federal level, described in chapters 1 and 3 as the "soybean pipeline." This began with expeditions to Asia sponsored by the USDA's Office of Seed and Plant Introduction (SPI), created in 1898; extended through the agency's Office of Forage-Crop Investigations, which sorted and distributed the varieties; and reached American farmers through the networks of extension agents and farm groups that burgeoned in the 1910s. This pipeline, carrying plant species from foreign lands to American farms, was not created with the soybean in mind specifically, of course, but it turned out to be one of its more consequential achievements. The fact that the soybean should take advantage of the apparatus so quickly, gaining traction in the Corn Belt by the end of the 1910s, strengthens the case that its success was a matter of destiny.

The case for contingency, in contrast, begins with the recognition of what was perhaps a deeper impediment to the soybean's spread than uncongenial geography or inadequate infrastructure. After all, other crops had flowed through informal channels and adapted to new climates. The problem, rather, was cultural: the soybean was not easily adapted to Western tastes. Its chief virtue—its bounty of protein—was accessed in Asia through a variety of traditional soy foods: *tofu, tempeh, natto,* and *miso.* Of such foods, only *shoyu,* or soy sauce, was a truly global commodity. It is not a coincidence that the first attempt to grow soybeans in America revolved around soy sauce or that, in the West, the sauce lent its name to the bean, not the other way around. Inroads by other traditional soy foods began before the turn of the twentieth century, carried by Asian immigrants, as described in chapter 1. With the Chinese Exclusion Act and other restrictions placed on Asian settlement, however, this remained a limited incursion. The other chief vector for soy foods was the work of Seventh-day Adventists, as well as other vegetarian, health, and "hygiene" groups. Throughout the early decades of the twentieth century, these groups not only offered and promoted traditional soy foods but also endlessly tinkered and innovated to create alternatives to meat and milk geared to a broader American audience. All told, however, this long remained a niche market sustained by religious conviction and its near relative, the enthusiasm of dietary converts.

Government promotion of soybean consumption also predated the beginning of the twentieth century. Charles Langworthy, the author of "Soy Beans as Food for Man," an appendix to an 1899 USDA bulletin, pointed that the "deficiency of protein" in rice-heavy Asian diets "is made up by the consumption of large quantities of . . . soy-bean products."[19] Although his article was reprinted in health-movement periodicals such as *The Hygienic Gazette,* Langworthy was not a vegetarian. He and his boss, Wilbur Atwater, in fact frequently sparred with vegetarians over minimum protein requirements, which they estimated to be 125 grams per day for a moderately active man.[20] (Rival researchers ultimately argued them down to a slightly more reasonable 70–100 grams per day.) Langworthy, a member of the founding generation of academic home economists, felt that the source of that protein allotment should be the most cost-effective possible, especially for the working classes. That meant cheaper cuts of meat and more beans. Ultimately, Langworthy did not attempt to adapt traditional soy foods. Rather, as chief of the USDA Office of Home Economics during World War I, he helped discover varieties that could be incorporated more easily into American-style bean dishes and casseroles. He also promoted soybean flour, at that time produced on a small scale for diabetics on low-carbohydrate diets, as an ingredient in mock meatloaves.[21] Home economics departments became a redoubt for this sort of soy recipe, which wartime emergencies brought to the fore. With soybeans a more widespread crop during World War II, it saw an even greater enthusiasm for soy as a substitute for meat.

Even in the midst of national emergencies, however, such attempts provoked resistance, often in the form of mockery. Surveying the Patriotic Food Show in Chicago during World War I, no less a humorist than Ring Lardner singled out soy for ridicule, with the wits at *New Yorker* magazine penning similar pieces during World War II. In both cases, the attacks on soy were mingled with disdain for the society women that the authors associated with soybean promotion—and dietary reform more generally. Indeed, in her 1945 book *The Useful Soybean*, Mildred Lager highlighted the "rebelling male" as an impediment to greater adoption of soy foods. And in fact, enthusiasm for soy foods faded rapidly after the war's conclusion. Even as a later generation began to embrace vegetarianism, films such as *Soylent Green* (1975) signaled the subconscious association of soy with a degraded standard of living. Later still, as soy foods spread in the 1990s, *The Simpsons* carried on the tradition of mockery, with vegan writers no less, as it imagined a near-future when family scold Lisa could buy Soy Pops ("Now with gag suppressant!") from a vending machine. Americans did not knowingly accommodate their food habits to soy products until late in the century, in any case. The most obvious route for soybeans onto American farmland, as a direct source of protein for human consumption, was largely foreclosed.

This is where the soybean's versatility proved to be a great advantage. Asian peoples had developed a wide array of products from soy over the centuries. Manchuria was long a center of an industry that pressed the oil out, mainly for nonfood uses such as lighting or producing paints and varnishes. The Chinese milled soy flour for bread. Europeans, as they gained interest in soy, found further uses—as a coffee substitute, for instance. These are nicely summarized by the USDA soybean expert William Morse in a diagram he included in a 1918 bulletin. With so many potential uses, there were many possible paths for the soybean to take until, through trial and error, it found its way to success. But far from being a matter of destiny, this process was shot through with contingencies, both long-term and short-term.

The long-term contingencies involve the centuries-long evolution of capitalist agriculture, beginning with the enclosure movement in England, which culminated in the Inclosure Acts of Parliament in the eighteenth and nineteenth centuries that ended the open field system of the Middle Ages and inaugurated a more intensive system of agriculture. In the open field system, livestock grazed on common pastureland, while encouraged to leave their manure on fallowed fields, in essence restoring the fertility of cropland by concentrating the nutrients of a much wider area. When fields were consolidated and enclosed, the fallow period was eliminated in favor of a rotation of fodder crops, often legumes such as clover or vetch, which added fertility to the soil either by their own right or by way of animal manure.[22] Americans were notoriously careless with their bounty of land, with a tendency to wear out the fertility of a parcel and then move farther west. In the American South, land was often treated more as a means to realize the value of investment in human slaves than the other way around.

By the early nineteenth century, however, there were movements of agricultural improvement afoot, built as before around the twin pillars of legumes and livestock manure, with added attention to liming and other methods of soil enhancement.[23] Agricultural societies and journals proliferated, and the period around 1820 saw the beginnings of a veritable revolution in farm equipment.[24] Farms in the Northeast, increasingly oriented toward providing nearby cities with produce and milk, and in the large wheat-producing regions in the American West, supplying the world market through commercial channels greased by a canal-building spree, alike adopted a more commercial orientation. It was the subsequent search for highly productive fodder legumes that led agricultural experiment stations to test soybeans in the late nineteenth century and the USDA's Office of Forage-Crop Investigations to work with soybeans at the beginning of the twentieth. There is abundant protein in the leaves and stems of soybean plants, as well as in the seeds, and it is as hay that it initially spread in many areas of the country. More generally, however, it was the desire for more profitable crops, and for government assistance in finding them, that helped create the soybean pipeline in the first place.

Short-term contingencies that aided the soybean's rise include many of the major events of the twentieth century, as indicated by figure 0.1, which charts how acreage for soybeans grown for beans—rather than hay—increased over the course of the century. Before 1924, estimates are largely guesses, but the rise was substantial. The increase was due largely to the boll weevil infestation spreading through the South, which roiled the region's

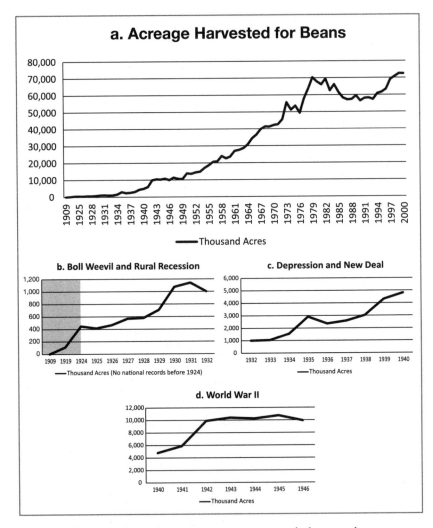

Figure o.i. Soybean acreage in America, 1909–2000, with three graphs highlighting key moments of growth. Source: Historical Statistics of the United States: Millennial Edition Online.

population and helped spark an African American migration north, as well as largely unsuccessful attempts to dislodge the South's cotton monoculture with alternative crops (see chapter 2). The real significance of World War I, soy-wise, was its aftermath: a rural crisis in the North to match that in the South, as wartime demand for wheat and corn collapsed, prompting several cycles of enthusiasm for the soybean, first as hay and then as an oilseed.

The soy processing industry, which "crushed" out the oil and fed the residual high-protein meal to livestock, got under way in the Midwest: the big jump from 1929 to 1930 represents the shift from growing seed for hay to growing beans for oil (chapter 3). This was the Roaring Twenties, so there was capital for such things.

That is, there was enough capital until the rest of the country caught up with the farm economy during the onset of the Great Depression, the depths of which is indicated by the dip into 1932. Then came President Franklin Roosevelt and the New Deal, ushering in a renewed expansion of soybeans as government policies restricted the planting of crops in oversupply. Though partly weather-related, the small peak in 1935 neatly divides the first New Deal from the second, when the government lost some power to restrict the use of farm acreage but during which protectionist measures against foreign edible oils was a big boost to soybeans and their processing (chapter 4). A steady rise into the 1940s turns into a sudden jump that marks America's entry into World War II and the mobilization of the soybean industry to provide protein for livestock to ramp up meat production for hungry troops (chapter 5). The technological advances and social transformations of the war would lead to a long postwar boom, reflected in an increase of soybean acreage dwarfing all previous advances (chapters 6 and 7).

This would hit the skids with the OPEC oil shock and subsequent stagflation of the 1970s, discernible on the graph. In the case of soybeans, however, globalization would create a strong export market to lift the crop through the rest of the decade until debt crises—both foreign and, particularly on family farms, domestic—would spell a difficult period in the 1980s for soybeans and for American agriculture more generally. Globalization would mean the rise of Brazil and Argentina as soybean exporters, squeezing the American crop even further. However, globalization also meant the rise of China as an industrial giant. China would more than make up for the increased competition with its strong hunger for soybeans, something reflected in the increasing acreage after 1992—and especially after 1996, when new farm legislation encouraged farmers to plant crops in high demand on world markets (chapter 9). The strength of China in the evolving world economy was a major factor in the American soybean's fate at the end of the twentieth century, much as China's weakness was a factor in the influx of new soybean varieties at the beginning of that century.

In the midst of these events, it is at first difficult to discern the crucial inflection point when the fate of the soybean shifted from being a matter of chance to something resembling destiny. Its initial forays largely stalled. It did not displace cotton in the South—although the notion that it might helped keep interest in the crop alive at the USDA during the crucial decade of the 1910s. In the Corn Belt, its initial boom as a hay to be "hogged down" in the field petered out by the early 1920s. The first attempts to start a processing industry—"crushing" soybeans into oil and protein-rich residual meal—likewise fizzled by the mid-1920s. What these developments held in common was a low-investment, easy-return strategy on the part of soybean adopters that squeezed a little more revenue out of existing assets, whether it was southern cottonseed mills hoping to make use of their equipment's downtime or Corn Belt farmers hoping to add a few more pounds to their hogs. The key moment came when a number of large enterprises—cornstarch manufacturers and seed merchants, as it happened—committed instead to incubating a soybean industry despite years of early losses. This kickstarted a virtuous cycle of investment, which gained momentum in both the private and public realms, with the University of Illinois conducting rigorous tests to improve the performance of soybean oil in paint and the USDA sending its first and only "soybean expedition" to Asia to find new varieties.

This is the moment that soybeans went from chancy—as likely as not to disappear from the scene in the face of competition from other legumes or oilseeds—to established. By the mid-1930s, the soybean was secure enough as a commodity to be traded on the futures market in Chicago. During World War II, it provided the quickest way to increase the protein available for animal feed, and additional investments in research and processing capacity put it on the path of its meteoric postwar rise. It went from established to entrenched, with the "soybean industry" emerging as an identifiable player both in the economy and in politics. The soybean gained momentum as a commodity not simply in terms of sunk costs, however, but as the result of a reinforcing loop of volume and value. This process is nicely illustrated by a midcentury graphic in *Fortune* magazine (figure 0.2) that accompanied a story on the Glidden Company, which at that time was active in processing soybeans (see chapter 6). The image is that of a delta, a river of soybeans dividing into smaller streams of by-products: crude oil and soy meal to begin

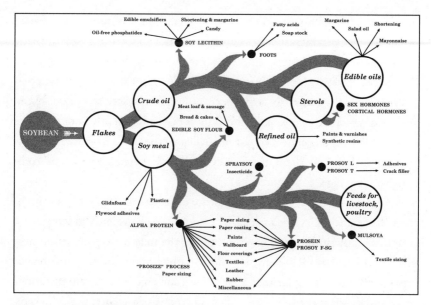

Figure 0.2. Glidden's fractionation of the soybean. From "The House That Joyce Built," *Fortune*, May 1949. Credit: Kurt Weihs.

with, which in turn split into more specialized substances. These include, on the far right of the diagram, sterols used as precursors for synthetic human hormones. The greater the volume, the greater the ability to fractionate soybeans into specialized substances: to derive one pound of synthetic progesterone from those sterols required an estimated 15,000 pounds of beans.

Especially if one imagines the origin point, labeled "Soybean," as having branched off from the soybean plant as a whole, one can scan the graphic from left to right—or at least its general form, if not all of the specific products—as the chronological tale of the soybean in twentieth-century America. At the outset, farmers mainly used the plants as a whole, plowing them under as fertilizer—taking advantage of one of the plant's three main attractions, the fixed nitrogen—or using them as fodder for animals. If the animals foraged in the fields, they returned the nitrogen in the form of manure while enjoying the second attraction, protein. By the 1930s, with the advent of combine harvesters and the growth of the soybean processing industry, the beans were neatly separated from the rest of the plant, which was left on fields as nitrogen-rich residue. At first, the oil and protein derived from the beans was crude, with the former used mainly for soap, but as time went on they were split into a greater number of specialized fractions, many of which began as waste products. By the century's end, not all soybeans had synthetic hormones as an endpoint—although some did—but there were other small derivatives to recover: tocopherols for vitamin E, for instance, or omega-3 fatty acids. As the volume of soybeans rose, even tiny fractions became cheap enough to compete against similar products derived from other sources. The more value that was squeezed out of soybeans, the more worthwhile it was to plant and process them. It was a cycle that ratcheted up soybeans' competitive advantage.

By the 1960s, the soybean was a fixture of American life, but in a way entirely distinct from its role in Asia. The bounty of its protein did not sustain people directly; it did so indirectly through the massive expansion of meat production. It was a key element—along with cheap grain, scientific breeding, and the use of antibiotics to spur growth and enable large concentrations of livestock—in systems of factory farming that emerged first with chickens, in broiler production, but that soon spread to hog farming and cattle raising. As Shurtleff and Aoyagi would lament, this entailed dumping possibly as much as 90 percent of the soy protein grown in the country into "the process of animal metabolism."[25] This explains in part how little noticed soybeans were as they went about their business. In past eras, when a large proportion of Americans were tied to farming, we might imagine that a newly adopted crop would appear simultaneously on the land, on people's plates, and in their awareness. By the 1960s, with an elongating food chain between farm and fork, this was no longer true. The soybean had insinuated itself thoroughly into the American diet, but either indirectly in the form of a growing meat supply, generically in the form of salad oil, or unobtrusively in the form of ingredients in processed food such as soy lecithin. It is true that farmers, at least in the Midwest and increasingly in the South, were well aware of soybeans, but they were now a small and shrinking part of the population.

By the end of the 1960s, however, the hippie counterculture took hold of soybeans and, in the process of trying to wrest them free from capitalist meat production, made them more visible (chapter 8). At the same time, their efforts would have been impossible without soybeans first having become so widespread as animal feed. The hippies who grew their own beans, often using organic methods at variance with the practices of their neighbors, had well-adapted, locally available varieties to choose from, a legacy of the crop development efforts of the USDA and state programs. They also relied on other homegrown legacies: that of Asian American tofu makers and that of Seventh-day Adventist soy-food innovators. Both served niche populations, for whom soy foods came to represent the bonds of community or religious devotion, and thus did not need to rest on broad market appeal. Tofu was a highly resilient feature of the Japanese American diet, for instance, persisting even as restrictions on immigration worked to more thoroughly American-ize younger generations—and making its appearance even during the ordeal of internment. Adventists, for their part, pioneered soy analogs of meat and dairy products in America, stalwartly ignoring any deficiencies in taste or texture. These existing communities would be a resource for soybean utopi-ans, much as they had been for generations of academic soy researchers who visited nearby Chinatowns or corresponded with Adventist institutions.

The 1970s were wild days again for the soybean. They were not a prelude to a postmarket society but rather to a renewed cycle of capital accumula-tion, product diversification, commercial promotion, and overall standard-ization. This time, however, the soybean did not hide behind the scenes but was front and center—or almost was. Through the 1980s, soy products did well to call themselves a variant of tofu rather than something soy. This was notably true of Tofutti, the soy ice cream that honed in on the yuppie ap-peal of Häagen-Dazs and that was taken to task at one point for no longer containing any actual tofu. By the 1990s, when soy gained a reputation in its own right for containing healthful properties, "soy" became more forthright on cartons of milk and wrappers of energy bars. By 2000, by which time it was common for people to order soy lattes at Starbucks, the soybean had completed its century-long transformation from an exotic import to a nor-mal, verging on ubiquitous, presence.

For a narrative historian, there is still something important missing from this extended account of the soybean's rise: the efforts of actual people who in the midst of their work did not consider themselves mere puppets of history or of capitalism. This is a crucial point. Societies, economies, in-novation, the unfolding of history: these are not things that run themselves but are kept in motion and given guidance by millions of separate metaboli-cally fueled imaginations. In fact, none of the transformations of the soybean came easily; it was an often recalcitrant object of improvement, requiring the independently motivated efforts of diverse actors. Their investment in the soybean was other than financial, involving personal career goals or dreams of an improved world. The bulk of the pages to come, in fact, are devoted to the people who, often in idiosyncratic ways, imagined beyond what was realistically achievable and, for the most part, failed to achieve it. The realm of aspiration always exceeds the realm of what comes to pass; after all, if it didn't, it seems unlikely anything would ever come to pass at all.

This book is about the transformation of the soybean by America during the twentieth century, a case study in the ways twentieth-century America went about transforming many features of the natural world. It also charts how these transformational processes themselves changed over time. As much as this had to do with the evolution of economies and technologies, it was also a matter of how people in different decades, beset by different worries and embedded within different cultural moments, variously imagined what changing society could or should look like. Whether it was a vision of gathering useful plants from around the globe to fuel the nation's economic growth; or of modernizing agriculture to supplant the boll weevil–plagued cotton monoculture of the South; or of countering rural decline with creative chemistry to upgrade farm products into valuable industrial inputs; or of transcending the cruelties of capitalism through the artisanal production of high-protein plant foods—in all of these diverse visions, the soybean was able to gain a foothold and, for some of its more ardent advocates, become a lifelong obsession: a magic bean that provided the path to a different world. This was perhaps its best, and in some ways most mysterious, secret of success and the key to its destiny.

CHAPTER ONE

CROSSING OCEANS

When she arrived in Hawaii in 1910, twenty-year-old Tsuru Yamauchi—
formerly Kamigawa—spent three tense days at the Immigration Bureau
waiting for the arrival of a husband she knew only from a photograph. Her
parents had been strict, warning her about boys and keeping her home when
the sun went down, so the prospect of leaving with a man made her tremble
so badly that the two other picture brides waiting at the bureau held on
to her shaking legs and comforted her. It was a relief, however, from the
seasickness of the fifteen-day voyage from Yokohama on the *Mongolia*: she
had been unable to eat rice or even drink tea, and she spent the days sleep-
ing below decks in a swing made of thick cloth. In an interview conducted
seventy years later, she would mention that the sight of a ship still made her
feel weak. When Shokin Yamauchi arrived and took her to the cane fields of
Waipahu, where he worked on a plantation, she felt a different kind of sickness, a desolate homesickness: "You couldn't see anything but cane and some
mountains. I felt lost without my parents and sisters. Here you couldn't see
anything, no view, no landscape, just fields and hills. Ah, such a place. The
sun was already going down. I thought, 'Is Hawaii a place like this?'"[1]

The soybean did not cross oceans on its own but was carried along by
the restless movement of humans. The turn of the twentieth century was
an era of surging globalization, enabled by steam-powered ships and trans-
oceanic communication cables, that pushed people in both directions across
the Pacific. American missionaries ventured in greater numbers to China—
and farther into its interior—as the Qing Dynasty, in a period of reform

following the Boxer Rebellion, loosened its restrictions on foreigners. The US Department of Agriculture, seeking to remain competitive in the trade of global commodities, likewise sent explorers to Asia and elsewhere in search of economically useful plants. Farmers in Japan and Okinawa, meanwhile, hard pressed by the Meiji reforms that modernized the Japanese economy, sought employment in the cane fields of Hawaii and, later, the farmland of California. Each of these groups carried a different incarnation of the soybean. The USDA explorers, and the networks of botanical correspondents they cultivated, sent physical seeds to be bred into an American crop. The missionaries, immersing themselves in Chinese life, brought home knowledge of soy foods and, in the case of vegetarian Adventists, the idea that they might be adapted to American tastes. Asian migrants, finally, obtained beans wherever they traveled in order to sustain their food traditions.

It is unclear whether they planted soybeans in their new homes or imported them to meet their needs, but the migrants to Hawaii managed to make tofu, as Yamauchi would attest in an oral history decades later. In the cane fields, she and her growing family were able to obtain tofu once a week—on lucky weeks twice—delivered on foot from the nearby town of Waipahu.[2] It provided more than physical nourishment, as indicated by the comfort that another familiar food provided her as she sat fearfully awaiting the beginning of her new life. When served a meal at the Immigration Bureau, she was overjoyed that "they have *konbu* (seaweed) in Hawaii, too."[3] In an alien land, food offered a taste of home—a taste that Asian immigrants, with great tenacity, kept alive in Hawaii and the mainland for the rest of the century.

A Taste of Home

Yamauchi had grown up in Okinawa, historically an independent kingdom that had only recently been incorporated as a Japanese prefecture, and Okinawans typically ate even more tofu than their vegetarian neighbors to the north. They also ate more pork, but this was harder to come by for the poorest families.[4] Yamauchi's own family often depended on the charity of neighbors, including a tofu maker who would call them over to "get some of the burned bottom part"—a reference, most likely, to the deep-fried tofu, or *agé*, customarily prepared by the wives of tofu makers—and "even that tasted good when there wasn't any food." Yamauchi learned to make tofu when she was thirteen or fourteen, grinding the beans by hand early in the morning and using it to make a kettleful of the bean curd. She would peddle it on the streets to friends. If the tofu went sour before she sold it, she and her family would eat it themselves.[5]

To make tofu as Yamauchi did as a girl required waking before dawn to grind soaked beans into *gô*, a purée that sluiced into a catch barrel from between heavy, hand-turned granite millstones. To make it more palatable, the *gô* was boiled in a wide-mouthed iron pot over a wood fire while the cook periodically beat down the rising foam with a paddle. She then poured the *gô* into a cloth sack, using one of the fifty-pound millstones and her own body weight to repeatedly press out the soymilk until all that remained inside the sack was a fibrous substance called *okara*.[6] The milk went back into the iron pot—carefully scrubbed beforehand to remove any residual *gô*, the oil of which interfered with curdling—to again be boiled. After she allowed it to cool, she stirred in a curdling agent such as *nigari*, magnesium chloride traditionally collected from the liquid that dripped from sacks of damp sea salt.[7] Clouds of white curds formed, floating in the pale yellow whey. She ladled the curds into a wooden, cloth-lined rectangular pressing box, a foot square by five inches deep, and placed a weight on its lid. Over the course of an hour, the remaining whey would flow through the holes in the bottom and sides of the box.[8] The result, old-fashioned farmhouse tofu, was beige, bore the imprint of the coarse cloth, and was so firm that it could be tied into a package with rice-straw rope.[9]

In practice, the process of making farmhouse tofu was too laborious for every household to do it on a daily basis. In small Japanese villages, specific women would make tofu for the entire community, mainly at festival times. In towns and cities, while girls like Yamauchi might peddle tofu on the street, for the most part it was prepared in small shops by male craftsmen. Likewise, the Japanese who settled in California and the intermountain West purchased their tofu from shops, making it easier in retrospect to trace the spread of tofu throughout the region than if it had been largely a matter of household production. English-language sources are not particularly helpful in this regard. Agricultural experiment station researchers, venturing into Chinatowns, occasionally described shops selling "white cheese" wrapped in

yellow cloth, or dyed yellow using turmeric.[10] One popular magazine unflatteringly portrayed tofu as a "bilious pyramid of yellow-green cakes of bean
cheese" displayed "in the window of almost every Chinese grocer."[11] They
did not mention Japanese tofu, which was generally white and softer than
Chinese tofu, which more closely resembled Japanese farmhouse tofu. City
directories, moreover, rarely listed Japanese tofu shops: a Portland city directory included a tofu business in several editions as early as 1915, listing it variously as a bakery, a restaurant, and a public bath but never as a tofu shop.[12]
It was an industry largely invisible to outsiders.

Japanese-language sources, however, provide evidence that wherever
Japanese immigrants settled tofu soon followed. In 1905, the San Francisco–
based *Japanese American News* (*Nichi Bei Shimbun*) began publishing annual
directories listing Japanese businesses throughout the region, including tofu
makers.[13] The first directory listed six shops, mainly in Los Angeles, San
Francisco, Sacramento, and San Jose, plus the small town of Isleton.[14] This
grew to eight in 1906, including two in Seattle. By 1907, shops appeared in
small towns such as Florin, Visalia, and Watsonville; not to mention Ogden,
Utah; and the Tesla Coal Mine outside of Livermore, in Northern California.
In 1908, the number was fourteen, with four in Los Angeles alone and a shop
appearing in Reno, Nevada. In general, this tracked the course of migration
as it shifted from cities to rural areas. Like their Chinese counterparts, many
early Japanese immigrants came as students or to work in restaurants and
hotels, but near the turn of the century an increasing number were farmers
who came by way of Hawaii and arrived as farmworkers.

This was due to geopolitical events. Even before its annexation by the
United States in 1898, Hawaii had an agreement in place that allowed sugar-
plantation workers to migrate to the American mainland. Before 1894, however, not many did: fewer than 900 out of the 30,000 who had ventured to
Hawaii since 1886 made the trip, mainly with the goal of returning home
after fulfilling three-year labor contracts.[15] After a war with China in 1895,
however, the victorious but cash-strapped Japanese government ceded management of migration to private companies. The *imingaisha* aggressively
recruited on behalf of Hawaiian sugar planters, whose demand for labor
increased dramatically after 1898 as they sought to bring in huge harvests
before their system of indentured servitude, prohibited by the United States
Constitution, was phased out in 1900. More than 150,000 Japanese arrived

between 1894 and 1908.[16] Once in Hawaii, this growing Japanese population was in turn lured by labor recruiters from California, where their skill in growing fruit and vegetables was in high demand, resulting in higher wages and far better working conditions than in the cane fields.[17] As the Hawaiian planters turned next to Okinawans—who were familiar with sugarcane, a major crop on their own island, and who withstood harsh labor practices in order to escape dire poverty[18]—ethnic Japanese settled in the California countryside as hired hands, tenants, and eventually as small landowners. Between 1901 and 1910, there were as many as 130,000 Japanese immigrants; *Nichei Bei Shimbun* put the total population in 1910 at around 100,000.[19]

In 1909, the listings of tofu shops in the *Nichi Bei Shimbun* directories suddenly doubled from fourteen to twenty-nine, with many in rural locales such as Alameda, Armona, Dinuba, Oxnard, Reedley, Santa Barbara, Selma, and Tulare. There are a number of possible explanations for this abrupt jump in the number of shops. There may have been a lag as the Japanese populations of these small towns reached a sufficient size to support tofu shops. Alternately, it may represent a change in the demographic composition of migrants after 1907, when the so-called Gentleman's Agreement between the American and Japanese governments curtailed the emigration of male laborers to Hawaii and the US mainland as part of a deal brokered by President Theodore Roosevelt to prevent the San Francisco School Board from consigning Japanese students to segregated Chinese schools. Wives, children, and parents were permitted to join current residents, however, resulting in an influx of women during the Period of Summoning Families (*Yobiyose Jidai*).[20] The arrival of wives and older Japanese may have raised demand for tofu. The labor of wives may have been crucial, moreover, in making tofu businesses viable; among other tasks, they customarily fried tofu for sale in the afternoon.

Another strong possibility is that the small-town tofu shops opened earlier than 1909 but were overlooked. That year, *Nichi Bei Shimbun* helped the California Bureau of Labor Statistics compile a comprehensive report on the state's Japanese population, as mandated by a California legislature alarmed at the new "yellow peril." Nine special agents of the bureau, all white, traveled to every Japanese community in California with surveys printed in English and Japanese, a high percentage of which were dutifully mailed back.[21] The resulting report, condemned in the press prior to its official release for its praise of the Japanese, was then scuttled entirely by the legislature that had commissioned it.[22] In the meantime, however, *Nichi Bei Shimbun* had gained access to the surveys, which may have aided it in locating tofu makers. Whatever the explanation, both the Gentleman's Agreement and the fate of the labor bureau report highlighted the anti-Asian sentiment that would eventually curtail immigration, although 80,000 Japanese would arrive between 1910 and 1920. It is also possible to imagine that such prejudice blocked tofu's adoption by Anglo Americans, but in truth it was so thoroughly ignored that it did not even figure into the "meat versus rice" mind-set of anti-Asian nativists.

After 1909, *Nichi Bei Shimbun* conducted business censuses of its own. These covered not only California but also a number of neighboring states. Its 1910 census located forty-two tofu makers, although its directory listed only twenty shops. Tofu was now being produced in Colorado, Utah, Idaho, and Wyoming, as well as in Washington State and Oregon.[23] These were modest businesses, typically with sales of between $500 and $1,000 per year, although one producer in Stockton, California, pulled in $4,000, and two in Los Angeles together earned $15,000.[24] Most were owned by men, although the 1913 census listed at least one shop owned solely by a woman.[25] There was a high churn rate. Only about a third of the shops listed over the years appeared in more than one directory, although certain locations were favored, with some addresses appearing in different years under as many as six names. Tofu shops were sometimes adjuncts to other businesses, usually food import companies and, in a number of instances, including the shop in Portland, public baths, presumably because both enterprises used large amounts of hot water.[26] Overall, the number of shops operating each year ranged between forty and fifty.[27]

It is impossible to determine whether homemade tofu, for household use or for sale, coexisted with the small shops listed in directories. In Hawaii, for instance, one of Yamauchi's fellow Okinawans later recounted how she made tofu as one of many means to earn a little extra money: "For fifteen years I made tofu. Every morning I got up at two o'clock to start making it. I also raised pigs. . . . In the afternoon I washed clothes for single men in the camp. I also learned dressmaking and tailoring. . . . I wanted to make enough money to send our children to schools."[28] The first official listing for a tofu shop in the Honolulu City Directory did not come until 1923, after which such businesses provided, in Hawaii as well as California, the bottom rung of the retail ladder, enabling proprietors to eventually move on to other ventures.[29] Yamauchi and her husband, with the assistance of their children, would operate such a shop beginning in July 1940, after years laboring in cane fields, cleaning houses, and working in factories. They would end up making a good living in tofu. One of their sons would venture to California, modernize and expand a tofu manufacturer to make it the largest on the West Coast, and lay claim to inventing the sealed water-filled plastic tubs that would one day become standard packaging.

There is also scant evidence to link the manufacture of soy foods in America at this time with the planting of soybeans. In 1909, *Nichi Bei Shimbun*'s Japanese American Yearbook estimated that the value of the US soybean crop back in 1900 had been $7 million, with the soybean crop of California alone worth over $1 million. The yearbook does not give a source for these figures, which seem higher than other retrospective estimates for how many soybeans were grown in 1900; the USDA did not start tracking the soybean crop until 1923.[30] By this time there was demand for soybeans from California shoyu factories, as well as tofu makers, and it is not unreasonable to imagine that Japanese farmers in America continued the custom of growing soybeans alongside—and often interspersed throughout—their fruit orchards and truck gardens. In Hawaii, for instance, the agricultural experiment station researcher F. G. Krauss reported in 1911 that local production of soy sauce and miso by Japanese immigrants had created "quite a demand" for the bean itself, with 2.5 million pounds imported annually from Asia. He also reported that coffee growers in the Kona district grew 200,000 pounds of soybeans each year planted among the coffee plants, although it is unclear whether these were for soy sauce or for livestock fodder, the use of greatest interest to Krauss.[31] His colleagues in California did not make similar reports, however. As early as 1897, the experiment station botanist Joseph Burtt-Davy recorded, among other interesting plants in the shops of San Francisco's Chinatown, "sprouted seeds of the Soy Bean, Glycine Soja [and] black, white and green seeds of Glycine Soja," but these may have been imports.[32] If Japanese Americans brought soybeans to the United States to plant, and if these varieties made their way more generally into American agriculture, the process remains as invisible to historians as it did to observers at the time.

CHAPTER ONE

An Idea before Its Time

In 1903, seven years before Tsuru Yamauchi's own ordeal crossing the ocean,
Harry W. Miller and his fellow medical missionaries on the *Empress of India*
felt confident that they would hold up well to sea travel. On the first leg,
crossing the Strait of Georgia from Vancouver to Victoria, British Columbia, they did not feel the least bit sick. Then, sometime after they had gone
to bed, they hit the open ocean. The two male missionaries, who shared a
cabin, were too ill to check on the state of their wives and two nurses. For
thirteen days, Miller could barely eat, drink, or walk; urged to get fresh air,
he managed to crawl up a gangway and lie plastered to a deck chair. As he
stood up again on terra firma in Yokohama, it seemed to Miller that the
buildings swayed and bucked. Even as he recovered, he vowed to himself
that, once in China, he would stay there: "Never will I cross the ocean again
[and] expose myself to such a fortnight of terrible sickness."[33] The next stop
after Yokohama was Kobe, where they spent an evening with a couple who
had been their classmates at the American Medical Missionary College
and who were hungry for news from home. The wife in turn prepared for
the group, still half-starved from their seasick passage, a sumptuous feast
of Japanese dishes, remarkably enough given that the couple had only been
overseas for a year themselves. One particularly caught Miller's attention: a
"nice roast" made from tofu. It reminded Miller of an egg soufflé. This was
the first time he had heard of the soybean.[34] The group "ate, and ate, and ate,
and visited," lingering so long that they almost missed the *Empress* as it sailed
for Shanghai.[35]

Miller joined a wave of Christian missionaries venturing to an unprecedented extent into the interior of China, encouraged by a reformist
government seeking to import Western expertise. It was a full-immersion
experience. Following the lead of the China Inland Mission, Miller and his
companions adopted full Chinese dress, including the *queue* and *mao-tze*,
the pigtail and cap that signified Han subservience to the Qing Dynasty, in
order to better connect with and convert the local population. He learned
to speak the language in a small village and to operate a Chinese press to
produce pamphlets. When his wife died from an intestinal illness, he lost
his last day-to-day contact with an English-speaker. He also undoubtedly
ate local food, and, according to one of his later accounts, he observed tofu

being made.[36] His church, fearing for his mental health, eventually called him home for a furlough. Traveling overland through Russia—to avoid the lengthy Pacific crossing—he gradually shed his Chinese trappings, adjusting to a Western suit and regaining his English fluency. What he ultimately carried home, when it came to the soybean, was less tangible than the physical beans by which Asian migrants preserved their food traditions in foreign lands. He returned with new knowledge of the food uses of soybeans, knowledge that—given the dietary practices of his denomination—had the potential to transform American foodways.

Miller was a Seventh-day Adventist, an offshoot of the apocalyptic Millerites (no relation), who had suffered what became known as the Great Disappointment when their prediction that Christ would return in 1844 proved premature. The church's dietary doctrines coalesced in 1863, when the church's founder and prophet, Ellen White, embraced the Water Cure, or hydropathy, movement. With roots in Austria, the Water Cure appealed to American temperance reformers, who saw water as a pure alternative to alcohol. Hydropaths also typically favored a vegetarian diet along the lines of that promoted in the 1840s by the health crusader Sylvester Graham, who counseled against the use of all stimulants: not just alcohol, but tobacco, tea, sugar, spices, white flour, and meat. White fell into a vision revealing that, in order to "take special care of the health God has given us," people should avoid "intemperance of every kind—intemperance in working, in eating, in drinking, and in drugging," and should avail themselves of "God's great medicine, water, pure soft water, for diseases, for health, for cleanliness, and for luxury."[37] Her vision gained institutional weight with the founding of the Western Health Institute in Battle Creek, Michigan, in 1866. As the Water Cure movement itself faded, however, the institute struggled for a decade until it fell under the direction in 1875 of John Harvey Kellogg, who renamed it the Battle Creek Sanitarium (or simply "The San").

Kellogg was a brilliant and charismatic young Adventist who, after the Whites paid for his training in hydropathy, insisted that they also send him to New York to receive training as a medical doctor. He became a skilled surgeon, specializing in the gastrointestinal tract; a prolific and influential author on science and health; and, in his efforts to provide a palatable vegetarian diet for his patients, a leading innovator of health foods. He invented granola—which, in its original incarnation resembled one of its surviving

imitators, Grape-Nuts—and flaked cereals, which formed the basis of his
brother William's food empire. (And although he did not invent peanut butter, as is sometimes claimed, he was key to making it popular.) While embracing medical science, he adhered in his voluminous writings to variants of
the nineteenth-century health philosophy of vitalism. Vitalism argued that
an organism's life force, and in particular the process that converted dead
matter—food—into living tissue, could not be reduced to mere chemistry.
Kellogg, in the Grahamite tradition, argued that food was healthiest when
it required the least energy to digest. He linked constipation, which trapped
decaying food in the body, to autointoxication, or self-poisoning, especially
if the decaying matter was meat.

In one instance, he took vitalism too far. In his 1903 book, *The Living
Temple*, he voiced a reverence for life, celebrating how "every drop of water,
every grain of sand, every snow crystal . . . speaks of an active, controlling
Intelligence possessed of infinite power and capacity,"[38] a position that was
later denounced by the church as heretical pantheism, leading to his expul-
sion in 1907. Trouble had long been brewing with Ellen White, who as early
as 1902 declared that The San, under Kellogg's cosmopolitan leadership, was
under a "sword of fire" for its indulgence in worldly luxury.[39] In the resulting
schism, The San went with Kellogg, while the Adventists founded a new
sanitarium near their new headquarters in the rural environs of Washington, DC, following White's proclamation to "let the light show forth from
the very seat of government."[40] Relieved of the increasing financial burden
of Kellogg's grandiose ambitions, a network of Adventist institutions spread
both in the United States and internationally. Even before the break, White
had shifted the emphasis of the church's work to rural schools, such as the
Nashville Agricultural and Normal Institute (NANI), founded in 1904 to
carry Adventist education to the American South, and Loma Linda College
in California. At the same time, White pushed for more international mission work, venturing herself to the hinterlands of Australia.

This institutional expansion is what made Adventism the cornerstone of
American vegetarianism for decades to come. As a fad, vegetarianism came
and went, and Adventists, like other Americans, regularly ate meat in their
own homes.[41] Ellen White had never made her health recommendations a
test of fellowship, although smelling of tobacco ruled out candidates for the
ministry, and she herself returned to eating meat before giving it up entirely

in her final decade.[42] The sanitaria and colleges, however, offered a vegetarian diet to patients and students as a matter of principle and worked to create new and appetizing vegetarian foods in order to maintain their appeal to those same patients and students. If they did not always operate their own farms and food factories, they were reliable customers to Adventist businesses that would then market their foods to a wider public. At the same time, missionary work in Asia exposed Adventists like Miller and his hosts in Japan to soy foods. Nonetheless, there would be a lag time of more than a decade before Adventists began experimenting with soybeans and soy foods.

This lag was particularly noticeable in the case of Kellogg himself. Throughout the 1890s, he sought to fashion a plant-based imitation of meat. These included Nuttose, which had the consistency of cream cheese, and Nuttelene, a "delicate white meat as dainty and juicy as the breast of a spring chicken."[43] In 1896, at the prompting of Charles Dabney, the assistant secretary of the USDA, who worried about the high cost of meat, Kellogg developed Protose, a product his health food company would continue to offer for decades. Protose combined powdered wheat gluten with peanut meal and cooked the mixture until its consistency and flavor were "changed in a remarkable way" to resemble the "dietetic and gustatory properties" of meat.[44] Striving to make his patent as broad as possible, Kellogg claimed that other glutinous cereals and "oleaginous" legumes could be used. But he did not consider using soybeans for Protose. He later claimed that he had simply not heard of them at the time.[45] Indeed, his earliest printed mention of them was in *The Living Temple*, in which he reported that the soybean "requires longer cooking . . . and is less well flavored than ordinary beans," mentioning in passing that it was "employed in China and Japan in making *bean cheese*."[46] Soybeans did not come up in a section on "vegetable milk," where he instead recommended nut milks, with almond milk commended for having the most delicate flavor.[47]

It is not likely, however, that Kellogg was altogether ignorant of soy foods in 1901. As early as 1899, Charles F. Langworthy of the Office of Experiment Stations had written an account of "Soy Beans as Food for Man," tellingly as a brief appendix to a USDA bulletin, *The Soy Bean as a Forage Crop*. Langworthy found only one reference to the use of soybeans as human food in the United States: a North Carolina Experiment Station bulletin reporting that boiling them with bacon made them palatable, just as with other beans more familiar to Americans.[48] Where widely eaten, he pointed out, soybeans were typically first transformed into "more or less complex food products" such as tofu; shoyu, or soy sauce; miso, a fermented paste; *natto*, whole soybeans fermented into a "thick, viscid mass [with] a peculiar but not putrid odor"; and *yuba*, "a sort of film [that] forms on the surface of soy-bean milk."[49] These foods filled an important gap in the Japanese diet, taking the place of "meat and other nitrogenous animal foods" to make up for the resulting deficiency of protein.[50] Langworthy and his boss, the famous experimental nutritionist Wilbur Atwater, in fact worried that meat would soon become too expensive for the American worker, requiring a similar substitute.[51] Beyond health-reform journals such as *Dietetic and Hygienic Gazette* and *Phrenological Journal of Science and Health*, little notice was taken of Langworthy's report on soy foods—but these were precisely the kind of journals Kellogg would have been familiar with.[52]

The real problem, it is reasonable to conclude, was less that Kellogg had never heard of soybeans but that they were not yet readily available in America. Some varieties circulated in small amounts among farmers and agricultural research stations, and beans suitable for food could presumably be obtained in Chinatowns and other Asian American settlements, but peanuts were much more plentiful. Kellogg would not take an active interest in the soybean, and the experience with soy foods of Adventist missionaries would not come into play, until it became an American crop. That, in turn, required that soybean seeds cross the oceans in large numbers with the purpose of being transplanted to US soil: a pipeline of soybean varieties. This would be the achievement not of immigrants or returning missionaries but of a concerted effort by the federal government.

The Soybean Pipeline, Stage One: Asian Expeditions

In the decades following its founding in 1862, the USDA's largest program, in terms of dollars spent, was the distribution of seeds on behalf of congressmen to their constituents. In 1880, this accounted for almost half of the department's $200,000 budget; in 1900, it alone cost $200,000, as seeds were distributed to an estimated 3 million farmers. This was rural patronage: the bulk of the seeds were widely available, most frequently labeled simply "vegetable seeds" or "garden seeds," rather than novel varieties.[53] Among those who considered the program petty graft was David Fairchild, a young plant pathologist and member of a cohort that, trained in the nation's land-grant colleges but inspired by European standards of scientific rigor, sought to remake the USDA into a research center devoted to the greater public good. Returning to the department in 1897 after a leave, he and his fellow pathologist Walter T. Swingle conceived a plan to earmark $20,000 of the congressional seed distribution budget for the purpose of introducing new and useful plants from overseas. In approving the appropriation request, Secretary of Agriculture James Wilson insisted on adding the word "seed" to the proposed Section of Foreign Plant Introduction—henceforth the Office of Foreign Seed and Plant Introduction (SPI)—in order to reassure congressmen that it was merely an extension of the popular existing program.[54] Despite his distaste for congressional seed distribution, Fairchild was alert to the needs, and political clout, of American farmers. Indeed, his father, the longtime president of the Kansas State College of Agriculture, was ousted by a Populist Party insurgency.[55] In contrast to some Populist tendencies, however, Fairchild envisioned a business solution to farmers' woes, boosting demand for their output by fostering industries based on new crops.

To achieve this, he proposed an effort, global in scope, to collect plants of potential economic value, as well as the many foreign varieties and closely related species of already important American crops. In a USDA bulletin, *Systematic Plant Introduction: Its Purposes and Methods*, written while awaiting the passage of congressional appropriation for SPI, he argued that "the rapid development of any new country" was due to the flourishing of introduced food plants—in the case of the United States, this encompassed virtually every major crop—and "seldom to the development of an endemic species." (He noted that even maize was an import from farther south.) Moreover, modern breeding techniques required systematic collection, gathering in one place as many varieties as possible of important crops. He criticized the "magnificent botanic gardens" scattered throughout European colonies for making no attempt "to establish, for example, specimens of all the species of coffee, which is the first step to be taken in the production of a better variety."[56] Collection had to be geographically extensive as well as exhaustive, as two closely related species of plant separated by distance might retain the ability to interbreed, and thereby produce desirable hybrids, whereas two species in close proximity would likely have developed mechanisms to prevent this kind of interbreeding.[57] All of this argued for the use of "trained explorers or specialists in the particular branches of plant industry" to carry out the work, rather than the ad hoc group of missionaries, military officers, diplomats, and naturalists who had previously introduced new plants to America. "If the work of this character were left to individual enterprises, only occasional expeditions could be expected, and no comprehensive exploration of the cultivated territory of the globe would be undertaken."[58]

Fairchild's project presumed that other countries would tolerate the work of American collectors. In some of his own early expeditions, he realized the need for discretion, as he was potentially robbing localities of their incomes. For instance, in the case of Jordan almonds, which he collected in Spain, he went so far as to secretly hope that his work would not "destroy the business of the poor growers of the mountains" near Malaga. In this case, the cuttings cultivated in California produced an inferior nut, preserving for the peasants "their means of livelihood."[59] Occasional misgivings like this did not shake his conviction that all nations would benefit from the global free exchange of plant species, although he emphasized that America's exceptional geography would help it benefit most of all. There was no other "country in the world tilled by progressive cultivators whose connected territory presents such varied conditions of soil and climate as ours." Plant explorers were to carry a map of this geography in their heads, linking each foreign region to a climatically similar region in the United States in the effort to find better crops for American farmers.[60] Of special interest were crops—including new varieties of traditional crops—that could thrive in the arid Southwest or frigid far North of the country. In Fairchild's vision, the United States was still a new country, its agricultural frontiers far from closed.

China held the most promise of any field of plant exploration. Its rich wild flora had not been touched by the last ice age that had covered much of North America and Europe, and it had a history of cultivation that stretched back thousands of years.[61] Its continental expanse matched that of the United States. Augustine Henry, a former Irish consular official in China and renowned botanical collector, wrote to Fairchild that "the interior of China is one vast treasure of plants, useful, ornamental, and unknown." There were few missionaries and diplomats in the Chinese interior, so Henry counseled "not [to] waste money on postage. Send a man!"[62]

In 1905, Fairchild settled on Charles Sprague Sargent of Harvard's Arnold Arboretum to lead the expedition, assisted by a man whose feats of pedestrianism and talent at plant propagation he had heard of through colleagues. Frank N. Meyer (photo 1), born Frans Meijer, had worked at the Amsterdam Botanical Garden under its renowned director, Hugo De Vries. When he immigrated in 1901, he found work at the USDA greenhouse on the National Mall in the nation's capital. Prone to a melancholy that found relief in travel, he moved on to a USDA plant introduction garden in California; and then to Mexico, where he undertook a 240-mile journey on foot, collecting plants at his own expense; and then to St. Louis, where he worked at the Missouri Botanic Garden.[63] When Sargent withdrew, Fairchild summoned Meyer to the capital for a meeting. In their interview Meyer related how once, while he was working at the plant introduction garden in California, a stubborn plant pathologist had refused to properly mulch bamboos sent by Fairchild and would not let Meyer do it, either. The bamboos had died. Meyer's eyes filled with tears as he related the story. Fairchild knew he had his man.[64]

The son of a sailor, Meyer did not suffer seasickness on his Pacific crossing, as had Tsuru Yamauchi and Harry Miller; in fact, he was uncharacteristically convivial during the passage. This was followed, however, by three years of hardship in the Chinese countryside. Plant exploration as a rule took place on foot, and Meyer was a heroic walker, but the roads in China were especially bad, and pack animals proved scarce. On long treks in the fall, he was exposed to icy winds and dust storms. At nights he slept on brick beds in inns that swarmed with lice, centipedes, and the occasional scorpion. In one inn, he saw on a wall, written in French, the "amusing and disgusting inscription: 'Hotel of 1000 Bedbugs.'"[65] He was also plagued by the bureaucratic demands of the USDA itself, whose accountants instructed him to record all transactions in Chinese currency—despite the fact that numerous brass, copper, and silver coins were in circulation, requiring him to carry hundreds of pounds of Mexican or Hong Kong dollars at all times—and to file all expenditures within twenty days of a transaction, despite the fact that he was often in the field for months at a time.[66] The department required that he use elaborate blue-and-white vouchers that Chinese merchants often refused to sign, and it routinely denied reimbursement for "excess" baggage.[67] "Have these gentlemen who drew up all these regulations," he inquired, "ever

Photo 1. Frank N. Meyer in Chinese Turkestan, ca. 1910. From the National
Archives and Records Administration.

been out in a foreign country like China?"[68] Whatever the rigors of his treks,
he invariably grew most depressed filling out paperwork.[69]

Meyer also faced the hostility of the population in the countryside—
some called him a "foreign devil"—and the ever-present risk of bandits. This
turned out to be a boon for Fairchild, who understood that the right publicity would increase the political popularity—and therefore funding—of SPI.
On the basis of Meyer's letters, he worked to transform the taciturn Dutch
botanist into a hero out of pulp westerns. Representative of the stories that
Fairchild circulated in the popular press were accounts appearing in *The
Outing Magazine* in 1908. In one account Meyer's party, while venturing into
a hilly northern region in search of the finest peaches in China, is warned by
soldiers that a band of robbers is roaming the country. On the following day
they encounter "a ragged mob gathered in a farm field making a pretense of
work, with bludgeons and huge swords ready to hand." When the sun glints
"on the long nickel-plated barrel of Meyer's biggest pistol," however, they decide to drop their bludgeons. In another incident, ruffians likewise flee from
Meyer at the "flash of his pistol-barrel," fearing the "world-wide reputation"

of Americans for "shooting to hit." When Meyer clears up a misunderstanding with these men, they make peace by sitting down "to a smoking of pipes like Red Indians."[70]

The evocation of the American frontier was not, in any case, unusual. Many Americans imagined at the time that, with their own frontier closed, China would provide an outlet for American enterprise and energy and opportunities for both adventure and reform.[71] In one way, at least, China was the Wild West. Among the myriad hassles and inconveniences Meyer noted, he never mentioned any harassment from Chinese officials about the valuable plant materials he was sending to the United States or any restrictions placed on their shipment. At a time when America was pursuing its Open Door policy to ensure that all European powers had equal access to the Chinese market, this was a botanical open door, and in the long run soybeans would be perhaps the most valuable crop to pass through it. At the time of Meyer's expedition, however, what would become a flood began as a trickle.

In 1898, when SPI began its work, there were only a handful of varieties of soybean grown in the United States.[72] Fairchild himself arranged in 1898 for the US minister to Japan to send him not only ten soybean varieties from Tokyo but also samples of the earth they grew in,[73] as researchers were beginning to understand the symbiotic relationship between legumes and nitrogen-fixing bacteria in the soil.[74] By the time Meyer reached China in 1905, SPI had logged fifty-eight foreign soybean introductions—not necessarily distinct varieties—at a rate of roughly seven per year.[75] In the three years of his expedition, Meyer would send forty-four.[76] This was a major accomplishment, but during the same period the growing network of correspondents sending plant material to SPI—the very kind of network dismissed by Augustine Henry as a waste of postage—contributed eighty-three soybean introductions. These arrived from private seed companies in Europe and Japan, from consular officials in Shanghai and Saigon, from missionaries in China, from directors of foreign agricultural experiment stations, and from an array of private individuals whose profession was not identified in the SPI's inventories.[77] It was indeed an important part of Meyer's mission in this and future expeditions to cultivate a network of contacts, if for no other reason than to aid future explorers. As Meyer noted, "If it weren't for the missionaries throughout the land, I wouldn't have obtained as many things as I have now."[78]

Meyer's soybean collecting started slowly, in part because he considered it primarily a food item: he found some in Tientsin "used to make bean cheese from" and some in Mongolia "esteemed for human food," including one type that required "but little irrigation, and is well worth trying in the arid West."[79] And, though he was always ready to eat strange foods himself, he doubted whether Chinese foods would find a market in America. He noticed Chinese eating lotus, water chestnuts, and bamboo and alfalfa shoots but sought Fairchild's advice about sending vegetables that Americans might consider "rubbish."[80] He next turned his attention to finding hardy cereals, fruits, and vegetables for the northern United States by traveling to Manchuria, which happened to be the soybean heartland of Asia.[81] Even here, he collected only three samples, noting that they were crushed for their oil, the remaining "cake" being sent to southern China as fertilizer.[82] He obtained one sample in Korea, and then, traveling farther north, nine in Siberia, six of which came from one farmer in Markoechofka.[83] Another was a gift from the Russian director of the agricultural experiment station in Khabarovsk, where he purchased two more samples in the town market. Finally, circling back through Manchuria in early 1907, he picked up three more. In all, it was only sixteen soybean samples collected in the span of nine months of travel. Even so, when he visited the Japanese agricultural experiment station in Mukden, Manchuria, he was amazed to find that the Japanese had collected even fewer.[84]

Meyer's soybean efforts intensified in early 1908, however, after he received a USDA bulletin, *Soy Bean Varieties*, which was the department's first systematic attempt to determine exactly how many distinct varieties it was actually growing on its experimental farm in Arlington, Virginia.[85] One of his contributions already made the list of named varieties. In fact, it was named "Meyer": "I see that my name has been immortalized in the christening of a humble, mottled bean," he wrote to Fairchild. "What a joy!"[86] More than this honor, it was most likely a push from the department that focused more of his attention on soybeans. By November 1907, he was "anxiously awaiting" a full set of soybean samples from Washington to help him avoid duplicates, although this was not a big worry for him. "You know that the Chinese have no seed-shops like what we have," he commented. "Every farmer saves his own seeds of all his crops and . . . there may be countless strains of plants here in existence of which an explorer gets hold only once in a while."[87] He was only beginning to realize just how many varieties of soybean there might be.

In all, he packed eighteen samples of soybean when he embarked for America on the Standard Oil steamer *Ashtabula* in early May 1908. They were the least of his worries, however, as Meyer struggled to pack and load some twenty tons of other material including seeds, cuttings, and live plants potted in soil. Hundreds of bamboo trees, representing thirty different varieties, were packed in a hundred large crates full of soil.[88] His cares did not end when he arrived at San Francisco, however: not yet a naturalized citizen, he was also visited by immigration officers. Even more distressing was the treatment of his precious bamboo trees at the hands of California horticultural inspectors. Noticing some scale insects, they fumigated the crates in a way that even Meyer, who always urged that his plant materials be fumigated thoroughly, found excessive. Many of the trees later died, a loss that Fairchild later wrote "nearly broke Meyer's heart."[89] He managed, just barely, to fit his collection onto a Southern Pacific freight car, which carried it to the USDA Plant Introduction Garden in Chico, California. There, he repacked part of the collection and shipped it back east to Washington. This included the eighteen packages of soybean that, having a limited shelf life before they lost the ability to germinate, now sought to take root in American soil.

At the turn of the twentieth century, the soybean entered America through several means: Asian immigrants to the United States and its territories, acting as agents of diffusion; Adventist missionaries returning home, acting as agents of cultural exchange; and the USDA's explorers and officials who, together with the network of correspondents they cultivated, acted as agents of seed propagation. For all of these actors, the soybean was far from the center of attention as they grappled with more pressing issues. Even USDA explorers, charged with systematically transferring the botanical wealth of the world to American shores, focused the largest part of their energies on other prospects. And even as it entered the United States in larger numbers, the soybean would continue to compete against other promising crops for space in agricultural research programs and, ultimately, on America's farms. The process of importing new commercial crops was open-ended when compared to efforts to maintain traditions or to transform the world according to a particular utopian vision, as it cast a wide net and sought to remake the world piecemeal according to the unpredictable dictates of market demand. For the product to be sustained during the first stage in this east to west transpacific pipeline, the soybean would need to find a novel and more commercially tangible use in the New World.

The Soybean Pipeline, Stage Two: The Big Sort

During one trip through Peking in 1905, early in his expedition, Frank Meyer collected a sample of soybean right around the same time that he also logged two varieties of apricot whose seeds, called "almonds," were "eaten as dessert and also used in confectionery"; a cowpea "roasted for confectionery"; and an adzuki bean "boiled, made in a pulp, sweetened with sugar, and baked in small cakes." The particular variety of soybean he obtained was likewise prepared as a treat, "roasted and sold in Peking as delicatessen."[90] It was not uncommon in China or Japan, in fact, for salted and roasted soybeans to be eaten plain or included in sweets. Given that the smells of Peking were especially troubling to the fastidious Meyer—"You people in America haven't any idea of the filth here,"[91] he wrote to a friend—it is pleasant to imagine that he found refuge during this period in the city's candy shops and among its street-food vendors. Although generally hesitant to collect Chinese food items that he feared Americans would disdain, he put the soybeans in a small sack. He tagged this with a number, "17a" (the "a" indicating that it contained seeds rather than cuttings), packed it in a tin with other sacks of seeds, and included it in a shipment containing more than a hundred other similar packages that crossed the Pacific to the USDA in Washington. There, the Office of Seed and Plant Introduction logged the seeds under its own inventory number, SPI 17852.

From there the seeds passed into the hands of the Office of Forage-Crop Investigations, created just that year to develop better grazing and fodder options for livestock.[92] Charles Piper had joined the USDA's Office of Farm Management two years earlier as an agrostologist, an expert in grass species. Indeed, one of Piper's later claims to fame would be to revolutionize the turf on American golf courses.[93] Crops that fed animals were his main focus, however, and that meant grasses such as sorghum. He would score the greatest success of his career, in fact, by discovering Sudan grass, a near relative of sorghum hardy enough to survive on the western plains. The key to this discovery was his skill as a taxonomist: he exhaustively researched the botanical relationship among plants in order to make fresh discoveries, missing links "whose existence seemed probable," as one of his colleagues put it, "but whose like had never actually been seen."[94] Piper had surmised that the link between sorghum and Johnson grass, a pernicious weed, would be found in North Africa, and he was proven right by the arrival of the parcel containing Sudan grass. Piper's work extended beyond grasses, however, and increasingly focused on promising legumes and thus to the soybean varieties that the USDA had amassed since 1898.

Legumes—a family of pod-producing plants that includes alfalfa, clover, and many species of bean and pea—gained favorable attention for two reasons. First, they are higher in protein than grains or grasses, whether left in the fields as forage, taken fresh to the barn as "soiling," combined with grains and stored wet in silos as "silage," or stored dry in bales as hay. As a USDA bulletin pointed out in 1898, a high-protein regimen was "much more economical" when milk production or "rapid and continuous growth" were the goals, a consideration that would only gain in importance as draft animals gradually gave way to meat and dairy livestock.[95] Second, legumes have the ability to draw nitrogen from the air contained in soil and "fix" it into compounds that plants can use. They accomplish this feat through a symbiosis with certain bacteria that are responsible for the actual work of nitrogen fixation. The plants nurture the bacteria within lumpy nodules on their roots, frequently called "tubercles" in the early twentieth century, linking them to the similar bacterial colonies that form in the human disease of tuberculosis. When plowed under, or left in the field as forage for manure-producing livestock, legumes add nitrogen to worn-out soils; when harvested for silage or hay, they at least deplete it less than grains or cotton do.

When Piper first encountered the USDA's soybean collection in 1903, it was in classificatory disarray. Characteristically, this is the first thing he addressed, assigning the work to an assistant, Carleton Ball, who would spend four years completing the job.[96] By the time Ball reviewed the situation, seed merchants and "private investigators" had joined experiment stations in circulating soybeans among themselves and farmers. The USDA gathered its collection from these sources, as well as directly from foreign experiment stations and merchants beginning with the founding of the SPI in 1898. In his 1907 bulletin, *Soy Bean Varieties*, he noted that the USDA had "secured from seven different countries of the old world no less than 65 different lots of soy bean seeds," adding that these contained around twenty varieties, or plants genetically similar enough to be interchangeable, if not indistinguishable, for the purposes of breeding and cultivation (photo 2).[97] The seeds collected by the USDA derived from lineages that in many cases had circulated through Europe and America for some time, something obscured by the lack of consistent naming practices. In 1903, soybean varieties were generally named according to a system based on the color of the seed—white, green, or black—and the time it took for the beans to reach maturity: "Early White" or "Late Black," for instance, with "early" meaning they ripened sooner and were therefore more suitable for northern states with short growing seasons.[98] This gave too few naming options to encompass the full range of differences among soybeans, even with the addition of such designations as "medium," falling between early and late, and "late medium."

Ball's first step, then, was to reform soybean nomenclature by giving each variety a single proper name. For the most part, each name was rooted in some aspect of the plant: its size ("Mammoth"), the appearance of its seed ("Buckshot," "Butterball"), the experiment station that first grew it ("Manhattan" as in Kansas, "Kingston" as in Rhode Island), the overseas explorer who first collected it ("Baird"), or the idiosyncratic name, oftentimes Asian in origin, already given to it by experiment stations or seed merchants ("Ito San," "Eda"). In addition, some varietal names honored men considered important in promoting the soybean ("Nuttall," "Haberlandt").[99] Ball then included a detailed description for each variety, with the thought that a consistent nomenclature—adopted, it was hoped, by seed dealers as well as researchers—would allow farmers to find soybeans that matched their needs and local climates.[100] Ball eventually settled on twenty-three distinct named varieties, some of which consolidated seeds from as many as sixteen different sources. It took him three years to make these determinations, in part because he relied on characteristics, such as the plant's height or its tendency to lean (*habit*), that he felt required at least three consecutive annual plantings to reach a state of "equilibrium" in any given location; initial differences, as plants responded to new environmental conditions, would often disappear.[101]

SPI 17852 did not have to wait three years to become a named variety. The beans arrived in Washington in February 1906 and were planted later

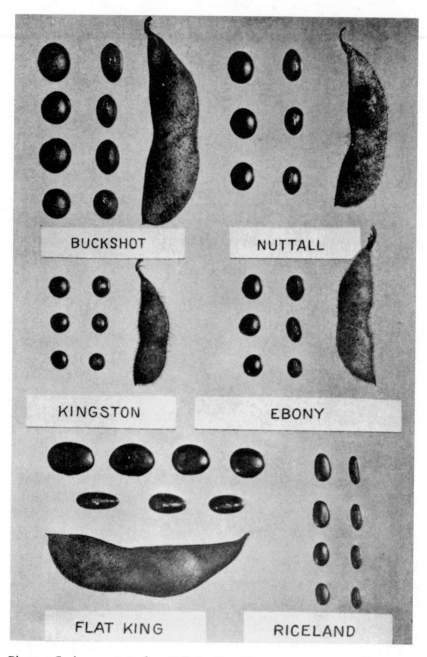

Photo 2. Soybean varieties from Ball, *Soy Bean Varieties*, 1907.

that spring. On the basis of their appearance alone, Ball was prepared to designate them a "distinct variety of the mottled group": rather than being a solid color, the seeds tended to be a mix of black and brown. He named the new variety "Meyer." This seeming haste pointed to what Ball had achieved, a definitive catalog of known varieties against which new introductions could be held up, thus providing an important baseline for the USDA's soybean work. As it turned out, his judgment that SPI 17852 was a single variety was indeed premature. Despite noticing differences among the seeds—some were "quite covered" in black, for instance, while others were mostly brown with "only faint lines" of black—he did not suspect the true amount of genetic variation that this represented.[102] After all, his job had been to address duplication among lineages of soybeans that had circulated for years among experiment stations, seed dealers, and American farmers. Confronting the variability of seeds arriving fresh from Asia would prove to be an entirely new phase of the work.

When the USDA published Ball's bulletin in 1907, he had already left Forage-Crops for the Office of Grain Investigations. Piper assigned soybeans to H. T. Nielsen, who also conducted the office's cowpea research; both were annual legumes suitable mainly for the South. The newly arriving samples of soybeans were of landraces, populations of roughly similar plants grown for generations in one locality. These typically contained a substantial amount of genetic diversity, to some extent deliberately preserved by farmers as a hedge against events that might otherwise wipe out entire harvests. By the fall of 1907, there were enough soy plants growing in the test plots at Arlington to evaluate them according to a much-expanded list of traits. These included height and two aspects of habit: bushy versus slender and "erect" versus "suberect." Nielsen also considered the color of the flowers (purple or white); the color of the pubescence, or plant hairs (tawny or green); the size of the pods and how swollen they were ("tumid" or "compressed"); the size and shape of the seed ("oblong," "elliptical," "flattened"); and the tendency of the pods to "shatter," or to break apart and release the seeds. He recorded whether the seed color was black, brown, olive-yellow, straw-yellow, chromium-green, or bicolored, at the same time noting the color of the hilum, the little scar joining together the two halves of the seed, and the color of the seed's germ once its outer skin was removed.[103]

For these plant immigrants, America was anything but a melting pot, as Nielsen sorted them out into "pure" selections that contained no discernible differences among the plants—except for height, within a certain range—and "mass" selections that were less uniform but still more genetically pure than landraces.[104] Once achieved, this genetic purity was easy to maintain by virtue of the tendency of soybeans to self-pollinate, which at the same time made it difficult for breeders to create new varieties through planned cross-breeding.[105] The diversity of soybeans arriving from Asia made this type of breeding largely unnecessary in any case, and for decades varietal development would consist of sorting rather than crossing. Between 1907 and 1908, the number of soybean lines grown annually on the USDA's farm near Washington grew from around 170 to 280. Fully sixty-four of the new lines were field selections, not fresh foreign introductions, out of which three became official named varieties.[106] From SPI 17852, for instance, Nielsen discerned as many as seventeen separate types, each designated by a letter.[107] Collectively they displayed remarkable diversity: seed color ran the gamut from black to brown to chromium-green to olive-yellow; some had white flowers, some purple, some both; some were bushy, though most were "slender, erect, the tips twining," good qualities for hay.[108] The most promising was 17852 B, a pure selection, which Nielsen named "Peking." As the Meyer variety fell by the wayside, Peking circulated widely in northern states over the next decade. Soybeans that began as Chinese food, perhaps roasted and sold on the streets of Peking, thus became fodder for American livestock.

In a manner that echoed Darwinian competition in the wild, different soybean lines vied for the advantages that came with being named an official variety: distribution to state experiment stations, mass propagation by seed merchants, and an increased chance of adoption by farmers. Likewise, soybeans as a whole contended with other crops for basic resources at the USDA, including space, funds, and the attention of staff. Because soybeans soon lose the ability to germinate, breeding lines had to be planted and harvested each year. After Congress transferred 400 acres adjacent to Arlington National Cemetery from the Department of War to the USDA in 1900, this was something that happened at the resulting Arlington Experiment Farm.[109] Each of the Bureau of Plant Industry's numerous and shifting divisions jockeyed for space at Arlington, where they could propagate plants and conduct field trials, usually carried out by a point person stationed on the farm itself. Beginning in 1907 a new employee, William Morse, played this role for the Forage-Crop Investigations Office. He conducted much of the painstaking soybean work that began that fall, and when Nielsen transferred to Field Crop Investigations in early 1909, Morse officially became the scientific assistant in charge of soybeans and cowpeas. The fact that he remained in Arlington at the disposal of the other assistants, still conducting their trials, indicated that soybeans may not have had the highest priority at the time.[110]

Indeed, having crossed the ocean to root on American soil, it was far from clear that soybeans would find a reason to spread beyond experiment stations. It competed with alfalfa, clover, cowpeas, and peanuts as a leguminous forage crop and was not widely considered promising as a food crop. For all this, legend had it that Piper would visit Morse on Sundays, evenings, and other odd times at the Arlington Experiment Farm while the young man carried on his work, reassuring him of its importance. As told in a 1942 book, *Soybeans: Gold from the Soil*, Piper painted "word pictures of a future agricultural economy" in which the soybean would play a "tremendous role." "Young fellow," Piper would say, "these beans are gold from the soil. Yes, sir, gold from the soil. One must truly stand in awe of their potential power in the life of the western world."[111] At this stage, this may have been merely a pep talk. Yet it was during this period, in 1909, that a new potential role emerged for soybeans: as a savior of the Cotton Belt.

CHAPTER TWO

JUMPING THE GUN

In his 1918 bulletin, *The Soy Bean: Its Uses and Culture*, William Morse included a chart listing four dozen soybean products, from hay to linoleum to smoked cheese (figure 2.1).[1] This chart was largely aspirational, a compendium of ways that the soybean had been used sometime, somewhere in the world, often on an experimental basis, but it provided Morse with an agenda that he rarely missed an opportunity to push. On one October day in 1920, for example, he found himself at loose ends in Biloxi, Mississippi, when his plans to review nearby test plots fell through. As he recounted in a letter to Piper, he decided to take a walk and happened across a "coffee roasting establishment." "Rather interested in seeing how they got rid of the fumes," he entered and struck up a conversation with the manager. Eventually, the conversation got around to soybeans and the possibility of roasting them for coffee: "I promised to send him some of our Mammoth Yellow seed. He said he would roast the beans and send us some samples." He added hopefully that it was "quite possible that we can get something started with them, although at the present time it is a small concern. I understand they are to enlarge in the near future."[2]

There is no indication that anything came from this encounter, and, truth be told, use as a coffee substitute was not the most promising avenue for the soybean. In the 1890s, when some farmers apparently prepared soy coffee for their own use, it was briefly a topic in agricultural bulletins. The head of the agricultural experiment station at Lafayette, Indiana, declared it "agreeable" and more nutritious than barley coffee, although he conceded

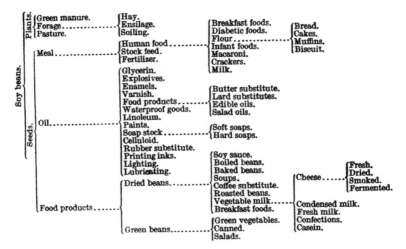

Figure 2.1. The uses of the soybean, ca. 1918, representing aspirational possibilities more than actual commercial products at the time. From Morse, *The Soy Bean: Its Uses and Culture.*

it would not have satisfied "the lover of high-grade coffee."[3] The secretary of agriculture, by contrast, thought it a "poor substitute . . . about equal to scorched wheat or rye."[4] By 1920, it would also have faced competition from the popular coffee substitute Postum.

The incident nonetheless provides a useful measure of two things. The first is Morse's worth as a champion of the soybean, rooted in his conviviality, his wide-ranging curiosity about technical matters, and his patience in exploring every commercial possibility. The other is the soybean's failure to live up to the expectations of the previous ten years. He and Piper had hoped and projected that there would be a thriving and growing soybean sector throughout the American South, crushing soybeans instead of cottonseed—and giving farmers, even tenants, a means to break the region's cotton monoculture. There were other bets placed on the soybean in the 1910s that similarly did not quite pan out: inventors patented processes for making milk out of soybeans, as an alternative to disease-ridden cow's milk; and the federal government promoted soybeans as a substitute for scarce meat during World War I, going so far as to send a Chinese national on a mission to her homeland to discover the secrets of making tofu. If these and similar efforts did not quite provide the soybean with a breakthrough, however, they did sustain interest and investment in the crop, a necessary precondition for its success in subsequent decades, when it would come to fulfill many of its proponents' early dreams.

A Hope for the South

Agricultural reformers in the South had long pointed to the soil exhaustion, rural poverty, and technological backwardness (the "one-horse plow") that resulted from an overwhelming dependence on one crop.[5] They called for a program of "lime, legumes and livestock" that would enrich the soil through nitrogen-fixing legumes and the application of limestone and manure. Diversified farming would also provide a better income—through the sale of hay, meat, and milk—than cotton alone. This, in turn, they argued, would lead to a general renovation of the southern economy and culture. "This system will enable us to build better roads, better homes, better schools and better churches," urged a North Carolina extension agent. "It will make us better citizens and better Christians."[6] It would also provide a defense against the boll weevil, an invasive beetle that began decimating cotton crops in southern Texas in 1892 and, carried by late-summer winds, spread inexorably to every cotton-growing county of the South by 1922.[7] The pest's impact in the years following its first arrival in a county was catastrophic, reducing the cotton crop by up to 50 percent.[8] Reformers saw this as the "paralyzing shock" required to induce southern farmers to make a "material change" and to adopt a program of lime, legumes, and livestock.[9]

In line with reformers, Piper sought a perennial legume for the South to match the clover and alfalfa that thrived farther north, estimating that it "would be of incalculable value." He considered kudzu a promising candidate, but only on land otherwise too rough or infertile to farm.[10] Pending new discoveries, this left annuals such as soybeans and cowpeas as the best options for leguminous forage. He therefore pinpointed the soybean's "region of maximum importance" as "south of the red-clover area."[11] But it was not the prospect of better hay that sparked interest in 1909; rather it was a special consular report issued by the US Department of Commerce at the behest of the American cottonseed industry. Over the second half of the nineteenth century, cottonseed had evolved from a waste product, sometimes used on fields as fertilizer, to a valuable by-product of the cotton industry. The refined oil of the seed was bland and palatable. With the advent of hydrogenation, which made liquid vegetable oil into a solid fat, it was ideal for shortening such as Crisco. Shortages of cottonseed and linseed in 1908, however, compelled British oilseed mills to import soybeans from Manchuria. They conducted a "series of tests to demonstrate the uses to which the soya cake, meal, and oil may be put, and it is claimed that the results have been eminently satisfactory," stated the consular report. "The seed crushers in England have been very active in seeking outlets for their products and have offered it in practically every market for such manufactures in Europe."[12]

This worried cottonseed oil producers, but the USDA perceived a revolutionary possibility for the South. In a 1909 bulletin, Piper proclaimed: "The recent enormous exportations of soy beans and soy-bean meal from Manchuria to Europe would seem to indicate that there is practically an unlimited market for this product [and that] the soy bean can be profitably grown in practically all parts of the cotton belt as a grain crop."[13] Soybeans, in short, were a plausible alternative cash crop for the South during the boll weevil crisis. The region's long growing season resulted in large crops of mature beans that were ideal as sources of oil.[14] Crucially, the infrastructure for producing crude oil—or *crushing* it out of the beans—was seemingly already in place. Crushing mills dotted the South, never far from the sources of the highly perishable cottonseed. The hope was that soybeans could initially supplement cottonseed—helping to lengthen the crushing season, which was compressed into a short period following the cotton harvest—and then gradually supplant it. Cottonseed oil production perpetually fell short of demand, as the quantity of cotton responded to the price of the fiber, not the seed. Soybeans, grown in sufficient quantities to fill the gap, might provide income to both tenant and landlord. In 1916, Piper and Morse prepared a bulletin that included a map identifying where the "soy bean is especially adapted for growing for oil," an area that included southern states up to southern Virginia, Kentucky, and Missouri.[15] By this time, there were some strong signs to support their prediction.

A breakthrough in soybean crushing had occurred three years earlier in North Carolina, although Morse learned about it only in 1914. The Southern Cotton Oil Mill of Elizabeth City, in the northeastern corner of North Carolina, had experimented "with soy beans as an oil proposition. I was not able to learn further than that experiment was successful." He added, in a letter reporting the discovery to Piper, that "if the farmer can be brought to realize the possibilities and value of the crop not only as a cash crop, but the value to his land, the oil mills will not lack for a cotton-seed substitute."[16] Farmers there had in fact grown soybeans in at least modest amounts since the 1880s,[17] and they increasingly harvested the beans to be sold in northern states where the favored hay varieties matured too late to supply a sufficient amount of seed.[18] Thus even before 1913, some North Carolina farmers were producing commercial soybeans, often using mechanical harvesters manufactured in Elizabeth City.[19] This unusual supply of commercial beans provided an opportunity for local mills, which would be able to continue operations outside of the normally short season for crushing cottonseed, which was highly perishable. A more complete utilization of its physical capital seems to have been the motivation, in any event, of the Southern Cotton Oil Mill in 1913.

Soybean crushing did not get under way in earnest until 1915, however, when the shortage of cottonseed became acute rather than merely seasonal. In July 1914, the onset of World War I had curtailed shipments of cotton to Europe. When cotton prices plummeted, growers planted soybeans instead. When the cotton trade reopened in 1915, with the supply now low and war boosting demand, the price for both fiber and seed skyrocketed. Relatively plentiful soybeans became a cheap alternative for oil mills. In December 1915, the Elizabeth City Oil and Fertilizer Company crushed 10,000 bushels of soybeans in a test run.[20] Its manager, William Thomas Culpepper, a future member of the North Carolina legislature, would later receive credit for founding the state's soybean industry.[21] Others followed Culpepper's lead, with mills in at least nine of the state's cities and towns crushing perhaps 100,000 bushels in the spring of 1916.[22] The price of soybeans rose after the 1916 harvest, as farmers saved more of the seed to plant in order to expand their harvests, causing mills to turn to cheaper Manchurian beans. Mills contracted with farmers for the more expansive 1917 crop, however, with imports from Manchuria falling in 1918. From then on North Carolina's domestic soybean industry became well established.[23]

This development was not the outcome of market forces alone. C. B. Williams, director of the North Carolina Experiment Station, was especially active in promoting soybeans in his state. His earliest request to the USDA's

Forage-Crop office for seeds of new soybean varieties was in 1907, soon after
he arrived in Raleigh, and over the next decade he worked to convince North
Carolina farmers to plant them. In Washington, in addition to developing
soybean varieties and coauthoring research bulletins with Piper, Morse sent
beans to any experiment station, scientist, or farmer who requested them in
return for any data they could provide in return. Beginning in 1910, he followed up with visits to these "cooperators" each autumn, traveling through
twenty states over the course of the decade and maintaining a correspondence with contacts in at least fifteen others.[24] During his annual tours, as
he recalled years later, he would carry along a "few bushels" of soybeans and,
venturing from train stops into the countryside on hired wagons, induce
farmers to "plant a few rows."[25] In October 1910, for instance, he visited the
farm of Fred Latham near Belhaven, about eighty miles south of Elizabeth.
Latham, a member of the state senate, had been pushing to diversify the
area's farming for several years and was excited to be "next to the man who
had the information for which I had been thirsting"; they talked "that whole
afternoon, that night, and all the next day."[26] Morse and Williams, as well as
the cooperators who planted soybeans and praised their virtues to neighbors, completed the pipeline of new varieties that originated in China.

In a flurry of bulletins, Morse sought to generalize the success of soybean
crushing in North Carolina to the rest of the South. These included *The
Soy Bean, with Special Reference to Its Utilization for Oil, Cake, and Other
Products* (with Piper) in 1916; *Harvesting Soy-Bean Seed* in 1917; and *The Soy
Bean: Its Uses and Culture* in 1918. In the USDA's 1917 *Yearbook of Agriculture*,
he reported that the "cottonseed-oil mills of the South saw the possibilities
of the soy bean as an oil seed, and many mills throughout the cotton belt
contracted with planters for seed of the 1917 crop."[27] Morse's references to the
"South" and "the cotton belt" belied the fact, however, that North Carolina
produced almost half of the nation's soybean seeds in 1917, more than double
the amount of neighboring Virginia. This meant that something less than a
third of the total was produced in the rest of the South combined—and an
unknown portion of this, certainly the majority, was to be planted for forage
rather than crushed for oil.[28] It is true that, by 1917, national soybean acreage
had increased tenfold from 1907: from an estimated 50,000 acres[29] to around
500,000 acres.[30] But this was scattered among the more than 300 million
acres of farmland harvested each year,[31] including some 30 million acres of

cotton. Thus soybeans had hardly made any progress in the South, especially when measured against the dominance of cotton. Even in North Carolina, which remained the leading soybean grower until 1924, the crop struggled to expand beyond the beachhead it had established in the Northeast.

The soybean's lackluster expansion in the South may have been due in part to difficulties in marketing soybean oil. Its physical properties lay somewhere between those of cottonseed oil on the one hand and linseed oil, produced from flax seeds, on the other. Slow-drying cottonseed oil was bland enough for edible purposes such as salad oil or shortening. Fast-drying linseed oil was valuable in paints because it left behind a solid film, but it was too "painty-tasting" to be readily used in food. Soybean oil was "semi-drying," which meant that it was too painty to wholly substitute for cottonseed in food but too slow-drying to wholly substitute for linseed oil in paint. Of the two options, it showed more promise as a partial substitute for linseed oil, but this entailed finding entry into an entirely different network of commercial links, which typically connected flax growers in the Midwest with paint manufacturers, not the one that connected southern mills to food producers.[32]

Some experiment stations took steps to remedy this. George Washington Carver, at the Tuskegee Institute in Alabama, first requested soybeans and cowpeas from the Forage-Crop office in 1911.[33] He planted the soybeans in 1912 and was impressed by their abundant forage "of the nicest possible kind." In 1914, he looked beyond forage and cooperated with a New Jersey paint company to test five varieties to determine the quantity of oil they provided.[34] C. B. Williams in North Carolina meanwhile contacted dozens of paint and varnish manufacturers, most of which were in the Northeast and Midwest, and circulated excerpts of their replies in a 1916 bulletin, *The Commercial Use of the Soybean*.[35] As it happened, during the shortages of World War I, some companies made too liberal a use of soybean oil, much of it imported from Manchuria and of low quality, and by some accounts this destroyed its reputation for use in paint for years to come.[36] Following the war, soybean oil found its main outlet in soap, a low-value use providing lower returns to mills than they would get with cottonseed oil.

What most limited the soybean's expansion in the South, however, was the competition from other crops. Above all, predictions of cotton's demise were markedly premature.[37] Given the boll weevil's slow eastward spread, unaffected areas had ample opportunity to expand their cotton acreage to make up for the shortfall in affected areas. And as the weevil approached a given county, its production of cotton skyrocketed as growers, aided by an influx of refugee labor from weevil-afflicted counties, tried to "squeeze out one last big crop."[38] It was this inflated amount that was reduced by 50 percent: within ten years, acreage typically crept back to something near what it had been before the anticipatory run-up. Some land was diverted to corn, but corn yields also went down, indicating that farmers were devoting more acres to bare subsistence, not to the improved methods that involved rotation with legumes.[39] The boll weevil put the cotton-growing South into turmoil, causing waves of internal migration that spilled over into other regions as well, but it left its dependence on cotton intact—for the simple reason that cotton remained the most valuable cash crop that could be harvested with hand labor.

In the case of North Carolina, the boll weevil did not arrive until 1920[40]—and was thus not a direct factor in the advent of soybean crushing there seven years earlier—but when it did damage the state's cotton, soybeans found themselves hemmed in by another cash crop. The cultivation of "bright-leaf" tobacco had begun spreading east from the Piedmont to the coast in the early 1900s. Valued for its sweetness, it was used widely in plugs of chewing tobacco and subsequently in cigarettes. It also upended the soil-enrichment program of rural reformers, as its color and taste were the result of being starved of nitrogen after the initial stages of growth. Tobacco farmers accordingly applied commercial fertilizer in strictly controlled doses to the most sterile land they could find[41]—and unlike some progressive cotton farmers, they refused to grow it in rotation with legumes precisely because they made the land too fertile.[42] As bright-leaf tobacco arrived in the northeastern part of the state, rates of tenancy rose and the average size of farms shrank,[43] reinforcing the sharecropping system. Soybeans earned relatively low returns per acre and, for decades afterward, were planted by small farmers as a cash crop of last resort.[44]

Finally, soybeans faced competition from other legumes: cowpeas and peanuts. These were familiar subsistence foods in the South, and George Washington Carver, who largely abandoned soybean research, was not alone in thinking that small farmers could be convinced more easily to expand their patches of these crops than to plant soybeans.[45] As a cash crop, peanuts also had the advantage of having become big business in the North well before Carver's famous peanut bulletin of 1915: roasted peanuts, shelled salted peanuts, peanut butter, and Cracker Jack were all in high demand.[46] Peanuts could also be crushed for oil. The soybean's chief advantage next to these legumes was its upright habit, making it easily mowed as hay or mechanically harvested for beans. Peanuts and cowpeas were viny, spreading along the ground. Morse, who devoted as much time to cowpeas as he did to soybeans, in fact worked to develop a hybrid cowpea, using breeding techniques more sophisticated than the sort-and-test procedures of soybean development, that was more upright, arguably undermining the competitive advantage of soybeans.[47] In truth, however, the soybean's habit was an advantage mainly for mechanized farms, the sort that could emerge in the South only by pushing tenants off the land. This is precisely what would happen later under the combined pressures of the Depression and the New Deal, providing room for soybeans to become a major southern crop after World War II, but before then the region's longstanding economic system would maintain a tenacious hold, as would its traditional mix of cash and subsistence crops along with it.

A More Hygienic Milk

Even as it largely failed to enter southern agriculture, there were other crises during the 1910s that offered opportunities for the soybean. One was a health crisis surrounding the nation's milk. The alarm was sounded most forcefully by Milton Rosenau of the US Public Health Service's Hygiene Laboratory in his 1912 book, *The Milk Question*. Rosenau argued that milk was the cause of an epidemic of child deaths in American cities, despite bans instituted during the previous century on the sale of "swill milk" from sickly urban cows fed the by-products of breweries. He in fact blamed milk's unwholesomeness on the distance it now traveled from the countryside: "To separate the mouth of the baby from the teat of the cow by several hundred miles is often a serious matter for the baby. . . . Dirt and bacteria enter, decomposition proceeds, poisons may develop, so that a glass of ordinary market milk may be very unlike the food that leaves the mammary gland."[48] Despite all these hazards, Rosenau insisted that milk was a necessary food:

"It is true that several large nations comprising millions of people get along reasonably well without the use of the milk of the cow or of any of our mammalian friends. . . . Western civilization, however, has come to depend upon cow's milk as an essential article of diet for children and it has become a very important article of diet for adults."[49] This quandary of milk being both dangerous and indispensable led some to search for a less risky but otherwise equivalent substitute, with the federal government playing a side role by granting patents.

There were several patents for soymilk approved in the United States during the decade. Some of these were filed by residents of Europe, who did not feel compelled to justify their invention on sanitary grounds. After all, innovations in artificial dairy products such as margarine, created to address wartime shortages or the needs of armies, had a long history in Europe. In his 1919 application, for instance, the Danish citizen Knud Erslev simply noted that "efforts have already been made to prepare artificial milk from vegetable products" and that his invention came closer to resembling cow's milk in composition and taste than these earlier efforts.[50] The earliest US soymilk patent was awarded in 1913 (filed 1911) to Li Yu-ying, a Chinese expatriate who operated a tofu factory outside of Paris and whose application was unusual in the variety of products it proposed to derive from the milk: not just tofu and several varieties of fermented cheese but also soy sauce and, for industrial purposes, purified soy "casein."[51] Like Erslev, Li did not mention public health concerns.

American soymilk innovators, however, routinely foregrounded the sanitary advantages of their products. Louis J. Monahan, a prolific inventor in Oshkosh, Wisconsin, best known for being a designer of automobile engines, submitted an application in 1913 for a "Process of Making Soy-Milk" that promised "the elimination of germ disease due to the animal secretions," as well as a product "free from elements harmful to diabetics."[52] American press accounts of German efforts to produce synthetic milk—in which "the Soya bean appears to be one of [the] important ingredients"—stressed that one of its advantages, "so obvious that the importance of the announcement of its achievement is manifest," was that it "would largely eliminate the danger of infection through milk." The key was that the preparation of vegetable milks, including soymilk, typically involved boiling the liquid, making it "absolutely sterile."[53] Dairy pasteurization, by contrast, maintained temperatures below the boiling point to avoid denaturing the proteins of cow's milk. It must be said, however, that the primary purpose of boiling soymilk in most of the patents was not to sterilize it but to improve the milk's flavor. A persistent, difficult-to-mask "beany" taste was the chief impediment to wide acceptance in the West and a spur to ingenuity. Li was an exception, perhaps because he was Chinese. He did not state the removal of a "beany," "nauseous," "disagreeable," or "raw" taste as a goal. And though he pasteurized the milk, he did not boil it.[54]

Boiling was not the only strategy for diminishing the beany flavor. Monahan, the automobile engineer, emulsified a fine soybean flour with lime water (that is, water with a high calcium content) and sodium bicarbonate, "the reason for using these agents [being] to counteract the taste of the bean as much as possible as well as to partially arrest the oily odor therefrom."[55] Gaston Thévenot, a resident of Milwaukee and later New York City, was among the most dogged in attacking this problem in four patents in the late 1910s and early 1920s. In the earliest, he simply boiled the soymilk, but by 1923 he also soaked the puréed beans in grain alcohol or other solvents.[56] The British applicant William Melhuish located the "nauseous" taste in the soybean's oil: he therefore thoroughly removed it using a centrifugal separator, then replaced it with better-tasting sesame oil. This, however, involved "considerable expense in separators [and] their cleaning and upkeep," so that even before his patent was approved, he submitted another for artificial milk made from peanuts.[57] The cow, however unsanitary it might be, would not be easy to supplant with the soybean. And as it happened, major reforms—including mandatory pasteurization, which was law in New York by 1914, and a thorough-going program for culling tuberculosis-infected cows—rehabilitated cow's milk in the public mind before soymilk could gain a foothold. If its path as a milk substitute was thereby blocked, however, the decade's largest crisis—a world war that eventually pulled in the United States, creating shortages 4of meat and wheat—provided a boost to its prospects as a solid food.

A Patriotic Substitute

When the Chicago Patriotic Food Show opened in January 1918, it was billed as the first of its kind in the nation or even, more grandiloquently, the world.

Organized by a special committee of the Illinois State Council of Defense, it received the blessing of Commissioner Herbert Hoover's wartime Food Administration.[58] Its floor plan expressed the principles of the era's nutrition science, consisting of five parallel aisles representing the "five food groups": Proteins, Fats, Sugars, Fruits and Vegetables, and Starches.[59] In the median of each aisle, running its length, was the demonstration space, where students and teachers from nearby home economics departments stood behind broad counters handing out samples, the recipes for which visitors could find in the *Official Recipe Book*, available for 5 cents. Flanking the demonstration spaces were commercial booths, frequently showcasing the products used by the demonstrators.[60] Ring Lardner, the humorist and sports writer, gently satirized the event in his *Chicago Tribune* column, summing up the overall message of the show this way: "The life-supporting principles in food are proteins, starches, sweets, and fats. . . . The purpose of the food show is to acquaint the public with victuals containing the aforesaid principles but transgressing none of the laws of patriotic conservation."[61]

Soybeans appeared in three of the five aisles: as a meat saver along with other legumes in Protein, paired with cowpeas in Vegetables, and ground into flour in Starches. It did not, however, appear in Fats among "various new oils" made from cottonseed, peanut, and coconut.[62] Twelve of the over 300 recipes in the official cookbook contained soybeans. Its Soy Bean Loaf recipe called for the use of "soy bean pulp," which required soaking the beans for twenty-four hours, simmering them with baking soda for two hours, placing them in a "fireless cooker" for an additional twelve hours, and then putting them through a meat grinder.[63] The recipe book did not recommend soybean flour for yeast breads, but it had several recipes for muffins, nut breads, cakes, and cupcakes that used soybean "meal," indicating that it was to be ground by the baker herself, in equal proportions to wheat flour.[64] The soybean's ubiquity made an impression on Lardner, who commented: "If you have a little soy bean in your home there is no danger of malnutrition. This little fellow appears to be an effective substitute for everything from the anchovies to the 'zert, or from a to z." Lardner went on to offer a mock menu "for a day's patriotic meals" that included many courses of soybeans. Breakfast, for example, consisted of: "PROTEINS. Soy beans. STARCHES. Stand-up or Turn-down hash. This is made by cutting two worn-out stiff collars into small flakes and mixing them with soy beans. FATS. Boiled Kaiserkopf.

Remove the brains from a Hohenzollern's head in a thimble and sterilize the balance in boiling water. SWEETS. Oney Fred potpie, with soy beans."[65]

Lardner's *Tribune* colleague, the food writer Jane Eddington, had a more sincere enthusiasm for the "truly and wonderfully educational" exhibits of the food show. Like Lardner, she highlighted the presence of soybeans, zeroing in on a commercial booth staffed by two Chinese women, Hattie Don Sang and Marion G. Moy, which showcased "bean bread": bread and rolls made, they said, with 10 percent white flour, only "enough to forward fermentation."[66] These were, in Eddington's estimation, "deliciously palatable, so much so as to provoke criticism of ordinary baker's products made of white flour and flavorless almost save for the fat." When she asked where she could get soybean flour, however, she was informed, "We only make enough for our own bakery." The booth also displayed "toufu" and soybean sprouts, with recipes. Eddington concluded, "If we watch out we may find out how to make the soy bean cheese or toufu,"[67] although the most she offered her readers in a subsequent column was an extended quote from one of William Morse's bulletins describing how tofu was made, not any kitchen-tested process of her own.[68] Recipes from the Chicago Bean Bread Company, including those that used tofu, eventually made their way into Charles Piper's 1923 book, *The Soybean*, cowritten with Morse.[69] At the time of the Patriotic Food Show, however, the USDA was pursuing its own initiatives to adapt the soybean to American tastes, at one point sending a mission all the way to China to discover the secrets of making tofu but, for the most part, focusing on incorporating soy into such things as muffins and meatloaf.

The key to the soybean's appeal to home economists was its high protein content, up to 40 percent of its weight, a nutritional treasure house that could provide a frugal alternative to America's extravagant meat consumption.[70] As early as 1911, a number of American newspapers, under such headlines as "WONDERFUL SOYA BEAN," publicized the work of Gilbert Brooke, a British health officer in Singapore, who praised soybeans for being cheap and disease-resistant. "Most important of all," Brooke emphasized, they contained "more nearly than any other known animal or vegetable substance all the essential and properly proportioned constituents of a perfect diet," a reference to their high fat, as well as protein, content.[71] In 1914, citing other British sources, Jane Eddington pointed out that "the very element, nitrogen, which is good for renewing soil, is the one we get from foods" via protein "to renew or mend or build up our muscles." In a follow-up column, she advised, however, that this virtue created a challenge: the soybean "must be gently cooked because of its high protein content, and it would seem to require several hours to reduce it to the required softness."[72] In 1917, with the price going up not only for meat but also for navy beans, she recommended the soybean but cautioned that it was "in the world of vegetable foods what the old hen is among meat foods. Both contain a rocky sort of protein which can be cooked soft and savory if you know how. A good many people have not known how, so have discarded the soy bean after a trial or two."[73]

At the USDA, Morse would address this problem in his customary manner: exhaustive varietal testing. In 1917, USDA staff began cooking trials on around 800 numbered introductions and eventually discovered that two cooked very soft: SPI 34702 (subsequently Easycook) and SPI 40118 (subsequently Hahto), both large, unusually starchy soybeans. While the average soybean required three to six hours to soften, Easycook was ready in twenty minutes.[74] Morse would also recommend both varieties, especially Hahto, as substitutes for lima beans if harvested while green, about three-fourths of the way to full maturation, though some researchers found the substitution disappointing.[75] In any case, it seems that the earliest Morse was able to distribute these beans to experiment stations came in 1919, as he sent the varieties to George Washington Carver and to the Adventist Nashville Agricultural and Normal Institute, which was interested in marketing canned soybeans.[76] Meanwhile, the most readily available soybeans were from seed stores and tended to be popular hay varieties, like Mammoth Yellow, which did not readily soften.[77] In a 1918 bulletin, Morse reported that, as early as 1916, before the discovery of Easycook, several companies had canned 100,000 bushels of soybeans as baked beans.[78] With the price of soybeans themselves rising in late 1917, it seems, however, that housewives as well as canneries, after initial enthusiasm, scaled back their use of soybeans.[79] By April 1918, Eddington was praising the pinto as a cheaper alternative; it was, moreover, "a digestible bean," while she had "doubts about the soy bean in that regard."[80]

If preparing soybeans the way Americans were accustomed to preparing navy beans proved challenging, soy products such as flour and tofu still held promise. The USDA's Office of Home Economics focused on the flour, for which the more available but harder beans, such as Mammoth Yellow, were well suited. The Chinese had long used ground roasted soybeans as flour, in particular to make confections, but it was the Germans in the nineteenth century who, following the lead of Haberlandt, pioneered the production of unroasted soybean flour as a cheap form of protein for Europe's poor.[81] The flour gained its greatest popularity, however, as a specialty food for diabetics, typically by being mixed with wheat flour to varying degrees as a way to lower the carbohydrate content of bread. With the advent of soybean crushing in Britain, flour also represented a higher-value use than feed or fertilizer for the press cake left over after the oil was removed. Morse, in fact, sought to interest northern flour mills and bakeries in this by-product of what he envisioned would be the South's soybean industry.[82] In May 1918, under the direction of the same Charles Langworthy who in 1899 had written about tofu and other Asian soy foods, Home Economics issued *Use Soy-Bean Flour to Save Wheat, Meat and Fat.*

This pamphlet offered recipes for quick breads, muffins, and yeast breads using soybean flour, though it cautioned that "it is rich in protein and fat and should be combined with starchy substances like, rice, potatoes, or corn flour"; but because even the defatted soy flour of the era still contained a fair amount of oil, it reduced the need for added fat.[83] The publication also instructed housewives to make "soybean mush" by cooking the flour in a double boiler for two hours. This was a "meat saver," as it could be sliced and baked as croquettes or used as an ingredient—along with actual meat—in the Soy-Bean Meat Loaf recipe.[84] It is hard to gauge the influence of a single bulletin, but USDA demonstrators, notably Hannah Wessling from the Bureau of Chemistry, also toured the country to show agricultural extension workers the uses of soybean flour.[85] Home economics departments at universities also worked with soybeans, and "soy loaf" recipes—either using beans or flour—were published frequently in newspapers. All of these efforts presumed that housewives could obtain beans and grind their own flour, as the commercial product was scarce. As she indicated in a column in 1914, and again in 1917, the *Tribune*'s Eddington could obtain it only by way of a "medical manufactory" that produced it for diabetic patients.[86]

The USDA did not rule out adapting Asian soy foods to American tastes. Unaware of domestic tofu makers, it seems, the department selected the singular figure of Yamei Kin (photo 3) to undertake its mission to China. Born in 1864 to Chinese converts who died in a cholera epidemic, she was raised in China and Japan by American medical missionaries.[87] At age sixteen, under the name Y. May King, she entered the Women's Medical College, part of the New York Infirmary for Women and Children founded by the pioneering physician Elizabeth Blackwell, and in 1885 she graduated at the top of her class—the first Chinese woman to earn a US medical degree.[88] She did a short tour as a medical missionary, married a Macao-born Portuguese musician, and moved to Hawaii, where she gave birth to a son, Alexander, in 1896.[89] She moved to California, deserted her husband—who sued for divorce in her absence—and took to the theatrical lecture circuit, where she amazed audiences with the combination of her elaborate Chinese costumes and flawless English.[90] At a time when the Chinese faced exclusion and discrimination, she was embraced by American high society. She returned to China to pursue a dream of being her nation's Elizabeth Blackwell, heading up the Imperial Peiyang Women's Medical School and Hospital in Tientsin, where she devoted herself to bringing Western medical and sanitary techniques to China.[91] She held on to the position through the overthrow of the Qing Dynasty and the establishment of the Chinese Republic, and she began traveling to the United States again in 1911, escorting Chinese nursing students for American training and once more touring as a lecturer.[92]

In keeping with her thoroughly scrambled national identity, she was now to be sent to China as an American emissary. On June 10, 1917, the *New York Times Magazine* featured a full-page story, "WOMAN OFF TO CHINA AS GOVERNMENT AGENT TO STUDY SOY BEAN: DR. KIN WILL MAKE REPORT FOR UNITED STATES ON THE MOST USEFUL FOOD OF HER NATIVE LAND." The article remarked that this was the first time the "United States Government has given so much authority to a Chinese" national, marveling further that it was "a woman in whom such extraordinary confidence now reposed." The rest of the piece was an extended quote from Kin herself, who reiterated what was the recurring theme of her lectures: whereas the West might be technologically dominant, in the matter of living wisely and resourcefully, "we Chinese have far outstripped you." She pointed out that, "instead of taking the long and expensive method of feeding grain to an animal until the animal is ready to be killed and eaten, in China we take a short cut by eating the soy bean, which is protein, meat, and milk in itself."[93] In a time of wartime shortages, this could prove an indispensable wisdom for the Western allies.

Photo 3. Yamei Kin, 1912. Courtesy of onceuponatown.tumblr.com.

Another press account reported that Kin would actively organize, with the cooperation of the Chinese government, an "effort to multiply the production of the soy bean [for export to] the United States, Canada, and Great Britain." She was even to recruit Chinese farmers to return with her (the Chinese Exclusion Act's ban on laborers notwithstanding) to aid "in opening bean patches, the Chinese being, she thinks, experts in the best mode of selection."[94] These plans did not come to fruition, and it seems that in addition to her soybean investigations Kin spent her time in China trying to set up cotton plantations under the direction of American experts in a number of northern provinces.[95] When she returned to New York in October, however, she set about creating what one newspaper account declared "one of the most interesting kitchens in the world" at the New York laboratory of the USDA Bureau of Chemistry, the precursor to the Food and Drug Administration.[96] Since 1904, this lab had tested foods, wines, and oils suspected of adulteration as they entered the United States at its busiest port.[97] Kin was engaged in another of the bureau's functions, which had expanded markedly during the war: the search for "meritorious substitutes" for scarce foods. A firsthand account was provided by Sarah McDougal, a syndicated reporter, who visited on a hot summer day in 1918.

A "Chinese lad had just finished milking the soy beans before I came in," she recounted, explaining that although that "may sound queer," it was "all very simple." The beans had been soaked overnight, then ground in a mill that "looks primitive, being made of two huge pieces of granite, imported from China. In its homeland this mill is worked by coolies, in New York by electricity." The "soy bean cheese" made from the milk—McDougal never called it tofu—was "a base for a series of camouflage experiments," the success of which was vouched for by a number of chemists from the floor's other labs who fortuitously dropped in. "We made ours into fish for dinner last night," reported one man. "My wife fried a couple of fish and then fried some soy bean cheese in the gravy, and honest to goodness I couldn't tell which was which. It has a way of absorbing the flavor of whatever it's cooked with." "We had ours with chops," remarked another visitor, who insisted that if he hadn't known better he might have thought he was eating an additional chop. "Everybody in the place was ready to root for soy beans," McDougal remarked. She herself was impressed by the array of soybean products displayed in a row of glass jars on a long table. "Talk about dual personalities! The soy bean has so many aliases that if you shouldn't like it in one form you would be pretty sure to like it in another."

McDougal was treated to an all-soybean luncheon at the apartment of Kin's son. Kin could not herself attend, but Wai, the Chinese youth, served her guest. With a gracious smile, he placed a plate with a stuffed green pepper in front of her. "Soy beans," he said, then disappeared silently. McDougal scarcely "believed that pepper was stuffed with anything that was even

a distant relation to the soy beans" that she had once prepared in the manner of baked beans, with disappointing results. Kin later told her the peppers were stuffed with chopped tofu, prepared like chicken hash. "Honestly
I've never tasted anything more delicious." The accompanying biscuits were
made with soybean flour. Wai brought out the dessert, a "trembling pyramid
of chocolate blanc mange topped with white sauce." "Soy beans," he said.[98]
The meal concluded with soybean cheese. This was not fresh tofu, which
Kin also tended to call "cheese," but a fermented product—bean curd put
through the "cheese process"—that resembled Roquefort.

In late July, about the time that McDougal toured Kin's kitchen, the doctor B. R. Hart, chief of the Bureau of Chemistry's Eastern District, sent a
letter to members of the National Canners' Association. The year before,
when first notified of her mission, Hart had argued that Asian soy foods—
shoyu, miso, tofu, and *yuba*—were "consumed only by the Oriental population, with the possible exception of a small portion of the shoyu. In fact, the
flavor of most of these foods is so distinctive and peculiar that there is little
likelihood of their ever being accepted by Occidental peoples."[99] Now he
informed the canners that Kin had developed soybean dishes "well suited for
canning, and in view of the present shortage of meat they can be added with
advantage to the preparation[s] you now have on the market." He added that
a "number of prepared dishes of various kinds have been made up ready for
use, and these as well as the process for manufacturing the curd have been
worked out quite in detail. . . . Dr. Kin would be glad to grant you or your
representative a personal interview and explain the whole matter."[100] There
is no indication that any canner took Hart up on the offer.

Kin also hoped to use tofu "to increase the bulk and food value of meat
dishes served to soldiers in training at near-by camps," even serving an all-
soybean meal to a group of army officers. This was hampered by wartime
logistics: she was unable to arrange for large-scale shipments of soybeans
from North Carolina on the government-controlled railroads.[101] Kin also
did her share of demonstration work, giving a lecture on the soybean to a
Home Demonstration Conference in Washington, DC,[102] and even traveling to places like Buffalo, New York, to "demonstrate the use of Soy Bean
Curd as a wheat substitute."[103] But the war did not ultimately provide the
opportunity for tofu that she sought. One clue as to why may lie in the way
she would regularly recommend tofu as a substitute for chicken or fish or

describe it as tasting "a little like brains and a little like sweetbreads."[104] This positioned it as a substitute for foods that Americans were already substituting for beef, pork, and mutton, the only meats that the Food Administration defined as "meat" for the purposes of conservation.[105] As an indication of her project's dwindling prospects, the USDA allotted only $500 to her work in fiscal year 1919, which included the latter half of 1918, funds that she moreover had to share with another bureau scientist.[106] In *The Soybean*, published in 1923, Piper and Morse simply noted that "attempts have been made during the past 5 years to introduce tofu to the American people, but without much success."[107] Kin returned to China for good in 1920, to be remembered among a small coterie of American soybean enthusiasts as a "particularly well-known exponent of bean curd."[108]

If World War I did not lead to a general embrace of tofu, however, there was some good news for American soy foods. Seventh-day Adventists, now that numerous cultivars were available from the USDA, finally emerged as soybean innovators during the war years. In 1918, Morse visited the Nashville Agricultural and Normal Institute and reported that the school's horticulturalist "has done a considerable amount of work with different food products from the soy bean. At the present time they have a factory for canning several different soy products from the soy beans which are grown on their farm,"[109] the outcome of experiments apparently begun in 1917. Their canned soybeans undoubtedly improved after Morse sent them Easycook seeds in 1919. In 1922, Madison Foods—the institute's commercial food factory—added Soy Bean Meat to its line of nut-based meat substitutes.[110] According to the recollections of Harry Miller's son, his father was making soymilk and tofu at the Washington Sanitarium, which Miller ran after his return from China as early as 1921 and adding soybean flour to its meat analogs—still mostly made of wheat gluten and peanuts—in 1923.[111]

As early as 1918, T. A. Gundy, an Adventist in California who had worked at the St. Helena Sanitarium Food Company and was now the foreman of a ranch near San Jose, produced Smoein ("smoked protein"), a bacon-flavored seasoning made from powdered, roasted soybeans. (The Sanitarium Food Company, near Loma Linda, introduced a similar product, "Smokene," in 1922, which included dry yeast in its formulation.) Gundy's daughter would later recount that her father's interest in soybeans had been sparked in 1915 by the Panama-Pacific International Exposition in San Francisco, where he came across them in one of the Asian exhibits and managed to buy a hundred-pound sack to experiment with.[112]

John Harvey Kellogg, no longer a member of the Adventist Church, had discovered soybeans by his 1917 *New Method in Diabetes*, citing their use in Europe as a "highly valuable food for diabetics,"[113] mainly in the form of soybean flour used to augment the protein and cut down on the carbohydrates in bread. Kellogg's nephew, John Leonard Kellogg, appears to have gained an interest in soybeans even sooner. Lenn, as he was known, was the scion of John Harvey's estranged brother, Will, who owned the famous cereal business in Battle Creek. Like his uncle, Lenn was fond of experimenting with foods and is credited with creating Kellogg's All-Bran cereal.[114] In 1915, he applied for a patent for the "Manufacture of a Food Product," which combined soybean flour and peanut oil to create what was essentially a peanut-butter substitute, one that, he argued, contained "much more protein" than peanut butter and was therefore "very desirable as a dietetic food."[115] There is no indication that this product was ever marketed. By 1921, in any case, when John Harvey Kellogg wrote his *New Dietetics*, he was a full-blown enthusiast, declaring that "the soy bean is the best of all the beans."[116] Quoting the growing body of literature on soy foods, he described soymilk, tofu, soy sauce, and sprouts. He described a recipe for "a quite palatable milk from the soy bean" that involved boiling the milk for ten minutes but not otherwise altering the flavor, which he acknowledged was "different from that of cow's milk."[117]

By the 1920s, Adventists were an important redoubt of soy-food production and consumption, while the rest of the nation largely ignored the soybean as a substitute for meat and milk. Adventists would develop soy products for decades to come, until the 1960s provided new opportunities for a breakout. In the near term, however, soybean expansion would not rest on the adoption by Americans of traditional soy foods but instead on the somewhat unexpected embrace of soybeans by the Corn Belt for its system of producing meat.

CHAPTER THREE

TAKING ROOT

Although it was perhaps not as momentous at the time as it would become in retrospect, the "First Corn Belt Soybean Field Day" was nonetheless bigger than anyone expected. The crop extension specialists at Indiana's Purdue University arranged the day as the culmination of a series of county soybean field demonstrations held throughout the summer of 1920. In the spirit of neighborliness, they also invited growers and experiment station staff from nearby Corn Belt states.[1] On September 3, more than a thousand midwestern farmers, farm advisers, and agricultural researchers crowded onto the Fouts family farm, also known as "Soyland," near Camden, Indiana. Visitors inspected 150 acres of soybeans planted alone for seed production and hay, as well as 200 acres of soy and corn sown together to be browsed by black-faced lambs. As the lambs happily dined on soybean pods, the local Presbyterian Ladies Aid Society provided a lunch for the human guests that featured, along with sandwiches and pies, baked soybean salad and roasted, salted soybeans. As entertainment, a quartet of local growers sang "Growing Soybeans to Get Along."[2] The lyrics were not reported, but they were likely along the same lines as an ode published ten years later by one of the day's hosts, Taylor Fouts:

> Soybeans! Soybeans! You're like a Musical Band
> To the Farmer who's tuned for the "Best on his Land."
> Microbic Composers, on the millionth wave length,
> Sing "love" to the Rootlets as they're reveling in strength. . . .

62

The "Pop o' the Pods" is Jazz to the Pigs—Puts pep in the Porkers—
    They grunt and grow big.[3]

The words reflect the fears and hopes that brought the crowds to Soyland that day. Following two decades of prosperity and growth, peaking
with high demand for farm products during the war years, the region was
now coping with collapsing crop prices. Agronomists worried that patholo-
gies usually linked to southern farming—overreliance on a small number
of crops, declining soil fertility—had now made their way north, thus the
hopes surrounding soybeans. As legumes, they could add fertility back to
the soil. As a new crop, they could diversify midwestern farming. And as
a high-protein hog feed that could be consumed in the field and added to
corn in silos, it promised at least to cut the cost of pork production, if not
solve the problem of oversupply. More than anything else, the day's events
showcased the organizational energy with which the region confronted its
challenges. This was a golden age of joiners, and indeed at the end of the
afternoon a group of attendees decided that the day's success should be followed up the following year not by a second Corn Belt Soybean Field Day,
but by a National Soybean Field Day, to be arranged by a newly formed
National Soybean Growers' Association (NSGA). This would later become
the American Soybean Association (ASA), to this day the chief voice of
soybean farmers.[4]

It would be a mistake, however, to draw too straight a line from that day
in 1920 to the region's eventual embrace of the soybean as a leading crop. The
task of convincing a substantial number of midwestern farmers to plant soybeans stretched over the following two decades, progressing in fits and starts.
The Corn Belt Soybean Field Day was a high point of the first wave of enthusiasm, built on the premise of pigs eating soil-enriching soybeans in the
field. By 1940, this would be an increasingly quaint notion, supplanted by the
growth of a soybean-processing industry whose diverse array of products
included commercial hog feed. In retrospect, it is easy to see the spread of the
soybean in the Midwest as something inevitable, but from the standpoint of
1920, the optimism of the crowds on the Fouts farm notwithstanding, it was
far from a sure thing.

The Soybean Pipeline, Stage Three: The Last Mile

The enthusiasm for soybeans in the Midwest at first took the nation's leading expert on the crop by surprise. About a month before he wishfully chatted up the Biloxi coffee manufacturer about soybeans, William Morse was
able to send a more heartening report from the northern leg of his annual
tour. On August 31, 1920, he wrote C. V. Piper from the Beardsley hotel in
Champaign, Illinois: "My trip thus far has been one of the best soy bean
trips I have ever experienced. It is remarkable how interest in the soy bean
has increased throughout the northern and central states." This was not the
region where he and Piper had expected soybeans to take off, but that hardly
dampened his pride at the outcome of a decade of evenhandedly promoting
the soybean wherever it might succeed. "It is rather gratifying," he noted,
"how the varieties sent out by our office are taking hold." Near Quincy, Illinois, he observed an eight-acre field of Virginia soybeans averaging six feet
tall. "Needless to say the grower is mighty proud." The next day he planned
to visit a farm where they produced seed on 170 acres, and the day after that
he would "leave with Prof. Hackleman by auto for Camden, Indiana, for a
visit to the famous soy bean farms of the Fouts Brothers."[5] Morse's presence
at the Corn Belt Soy Bean Field Day appears to have been by chance, with
no indication that the organizers thought to invite him, although once there
he obligingly reported on the breeding work under way at Arlington Farm.[6]

It was fitting that Jay Courtland Hackleman, of the University of Illinois, provided the crucial link between Morse and the nascent ASA. The
relationship he would cultivate with Morse over the next decade was one
reason that his state would take the lead among soybean producers. "Hack,"
as he was known to colleagues, was born in 1888 on a farm near Carthage,
Indiana. His pluck and enterprise was apparent from an early age, with a
particular talent for leading organizations. He attended college at Purdue,
where at various times he was president of the Agriculture Society, editor
of the *Purdue Daily Exponent*, organization editor of the Purdue yearbook,
and president of the Emersonian Literary Society. At the University of Missouri, where he earned a master's degree in 1912, he served as an instructor in
farm crops until 1917 and as an assistant professor in crops extension until
1919.[7] He was also secretary and treasurer of the Missouri Corn Growers'
Association from 1914 to 1919—in which capacity he proved to be a valuable

intermediary between drought-stricken Missouri farmers and seed merchants, whom he convinced to donate thousands of dollars' worth of seed.[8]
When he joined the University of Illinois in 1919 as the assistant professor
in charge of crops extension,[9] an office established only a year earlier,[10] he set
about his work with customary vigor. He eventually was best known for his
Better Seed Corn campaign, which promoted improved corn varieties, and
for his role in founding the Illinois Crop Improvement Association.[11]

Hackleman was one of a growing cohort of extension workers. The farm
demonstration movement, in which volunteer farmers would exhibit new
crops and methods under the direction of agricultural experts, had its roots
in Texas early in the century, when USDA agent Seaman A. Knapp persuaded a farmer to practice diversified farming in the face of the boll weevil
invasion. The farmer's methods—and profits—were showcased to others in
the area. The first agricultural agent devoted to a single county, and whose
salary was provided in part from farmers and businesses from that county,
appeared in Smith County, Texas, in 1906. These early county agents were
itinerant teachers, usually farmers from the counties they served, who coordinated demonstration work according to Knapp's dictates.[12] In the North
and West, where demonstration work developed more slowly, state agricultural colleges were more commonly involved. Agents, sometimes known as
"farm advisers," were typically college graduates versed in scientific agronomy.
At the same time, the approach was less top-down than it was in the South,
as agents focused on publicizing and disseminating the existing practices of
the most productive local farmers.[13]

In 1914, the Smith-Lever Act increased federal funding for county agents
as a supplement to their state and county support, meanwhile consolidat-
ing the system under the joint control of the USDA's Office of Extension
Work and state agricultural colleges. This helped boost the number of
county agents from 928 in 1914 to 1,436 by the outset of World War I. Even
as the war curtailed demonstration work, it enhanced both the number and
prestige of county agents as they engaged in national campaigns to increase
food production. By the end of the war, there were 2,435 of them, serving
in almost two-thirds of US counties.[14] This growth was matched by that of
county farm bureaus, which were voluntary associations of rural citizens
that provided additional financial support for county agents. With the encouragement of agricultural colleges, there were hundreds of farm bureaus

by 1919, with an aggregate membership in the hundreds of thousands.[15] County agents were also instrumental in organizing, advising, and sometimes operating the purchasing and marketing cooperatives that emerged following the war. These pooled money for fertilizer, seeds, and other inputs or collectively marketed poultry, produce, or dairy products.[16] This kind of associationalism was especially robust in the North, increasing its potential relative to the South as a proving ground for novel crops.

Every distribution system needs to solve the costly problem of the last mile, where trunk lines split up to transport cargoes to numerous final destinations. In the case of new soybean varieties—which traveled through feeder networks to the central pipeline of Morse's office in Washington—this meant getting them to seed merchants, who would expand the supply of seeds, and finally into the hands of individual farmers. The growing network of extension workers, county agents, farm bureaus, and voluntary associations constituted this last mile for soybeans, and nobody proved more effective at this than Hackleman. By the time he joined the University of Illinois in the fall of 1919, soybeans had become a priority. Undoubtedly realizing that, although new corn varieties could be bred locally, the best source for new soybean varieties was Asia by way of Washington, and he set about actively courting Morse.

In his new post, Hackleman first wrote to Morse in late November 1919, reminding him with a touch of flattery of their prior correspondence: "As you will notice, I have changed my location somewhat, but have not changed my source of soybean information."[17] (He had conducted soybean variety tests with local Missouri farmers in 1914.)[18] In January, he wrote to ask, "Do you have any new variety or strain of soybeans that you think especially promising and which you would like to have propagated here in the Corn Belt?" He assured Morse, "I am going to do all I can to foster soybean production in Illinois, and the county advisers are already working on the subject very vigorously." Morse replied tentatively that it would be possible to cooperate with Illinois in variety testing if the work was "not too extensive, as our supply of seed of the various varieties is somewhat limited."[19] Hackleman was able to report to Morse in February that, at a conference with farm advisers, he lined up demonstrations in two counties in southern Illinois, across from St. Louis. Morse agreed to send seeds of seven varieties directly to the advisers. Losing no time, Hackleman mentioned in his reply that he was now taking a trip to the northwestern section of the state and would write upon his return "as to the varieties and the amount of seed that will be needed."[20]

Pressing harder, Hackleman wrote in June to invite Morse "to take a day off and visit us here at Urbana" during Morse's customary tour of northern and western states in the fall. In a later letter, he expanded this invitation to include a tour of demonstration plots in the southern counties. As with sending seeds, Morse's first response was polite but noncommittal: "If I am in that region during the season, and can manage it, I shall be pleased to drop in and see you." Finally he relented, agreeing to meet up with Hackleman in St. Louis in late August and from there embark on a tour of several Illinois counties where cooperating farmers hosted soybean demonstrations.[21] This was the tour that culminated with the Field Day at Soyland and the founding of what would become the ASA. From that moment on, Morse's attention would decisively shift to the Corn Belt, and he and Hackleman would become active collaborators. Morse no longer begrudged his new friend seeds, fulfilling annual requests that amounted to as much as 100 pounds each of several varieties. These were used for demonstrations in a growing number of Illinois counties: sixteen in 1921 and 1922, twenty-seven in 1923.[22]

Hackleman provided a valuable conduit for new soybean varieties at a decisive moment. He reported that, during one meeting with county farm advisers to plan the upcoming year's demonstrations, one adviser hesitated to buck the popular sentiment in his southern Illinois county favoring cowpeas over soybeans. Other advisers spoke up to say that they had been in the same position a year earlier but that "one or two demonstrations had changed things materially."[23] Hackleman and Morse also worked together to firmly establish the association founded at Soyland. Its annual Field Day was held in Champaign in 1921, and Hackleman led a large Illinois delegation to Washington for Morse's turn to host in 1925.[24] The two men also traveled each winter to the Chicago International Stock Show, during which the NSGA held its first several business meetings, mainly for the purposes of electing officers and planning the summer Field Days. They both sat on the Soybean Nomenclature Committee, where they sought to regularize the provision of new varieties. This involved working with seed companies to increase the supply of new strains, all the while pressing them to use official varietal names rather than inventing new names for old varieties, a common practice to garner repeat business from farmers who might otherwise save and plant their own seed. Even before Morse visited Champaign, Hackleman had addressed this issue by founding a local soybean seed growers' organization that pledged participating farmers to grow only approved beans.[25]

Hackleman and others like him were key to ensuring that new varieties made their way onto farms, but they did not create the first wave of soybean enthusiasm by themselves. Rather, there were larger forces at play that led agronomists at Corn Belt colleges to make soybeans a priority and that made farmers eager to plant them.

Hay in the Field

Prior to World War I, there was a small but steady interest in soybeans among Corn Belt farmers, spurred by pioneer enthusiasts such as Dr. Isaac "Soy Bean" Smith of Huntington County, Indiana, and E. F. "Soybean" Johnson of Stryker, Ohio. Smith, a physician who inherited his family farm and decided to run it along scientific lines, obtained beans directly from the USDA in 1905 and initially found them problematic. Alerted by a Purdue bulletin of the need to inoculate his field with the appropriate bacteria, he persuaded the experiment station to give him soil with which to experiment. In one account, on his way home "he told several farmers of his intention to inoculate his farm and they laughed at him." By 1914, however, having gradually inoculated new land with soil enriched by successive harvests, he had sixty acres planted in soybeans and was "making money out of them." His chief dilemma as early as 1911, in fact, was whether to use the beans to fatten hogs or to sell them—along with inoculated soil—to the farmers who had once laughed at him but who now clamored for seed.[26] By 1916, E. F. Johnson similarly claimed that "probably no crop has ever made such rapid progress in winning favor with corn-belt farmers, as has the soybean." Unknown ten years earlier, "it is fast becoming a necessity in every system of rotation as a soil builder."[27]

Given that they were aggressive salesmen and promoters, however, Smith's and Johnson's claims should be treated with some caution. Cyril Hopkins, professor of soil chemistry at the University of Illinois, gave a more measured assessment in 1916 of the soybean's popularity. Responding to a request from Morse for state statistics, Hopkins wrote that "we regard both the cowpea and the soybean as valuable crops in Illinois, primarily as substitution crops in years when the farmer has no clover in his rotation because of clover failure." As was typical for these years, soybeans were part of a spectrum of legumes valued for enriching the soil and providing hay, but they ranked lower than clover and were, it seems, less common than cowpeas. Though lacking hard data, Hopkins guessed that "about one farmer in ten in southern Illinois grows some cowpeas, perhaps on one-tenth of his cultivated acreage. Possibly half as large a proportion of soybeans is grown in central and northern Illinois [north of the cowpea's typical range] in seasons when there is little or no clover, but, in normal seasons when clover is abundant, the soybean is correspondingly more rarely grown."[28] If it was any indication of the priority given to soybeans at the university itself, W. L. Burlison of the College of Agriculture, addressing his response to "Mr. W. J. Moore," turned down an offer from Morse of thirty new Manchurian varieties for testing.[29] Aside from a few requests for older varieties, similarly directed to W. J. Moore, correspondence between the University of Illinois and Morse did not pick up until Hackleman came on board in 1919.

Hackleman's arrival happened during a postwar farm crisis in the Corn Belt. Prices for corn and wheat had collapsed after the war, corn dropping from $1.52 per bushel in 1918 to 60 cents per bushel in 1920. Hackleman estimated that even oats "seemed to offer less returns each successive season."[30] To make matters worse, the amount of corn that farmers were able to harvest from each acre of land was growing smaller. Hackleman attributed this decline in soil fertility to wartime demand. Farmers had overplanted corn and wheat at the expense of other crops in traditional rotations, particularly nitrogen-fixing legumes such as clover. Soil became acidic as it was likewise depleted of calcium-containing minerals, collectively known as "lime," which in turn led to lower yields of clover when farmers returned to planting it after the war and therefore to a smaller gain in soil nitrogen.[31] The subsequent lower yields of corn, combined with reductions in land devoted to the crop in such states as Ohio—where acreage fell 39 percent between 1919 and 1924—might have led to higher prices, but corn grown in states farther west and north helped to sustain a national glut.[32] Corn Belt farmers could not hope to increase their income by idling their acres and restricting supply. They needed to divert their land to something profitable, and soybeans were a promising alternative.

By March 1919, W. L. Burlison, the new head of the University of Illinois agronomy department, was markedly more bullish about soybeans than he had been in 1917, when he responded so tepidly to Morse's offer of new varieties. In an article in the *Orange Judd Farmer*, he lauded the tolerance of soybeans to acidic soil, enabling them to grow on land where clover failed and to take over the role of increasing soil fertility for the crops that followed.[33] It was to spearhead a soybean campaign, then, that Burlison hired Hackleman and the plant scientist C. M. Woodworth, who performed much of the actual breeding work at the university over the following two decades.[34] If Burlison's primary goal was to save the fertility of the state's soil, however, this was not necessarily enough of a reason for farmers to adopt a new crop. The soybean would have to pay its way beyond providing a cheap alternative to fertilizer. The key to the first wave of its popularity among Illinois farmers, in fact, was that it also seemed to provide a cheap way to fatten hogs.

The Corn Belt did not so much produce corn as corn-fed meat, using practices that originated in Virginia and Kentucky in the early nineteenth century. Settlers carried the system to the Midwest soon thereafter. The highest-value destinations for Illinois corn after World War I were the state's cattle feedlots and Chicago's famous packinghouses, but a reliable fallback for farmers when the market for corn faltered was to use it to fatten hogs on their own farms. Unfortunately, the postwar prices of slaughtered hogs also fell due to oversupply.[35] According to the *Chicago Tribune*, many Corn Belt farmers in 1920 "closed the gates to their feedlots, declaring they would stay out of the game until conditions improved."[36] Rather than abandon hogs altogether, however, they took to sowing soybeans among fields of corn and then "hogging down" the fields in the late summer, when the plants were young enough to provide easy forage but the beans were mature enough to supply the concentrated protein ration that, in feedlots, was typically provided by tankage (processed meat scraps) or oilseed meal.[37] Farmers who did not want to hog down corn and soybeans in the field might alternately harvest the combined crops for fresh feed ("soilage") or winter silage. Hackleman estimated that soybean production in Illinois grew from less than 300 acres in 1909 to 40,000 acres in 1919. In 1923 it reached almost 900,000 acres.[38]

The expansion of acreage grown for feed triggered a secondary boom in soybeans grown for seed. One indication of this was the increasing percentage of acres on which soybeans were grown alone rather than mixed with corn or other crops. While in 1919 these constituted a tenth of soybean acres, in 1923 they represented a full quarter of the vastly increased acreage.[39] This raised the worrisome possibility, however, that the soybean boom was a bubble. Just as farmers began producing seed to sell to other farmers for the purpose of growing yet more seed, the ultimate market for all of those seeds was showing signs of weakness. Problems had emerged with feeding hogs whole soybeans. Most damaging was that the high oil content of soybeans resulted in "soft" pork that was flabby in appearance. When hogs were fattened for lard this was not a big detriment, but market demand was shifting to favor leaner hogs for bacon. One solution, as with hogs fed peanuts, was to finish them off with several weeks of corn alone. But other producers instead limited whole soybeans to no more than 10 percent of the hog's ration, potentially putting a drag on the crop's expansion.[40]

In a talk to the Society for Agronomy in 1923, Hackleman cautioned that some of the other early selling points of the soybean had also been overstated. Soybeans indeed grew in sour or acidic soils where red clover failed, but high yields nonetheless required a generous application of limestone. In fact, he estimated that it took more limestone to produce a ton of soybean hay than a ton of red clover.[41] Likewise, "much has been said about the merits of the soybean as a soil builder, and great promises have been made for it. In fact, it now seems that entirely too much emphasis has been given to this characteristic of the crop." While it did make a considerable amount of "its own nitrogenous food" given the right conditions, he noted that, in the rush to expand acreage, "a comparatively small percentage of the corn belt farms producing soybeans are really raising the crop as a legume." They did not inoculate their seeds properly with symbiotic nitrogen-fixing bacteria, in the absence of which soybeans consumed almost twice the nitrogen of oats and substantially more phosphorous and potassium. Even when inoculation was thorough, evidence suggested that soybeans provided little more benefit than oats to subsequent stands of wheat.[42]

Hackleman concluded that it was time for a fundamental reassessment of the soybean "to determine its real value and to ascertain its proper place in the farming system." As Hackleman now saw it, a system of hogging down beans in the field would not sustain an expanding soybean crop. To get sufficient value out of soybeans meant investing more labor or capital in them.

The return on soybean hay, which needed to be harvested and cured, compared favorably to alfalfa hay. The soybean's greatest value, however, lay in pressing out the oil—the cause of soft pork—and using the meal as a high-protein additive to feed rations. In this role, it was a viable alternative to flaxseed and cottonseed meal. But this use ultimately required more than investments by farmers. It required a local crushing industry. This is where the networks of farm advisers, bureaus, and associations finally proved insufficient. They would be unable, on their own, to create such an industry from the ground up. All the same, when a crushing industry did begin to emerge, these networks would provide necessary support at a crucial junction.[43]

A Sustained Crush

In 1927, the Illinois Central rail line introduced the Soil and Soybean Special, a rolling exhibition of soybeans and soybean products with accompanying lectures by "soil doctors and soybean specialists."[44] Two cars contained exhibits prepared by Hackleman, two were converted into motion picture theaters, one was for lectures, and one, in the rear, was where officials dined and slept. The Soybean Special traveled 2,478 miles, made 105 stops, and attracted almost 34,000 people to, among the other things, compete in a contest to guess the number of soybeans in a five-gallon glass jug—the prize being 50 tons of limestone for improving soil.[45] It was the latest in a long line of agricultural demonstration trains, extending back to the 1904 Seed Corn Gospel Train. In 1911 alone, seventy-one trains traveled through twenty-one different states with a collective attendance of almost a million people.[46] It is not clear which movies were shown in the cinema cars. Perhaps they included *Four Men and the Soy*, a twenty-minute film that debuted at the 1925 meeting of the ASA and that followed four farmers as they attended field demonstrations at the Ohio State University Soybean Day.[47]

One of the biggest draws was an appearance by A. E. Staley, cornstarch magnate and chief organizer of the Soybean Special. Born sixty years earlier in North Carolina, he liked to recount how in 1880 his father attended a Methodist camp meeting where he received a handful of soybeans from a missionary returning from China. "My father turned them over to me to play with. I planted two rows of the beans in the family vegetable garden. I was proud of them. I weeded them and picked them. Then I planted some more. The missionary said they would be good for the soil. I believed it—even if no one else did." He claimed that there were still some soybeans in North Carolina "parented by that original handful from China."[48] When a reporter covering the Soybean Special asked if he had any hobbies, his answer was to the point. "Soybeans—just soybeans, I guess." This was not entirely true: soybeans were not really a hobby for Staley but rather a business venture struggling to make a profit. Taking to the train to convince farmers to plant more soybeans—and to harvest them for beans, not hay—was one part of a multipronged strategy to build a soybean crushing industry from scratch.

The earliest attempts to establish soybean mills in the Corn Belt began seven years earlier, just as the first wave of soybean enthusiasm swept through the region's farms. The region lacked the ubiquitous cottonseed mills of the South, which were a natural basis, to Piper and Morse, anyway, for founding an industry. There were a number of small mills, such as the Chicago Heights Oil Manufacturing Company, established in 1907, that relied on cottonseed and flaxseed from other regions, which it would process into oil and meal for nearby industries and feed operations. In the early years of the century, however, it was given the chance to crush a local product: corn germ. The germs constituted only 10 percent of corn kernels by weight but contained fully half of the oil. To prevent products from going rancid in an era when nationally marketed brands required greater shelf life, corn mills increasingly removed the germs before grinding the corn into hominy products: cornmeal, grits, and flour. Initially, the germs went into livestock feed, but the rising demand for vegetable oil, along with shortages of olive oil during World War I, made it more profitable to press them. Like cottonseed, however, corn germ was a by-product, and its availability fluctuated with the demand for corn products. The end of the war drastically reduced demand for corn, and to make matters worse, Prohibition threatened the principal use for corn grits, which were combined with malted barley for brewing beer.[49]

Looking for an alternative to corn germ, Chicago Heights experimented with crushing soybeans in the fall of 1919.[50] The results were disappointing. Illinois and Indiana farmers tended to sell beans that were cracked or otherwise unfit for planting. The company's operators were, moreover, still trying to figure out how to adapt corn-oil equipment for soybeans. "The few drums of oil produced," by one account, "were as sorry-looking as the beans." During the 1920 harvest, there were simply no soybeans to be had because farmers saved them, or sold them, for seed. The company ended up bringing in ten carloads of soybeans from North Carolina and Virginia. It sold the resulting twenty barrels of oil to an oil-compounding company, its product now good enough, it seems, to mix with oils of higher quality without being noticed.[51] The company also tried to foster a market for the other end product of the soybean crush. It "coaxed and forced feeders to try the meal," in the words of one of the company's operators, I. C. Bradley. It gave away free samples of meal to farmers and experiment stations, exhibited it at county and state fairs, and blended it with wheat flour in five-pound bags to sell at grocery stores, at least the few "who would consent to accept it."[52]

A. E. Staley turned his attention to soybeans at about the same time. Staley had begun life as a farm boy eager to leave the farm. As a teenager, he advanced to small-town clerk in a dry-goods store, the first step in a logical, upward progression. He went from clerk to traveling salesman, which alerted him to the national trend of packaging and branding what had until then been sold in bulk—for example, boxes of Nabisco products supplanting the cracker barrel. He established a popular brand of his own, Cream Corn Starch, in Baltimore. Then, to secure his supply of raw material, he ventured into cornstarch manufacturing in 1908 by purchasing a bankrupt starch plant in Decatur, Illinois. By dint of his considerable powers of salesmanship, he managed to weather a number of near-bankruptcies himself until, by the 1920s, the original six-acre site in Decatur had grown to forty-seven and the number of manufacturing buildings from eight to forty-one.[53] Because "wet millers" of cornstarch—like "dry millers" of hominy—removed the germs, one of these buildings likely held a corn-oil plant. Like Chicago Heights, his mill was well positioned to diversify into soybean crushing. When Staley did so, however, he insisted that it was not primarily in pursuit of additional profits.

Staley chatted regularly with local farmers, who complained to him of low prices and the declining fertility of their land. Agreeing with the state's agricultural researchers, Staley concluded that the region was being "corned to death," in part to supply his own business. On his return from a visit home to North Carolina in 1919—during which, by his account, he was reminded of his boyhood experience planting soybeans—he reportedly pulled out a handful of beans from his pocket and declared to a business associate that "farmers need something to rotate with corn and I think soybeans are the answer." At first, he believed there would be value in removing green soybeans from their pods and plowing them into fields as manure, an idea he later attributed to a "bum steer." He soon received more reliable information from the University of Illinois, which he disseminated through leaflets given out to the farmers who supplied him.[54] This was around the time that Hackleman, worried that the soybean expansion might fizzle, wrote to Morse urging that uses be "found for the seed in addition to its present use," which was "almost one hundred percent" for replanting.[55] In 1920, perhaps at the urging of Hackleman, Staley acquired two corn-oil expellers that he directed his plant superintendent, George Chamberlain, to adapt for soybeans.

Through 1920, Chamberlain modified the expellers. He also tinkered with the equipment that dried the beans. His work in 1921 was devoted to providing truck access, as too few beans were expected to arrive to justify the use of railroad freight cars. Then there was a business downturn, which made money so tight that Staley borrowed against daily invoices to cover payroll. It was not until June 1922, late in the season but still in time for farmers to plant soybeans, that Staley officially announced the construction of the plant. In October, it opened, hailed by Staley for "inaugurating a new industry for Central Illinois and providing the growers of this territory with a market for their beans." With characteristic bravura, he predicted that "the day will come when our plant will process more soybeans than corn," this at a time when his company was handling 40,000 bushels of corn daily.[56]

By the time it opened, Staley's plant was one of several new operations. Farm advisers from Piatt County helped to organize a cooperative mill in Monticello, roughly halfway between Decatur and Champaign, that would use the cutting-edge method of solvent extraction to process a projected 50,000 bushels during 1922–1923. The Piatt County advisers had themselves been inspired after touring a new mill in Peru, Indiana.[57] Chicago Heights signaled its confidence in soybeans by increasing its crushing capacity with two new hydraulic presses. Meanwhile, the East St. Louis Oil Company also geared up to process soybeans.[58] With Hackleman's encouragement, the four Illinois mills—Staley, Monticello, Chicago Heights, and East St. Louis Oil—issued a joint guarantee to farmers that they would purchase 250,000 tons of soybeans for crushing.[59]

But the farmers did not cooperate with the plan. The harvest was large, but this led many to worry that this would glut the market for milling. They decided instead to store their beans until the spring for what they hoped would be robust demand for seed. As a result, the four companies received only a few thousand tons of beans.[60] In early 1923, in a letter to Morse, Hackleman lamented that he did not understand "how the rumor started" that Indiana and Illinois had an overproduction of beans. Mills were paying up to $1.45 per bushel and still "not getting enough beans to pay them to run."[61] The Monticello plant operated for only six months in 1923–1924 and then shut down entirely until new owners purchased it in 1929.[62] Chicago Heights ended up selling its machinery to the Funk Brothers Seed Company in Bloomington, Illinois, which hired I. C. Bradley to operate it.[63]

Staley, who at first was able to purchase beans for less than a dollar a bushel, operated seventy-four days in 1922 and fifty-seven days in early 1923.[64] The situation was no better during the 1923–1924 season, when Staley paid $1.50 per bushel. He noted in 1924 that a number of new mills had opened and, not having the luxury of idling their plants as he did, were driving up prices to $1.80 per bushel. "Our experience so far has been both unprofitable and discouraging," he reported. Calculating the costs of investment, depreciation, and plant idleness, he estimated that "our loss for one month's operation amounted to approximately twelve thousand dollars." Convinced that the 1924 harvest would also go for seed, Staley closed down the mill that fall. He made plans to "dismantle the plant and discontinue the soybean business" if prices did not fall.[65]

Eventually they did, but only because the market for seed faltered. In the spring of 1925, farmers "could not dispose of their soybeans at any price," reported Frederick Wand, the head of Staley's soybean department, to the fall 1925 ASA field meeting.[66] This was the case even though the production of soybeans had not gone up much: farmers had increased their plantings by 25 percent, but poor yields meant the harvest was only 7 percent higher. Wand described the problem as a matter of mutual trust. Farmers would not grow soybeans on an extensive scale, creating a buyer's market in the crop, unless they had confidence "in the honesty and integrity of the manufacturer" to "handle their beans with only a small margin of profit"—that is, to pay a fair price. The manufacturers, for their part, could not offer reliably high prices for beans unless growers produced them "in large enough quantities to keep the mill operating throughout the year." This was the only way to hold down overhead costs and, more important, to establish a year-round market for soybean products. Ultimately, Wand argued, farmers would find that growing beans in high volume for crushing was a much more reliable way to make money than gambling each year on getting a premium for seeds. Farmers, however, did the opposite, shrinking their soybean acreage in 1926. But this time good yields actually pushed up the production figures, and prices declined steeply. All told, Staley found it worthwhile to run his mill for seven months in 1925 and eight in 1926.[67] This saved farmers from a total loss but did not necessarily do much to build mutual trust.

The problem for the nascent soybean industry went beyond whether farmers would plant more land in soybeans. It was a matter of their willingness to invest a substantial amount of labor and capital to take full advantage of the crop. To get high yields of soybeans and the crops that might follow them, for instance, farm advisers were at pains to emphasize the necessity of inoculating the soil, either mixing bacteria-laden dirt into their fields or coating seeds with inoculated soil or pure bacterial cultures. Minimizing losses of beans during harvesting, furthermore, required an expensive upgrade in equipment. Conventional binders, which gathered plants for later threshing by a grain separator, resulted in a high number of shattered pods. A potential alternative was the combine, a harvesting machine able to both cut and thresh beans in the field, leaving behind the straw. Already used to harvest wheat in the American Southwest, combines were widely perceived as too large for the needs of Corn Belt farms. After witnessing a demonstration on 200 acres in central Illinois, however, Frederick Wand traveled in 1924 to the Massey-Harris Harvester Company headquarters in Batavia, New York. He urged its directors to expand their sales organization to Illinois, where it soon succeeded in selling eight combines, a small but meaningful start for the state.[68] In a 1928 bulletin, Hackleman praised combines for lowering shattering losses; shortening the harvest season, thus reducing the risk of bad weather; and leaving behind a litter of stalks, leaves, and pods that fertilized the soil. Still, he remarked that "combines are costly" (photo 4).[69]

Commercially oriented midwestern farmers had long shown a willingness to adopt capital-intensive innovations, but in the early 1920s soybeans were a fallback crop. It was planted alongside corn as a forage crop or, when corn prices were low, planted in its place.[70] Many farmers did not bother to

Photo 4. Combine harvesting Manchu soybeans in Illinois, ca. 1928. From
J. C. Hackleman, *Soybean Production in Illinois.*

inoculate their soil, and many stuck to planting oats in traditional crop rotations, even when urged by farm advisers to substitute more highly profitable
soybeans. Oats were an easy crop to plant and market, whereas soybeans, in
the estimation of one mill manager, required "more information, labor and
machinery." In the absence of a "standardized market," soybeans were not
worth the investment.[71] Private and public capital had in fact gone into creating such a market—with resources invested by universities, governments,
and mills to build a soy-processing industry—but if it was not enough to
trigger investment by farmers, it would be for naught. Staley, for his part,
made a sustained pitch to farmers, distributing posters and free booklets to
stores, grain elevators, and banks. This strategy culminated with his work
to organize the 1927 Soybean Special.[72] That year, in fact, farmers did plant
more soybeans, but mostly because of poor conditions for corn. Unusually
dry weather and the incursion into the Midwest of a new insect pest, the
European corn borer, made soybeans once again an attractive fallback.

The true turning point for the industry came in 1928 with the "Peoria
Plan," a development from which Staley stood aloof. The plan percolated
up through the era's rich network of voluntary associations. H. G. Atwood,
president of the American Milling Company, happened to attend a meeting

of the Peoria Chamber of Commerce's Rural-Urban Committee, where a farmer complained about the shortage of market outlets for soybeans. Atwood took up the matter with the president of the Peoria County Farm Bureau, proposing that his company join with several others to provide a guaranteed outlet. They arranged a meeting attended by, among others, representatives of the Funk Brothers Seed Company, the Grange League Federation Exchange (GLF), and the Caterpillar Tractor Company. Hackleman and the editor of the Chicago *Prairie Farmer* also attended. Funk Brothers, American Milling, and the Grange League Federation agreed to contract up to 50,000 acres of Illinois soybeans—equivalent to roughly 1 million bushels—for a guaranteed price of $1.35 per bushel. The agreement allowed farmers to sell to other bidders for more, as long as they gave the three mills the first option to buy at the higher price. The contracts, signed by individual farmers who each indicated the acreage they planned to devote to soybeans, were distributed through a Farm Bureau Committee created at a meeting of Illinois county agents. By the beginning of August, the committee had collected over 1,000 signed contracts representing more than 40,000 acres.[73]

The lynchpin of the whole scheme was its distinctive marketing plan. Rather than push the oil—which, if not of consistently high quality, was not deemed fit for anything beyond the "soap kettle"[74]—the mills cultivated a reliable and profitable outlet for the meal, for which standards were less stringent. All three mills produced large amounts of mixed or "formulated" feeds. Consisting largely of ground corn, these typically included cottonseed or flaxseed meal as a concentrated source of protein, but soybean meal also sufficed in most cases. Because it retained a fair amount of oil even after crushing, it was still not a good choice for hog feed—soft pork would be the result—but it was suitable for dairy cattle. The market for dairy feed, moreover, extended well beyond the Corn Belt. The Grange League Federation, for one, had contacts with the New York Grange League Federation and its dairy farmers. Such outlets proved so lucrative that the mills ended up offering the contract price to all farmers, whether they had signed a contract or not. As a result, they scrambled to find storage space for 40 percent more beans than originally anticipated. This forced other mill owners to pay a similar price—even Staley, who had refused to join the plan on the principle of never contracting for beans more than thirty days in advance.[75] Like the Peoria Plan mills, he ultimately courted new customers for the

meal. Ranchers in western states such as Colorado provided a ready market
for Staley's innovative feed pellets, designed to be easily found by cattle and
sheep when scattered on snowy fields.[76]

The impact of these new arrangements went far beyond short-term sales.
Their greatest importance was to provide the steady revenue—and bright
outlook for the future—that drove new investments in soybeans by everyone
involved in production, from farmers and mills to agricultural experiment
stations and the federal government.

Capital Investments

The impact of the Peoria Plan extended into the next decade. The number
of Illinois acres planted in soybeans rose modestly from 465,000 in 1927 to
497,000 in 1928 and then, following two good years of high yields and strong
prices, up to 719,000 in 1930. The amount grown for beans rose even more
markedly, with increases in production from around 2 million bushels in
1927 to just over 3 million in 1928. The output of beans in 1929 grew by only
a couple of hundred thousand bushels, but the unusually high proportion of
the harvest sold as seed that year set the stage for an enormous expansion in
1930, to just shy of 6 million bushels.[77] The shift was most dramatic in the
tier of counties closest to the crushing mills of Peoria, Decatur, and Bloomington, where from half to two-thirds of the harvest went to beans rather
than to hay. In counties near the northern and southern borders of the state,
by contrast, 70–80 percent of soybeans were still harvested for hay. That
this went hand-in-glove with greater investment is suggested by the fact
that yields were also highest in the most heavily bean-producing counties:
19 bushels per acre versus 11 bushels per acre in the southernmost counties.[78]
Sales of combines were up, with their use for harvesting soybeans being a
driving factor.[79] Farmers were also taking more care to inoculate their fields,
as indicated by the increasing availability in 1930 of commercial products
such as Dickinson's New Pure-Culture Humus Inoculation for Soy Beans.[80]

This increased investment in soybeans by farmers, underwritten by
guaranteed purchases, reinforced a virtuous cycle of capital investment by
commercial processors, universities, and governments, mainly in the form
of research and development. Although feed pellets produced from soybean

meal brought in a steady income, Staley believed that the highest profits
would come from improving the quality of the oil for use in human food.
He brought in Maurice Durkee, who had worked with his fellow chemical
engineer David Wesson at the Southern Cotton Oil Company. Methods for
refining cottonseed oil—neutralizing its free fatty acids with alkalis, bleaching it with fuller's earth (a special clay), and deodorizing it with superheated
steam—resulted in a clear, bland oil that, in liquid form or hardened into
shortening through hydrogenation, became the gold standard for edible
uses.[81] During the 1920s, corn oil was successfully refined to the point of
being competitive with cottonseed oil for food uses. Early attempts during
World War I to similarly refine soybean oil—using beans imported from
Manchuria—largely failed, ending up with something that tasted "fishy" or
"painty."[82] Durkee, working with the more consistent output of Corn Belt
farmers, and adapting the system used for corn oil, managed to produce soy
oil he later described as "surprisingly good": colorless, sweet, and bland, although with an unfortunate tendency to develop "grassy" or "beany" flavors
after a few weeks of storage.[83] This limited the degree to which soy could substitute for cottonseed or corn in salad oil, shortening, or margarine, but those
products nonetheless provided more profitable outlets than the soap kettle.

Similarly, utilization research intensified at the University of Illinois.
The home economics department investigated edible uses for people, and the
animal husbandry and dairy husbandry departments studied the use of the
meal for livestock. The biggest payoff, however, came from the Department
of Agronomy's trials of indoor and outdoor paints that incorporated varying amounts of soybean oil. As in the case of food uses, experiences during
World War I using beans from Manchuria had given soy a bad reputation as
a substitute for linseed oil in paint. Moreover, while linseed was a fast-drying
oil, resulting in a strong film, soybean oil was "semi-drying" and required
additional chemicals, known as "driers," to be added to the paint. This was
another focus of research.[84] In addition to utilization studies, the university
produced a vast number of circulars and reports advising farmers how to
select varieties for planting, inoculate fields, combat plant disease, harvest
beans, and in general maximize yields. This included financial yields, with
the Farm Organization and Management Department issuing detailed anal-
yses of the costs of growing and harvesting soybeans using various methods,
as well as the gains to be made in comparison to other crops.

Increased investment in soybeans was evident at the federal level as well. Some of this was regulatory, with the USDA conducting a series of tests to establish quality grades for soybeans, a move to facilitate the trading of soybeans as a bulk grain. When sold as seed, soybeans by necessity had to be of high quality, with the fewest possible damaged or "split" beans—which would fail to germinate—and the smallest quantity possible of "foreign material," which commonly included weed seeds. Beans destined for the mill did not need to germinate. The standards rolled out in September 1925 were nonetheless still rather stringent about the number of split soybeans, which were limited to only 1 percent by weight in No. 1 soybeans and 10 percent in No. 2. As J. E. Barr, the official in charge of developing the standards, explained at the 1925 ASA field meeting, even though a high percentage of split beans did not necessarily make a difference when it came to industrial processing, it should still be included as a factor for establishing grades. To do otherwise, he argued, "would be to encourage careless handling of the crop at thrashing time," whereas grading standards should provide an "incentive for the production and marketing of the highest quality product."[85] The public investment in establishing standards was aimed primarily at sparking greater private investment.

The most dramatic federal investment, however, was the USDA's 1929–1932 Oriental Agricultural Exploration Expedition, known informally as the Dorsett-Morse Expedition. P. H. Dorsett, an old hand at the Foreign Seed and Plant Introduction Office and an experienced botanical explorer, had sent a bumper crop of new soybean varieties to Washington during his travels in China from 1924 through 1927 in search of novel persimmons. During the fall of 1925, he received 100 single-plant selections—seeds still in the pods—as a gift from Russian botanists at the Manchurian Agricultural Society of Harbin. These quickly made their way through the soybean pipeline, so that Hackleman was planting some of these varieties in Urbana, Illinois, by the following spring.[86] Dorsett also arranged for the Manchurian postal commissioner to have postmasters throughout the region collect samples of soybeans and mung beans from their villages. As a result, as Morse reported to Hackleman, by early 1927 he had "received in the neighborhood of 1,200 introductions from Manchuria and China."[87] Dorsett's soybeans came mostly from northern Manchuria and would prove valuable as the American soybean frontier pushed north into states such as Minnesota.

In fact, as crossing varieties became a more common practice in soybean breeding, a small number of Dorsett's contributions would have a disproportionate impact on the genetic makeup of American soybeans.[88] At the time, however, Dorsett felt he had barely skimmed the wealth of Asian soybean varieties, and he advised a separate expedition led by the USDA's top specialist.

By 1929, that was indisputably William Morse. In 1923 McGraw-Hill published *The Soybean*, an indication of the growing importance of the crop as it gained momentum in the Midwest. Charles Piper was the lead author, with Morse in the junior role. Piper died in 1926, by which time Morse had been president of the newly renamed American Soybean Association for two years running. As originally conceived, the Dorsett-Morse Expedition encompassed southern China, the Dutch East Indies, Singapore, and Ceylon, reflecting Morse's ongoing commitment to finding varieties that would thrive in the American South, both as food and fodder. A number of factors, including Dorsett's failing health and tightening budgets as the Great Depression deepened, eventually pushed the southern regions of Asia off the itinerary. Even as tensions between the United States and Japan emerged, Morse focused his trip on areas under Japanese control—Japan itself, southern Manchuria, and Korea—often benefiting greatly from the assistance of Japanese agronomists. The geographical focus, roughly along the same latitudes as the American Corn Belt, also reflected the growing significance of the crushing industry. Morse lingered in southern Manchuria longer than originally planned in part to more fully document its soybean-oil industry (photo 5). The growth of private investment now partially determined the goals of public investment. The expedition eventually logged 4,500 new introductions, many of them well suited for oil production.[89]

With the expansion of investment at all levels by 1930, numerous mills joined Staley, Funk Brothers, and American Milling in processing soybeans, including the Iowa Milling Company of Cedar Rapids, the first to crush soybeans west of the Mississippi (1928); the William O. Goodrich Company of Milwaukee (1926), which was acquired by Archer-Daniels Midland (ADM) in 1928; and the Shellabarger Grain Products Company, joining Staley in Decatur (1929). In May 1930, ten years after soybean growers established the ASA, Corn Belt crushers formed their own trade group, the National Soybean Oil Manufacturers Association (later the National Soybean Processors

Photo 5. William Morse in Dairen, Manchuria, 1930, examining soybean "oil cake" (from which oil has been expelled) from a Chinese oil mill. Courtesy of Soyinfo Center.

Association, or NSPA). This was in part a response to the formation a year earlier of the Soybean Marketing Association, a short-lived cooperative created to ensure that farmers got the highest possible price for their soybeans, but with which only Funk Brothers, among the Peoria Plan mills, agreed to negotiate.[90] The processor's new association, like the ASA, would become a permanent fixture.

At the outset of the new decade, a virtuous circle of public and private investment had likewise ensured the soybean's long-term place in American agriculture. The stage was set for the 1930s, when the soybean truly took off in what might have seemed the unlikeliest of times, when the prospects for so much else in American life looked so bleak. The soybean not only expanded as a crop, however: it gained prominence in the American imagination as the symbol of a social movement headed by the nation's most famous businessman.

CHAPTER FOUR

EXPLORING ALL AVENUES

In 1934, during the second year of the Century of Progress International Exposition, popularly known as the Chicago World's Fair, no exhibitor garnered more attention than the car manufacturer Henry Ford. He had boycotted the fair in 1933 to protest General Motors's exhibit of a working assembly line, something that he considered to be the theft of his idea.[1] When he decided to be part of the fair's return engagement in 1934, however, Ford went all-in. He invested $2.5 million, an unprecedented amount, to create a fair exhibit on a monumental scale. The Ford Building's central rotunda, in the form of enormous, concentric gears, rose twelve stories. At its center was a giant revolving globe and an array of dozens of vehicles charting the history of wheeled transportation. Around its sides were epic photo murals. And from its top, open to the air and lit at night with thousands of colored lights, emerged a pillar of white light that, under the right conditions, reached a mile into the air and was visible twenty miles away. The building's wings, including the Ford Museum and the Industrial Hall, extended hundreds of feet.[2]

For all its grandiosity, one of the exhibit's most popular attractions was a modest, weather-beaten hay barn adjacent to the main building (photo 6). Built in 1863, the year Ford was born, it had been carefully transplanted from his boyhood farm. If the fair as a whole represented a technologically optimistic antidote to the Great Depression, the Ford Industrialized Barn embodied Ford's own solution to the nation's farm crisis. The barn dispensed with stalls and haylofts, featuring instead an immaculate arrangement of

Photo 6. The Ford Industrialized Barn exhibit at the 1934 Century of Progress World's Fair in Chicago. From the collection of The Henry Ford.

machinery and pipes that washed the oil out of soybeans using a hexane solvent (photo 7). Threshed soybeans were gravity-fed into rollers that flattened them into flakes. Traveling through a pipe set at a 10-degree angle, the flakes were carried upward by a screw-like conveyor through a stream of solvent flowing down in the other direction. At the top of the pipe, the meal passed over hot steam that removed traces of solvent. The oil-solvent mixture that came out the bottom at the other end was then forced upward through a thin neck and then downward through a still, where the solvent was carried upward by steam, leaving behind the oil. The system held around 100 gallons of solvent, which was cooled and recirculated. "As every seam and vent is closed," one brochure pointed out, "there is very little waste of gasoline and very small fire hazard."[3]

Shortly before the fair opened in late May, Ford inspected the exhibit and took the opportunity to explain its meaning to a group of corn, wheat, and dairy farmers on a guided tour. As recounted in a pamphlet issued by the Ford Company, one farmer, struck by the "oddity of the exhibit," asked for "the REASON of it all." Ford responded that he wanted to give "the

Photo 7. Interior of the Industrialized Barn. From the collection of The Henry Ford.

American farmer a new idea to work with" to help give him and his family "an abundant livelihood" and "a cash surplus with which to buy the things that he and his family need and want." This new livelihood rested on the use of farm products in industry. In terms similar to his promotion of the five-dollar day twenty years earlier—when Ford workers were offered an unprecedented wage as a means of boosting their ability to buy, among other things, Tin Lizzies—Ford told the farmers that "business is only exchange of goods. If we want the farmer to be OUR customer, we must find a way to become HIS customer."[4] An agricultural revival would in turn go a long way to ending the Great Depression: "Just as soon as the individual farmer can make money the farm problem will vanish, and so will most of our other economic problems."[5] Implicit in this was a not-so-subtle rebuke of New Deal farm policies, which sought to raise the value of crops not by finding new and better uses for them in industry but by curtailing production.

Beyond economic recovery, the Industrialized Barn offered a means to fulfill Ford's goal of preserving the virtues of rural life while jettisoning everything outmoded about farmwork. Solvent extraction of soybean oil was a modern, industrial process that could be scaled down, he argued, to fit comfortably on a farm. As the pamphlet explained, "The machinery is simple and easily installed. It can be obtained almost anywhere, at small cost. Much of it is standard piping." In part because tractors were replacing draft animals, there were "many barns in the United States, now standing abandoned, that could easily be converted into factories such as is shown at the Exposition."[6] As much as Ford personally wanted this to be true, however, there were reasons to doubt that the industrial processing of soybeans would defy the usual advantages of scaling up. Were the tanks of highly volatile hexane safe, especially when the average farmer lacked the safety resources and expertise of the Ford Company? An answer of sorts came one night in mid-August. Even with precautions, such as placing the boiler in a separate brick enclosure outside of the barn proper, the seventy-year-old barn somehow caught fire and nearly burned to the ground, in the process severely injuring an exhibit attendant.[7] Ford continued to exhibit solvent extraction equipment at state, regional, and world's fairs for the rest of the decade, but it is not clear if he ever again showcased the Industrialized Barn.[8]

The 1930s were heady years for the soybean. Ford provided it with a high public profile that it would not enjoy again for decades. And he was not the only one during desperate times for whom it symbolized the possibility of a revolutionary new world. While a group dubbing themselves "chemurgists" saw its promise as an industrial input, the Adventists increased their efforts to make it the basis of new American foods. All the while, however, the soybean was inexorably heading toward a staid postwar existence that, in a peculiar way, brought these two dreams together, as it became a key, but little remarked upon, input for new types of industrialized food.

Industrial Uses

They called their shared vision of new industrial uses for farm products "chemurgy." In May 1935, Henry Ford hosted several dozen millionaires, industrialists, farmers, and scientists at Greenfield Village, his outdoor repository of historical buildings in Dearborn, Michigan. Attendees entered a replica of Independence Hall to sign a "Declaration of Dependence upon the Soil and of the Right to Self-Maintenance." In order to "enjoy and to secure this latter right," an extension of those listed by Thomas Jefferson,

the document argued that "man must recognize that his basic sustenance issues from the soil and not from merchants' shelves; that, whenever industrial
centralization causes harmful human congestion, and becomes destructive
of the right of self-maintenance, man must turn again to the soil from which
all new wealth springs except that from fisheries and mines. Otherwise the
right of self-government cannot endure."[9] Given Ford's personal antipathy
toward FDR and his policies, and attendees' hostility more generally to the
Agricultural Adjustment Act (AAA) of 1933, New Deal leaders were pointedly not invited.[10] But the meeting proved that, as idiosyncratic as Ford could
often be, the ideas embodied in the Industrialized Barn were not his alone.

If the worlds of cutting-edge organic chemistry and rural production
were not often yoked together, William Hale considered that simply a failure of imagination. Hale, a researcher with the Dow Chemical Company
in Midland, Michigan, lamented in a 1926 article in Ford's *Dearborn Independent* newspaper that everyone seemed to view farming "through the haze
of bygone days," when farmers "solely and almost directly [provided] food
and raiment for mankind." He proposed instead that farmers be defined as
an "organic chemical manufacturer" who produced raw materials—starches,
proteins, cellulose, oils—that could be transformed by the ingenuity of
chemists into an array of substances whose collective value would soon
place "the feeding of corn to hogs" in the same class "as that other unholy
act, the feeding of raw bituminous coal to a furnace for heat supply." And
just as coal tar, long considered a waste product, had provided the basis for
organic chemistry in the nineteenth century, Hale predicted that what were
considered agricultural wastes would revolutionize it in the twentieth.[11] In
1934, after some misfires—such as "chemo-genetics"—Hale coined the term
"chemurgy" to embody his principles: just as metallurgists derived valuable
materials from mixed ores, so would chemurgists, as distinct from academic
chemists, derive new products from organic sources.[12] Crucially, in a way
that appealed to Ford's populism, Hale argued that the value thereby added
to farm products should redound to the benefit of the farmers themselves,
rather than further enrich industrialists and financiers.

Other leaders of the movement, all in attendance in Dearborn, included
Dr. Charles Herty, Wheeler McMillan, and Francis P. Garvan, the conference's chair. Herty, considered a co-originator of chemurgy, was an academic
chemist who sought to revitalize the South by developing a method for

converting slash pine—a weedy, fast-growing tree that could be farmed—
into newsprint, at that time made from northern old-growth forests. McMillan was editor of *The Country Home*, which had sponsored a Model Farm
House at the Century of Progress, designed using modern methods and
materials (including soy paint) with an eye toward convenience and business
efficiency.[13] Garvan, a lawyer by training, was the director of the Chemical
Foundation, the trustee of US patents confiscated from German chemical
companies during World War I, patents whose methods became the basis of
the American dye industry. Garvan was a relative latecomer to chemurgy, but
the Chemical Foundation's support, along with Ford's publicity machine, was
considered crucial to the nascent movement's health. If their backgrounds
varied, all of the leaders subscribed to the belief that farm products could
undergo a Rumpelstiltskinesque transformation into high-value inputs to
industry in a way that both enriched the farmer and conserved nonreplen-
ishable resources. Hence they were early advocates for corn-based alcohol
as fuel, and they celebrated the hundreds of useful substances derived from
the peanut by George Washington Carver, who was invited to Dearborn to
meet Ford personally.

While in his 1926 article Hale singled out the soybean as "of greatest interest," citing the oil's use in soaps, inks, varnishes, and enamels,[14] it was Ford
himself who most energetically promoted it as uniquely suited for industrial
use. In 1929, in honor of his mentor and friend Thomas Edison, he founded
the Edison Institute at Greenfield Village, which included a chemistry lab
and an experimental farm dedicated to Hale's mission. To perform this
work, Ford chose a bright, energetic young man with no university training
in chemistry. Robert Boyer, a twenty-one-year-old graduate of the Henry
Ford Trade School, headed a staff of a dozen of his former classmates.[15]
They experimented with numerous crops before Ford instructed them in
1931 to focus their efforts on soybeans, reportedly after he wandered into
the lab one day and idly picked up, and then perused from cover to cover, a
copy of Piper and Morse's *The Soybean*.[16] By 1933, work had progressed to
the point that Ford announced that the following year's car models would be
painted with enamels produced from synthetic resins and soybean oil.[17] This
struck some newspapers as humorously incongruous, with one announcing Ford's "inauguration of another automobile plant. It is the soy bean."[18]
Boyer and his chemists soon developed ways to use soybean oil in foundry

cores—mixtures of sand and oil baked solid into the hollow spaces of metal castings, then pulverized and removed after the metal cooled—as well as in shock-absorber fluid.[19]

Then there was the meal left over from oil extraction, a bulky by-product for which there was often an insufficient local market to profitably sell to as livestock feed. In search of a higher-value use, Ford chemists turned it into plastic instead. During this era, there was nothing unusual about plastics produced from natural products: celluloid, cellophane, and rayon were all made from cellulose, a major component of the walls of plant cells. Plastics made from soybean protein were also not entirely novel: patents had been issued in Great Britain and France as early as 1913, and the first US patent for a soybean plastic was issued to a Japanese citizen in 1917.[20] In contrast to the popular plastic Bakelite, which was synthesized from coal tar derivatives and was heat-resistant, waterproof, and well-nigh indestructible, soybean and other natural plastics tended to absorb moisture from the air, causing them to warp and crack, thereby consigning them largely for use in small objects such as buttons. Boyer's team addressed the moisture problem by creating a composite material: part soy-protein plastic hardened by formaldehyde, part synthetic phenol-formaldehyde resin, and part "wood flour."[21] Lighter than Bakelite, this could be molded into small, durable automobile components such as horn buttons, gear-shift-lever balls, light-switch handles, and window-trim strips.[22] By one estimate, providing fifteen pounds of this plastic to each of the 1 million Ford cars that rolled off the assembly line each year required roughly 28,000 acres' worth of soybeans.[23]

A. E. Staley had once claimed, rather disingenuously, that soybeans were his hobby. This was far truer of Henry Ford. It was just that, given Ford's wealth, fame, and de facto control over a major manufacturing company, his private hobby had an enormous impact on how soybeans were used by industry and perceived by the public. What was less certain was whether, absent the push provided by Ford's utopian obsessions, the rational workings of capitalism would continue to find uses for the soybean. Paint companies were the most likely source of demand. Not only did soybean oil have some intrinsic advantages, such as less of a tendency to yellow over time than linseed oil; it also provided the basis for a pitch to farmers, a major market: we will use your soybeans if you in turn buy our paint. However, soybean oil's poor drying quality severely limited how much could be substituted for linseed oil.[24] The companies that incorporated soybean oil into paint, in fact, mostly did so because they had plentiful supplies of it on hand as a by-product. Swift and Company, the famous Chicago meatpacker, had a side-line in paint to make use of the oil left over from feed production. Nowhere was this truer, however, than in the strange case of the Glidden Company.

Founded in 1875, Cleveland-based Glidden had for many years been a one-factory varnish operation best known for its Jap-a-Lac brand. In 1917, however, it was taken over by Adrian Joyce, an Iowa farm boy whose busi-ness apprenticeship was in Chicago at Swift. If developing valuable by-products through creative chemistry was a credo for the chemurgy move-ment, it had long been a standard operating procedure among meatpackers, who made money turning wool and hair into brushes, viscera into sausage casings and violin strings, bones into combs and glue, and fat into candles and margarine.[25] Joyce himself helped establish Swift's fertilizer division, which turned scrap meat ("tankage") into plant food and livestock feed.[26] Likewise, when he took charge of Glidden, not only did he expand it into a national paint manufacturer through standardization and vertical integra-tion; in addition he actively sought profits from the "shards and stinks of industrial processes."[27] It was this search that would eventually lead to an ambitious plan to process soybeans in a giant new plant in Chicago.

Glidden ventured into new businesses in part to realize hidden value in existing operations. To get the most out of his linseed-oil mill, for instance, Joyce directed it to crush copra from the Philippines in the off-season to produce coconut oil, used mainly for soap. Seeking a more profitable outlet for coconut oil, he refined it for use in shortening and margarine. Having entered the margarine business in a small way, he quickly decided to compete with General Foods by acquiring a national distribution system. In 1929, Glidden acquired several food companies throughout the country, including E. R. Durkee and Co. on Long Island, which provided a trade name, Durkee Famous Foods, for the division's products.[28] The new food division joined three others, all of which produced some products that could be utilized by the others: paint and varnish; naval stores; and chemicals, metals, and min-ing.[29] Two of these divisions were potential markets for soybean oil, which could be used as a substitute for linseed oil in paint and coconut (or cotton-seed) oil in margarine. Tellingly, however, it was not the value of the oil that convinced Joyce to create a Soya Products Division but potential uses for the meal. While not exactly a "shard or stink," the meal was generally worth less than the oil in the 1930s, something of a reversal from the 1920s. It was by augmenting the meal's value that Joyce now hoped to make the whole enterprise profitable.

During a research trip to Europe to observe advances in industrial chemistry, Joyce and Glidden vice president William O'Brien spotted a German process for extracting protein from soybean meal, resulting in a product of high enough quality to be a plausible substitute for a milk protein called casein.[30] Casein itself was a hobbyhorse of the chemurgy movement. It was a crime to discard skim milk when making butter, the chemurgists lamented, when casein had found use in molded plastics as far back as the 1890s. They also cited the Italian success, as part of the fascist push for import independence, of developing imitation wool out of spun casein. Italy's ambassador to Great Britain once appeared in London sporting a suit he boasted contained forty-eight pints of skim milk.[31] Ford's researchers would in fact later imitate this feat using soy protein, but Joyce and O'Brien had a more practical goal in mind. They had their eye on the market for paper sizings, protein-based coatings—ranging from matte to glossy—largely responsible for how ink adheres to paper. When casein found a use at all in America, it was primarily as an ingredient in sizings. Because the Americans largely threw it away, casein was mainly imported from Europe. It tended to be expensive and highly variable in quality, something that would likely be even truer of an American product given the decentralized nature of the dairy industry, even if Americans decided to conserve it.[32]

Joyce reasoned that a suitable soy protein could be mass-produced to provide a uniform product to an underserved market. And as a side benefit, crushing would provide low-cost oil to Glidden's paint and food divisions. Research on protein extraction began in Cleveland in 1932. O'Brien later reflected that "if the Glidden Company had known of the many difficulties to be encountered and the heavy expenditures involved to bring the problem to the present point of completion, [it] would have hesitated before embarking on such a program."[33] The task at hand was not simply to remove the casein-like protein from the meal without damaging it—which proved difficult enough if the soybeans had been subjected to excessive heat or pressure when crushed[34]—but to then subtly alter, or denature, the protein in just the right way to produce desirable characteristics. This involved breaking some of the chemical bonds that determined its three-dimensional structure. Done right, the protein, when dissolved in a weak alkaline solution, would produce a coating with good "color, viscosity, and adhesion." Done wrong, the end result was too dark, too gummy to be sprayed, and either too sticky or not sticky enough to hold ink properly. These difficulties were compounded by the multiplicity of proteins in soybeans, only one of which, glycinin, was soluble in weak alkalis.[35] The project struggled until 1934, when Glidden acquired a patent from two Seattle chemists for a process that not only denatured glycinin in what seemed like the right way but also expeditiously filtered out the other proteins.[36]

Glidden named the end result Alpha protein to distinguish it from two lesser proteins (Beta and Gamma).[37] By late 1934, Joyce and O'Brien were confident enough in the product to invest $650,000 in a new soy-processing complex on the west side of Chicago, next to the paint factory of one of its subsidiaries.[38] A remodeled, six-story former brewery—operated clandestinely, the rumor went, during Prohibition—held the giant tanks where solvent-extracted soybean meal was agitated with an alkaline solution to create Alpha protein, which was then pumped into an adjoining building to be dried and bagged.[39] On the other side of the tank building, separated from it by a firewall, were two four-story buildings: the raw beans were cracked and flaked in one, and then solvent-extracted in the other.[40] A final building removed lecithin from the soybean oil. The new facility had the capacity to process 130 tons of soybeans a day, but a flaw in its design would cut those days short.

It began production in early 1935 but was shut down for prolonged periods of maintenance and fine-tuning. Then, shortly after operations resumed, a little before noon on October 8, 1935, an explosion razed the plant. Showers of brick and steel crushed five cars parked in an adjacent alley and two railcars on a nearby spur. Windows within a radius of several blocks shattered, and the detonation was felt three miles away. Forty-three people were injured, and by the next day, crews working through the night had found six bodies.[41] The death toll would eventually reach eleven.[42] As bodies were being pulled from the wreckage, O'Brien arrived from Cleveland to investigate the cause of the blast. The police and fire departments, state attorney's office, coroner's office, and experts from the USDA launched separate investigations.[43] As in the case of the Industrialized Barn, hexane was the likely culprit, a theory made more plausible in everyone's minds when a second soybean plant—not owned by Glidden—similarly blew up on October 22.

In contrast to Glidden's operation, the plant in Momence, Illinois, fifty miles south of Chicago, was a modest affair, a pilot project intended to prove the feasibility of processing soybeans in small rural towns. The owner designed the apparatus himself and had it fabricated at a local ironworks. It apparently leaked hexane fumes undetected through an open door into the boiler room, destroying the building—and killing the owner and his assistant—about an hour after operations got under way.[44] Glidden's facility, as well-financed and state-of-the-art as it was, was apparently similarly brought down by the interconnectedness of its buildings. Hexane fumes from the extraction building leaked, either over the firewall or via a water pipe, into the tank building. Meanwhile, a spark in the building where soybeans were flaked set off either dust or gas in a blast that traveled into the tank building through a doorway. Thus spark and gas, originating in two well-separated buildings, found their way to each other in a third.[45]

Glidden's response to disaster, which had been covered by insurance, was to rebuild the plant in five separate, "explosion-proof" buildings. A construction engineer assured the press that a "mechanical process will be used instead of the former chemical process in the treatment of soy bean products"—a reference to five new presses—but in fact Glidden installed two new solvent extractors as well, without which the production of Alpha protein would not be possible.[46] In place of the six-story protein unit, Glidden now built a smaller pilot plant. This was a sign that, even before the explosion, not all was well with protein production. In fact, the quality of the Alpha protein that had been produced over the first nine months of 1935 was considered unsatisfactory, and it had been unable to attract customers. In the wake of the blast, Glidden took the opportunity to go back to the drawing board, which meant scaling back its ambitions for the time being.[47]

If, as the chemurgists insisted, the best hope for the soybean—and, by extension, American farming—was to provide raw materials for nonfood manufacturing, its prospects at mid-decade were decidedly mixed. In the case of the Ford Company, economic rationality was beside the point, but Henry Ford would not live forever. Glidden was making a more carefully calculated bet on returns but would not long continue to throw good money after bad. At the same time, however, other economic forces enabled the soybean to cross an important milestone on its way to becoming a major American farm commodity.

New Bets

On October 2, 1936, members of the Chicago Board of Trade voted 633 to 23 to establish a futures market in soybeans. Most cast their ballots in the forty-five-story Board of Trade Building, then the tallest in Chicago, completed just as demand for office space collapsed with the onset of the Great Depression.[48] Activity on the twelfth floor, where the board's trading room was located, had also declined in recent years, particularly in the octagonal pits where futures contracts were traded. This was the result not only of the Depression itself but also of New Deal policies that, by providing support prices for grains like wheat and corn, undermined the need for grain dealers to use futures to insure, or hedge, against price changes.[49] The board was therefore on a mission to drum up new business, and soybeans were a good prospect, given their increasing presence on farms and in crushing mills. Anyone who stored or transported soybeans was a potential hedger. Recent publicity by Ford and others had meanwhile sparked the interest of speculators, whose trades made up the bulk of transactions. For all of this, it took almost five years of exploring the possibility before soybean futures became a reality, a step made possible in part by the same New Deal policies that both Ford and the board detested.

The board's futures contracts, like the grain they represented, were a bulk commodity.[50] Created in the mid-nineteenth century, they had their origin in "forward contracts" between individuals who agreed on a price for grain to be delivered on a designated future date, enabling both buyer and seller to lock in a price in advance. These face-to-face contracts suffered from many limitations, however. Not every seller could find a buyer, and changing market conditions often prompted parties to these agreements to renege. A futures contract, by contrast, was a standardized product issued by the board that specified delivery of a certain amount of a given grade of grain by the last day of a given month. As it happened, very few of these contracts were fulfilled by actual delivery, as traders could instead settle their accounts by simply selling the interchangeable contracts back to the market. Whether they made or lost money depended on how the price of the contract had changed in the meantime. For hedgers, futures functioned like forward contracts, locking in what the collective market guessed would be the price of a bushel of grain on a specific future date.

For speculators, buying and selling futures was purely a bet on future prices without any intention of handling grain. They faced the risk, however, of a so-called corner, in which a holder of futures contracts would demand the delivery of physical grain, having bought up the available supply in advance, and thereby make handsome profits as speculators scrambled to fulfill their contracts. The decision to create a futures contract for soybeans therefore rested in two ways on the likely volume of trade. The overall volume of futures trading had to be high enough to justify the investment by the board in managing the process. Volume was driven by hedgers and speculators alike—but mostly by speculators, who thus injected liquidity into the market, the key to making it more flexible than the old forward contracts. More narrowly, then, the volume of trading in physical soybeans had to be large enough to make it difficult for any one trader to corner the market. Otherwise, speculators would be leery of placing their bets.

The first time someone broached the idea of soybean futures, the volume of soybean production had not crossed the magic threshold. In 1931, Eugene Funk of the Funk Brothers Farm in Bloomington, Illinois, hosted a board committee investigating methods of corn breeding. He took the occasion to push the idea of soybean futures, complaining that farmers, grain elevators, and processors were all hampered by the lack of hedging opportunities.[51] W. L. Burlison, in a bulletin published the following year, similarly noted that some creative elevators and processors hedged soybeans with flaxseed futures and soybean oil with cottonseed-oil futures, but that the "movements of prices of these two types of products have not been sufficiently parallel" to make this approach viable.[52] When the group that had visited the Funk Brothers contacted the Chicago Board of Trade's president, he duly appointed a committee to investigate the proposal.[53] Nothing came of it, and the fact that acreage of soybeans harvested for beans declined slightly from 1931 to 1932, and was stagnant in 1933, made it unlikely that there would be action any time soon.[54]

Then came the Agricultural Adjustment Act of 1933. It was passed in May, too late for farmers to significantly change their mix of crops. To the

scorn of chemurgists, the AAA sought to raise the price of certain commodities—wheat, cotton, corn, hogs, rice, tobacco, milk—by reducing the
supply, initially by simply plowing under crops. To receive benefit payments,
the law obliged farmers in 1934 to reduce their acreage of these crops, usually with the proviso that they could not be diverted to other crops. This
condition was relaxed, however, when it came to food for home consumption or crops deemed to be soil-improving. Soybeans plowed under as green
manure contributed nitrogen to the soil and protected it against erosion,
thereby qualifying it as soil-improving, and indeed there was a substantial
increase in soybeans used this way after 1934, largely at the expense of hay.[55]
Soybeans harvested for beans or hay, however, were not normally considered
soil-conserving but were increasingly permitted in the face of drought and
the other difficulties faced by farmers.[56] As one agent for a trading house
reported in early 1935, "the Stoddards . . . who have possibly 5000 acres scattered over Illinois are going to take the full 30 per cent reduction of corn
acreage allowed by the Govt. and plant it all in soy beans. This idea is general."[57] Another observer noted somewhat acerbically that in "Illinois, Iowa,
Indiana and Missouri, almost all of the acreage forced out of production
of bread and feed grains" under the "AAA 'prosperity through scarcity' contracts" was planted in soybeans.[58]

   It was not just restricted crops that made way for soybeans. Oats, though
not covered by the AAA, declined even more rapidly than corn. Both crops
were highly susceptible to dry conditions, as well as to the invasion of the
North American chinch bug. Soybeans, in contrast, were highly resistant to
chinch bugs and better able to withstand drought.[59] Unlike oats, soybeans
could also be planted late in the season, making them an ideal fallback crop
when corn failed. The biggest problem for oats, however, was that increasingly mechanized farms employed fewer of the draft animals that needed
them for fuel. Soybeans, in addition to benefiting from mechanization, also
helped accelerate the trend. In 1933, "baby" combines, capable of being pulled
by a single tractor rather than a team of horses, began appearing on medium-
sized Corn Belt farms,[60] and by 1935 manufacturers even offered combines
specially designed to meet "the peculiarities of soy bean harvesting," as the
Wall Street Journal put it.[61] In 1936, the number of threshers produced nationwide more than quadrupled from 4,000 to over 16,000.[62] The use of
combines helped diminish the loss of beans during harvesting, thereby

increasing profits.[63] Combines also helped enrich the soil, a further financial as well environmental benefit; unlike binders, which removed soybean plants for later threshing, combines left a great deal of litter on the ground.[64] These factors increased the soybean's competitive edge, making it a good bet for farmers.

The AAA aside, however, what most benefited soybeans was an increase in the demand for soybean oil. This in turn was the result of another federal policy. In the early 1930s, two bitter adversaries—butter and margarine producers—united momentarily to oppose a third product. So-called cooking compounds, although labeled as substitutes for lard, happened to be the color and consistency of butter. Because the color came naturally from Javanese palm oil, these compounds were exempted from a federal 10-cents-per-pound tax levied on "artificially" colored margarine. This loophole briefly benefited domestic soybeans as well. In 1930, having discovered that the addition of unbleached soybean oil lent margarine an attractive yellow tint, A. E. Staley sold out his entire output of oil that year. Foreign palm oil would outcompete soy by 1932, however, the year the loophole was closed.[65] Then, in addition to having thus leveled the playing field, the federal government in 1934 subjected all foreign oils to a 10 percent tariff (on top of taxes levied by individual states).[66] This ensured that domestic oils, mainly cottonseed but a growing quantity of soybean as well, were the primary ones used in margarine and other butter substitutes.[67] Like the AAA, the tariff represented an antimarket measure that helped establish a market in soybeans.

From 1933 to 1934, harvested acres of soybeans jumped nationally from 847,000 to more than 1.1 million acres, and the amount of beans harvested increased even more markedly from less than 12 million to almost 18 million bushels.[68] The increase in Illinois was particularly dramatic: from 4 million bushels in 1933 to 11 million bushels in 1934. Moreover, a somewhat larger percentage of the beans harvested were crushed rather than sold for seed: from 30 percent in 1930 to 40 percent in 1934.[69] The Chicago Board of Trade took notice. In late 1934, it instituted cash trading in soybeans on the same terms as wheat, corn, oats, rye, and barley.[70] And it once more appointed a committee to take up the question of futures trading in "Soya beans."[71] In the early months of 1935, this committee sent out questionnaires to the largest handlers of soybeans and held a hearing that invited Board of Trade members to give "facts, figures and reasons for and against trading in soybeans."

The hearing was poorly attended and the survey results mixed, leading the committee to recommend against soybean futures in its March 1935 report. The crux of its findings was that, even with the growth of the crop in 1934, there were still too few beans sold on the market.[72]

If farmers were selling too few beans for the board's liking, it was only because—as in prior cases when production increased dramatically—they were saving them to plant.[73] In 1935, production again doubled to 22 million bushels,[74] and by 1936 almost 70 percent of these were crushed rather than sold for seed.[75] This explosive growth meant that in January 1936, less than a year after one committee had issued its report, the board's president appointed another Special Soybean Committee.[76] This committee sent out 1,500 questionnaires.[77] Of the 384 that came back, 331 were in favor of establishing a futures market. A similar consensus was expressed at four meetings held with various representatives of the grain trade—elevator operators, cash-grain receiving houses, processors—and officers of several large commission houses, who represented speculators.[78] The only group to express some reservation was processors, some of whom in prior years had rejected the idea outright. Although they were all now in favor of soybean futures in principle, they differed on whether to offer them immediately or at some later, unspecified date.[79] The processors' hesitance may have been rooted in a lingering worry that a possible corner would disrupt their business operations, in part by diverting beans to Chicago. Glidden notwithstanding, the movement of physical soybeans centered on Decatur, not the Windy City.

The Special Soybean Committee recommended an immediate futures market to the Board of Trade's directors, who put it before the membership in October. The vote was preceded by a twenty-part series in the *Chicago Journal of Commerce and LaSalle Street Journal*, "Soybean—The Magic Plant," which extolled the crop's expansion and, in good chemurgical fashion, its "manifold uses."[80] The futures contract that the membership approved on October 2 stipulated that Chicago be the only delivery point for futures contracts; that the unit of trading be 1,000 bushels; that the contract price refer to No. 2 Yellow Beans, while allowing No. 3 Yellow Beans to be delivered in their place at a 2-cent discount; and, finally, with respect to other matters, that the soybean contract conform to the contract for corn futures.[81] The membership also voted on a rule change that included soybeans in the list of commodities, including corn, covered by trading limits: soybean futures could not be traded for more than 4 cents per bushel above or below the previous day's closing price.[82] The membership had already voted in July to include soybeans in the "to-arrive rule" that prohibited Board of Trade members from overbidding the "last posted" market price.[83] In short, individual transactions between buyers and sellers, for both cash soybeans and futures, were strictly tied to the prices established by the collective market.

And though trading in soybean futures began modestly, amounting to less than 30 million bushels in 1937—compared to 2.5 billion bushels of corn and almost 11 billion bushels of wheat futures[84]—it signaled that the soybean had come of age as a farm commodity. This maturation of the soybean market increased its availability and lowered its price, making it even more attractive to Ford and Glidden, both of whom were moving forward with their ambitious plans for the crop.

Protein Products

By early 1936, Glidden, in the process of rebuilding its plant in Chicago, was in need of somebody to breathe new life into its research on soy protein. While attending a meeting at the Institute of Paper Chemistry, in pursuit of Glidden's work on paper coatings, William O'Brien got wind of the perfect candidate: one of the nation's top organic chemists, a specialist in isolating and synthesizing substances from beans, and a fluent speaker of German (a boon when so much of Glidden's soybean equipment was German-made). The Institute of Paper Chemistry, located in Appleton, Wisconsin, was itself in the process of offering him a job but had come up against a legal hurdle. Appleton was a so-called sunset town, one that prohibited African Americans from spending the night, much less buying a home, within its borders. The candidate, Percy Lavon Julian, was black. While the institute's board grappled with what they considered an archaic statute, O'Brien slipped away to interview Julian by phone. He made a job offer on the spot without having met Julian in person, in part to be able to later claim to Glidden directors that he had no idea of Julian's race. The position he offered was assistant director of research of the Soya Products Division.[85] According to one account, Julian was so surprised by the offer that he took several days to prepare his acceptance, at which point Joyce and O'Brien, thinking that he was holding out, offered him a higher salary and the role of full director of research.[86]

Julian was a remarkable member of a remarkable family—Alabama slaves and later sharecroppers who tirelessly pursued educational opportunities, however meager at times. Julian himself attained what was then the pinnacle of educational achievement: a scientific doctorate from a German university. He headed the chemistry department at the nation's flagship black university, Howard University in Washington, DC, before scandal and divisive campus politics forced him to resign. He landed at his alma mater, DePauw University in Indiana, where his research flourished but where racism—combined with divisive campus politics—blocked his path to a full professorship. Seeking a job in the private sector, he was deemed overqualified by DuPont and other companies, who argued that no white chemist would agree to work under his direction. The Institute of Paper Chemistry was hampered by Appleton's sunset-town ordinance, leaving it to Glidden, which so often recognized undervalued resources, to employ him.[87] Thus by a process of diminishing options did Julian become, for the next eighteen years, the nation's most famous "soybean scientist." He largely avoided comparison to another black chemist, George Washington Carver,[88] despite a shared chemurgical commitment to deriving manifold substances from legumes. Carver's imaginative uses for the peanut, in any case, rarely found commercial success, whereas Julian was driven from the outset to develop products with immediate market value.

Julian's first task was to improve Alpha protein. He examined Glidden's rebuilt pilot plant and, when asked by Glidden executives what he thought, responded matter-of-factly: "Gentlemen, it's lousy."[89] He was more specific about Alpha protein's shortcomings in his patent application for his improved production method. It had a "high dispersion residue," failing to dissolve completely in the alkaline solutions used to make paper coatings. Even when well dispersed, the resulting solutions were "highly viscous" and prone to becoming "stiff gels even at a relatively low concentration of protein." To paper manufacturers, this meant excessive energy devoted to stirring the liquid coatings, which, when they inevitably did gel, required "considerable expense in bringing them back to working consistency." Even more damning for what was supposed to be a casein substitute, the soybean coatings had "relatively poor adhesive qualities as compared to milk casein."[90] Up to this point, Alpha protein had been extracted by soaking oil-free soybean flakes in strong alkalis such as lye, the reasoning being that this was the best way to end up with a protein that readily dissolved in weak alkalis. It was perhaps a sign of Julian's genius—or at least his experimental boldness—that he did exactly the opposite, first treating the flakes with hot acid in a method that it took Julian and his team more than a year to perfect. The result was a "derived" protein that was distinct from the soybean's unaltered glycinin.[91] This protein was extracted and again treated with acid, which curdled it. Pressed into cakes, it was not unlike tofu, except that it consisted purely of protein.

Julian's method finally produced an Alpha protein that could plausibly substitute for high-quality casein and that resulted in low-viscosity coatings, with no tendency to gel, that were highly adhesive.[92] The relatively high cost of its production hampered its financial success, however, meaning that most of the Soya Division's profits were from cheaper, less highly purified protein. Two members of Julian's lab, Arthur Levinson and James L. Dickinson, received a patent for remedying the defects of solvent-extracted soybean flakes when used as livestock feed. Unlike the cake from oil expellers, solvent-extracted flakes were loose and dusty. Because the process did not involve heating, the flakes moreover retained the bitter and beany flavors plaguing all edible soy products. Levinson and Dickinson addressed these problems by sending the flakes through an expeller while using lower temperatures and pressures than when expelling oil. The result was a uniform cake, easily broken into dust-free bits, that was sufficiently toasted to remove most of the disagreeable flavors. They also pointed out that the amount of fat in the meal could be precisely regulated by adding any desired amount of oil to the fat-free meal before sending it through the expeller.[93] Once the bitter flavor was eliminated, soybeans accounted for an increasing share of the protein in Red Heart Dog Food, which, according to one account, was evaluated by taste tests that required human lab members to personally sample the product every hour.[94]

These improvements aside, and reversing its original business model, Glidden ended up earning less revenue from the soybean's protein than from its oil, with its uses in margarine and paint, and in particular from lecithin, a valuable fraction of the oil. First isolated from egg yolks at the turn of the century, lecithin was widely used as an emulsifier—a substance preventing oil from separating out from water—in such foods as margarine and choco-late. Soybean lecithin was at first considered no more than a gummy waste to be removed from the oil during refining. Part of the problem was that, when the oil was pressed or expelled from the bean, the same heat that toasted the meal into something more appetizing ended up damaging the lecithin. When the oil was extracted with a solvent, however, the lecithin could be recovered in usable form, something first discovered by researchers in Ger-many. Julian had access to this information through a joint pool of German and American patents available to members of the American Lecithin Cor-poration, which included Glidden and Archer-Daniels Midland.[95] Julian, aided by his fluency in German, oversaw and improved the extraction pro-cess at Glidden. He and a member of his lab soon patented a way to recover more lecithin from the oil. This was only one advance to come out of Julian's lab, which eventually filed 100 patents covering all aspects of soybean tech-nology,[96] forming the basis for Glidden's boast in its advertising that it used soybeans in a dizzying array of products, including paint, shortening, paper coatings, dog food, confections, baked goods, alcoholic beverages, cosmetics, automobiles, packaging, and plastics.[97]

In 1939, however, when Glidden tried to spin fiber out of Alpha pro-tein[98]—and thereby duplicate the accomplishment of the Italian ambassa-dor's casein suit—it was beaten to the punch by the Ford Company's Robert Boyer. At the 1938 meeting of the American Soybean Association, he an-nounced that his team had just succeeded in producing the first artificial fi-ber produced from vegetable protein, a skein of soybean fiber that resembled wool or mohair.[99] Boyer's method involved spraying a solution of soybean protein through the tiny holes of a "spinnerette submerged in a coagulating bath" so that it instantaneously precipitated into strands.[100] The imitation wool, slated for the sidewall upholstery of Ford cars, garnered its great-est publicity for its use in Henry Ford's own clothing, at first in a tie made of 50 percent soybean fiber. In 1941, Ford appeared in a "soybean suit"—actually one-quarter soy fiber and three-quarters sheep's wool[101]—which cost an estimated $39,000 to make and with which he was, as the *Detroit Times* reported, "as delighted as a boy with his first pair of long pants."[102] By 1942, a pilot plant was making 1,000 pounds of soybean wool daily, with a new plant under construction with five times the capacity. Ford tried unsuc-cessfully to persuade the armed forces to make uniforms out of soy fiber, and in 1943, unable to develop a product that could compete with the price of wool, he sold the process and machinery to the Drackett Company of Cincinnati, which similarly failed to successfully market the fiber.[103]

Boyer's most notable achievement during these years, however, was to fulfill Ford's vision of a car body made of soybean plastic. He produced hundreds of experimental rear-compartment panels for a Mercury sedan, which Ford then personally attacked with an axe until they were cracked or nicked. The one that finally withstood the axe consisted, beyond soybeans, of a wide variety of farm products. First, Boyer created a matting of "long and short fibers obtained from field straw, cotton linters, hemp flax"—which by the late 1930s Ford had to obtain a special license to grow[104]—"ramie and slash pine." With an eye to mass production, he floated this "cellulosic mass" on water and lifted it out on "screens which preformed it into a rough approximation of the finished panel." He eventually learned how to make six of these frames at a time. He added soybean meal, synthetic resins, and color and then plasticized it all in a hot press. Ford engineers eventually produced a prototype "plastic car" that supported fourteen of Boyer's panels on a tubular steel frame.[105]

Henry Ford unveiled the plastic car in stages. In 1938, calling in reporters to respond to a National Labor Relations Board ruling against his company's labor policies, Ford took them on a factory tour and, "picking up a curved sheet of a composition which he said was made from soybeans, the angular old man jumped enthusiastically up and down on it," pointing out triumphantly that "if that was steel it would have caved in."[106] In November 1940, he again called in reporters and proceeded to startle them, first with his axe demonstration on the plastic lid of a car, then with a prediction that his company would start producing "plastic-bodied" cars within three years. *Time* and *Fortune* magazines each ran articles with prominent photos and touted the virtues of Boyer's material: It looked like polished steel but was half the weight and ten times more dent-resistant; and its color, integral rather than painted on, was as enduring as the panel itself.[107] Finally, in August 1941, at the Dearborn Homecoming Day celebration, Ford proudly displayed a prototype and invited reporters to a fourteen-course soybean luncheon. The press was again largely adulatory: It "will revolutionize the automobile industry" and bring about a "peaceful agricultural revolution"; "here is something an America on wheels has been waiting for. Please hurry it, Mr. Ford; hurry! Hurry!"[108] Introduced when wartime steel shortages loomed, the plastic car rehabilitated Ford's standing as a visionary.

The specific uses of soybeans were ultimately less important to Ford, however, than the way they could enable his vision of a modernized rural landscape. Beginning in 1918, he established a series of what ended up totaling nineteen "village industries" in southern Michigan. These were small operations supplying auto parts to his central factories that were constructed on the sites, or in the renovated buildings, of nineteenth-century water-powered mills.[109] They were intended to provide income to farmers during the year's slack times, although the calendars of farm and factory rarely accommodated each other so neatly. In 1938, he opened two such plants, both on the Saline River, to process soybeans using a scaled-up version of the solvent-extraction equipment he had installed in the Industrialized Barn.[110] These ended up being shuttered in 1947, the year of Ford's death. Likewise, the plastic car never progressed past the prototype, as the onset of war curtailed all new domestic car production. Always a hobby writ large, Ford's soybean projects did not end up as a permanent part of the company's ongoing work.

Perhaps the most enduring of Ford's legacies, and indeed of the chemurgy movement overall, was a proviso of the 1938 Agricultural Adjustment Act that established four regional laboratories under the USDA to investigate the industrial utilization of crops.[111] The Northern Regional Research Laboratory in Peoria, Illinois, prioritized soybean research. Meanwhile, the Federal Regional Soybean Industrial Laboratory had been established at the University of Illinois two years earlier, where attempts to create a true soybean plastic—rather than phenol-formaldehyde plastics that used soybean meal as filler—continued for some time, without a breakthrough.[112] Ford's other legacy was the publicity he generated for the soybean, but this may have had an unexpected effect. While newspapers at the time had fun with the notion of vegetable plastic, suggesting that it be strengthened with spinach or that a car made out of it could run on pepper and vinegar,[113] during the later wartime push to eat more soybeans there was some indication that people had come to think of them more as industrial inputs than as food. This is ironic, as Ford himself was an avid soy-food enthusiast, joining a select company comprising mainly Asian Americans, Seventh-day Adventists—and the USDA soybean specialist William Morse.

Culinary Inventions

When he embarked on the USDA's Oriental Agricultural Exploration Expedition in 1929, William Morse was already familiar with traditional soy foods. His 1923 collaboration with Charles Piper, *The Soybean*, included Frank Meyer's photographs of various kinds of tofu. Drawing on the USDA's collection of books on Chinese agriculture, the chapter "Soybean Products for Human Food" provided information on six varieties of tofu—including "bean curd brains" (*Tofu Nao*), "dry bean curd" (*Tofu Khan*), "thousand folds" (*Chien Chang Tofu*), and "fragrant dry bean curd" (*Hsiang Khan*)—in addition to *natto* (fermented bean curd), *hamanatto* (soy cheese), *yuba* (soymilk skin), miso (soy paste), and green or vegetable soybeans eaten directly from the pod. A five-page spread illustrated the traditional method for making shoyu (soy sauce).[114] In addition to soybean loaf and bread recipes provided by various departments of home economics, Morse also included tofu recipes from the Chicago Bean Bread Company (most likely gathered during the Patriotic Food Show) and something called the Soy Products Company.[115] His experience was not always secondhand. One table presented the results of tests, conducted by the book's "junior author," to determine the quality of bean curd made from different soybean varieties. Variety 37050, with a black seed, provided a good yield of tofu, although the color of the curd was "slate." Likewise 37282, with a green seed, produced a "greenish" curd.[116]

All the same, Morse's trip through Asia was an eye-opener. As he reported in a letter to the tenth annual meeting of the American Soybean Association (the first he missed), "It is amazing, the extent to which the soybean is used for food in Japan." Uppermost in his mind were green vegetable soybeans. He described his surprise, when hunting down varieties at groceries and seed houses, "to find the soybeans listed with the garden beans." And, indeed, he noticed during forays near Tokyo that "in 95 percent of the cases there are other crops planted between the bean rows, such as early cabbage, onions, lilies (for the edible bulbs) . . . and other early truck crops." As early as May, "small bundles of plants with full grown pods were seen on the market. . . . The pods are boiled in salt water and the beans eaten from the pods."[117] He would eventually learn that the Japanese classed these garden varieties as *mame*, as opposed to *daizu*, or field soybeans grown for grain and forage.[118] This amazed him, even though he had pushed for over a decade for the use of Easycook and Hahto soybeans in the United States as canned or garden vegetables.

During the ensuing two years of the expedition, he eagerly collected as many soy foods as possible. In addition to miso, natto, and tofu—including numerous types of deep-fried and "dried-frozen" tofu—he investigated and collected endless varieties of soy sauce, *yuba*, sweet bean paste, soybean flour, soybean vermicelli, pickled vegetable soybeans, vegetable soybean in the pod, roasted beans used in numerous confections, and such miscellaneous products as Almen, a canned health-food beverage sold in Korea made from soybean flour.[119] While touring the Tokachi experiment station in Hokkaido, Japan, he happened upon a crowd of women attending a demonstration, his guide informed him, for making a fermented soybean beverage. In Washington, his colleagues had kidded him about wanting to make everything out of soybeans except Prohibition-era "home brew." Now, having obtained the recipe—he was unable to taste the finished product, as it had yet to ferment—"no more can they taunt me about not making soybean beer."[120] Morse forwarded samples of food to his office at the USDA, sealing the more perishable items in tin cans. He expected that, when he returned to Washington, he could open "a candy store, bakery, drug store, meat shop, feed store, and a voodoo shop"—a voodoo shop, he explained, because the Japanese loudly scattered parched or roasted soybeans in their homes and temples to scare away demons during the seasonal festival of Setsubun.[121] For all this, he remained sober in his outlook, doubting that the soybean would find acceptance "in the United States in all of the ways used here."[122]

This prediction was more than borne out when he returned home, where he promoted vegetable soybeans for the next decade without much effect. Whatever their lack of wide crossover appeal to non–Asian Americans, however, traditional soy foods did find a niche among one group: vegetarian Seventh-day Adventists. When Morse was diagnosed with an ulcer in the early 1940s, he went on a diet of soft, bland foods, including tofu, soymilk, and soy ice cream. To purchase these, he had only to travel a short distance from his DC neighborhood to the Adventist-run Washington Sanitarium, located in the adjacent town of Takoma Park, Maryland.[123] The Adventists had not simply adopted soy foods from Asia, however. As the inclusion of soy ice cream—and even soymilk—on Morse's shopping list indicates, they had made innovations of their own.

By the early 1930s, a number of Adventist food companies turned out soy products, primarily for consumption at nearby denomination-run colleges and sanitaria. The fact that the companies also sought to appeal to a wider, national market for "health foods"—a coinage of J. H. Kellogg—is indicated by the names of their products. Madison Foods, affiliated with the Nashville Agricultural and Normal Institute near Madison, Tennessee, offered Vigorost (analog steak), Zoyburger Loaf, Stake-Lets, Yum (similar to bologna), Breakfast Crisps, and Cheze-O-Soy (very firm, seasoned tofu) (photo 8). Most of these were developed by Perry Webber, a former missionary who had encountered soy foods in Japan. NANI, a self-supporting college that thrived during the Depression, included among its faculty Frances Dittes, a nutritionist who published numerous soybean articles and recipes in the college's *Madison Survey*.[124] Near Los Angeles, Loma Linda Food Company and La Sierra Industries—founded by T. A. Gundy near La Sierra Academy—both marketed similar lines of products. La Sierra offered toasted Soy Cereal, B-Nuts (soybeans roasted like peanuts), soybean Sandwich Spread, Soy Gluten (which resembled Kellogg's Protose), Soy-Co (an imitation coffee), raw and toasted soybean flour, and Soy Cheese (canned tofu with pimiento added to prevent graying).[125] For its part, Loma Linda produced Soy Bean Wafers, Soy Beans with Proteena, and Soy Mince Sandwich Spread.[126]

Although health-food stores cropped up throughout the nation, the health-food culture was in fact particularly strong in Los Angeles, due in part to an influx of German and Austrian émigrés associated with the Lebensreform ("life reform") and Naturmencshen ("nature men") movements, whose mystical reverence for sun and mountains drew them to California.[127] The opportunity this gave to soy foods was documented by Mildred Lager, who opened The House of Better Living, a "natural foods" store and information clearinghouse, in 1934. Influenced by area Adventists, she took a special interest in the soybean, and her 1938 *House of Better Living Catalog* listed forty-two soy products available for purchase, including Dr. Fearn's Proteinized Cocoa, Dietetic Soyrina Cereal, Bill Baker's Prepared Soy Bean Pancake and Waffle Flour, and Cubbison Soy-Gluten Crackers, as well as her

Photo 8. Advertisement for Adventist food products from Madison Foods, 1940. Courtesy of Soyinfo Center.

own Mildred Lager's Quick Cooking Cracked Soy Beans.[128] Soy products were also sold in grocery stores in Los Angeles. An ad for the Grand Central Public Market listed "Soy Bean Flour, For Patients with Diabetes" in 1932, and an ad for the May Company Modern Market in 1934 listed "Soy Bean Bread, for your health's sake," also hinting at a diabetic target audience.[129]

Soybean flour as a food for diabetes sufferers had roots in nineteenth-century Europe and had been the use of soybeans that first piqued the interest of J. H. Kellogg. Beyond diabetes, however, the Adventists imagined a wider role for the soybean in what Lager would call "corrective nutrition" in her 1945 book, *The Useful Soybean: A Plus Factor in Modern Living*. This concept was rooted in a vitalist tradition that, even as it adapted to new scientific discoveries such as vitamins, remained committed to a central insight: living processes could, if properly nurtured, displace disease. This required that the "life-giving properties" of food not be destroyed in processing and that food be easily digested so as not to overly tax the life force that assimilated it into the body. By the 1930s, vitalists also favored "alkalinizing" foods thought to shift the pH balance of bodily fluids to be inhospitable to disease. Prime among the soybean's virtues for Lager, in fact, was its "wonderful combination of highly nutritious protein and an alkaline ash [that] aids in building resistance to disease and infection and in relieving acidosis."[130] Jethro Kloss, who had formerly run the Nashville Sanitarium Food Company before it was taken over by Madison Foods, wrote in 1939's *Back to Eden* that the bloodstream, "if pure and alkaline, will dissolve and carry away all poisons." The soybean, which appeared in more than fifty recipes in the book, was "king of the beans" in part because "it is a fine alkaline food."[131]

Adventists also embraced the arguments of the Russian immunologist Élie Metchnikoff, in his 1907 *The Prolongation of Life*, that beneficial gut microbes safeguarded the body from the harmful bacteria of putrefaction. The good microbes, moreover, could be planted and nurtured in the intestine through yogurt.[132] This was another variant of a vital principle displacing a source of disease and death. It was also key to converting J. H. Kellogg to soymilk. He had always been ambivalent about cow's milk, on the one hand praising "milk fresh from the bovine font" in 1916 for "its rich store of vitamines and enzymes" and high-quality protein, but on the other cautioning that, if swallowed too quickly, it formed large, hard curds in the stomach and should instead be sipped slowly and thoroughly "chewed."[133] He was doubtful, however, about the taste of soymilk as a substitute. Taking Metchnikoff's lead, however, he found that soured soymilk had a pleasant, tangy flavor. It was also a far more effective substrate for the bacteria he and Metchnikoff preferred. By his estimation, *L. acidophilus* grew much more vigorously in soymilk than in cow's milk, with five to ten times more organisms per unit volume in the former.[134] He reported in 1935 that the Dionne quintuplets had successfully recovered from bowel troubles after their attending physician treated them with Kellogg's acidophilus soymilk, and by 1936 Battle Creek Foods offered it for sale.[135] Even earlier, in 1934, Therapy, Ltd., out of Pasadena, California, was advertising Theradophilus, a brand of "palatable soy bean acidophilus culture" that promised "a new army of Lactobacillicus Acidophilus to fight and destroy the harmful bacteria" that cause "Constipation, Indigestion, Colitis."[136]

To Adventists, alkaline soymilk offered advantages over cow's milk even when not cultured with friendly bacteria, but there were also drawbacks. It was deficient in both sugars and fats when compared to either mother's or cow's milk and had a bitter taste and tendency to cause intestinal discomfort that made it difficult to consume in large amounts.[137] Madison Foods in Tennessee and La Sierra Foods in California both produced soymilk as early as 1929, but it is unclear how well they addressed these problems.[138] In *Back to Eden*, Kloss offered a simple remedy to "remove the soybean taste" that involved changing the water a couple of times while boiling the beans, then additionally boiling the milk for twenty minutes after squeezing it from the pulp.[139] While this deactivated the proteins causing indigestion, however, it is likely that off-putting tastes remained. Therefore, a considerably more complicated process for improving the flavor of soymilk was undertaken by Harry Miller, the China missionary and former director of the Washington Sanitarium who during the 1930s was the director of the Shanghai Sanitarium. Miller would recount in later years that, from his first forays into China in the early 1900s, he had wondered why the Chinese curdled soymilk into tofu rather than drinking it. An avid drinker of cow's milk during his own student days, he also sought a substitute for his students in Shanghai from a local source. Finally, he reasoned that a better milk supply might combat protein deficiency in Chinese children when they were weaned.[140]

Miller later gave differing accounts of the steps by which he made soymilk more palatable. His first attempts involved little more than adding sugar, which covered up the bitter taste but did not help make it more digestible. Having consulted agricultural experiment station bulletins, he experimented with cooking his soymilk longer than was customary in China, where making it into tofu instead helped conserve scarce fuel.[141] Miller found that more prolonged cooking resulted in better digestion and less gas, although the off

flavors and nutritional deficiencies remained. The breakthrough innovation
came to him one day as he worked with soybean slurry, prior to straining out
the okara: "I heard a divine voice behind me that said, 'Why don't you cook
it longer with live steam?'"[142] In refining vegetable oils, including soybean
oil, it was in fact already common practice to force steam through the oil to
deodorize it. The turbulence created in the oil by the steam meant that volatile organic chemicals, responsible for off tastes and bad odors, evaporated
more readily at temperatures low enough to prevent burning the oil. Miller
saw this in action, as it happened, when he toured a copra-processing plant
during a visit to the Philippines. He noted that, while a mass of dried copra "smelled like a slaughterhouse," steam distillation removed disagreeable
odors from the oil.[143]

It is not clear if he had already discovered this method in 1936, when
he went in person before the US Commissioner of Patents to defend his
method of "debittering" soymilk. As Miller told the story, the commissioner
and his expert taster "admitted having tasted many soy products, and this
was the first time there had come to them a truly debittered soya milk."
The patent office approved Patent No. 2,078,962 in May 1937.[144] Miller did
not mention steam in his application, writing instead that the milk should
be "heated to a boiling point" while "the fluid is agitated . . . for a period of
time to cause the entire taste of the milk to be changed from a beany flavor
to what may be termed a 'nutty' flavor."[145] His emphasis in the patent was on
another innovation, inspired by a transpacific journey during which he witnessed the use of a small homogenizer to reconstitute milk from skim-milk
powder, water, and melted butter. Miller realized that by similar means he
could add any amount of any oil to his soymilk and not have it separate out.
To this end, he purchased a colloid mill, which broke up particles in a liquid
so that they would remain in suspension, and used it to incorporate "cereal
sugar," vegetable oil, and a small amount of salt into his milk.[146]

In 1932 Miller established the Vetose Nutritional Laboratory at the
Shanghai Sanitarium, and in 1935–1936 he carried out tests in which he
fed his formulated soymilk to hundreds of small children at the Shanghai
Clinic—in some cases, as the sole food for six months starting from birth—
with control groups consuming cow's milk and various American and European baby foods. Results were printed in the English-language *Chinese
Medical Journal* in April 1936. These showed, according to Miller, that "soy

bean milk was second only to mother's milk in the feeding of infants" from birth on.[147] To provide the milk more widely to residents of Shanghai, he and his adult son Willis imported the equipment to establish a factory to produce Vetose Soya Milk. Among other things, they obtained an "in-bottle sterilizer" so that they could distribute milk in bottles to be returned and reused. They set up delivery routes throughout Shanghai, with boys on bicycles pulling carts that distributed 3,000 quarts and 4,000 half-pints of milk per day. They eventually expanded their offerings to include chocolate milk and acidophilus-soured soymilk (for which Kellogg held the US patent) and added spray-drying equipment to the factory to make powdered milk that could be delivered more widely. Miller envisioned having an impact on childhood nutrition throughout China, providing an alternative for the majority of families too poor to afford dairy milk.[148] In August 1937, however, Japanese bombs destroyed the Vetose factory just eight months after it started production. In early 1939, Miller and his family was forced to flee China, the Shanghai Sanitarium having become a refugee camp.[149]

Miller settled in Ohio, where he set up a food factory that exported tinned soymilk powder to the Philippines and the Shanghai International Settlement, which had not yet been invaded.[150] When these outlets in turn were cut off by the Pacific War, Miller faced an unexpected challenge: selling soymilk to an American public well supplied with cow's milk while facing opposition from the dairy industry that so abundantly supplied it. Miller produced two products, Soy-a-Malt for adults and Soyalac for infant feeding. Even with a taste mellowed from beany to nutty, however, Soy-a-Malt did not taste enough like cow's milk for American palates, pushing Miller to conclude "that it takes more than the scientific fact that a thing is good nutritionally to put it across." Babies, however, did not know to mind the taste of Soyalac, and Miller asked the American Medical Association to endorse it as the equal of cow's milk for infant feeding, but the medical association restricted its recommendation, applying it only to babies with milk allergies. The era in which soy would be widely used in infant formula—as well as be regularly consumed by grown Americans—was decades away. During the war, in fact, Miller's best-selling products were Miller's Cutlets, a meat substitute made with wheat gluten, and canned green soybeans.[151]

If Adventists like Miller were the most active in developing soymilk and other novel soy foods, they were not quite alone. There was also Henry Ford.

As early as the 1920s, Ford had famously proclaimed that he would do to the cow what he had done to the horse: replace its primary function with a more efficient machine. By 1934, in fact, he had a demonstration plant in Greenfield Village producing several hundred gallons of soymilk daily, a product said to be popular with the Ford Company's Filipino workers.[152] To this extent, his pursuit of soymilk was consistent with his other goals for the soybean. He sought to modernize food production and to reduce farm drudgery. However, his interest in soybeans as a food was also rooted in his being that most American kind of eccentric: a dietary crank.

Like the Adventists, Ford was a strict teetotaler and opponent of tobacco; and, like them, he argued that these vices were the outcome, not the origin, of dissipated habits rooted in bad food. He may have absorbed these ideas, as well as his interest in soybeans, from J. H. Kellogg: he has frequently been included in lists of The San's notable guests and at one point stated, "I like Mr. Kellogg's philosophy."[153] But Ford, who flirted with but never embraced vegetarianism, did not require Kellogg's tutelage. He tended to view the body as he did one of his durable Model T's: capable of running smoothly with only minor repairs if given the proper fuel and regular maintenance. As he put it, using an automotive analogy, anyone could "live to 125 or 150 if we would keep the carbon out of his system."[154] Ford's notions, moreover, were generally stranger than Kellogg's. In the 1890s, Ford was convinced that sugar crystals lacerated the digestive tract. In the 1920s, he insisted that bread should be eaten only after it had sat out for a day, that "chicken is fit only for hawks," that it was harmful to combine starches, proteins, and fruit acids during one meal, and that people should not eat anything until 1:00 P.M.[155]

In 1926, he hired a boyhood friend, Dr. Edsel A. Ruddiman, former dean of Vanderbilt University's pharmacy school, to conduct nutrition experiments at a laboratory in Greenfield Village.[156] Ruddiman began experimenting with soybeans in 1928, gauging the dietary value of their protein, fat, and carbohydrates by feeding them to rats.[157] In 1932, he visited Madison Foods and took home samples of Adventist soy foods, including Vigorost and Soy Cheese, a very firm seasoned tofu; his wife made croquettes from the Soy Cheese that, he wrote to Madison, he enjoyed very much.[158]

By the time of the Century of Progress exhibition in Chicago, Ruddiman himself had created enough foods from soybeans to serve a five-course dinner to thirty guests in the Ford Building's executive lounge. The dishes, which may have been developed in collaboration with Jan Willemse, Ford's executive chef,[159] included celery stuffed with soybean cheese, salted soybeans (eaten like peanuts), soybean croquettes in tomato sauce, buttered green soybeans, soybean coffee, and assorted desserts—apple pie, cakes, and cookies—made to some degree with soy flour.[160] The *Christian Science Monitor* reviewed the dinner favorably, noting that "no meat was served and it was not missed" during "an excellent dinner in which every dish and drink was made in whole or in part from the little legume." One guest reportedly commented that the "soy bean cake is delicious, but after the soy bean croquettes, soy bean apple pie and soy bean coffee, you know, one isn't really hungry."[161] Ruddiman and Ford hosted at least two other soy banquets geared to journalists during the 1930s, as well as a fourteen-course soybean luncheon in 1941 when he introduced his prototype plastic car. Many of these dishes appeared in a nineteen-page booklet containing fifty-eight soup-to-nuts soybean recipes.[162] In contrast to this variety, Ford urged Ruddiman to develop a compact, all-purpose soybean biscuit that contained all of the nutrients necessary for human health. Ford professed to enjoy the result—as did Ruddiman's rats—but one of Ford's secretaries, pressured to eat one, described the biscuit as "one of the most vile things ever put into human mouths."[163] The experimental biscuit was largely forgotten by the time similar products were developed during the war.

Despite the efforts of Ford, Morse, Adventists, and a scattering of health-food enthusiasts such as Mildred Lager, the soybean did not succeed in the 1930s as a food that people knowingly sought. Neither did it fulfill the chemurgical dream of becoming a nonfood industrial input. Rather, its greatest success was as an ingredient whose identity was obscured by the growing industrialization of food production, a path it would continue to chart in later decades. And even though America's entry into World War II, with its attendant shortages of meat, would revive interest in soy foods of the sort advocated by Adventists, the war's ultimate effect would be to use the soybean itself to render such soy foods unnecessary, as it helped to augment the nation's supplies of meat and milk rather than supplant them.

CHAPTER FIVE

ANSWERING THE CALL

On a June afternoon in 1943, New York governor Thomas E. Dewey hosted a well-publicized lunch billed as a "war-diet luncheon," but which soon became popularly known as Dewey's "soybean luncheon." Albany's Executive Mansion, whose shadowy oxblood-red corridors once reminded Franklin Roosevelt's children of a Hollywood haunted house, had a formal dining room said to seat thirty-two, but which held sixty-seven guests on this day, including newspaper, magazine, and radio journalists. The proceedings lasted two hours as various members of the New York State Emergency Food Commission made speeches. Meanwhile, the press had the opportunity to ask participants what they thought about a menu dominated by what the New York Times called "the humble soy bean." It came in several guises: chicken and soybean-sprout soufflé, sprouted soybeans and onions, soybean bread, and perhaps as sprouts in the tossed salad. There was soybean-free strawberry shortcake for dessert. Only one guest—a man—refused to touch the soybean dishes, while most of the others "did justice to their full portions, although the majority never before had eaten soy beans." The meal was prepared by the mansion's staff, and Dewey told reporters that he and his family had been consuming soybeans in increasing quantities since he had taken office in January. "We had some soy bean gingerbread the other night; it was excellent," he reported. He hoped to set an example for other New York families, explaining that change "is being forced upon us by the war," prompting a search for "new and palatable foods which will maintain health and energy."[1]

The soybean lunch was not completely free of political intent. At the beginning of what would be twelve years in office, Dewey was eager to reduce state expenditures and fight corruption, while at the same time demonstrating that the state government could actively and efficiently promote the welfare of citizens. He sought to provide a counterweight to what he saw as Washington's overly bureaucratic control of the war effort. He charged the Emergency Food Commission with addressing logistical problems, from implementing a system to rush tractors and trucks wherever they were most needed to locating millions of bushels of barley and coaxing chickens to eat it.[2] Beyond these momentary problems, however, the commission foresaw a looming crisis. It submitted a report to Dewey a week before the luncheon projecting that "there will not be available enough food in this country to feed both its human and its present animal populations. Therefore much of the animal population will inevitably be liquidated." To help New Yorkers conserve and find alternatives to the "animal products (milk, eggs, meat, butter and lard)" that were at risk, the commission advised such measures as importing grain to boost the milk supply, issuing bulletins to let citizens know what foods were in short supply, and researching new foods, in particular soybean sprouts and soybean bread.[3] These recommendations, in keeping with Dewey's philosophy, were active, positive, and largely devoted to encouraging voluntary citizen action at the same moment that the federal government was implementing a widely resented rationing program.[4]

Because it had so often been the stepping-stone to the presidency, the New York governorship gave Dewey a national stature that ensured that his soybean luncheon received widespread coverage, surpassing even the publicity Henry Ford had garnered nine years earlier for a similar event. *Life* magazine featured photos of Governor Dewey and his wife mid-bite, Dewey "practicing what he preaches" by lunching on sautéed Cayuga soybean sprouts. Mrs. Dewey finished "all of her soybean soufflé" before having "a second helping of soybean-flour muffins." Praising Dewey's initiative, the accompanying article informed readers that the commission would send a free pamphlet on how to sprout soybeans to anyone interested. Several pages of photos followed showing the process of growing sprouts (photo 9) and preparing them into such dishes as aspic of soybean sprouts—"a cool and nutritious summer dish" that was also visually striking, with the sprouts seemingly captured midswim within the transparent mold. A final photo

Photo 9. Technique for sprouting soybeans. From "Soybeans: Governor Dewey Sponsors Them as Partial Solution to Food Crisis," *Life*, July 19, 1943. Nina Leen/ Contributor/Getty Images.

showed Lassie, a healthy Cairn-Scottie who had never been fed any meat, eating from a bowl of sprouts. This demonstrated the degree to which meat could be dispensed with, although showcasing sprouts as dog food may have carried a less than positive message about them to some readers.[5]

The role of soybeans during World War II turned out to be more complicated than Dewey or the commission expected. They did end up on the menu for both civilians and soldiers—as well as for the Japanese Americans struggling to maintain their lives in remote internment camps—but a massive expansion of both the soybean crop and the nation's crushing capacity forestalled the direst predictions of the commission. Unlike the previous war, World War II proved to be a decisive factor in the rise of soybeans in America, despite the logistical hurdles that the government's soybean program faced early on.

Feed for Livestock

World War II affected the demand for soybeans well before the Dewey luncheon or, in fact, the US entry into the war. In the late 1930s, the Sino-Japanese War shut off supplies of tung oil from China, with soybean oil—or at least the fast-drying fraction of it—stepping in to replace it in lacquers and varnishes.[6] The German invasion of Norway in the spring of 1940 similarly eliminated imports of fish oil, primarily cod-liver oil, and Germany's expansion into Mediterranean countries cut off the United States from 100 million pounds of olive oil. These losses represented perhaps 10 percent of total oil imports[7] and may have played a role in the marked increase in soybean planting in 1939 and 1940, although this was mainly the outcome of longer-term trends: soybean oil's increasing use in margarine and the limits placed by the Agricultural Adjustment Administration (AAA) on other crops. Indeed, when the AAA increased its quotas for corn and hog production in 1941 in response to demand from Europe, soybean acreage suffered, something that had not happened for half a decade. Consistent with strong demand for soybean oil, however, corn displaced acreage devoted to soybean hay. The number of acres planted for beans continued to rise, just not as fast as the acres for hay fell.[8]

The USDA sought to further accelerate this switch from hay to beans in June 1941 by redefining soy harvested for beans as "soil-conserving" rather than "soil-depleting," part of a more general relaxation of AAA limits.[9] In August, the government began purchasing soy flour for shipment to Britain under its Food for Freedom program, and by September the AAA set

a goal of 7 million acres harvested for beans in 1942, an increase of more
than a million acres over 1941.[10] In December 1941, *Soybean Digest* polled
state AAA committees for the results of intention-to-plant surveys of farmers and found that the three leading soybean states—Illinois, Indiana, and
Iowa—were set to exceed their AAA goals by more than a million acres,
planting more soybeans to harvest as beans than the entire nation did in
1941. The magazine projected a national total of 8 million acres.[11] The poll
was likely conducted before the attack on Pearl Harbor, in the wake of which
the AAA encouraged farmers to join the "Battle of the Soybean," with a new
national goal of 9 million acres.[12] Japan's conquest of the Philippines, East
Indies, Malaya, and additional territory in China spelled a loss to the United
States of a billion pounds of coconut, palm, and tung-oil imports.[13] To make
up for this loss, the federal government urged farmers to plant more peanuts,
flax, and soybeans.

This urging was accompanied by both financial incentives and calls to patriotism. The Commodity Credit Corporation (CCC), a New Deal agency
whose mandate to boost farm prices complemented the AAA's efforts to
limit and manage production, pledged to purchase soybeans for $1.60 per
bushel.[14] *Soybean Digest* disagreed, however, that an appeal to material interests was the best way to motivate farmers. For one thing, even with the
price guarantee, soybeans were still not as profitable as corn on suitably level
ground. Such an appeal also seemed to "discredit" farmers' patriotism. Better
was the approach of the Iowa Agricultural Extension Service. It distributed
25,000 pamphlets pointing out that, by USDA estimates, the nation would
need 3 billion more pounds of domestically produced oil in 1942 for "our
armed forces and hard-working civilians," who "need more fat in their diet
for energy." The United States was also now the only large source of edible
oils for allies Britain, Canada, and Russia as well. "The American farmer has
never let down his country," *Soybean Digest* concluded, "particularly when
the facts of a situation are presented to him straight from the shoulder."[15]
Crop improvement societies meanwhile tapped into an even simpler kind of
pride, holding local contests to see which farmers—and, on average, which
state—could produce the highest yield of soybeans per acre.[16] Ultimately, 10
million acres of soybeans were planted for beans in 1942. Some of this was
at the expense of soybeans planted for hay, but much of it represented new
acreage for the crop.[17]

This massive expansion created problems of its own. There was concern, first of all, that the planting of new, more marginal acres to soybeans might increase erosion. Unlike deep-rooted, perennial legumes such as clover, soybeans tend to loosen soil, doing substantial damage when planted on a slope. The Soil Conservation Service, noting that "all soybeans cannot be grown on flat land for the same reason corn can't"—there was not enough of it—recommended contour plowing when necessary.[18] Of greater immediate concern were a number of logistical challenges. Wet weather conditions were conducive to planting and growing soybeans in 1942 but created problems during the harvest. There were shortages of labor and combines, as both machinery and workers were in high demand for the war effort. In an address to the 1943 Farm Chemurgic Conference, former ASA president G. G. McIlroy recounted his troubles with a ten-foot combine that he intended not only to use for himself but also lend to neighbors. It broke down in October, but he was not able to get replacement parts until December, after the optimal time to harvest beans.[19] One Illinois county that requested 120 combines from the War Production Board was allotted only twenty.[20] A cold snap in November 1942 further interrupted fieldwork and lowered the yield of beans when they were harvested.[21] Finally, there was a shortage of storage for what was still an unprecedented harvest, forcing farmers to build makeshift bins.[22]

The largest bottleneck, however, was that the Corn Belt, where most of the new soybeans were grown, did not have enough mills to process the crop. In March 1942, *Soybean Digest* did a back-of-the-envelope calculation of the nation's crushing capacity and concluded that it was enough to convert an estimated 150 million bushels into oil and meal—or at least "nearly so." Soybean processors themselves could currently handle at least 105 million bushels, to which could be added 20 million bushels that cottonseed crushers in the South would be able to handle, plus 11 or 12 million that could go to West Coast copra and linseed mills, bringing the total to 137 million bushels. This understated the problem, however, as the tables accompanying the article themselves projected that the top three soybean states alone— Illinois, Indiana, and Iowa—would produce 105 million bushels, with only the crushing capacity for 76 million.[23] *Soybean Digest* also underestimated the yield per acre in their calculations: as it turned out, the nation produced 187 million bushels of soybeans in 1942, of which 20 million were held back for seed for the 1943 planting.[24] The resulting need to export Corn Belt soybeans for processing in other regions, in addition to putting a strain on the wartime freight system, in turn contributed to another persistent problem, alluded to in the pages of *Soybean Digest* as "the meal situation."

Prior to the war, soybean farmers with livestock typically bought soybean meal from the same processors who purchased their beans, using it as a high-protein supplement to other crops, such as corn or oats, held back on the farm for feed. This was a small market for the crushers, however, who sold most of their output to the growing number of mixed-feed manufacturers, typically in forward contracts arranged months in advance. The wartime situation upset these arrangements. The demand for meal went up dramatically, as farmers not only raised more livestock for the war effort but also were encouraged to feed each cow or chicken a larger protein ration to increase milk, egg, and meat production.[25] At the same time, the CCC established a price ceiling on meal. This made it cheap for the manufacturers of mixed feeds, who were soon accused of using too much of it not only to boost the protein content of their formulations but also to substitute for more expensive ingredients.[26] Because the mixed-feed industry locked down the supply of meal through forward contracts, there was little left for local feed dealers and farmers. The situation was made worse by the beans making their way to other regions, from which the meal never returned. Resentful farmers forced to buy expensive mixed feeds decided the following year to keep back more whole beans to use as feed—despite the risk of producing soft pork. This in turn created a shortage of beans for local processors to crush, thereby threatening as well the supply of much-needed soybean oil.[27]

The resolution of these problems was neither easy nor quick. The CCC and the national Office of Price Administration calibrated the price ceiling for soybean meal, while the War Production Board developed a distribution plan that reserved half of the meal processed outside of the Corn Belt for shipment to areas facing shortages.[28] There were efforts in 1943 to promote soybeans in the South, near to excess crushing capacity.[29] When the feed industry and USDA concluded in a joint study that available protein in 1943 would meet only 80 percent of requirements for livestock, feed manufacturers agreed to voluntary limits that the War Food Administration (WFA) soon made mandatory over their protests.[30] The manufacturers insisted that instead it was farmers who were squandering protein. In a full-page ad in *Soybean Digest*, Allied Mills prodded farmers to declare war on a cartoon

"weasel of waste," who along with the "wurst" and "wop" weasels—carica-
tures of Adolf Hitler and Benito Mussolini in weasel form—represented a
wartime enemy. The ad recommended, among other measures, frequently
culling poor egg producers, utilizing pastures to their fullest, and using
troughs or hoppers for feed rather than scattering it.[31] Eventually all sides
were forced to acknowledge, however, that shortages were less a matter of
waste or overuse than simply the result of a rapidly expanding population
of hungry animals. These circumstances were what prompted the New York
State Emergency Food Commission to predict in 1943 that livestock would
have to be killed off in large numbers.

In February 1944, even after the WFA imposed limits on the amount
of meal that processers could forward-contract, creating a reserve that the
WFA could distribute as needed, *Soybean Digest* reported that "everybody is
short" of meal.[32] By August 1944, however, the protein crisis had eased. By
October it was largely over, mainly because there was finally enough processing capacity in the Corn Belt. In December 1943, the War Production Board
had approved priority allocation of materials to build and expand thirty-
three soybean plants: eighteen in Iowa, five in Illinois, and the rest scattered
throughout other northern and midwestern states.[33] The number of mills
specializing in soybeans increased from 100 to 137 by mid-1944, with the
capacity to crush 172 million bushels per year.[34] These plants were operated
by the soybean pioneers of the 1930s—Staley, Glidden, and Swift in Illinois,
Ralston Purina in Missouri, Central Soya in Indiana, and Archer-Daniels
Midland in Minnesota—but also by smaller concerns. At the end of 1944,
quotas on meal were loosened, in part because numbers of chicks and hogs
fell much as the Emergency Food Commission had predicted.[35] In 1945, however, the supply of soybean meal kept up with growing livestock populations.
Beef topped 10 million pounds for the first time, and record-high numbers
of cattle, hogs, and chickens went to slaughter without a dampening effect on
the following year's production.[36] The region's increased processing capacity
also permitted plant breeders to introduce more productive varieties such as
the Lincoln soybean, high in both yield and oil content.[37]

The successful expansion of the soybean industry, whatever the hiccups
along the way, contributed enormously to America's unparalleled food supply during wartime. Even when meat rations were imposed in 1943, the allotment of two pounds per person was double that of Great Britain and

incomparably more than what Russian, German, Italian, French, or Japanese civilians could expect.[38] According to government surveys, in fact, meat consumption generally rose during the war from its low point during the Depression, with the poorest third of the population eating 17 percent more meat and poultry in 1944 than in 1942, and the middle and upper thirds eating only 3–4 percent less.[39] Still, this was far less meat than Americans had eaten at the beginning of the century, and it was less than they might have purchased with the rising incomes provided by the wartime economy. The sense of belt-tightening was real, and rationing to conserve meat for the armed forces and for America's allies was more stringent than during World War I. Calls to eat alternatives to meat were accordingly more vigorous, with governments at all levels urging Americans to, among other things, consume more of their soybeans directly, rather than via their role in feeding livestock. The response by citizens ranged from patriotic enthusiasm to bitter scorn.

Soy Foods for Civilians

In theory, any period of national belt-tightening might have provided soy foods an opportunity for greater acceptance. During the Depression, when meat consumption went down dramatically, university home economics departments experimented with soy flour. In this vein, J. A. LeClerc of the USDA's Agricultural Chemical Research Division pointed out in a speech to the ASA in 1936 that "one pound of soya flour is equivalent to two pounds of meat in protein content" and that simply switching from ordinary to soy bread could painlessly replace one-fourth of an American's daily meat intake.[40] Wartime shortages, however, provided a more effective spur to adopt such recommendations by couching them in calls to patriotic duty. Efforts to promote soybeans were also more effective during World War II than World War I, largely because a greater variety of soybeans and soy products were now readily available. Soy flour, the primary ingredient in Americanized soy cuisine, was produced by a number of companies by the early 1940s, primarily for the diabetic-foods market, and received an additional boost from direct government spending in 1942. The Agricultural Marketing Administration made large purchases of soy flour and soy grits to send to the Allies under the Lend-Lease Program and domestically for use in dehydrated soups provided by the School Lunch Program.[41] In March 1943, fresh meat was added to the list of rationed foods after the failure of the voluntary 1942 Share the Meat campaign. The USDA encouraged soy processors to increase the output of soy flour threefold in 1943, with the department's Bureau of Human Nutrition and Home Economics encouraging consumption with a sixteen-page booklet in October, *Cooking with Soy Flour and Grits*. By 1945, the revised booklet would contain 130 recipes.[42]

Much of the action was at the state level, however, with the state of New York taking the lead in soy-food promotion largely due to the work of the husband-and-wife nutritionists Clive and Jeanette McCay. Jeanette had a PhD in nutrition, but the formative experience of her youth had been as an in-store demonstrator for Gold Medal Flour,[43] and she retained a focus on communicating and promoting dietary ideas. In 1942, she was working with colleagues in Cornell's Child Development and Nutrition departments writing articles, radio addresses, and bulletins when she was offered a full-time position as an extension professor. Soybeans were a frequent topic of her lessons and demonstrations, and in 1943, when she was put in charge of publications for the new Emergency Food Commission, she soon became the chair of its Soybean Committee.[44] In the wake of the Dewey luncheon, which proved to be a major catalyst for public interest, the committee logged over 22,000 letters inquiring about soy recipes in the months that followed the lunch, peaking in July (the month the *Life* magazine piece came out) with almost 10,000. Although the largest number came from New York residents, letters arrived from every state in the union (plus Hawaii, Alaska, and Washington, DC), as well as Canada, Mexico, and a smattering from England, Cuba, Puerto Rico, and other places.[45] In response, Jeanette and her team produced and distributed more than 90,000 leaflets about soybeans by the end of 1943—some sent in bulk to home demonstrators and nutrition teachers—and around a million by the end of the war.[46]

These included *The Miracle Bean*, which featured recipes using whole soybeans or grits as meat extenders, such as "Chile Con Carne with Soybeans" and "Peppy Meat Loaf," as well as recipes for baked goods such as "Soy Grit Cookies," "Helen's Birthday Spice Cake," and "Lucille Brewer's 'Open-Recipe' Bread." She also issued a special pamphlet on sprouting written by Clive, *Soybeans for Fifty* (for restaurants and cafeterias), and *Desserts with Soy*.[47] These efforts culminated in *Soybeans*, a sixty-three-page Cornell extension bulletin issued in February 1945. All of these publications were enlivened by the drawings of Kenneth Washburn, an art professor at Cornell, and other artists who devised striking pictorial graphs to chart soybean production figures and nutritional data, as well as more whimsical illustrations: for instance, of a quartet of sprouts in top hats and bowties singing "a song of soy sprouts" on the cover of Clive's pamphlet.[48] The governor's lunch also inspired imitation throughout the state. As Jeanette reported in *The Food Commentator*, a newsletter distributed to home demonstrators and teachers, similar meals were held in nearly every county. More than 250 community soybean dinners attended by some 7,500 people were held in churches, grange halls, and Masonic halls.[49]

By the 1940s, Clive McCay was already well known in the world of nutrition science, having received his PhD in biochemistry from Berkeley in 1925 and subsequently worked with the renowned researcher L. B. Mendel at Yale. His main interest was in developing optimal diets for animals, ranging from young fish in Connecticut hatcheries to the nation's canine companions; his 1943 *Nutrition of the Dog* was a popular success. One of his most notable discoveries was that young mice stunted by severely calorie-restricted diets not only had the ability to restart their development once fed normally but also ended up substantially outliving their peers. This contributed to his opposition to what he would be among the first to call "empty calories" and led him to promote fortification as a means to make the calories Americans consumed more nutritionally full.[50] Likewise, his work creating balanced feeds for dogs convinced him that "the dogs of this country are, as a whole, probably better fed than the children, and this is particularly true of dogs kept in kennels where good mixed feeds are used."[51] In a speech in November 1942 to the State Federation of Home Bureaus, he likewise insisted that "the housewife should be as particular about what she feeds her family as the farmer is concerning the feed for his livestock." Bread being a common staple, he in particular urged that bakers include the "percentage composition," or proportion of each nutrient, on bread labels, much as might appear on formulated feeds sold to farmers.[52]

Beyond labeling, the analogy to formulated feed suggested that bread, too, could be scientifically formulated, with ingredients such as soy meal added to make up for deficiencies in protein and other nutrients. The impetus for Clive's work came from Carl E. Ladd, dean of the agriculture school at Cornell, where Clive taught, who suggested a survey of bread available in the local town of Ithaca, New York. Initially, Clive's team analyzed percentage of milk solids, an indicator of protein and vitamin content, and deemed twenty-eight of the twenty-nine varieties to be nutritionally deficient, with less than 6 percent milk solids.[53] Ladd urged Clive and his colleagues to study how the addition of soy flour would improve the food value of white bread. The Cornell team found that white rats grew better on white bread enriched with 5 percent soy flour, even if it already contained the optimal level of milk solids.[54]

Clive asked Lucille Brewer, a home economics professor who had been developing bread recipes for decades—and who had already experimented with adding soy flour to loaves—to devise a loaf enriched according to his specifications. He insisted, as he had in his speech, that the percentage of each ingredient be printed on the label of any commercial bread made according to the formula and that the recipe be widely available to home bakers. Thus the bread was variously called Lucille Brewer's Open-Formula Bread (again, a nod to animal feeds) or Open-Recipe Bread.[55] This was the bread served at the Dewey luncheon, and the *New York Times* duly published its recipe, which included nine tablespoons of high-fat soybean flour.[56] The goal was to provide complete nutrition in a staple food—white bread—without substantially changing it. "When a nation runs short of food its people usually have to retreat to eating more cereals," stated the label on Open-Formula Bread, and the "most practical way to take up the decline in the nutritional value of the diet . . . is to fortify the quality of bread—the principal cereal food."[57]

Clive also promoted soybeans in the more overt form of bean sprouts. Beginning in early 1942, he and a Chinese postdoctoral researcher stranded in Ithaca by the war, Peng Cheng Hsu, ventured to New York City to observe sprouting methods in Chinatown cellars.[58] They then experimented with different varieties and sprouting methods, including a system in their laboratory that watered 100-pound lots of sprouting soybeans.[59] They began test-marketing sprouts at the Ithaca Food Co-op, a Depression-era self-help venture that presaged the health food–oriented co-ops of later decades and that also sold Open-Formula Bread and soy flour. The university's cafeteria and meat shop also offered the sprouts.[60] Clive envisioned commercial sprouting operations set up in canneries and creameries,[61] but he also publicized home methods: the Dewey luncheon article in *Life* offered a step-by-step guide, accompanied by photographs, demonstrating the use of milk bottles and chlorinated lime water (to prevent the growth of mold) to sprout soybeans.[62] While sprouts were more exotic to Americans than white bread—even as they widely consumed mung-bean sprouts as an ingredient in chop suey—Clive's pitch was not altogether different. The point was to transform soybeans into something else, in this case a fresh green vegetable that was unexpectedly high in protein, although soybeans proved more recalcitrant than mung beans in completing the transformation. The sprouts remained stubbornly beanlike at one end. However, they contained an abundance of protein, vitamin C, niacin, and riboflavin[63] and had the additional advantage of being more widely available than mung beans.

Clive's work hoped to skirt what was emerging as the main obstacle in the wider adoption of soybeans as food. This problem was highlighted when, around the time of the Dewey luncheon, the National Research Council's (NRC) Committee on Food Habits conducted a study to gauge the best strategies for promoting soy foods. The researcher Patricia Woodward and her colleagues designed a number of posters that extolled the virtues of soybeans: one emphasized the variety of foods that could be derived from them, for example, and another their nutritional benefits. The researchers hung their posters in a number of government cafeterias. At the same time, they arranged for soybean-enriched options to be offered on the menu, including meatloaf, muffins, macaroni and cheese, and split-pea soup. Little enough soy was added to each item to leave the taste unaffected, ensuring that any preference among patrons would be the outcome of the mere idea of soybeans. They served the foods for a week without labeling them as soy products. When the soy labels appeared the following week, consumption of the items went down (except in the case of the muffins). Surveys suggested that this was due in part to the success of Henry Ford and the chemurgy movement, with some respondents objecting to eating "paint or steering wheels." It also appeared that the posters had at best no effect, with the ones emphasizing nutritional appeal actually seeming to discourage people from eating the soy foods.[64] This finding might give pause to anyone designing educational campaigns to promote healthy eating.

Americans seemed to like soy best when they were unaware of its presence. Indeed, because it held water, soy flour visibly increased the size and

improved the texture of loaves. The Soya Foods Research Council in Chicago, which offered bread containing as much as 7 percent soybean flour in
the cafeterias of Illinois mental hospitals over a thirty-day period, found
that it was consumed more avidly than standard bread.[65] This was consistent
with the experience of a Canadian mill that achieved a sixfold increase in its
output of soy flour by adding it to white bread in small amounts—ranging
from 1 to 2 percent—such that it did not alter "in any way the characteristic
color and flavor that the consuming public was used to."[66] Given Woodward's
findings, Clive's open-formula strategy was perhaps counterproductive. The
ASA certainly objected strenuously when the Food and Drug Administration (FDA) ruled in August 1943 that any bread using more than 0.5 parts
dehulled ground soybeans per 100 parts flour (an amount commonly used
as a bleaching agent by bakers) could not be sold as "white bread." The ASA
wished for the threshold to be 3 percent, and *Soybean Digest* alerted its readers that "SOYBEAN GROWERS OF AMERICA HAVE A MAJOR MARKET AT
STAKE" and sent the FDA commissioner a letter of protest.[67] Because the
WFA was at the same time encouraging greater use of soybeans as a source
of protein, the FDA ultimately relented in 1944 to put off any enforcement
of the standard.[68]

In her 1945 book *The Useful Soybean*, Mildred Lager noted that, although
the average American man was not at all interested in trying soybeans, feeling that he could "get along nicely without them," such a "rebelling male"
would eat gladly his beans "without suspecting their presence" if they were
artfully masked.[69] The job of hiding the soy, in Lager's scenario, rested on the
shoulders of housewives, the targets of Jeanette's messages. This dual strategy of promotion and concealment proved difficult to carry out in practice,
however.

As Lager observed from Los Angeles, "The sudden limelight [on] the
sprouted soy" as a result of the Dewey lunch "is enough to make the soy
pioneer and some of the slighted nutritionists rub their eyes in amazement";
she also knew all too well that "it is never easy to change food habits."[70] A
backlash was most noticeable among "rebelling males" in the press who, like
Ring Lardner during the previous war's Patriotic Food Show, found much
to mock. The *New Yorker's* Russell Maloney savaged the commission's report and its director of nutrition education for the New York area, the "well-
coiffed club-lady" Mrs. Roger W. Straus. He was puzzled by the very concept

of a "food substitute," writing that it "isn't meat, and it isn't potatoes, and it isn't butter, and Mrs. Straus will be damned if she knows what it is, unless it's soy beans." His "delicatessen man sells soy beans," he continued, "but the trouble is you go in to buy some soy beans and you're distracted by a lot of—well, pardon the expression, but *food*." He did claim to have recently served guests his "favorite soybean recipe," salted soybeans served with martinis and highballs—suggested by the *Life* article—followed by a dinner of cold tomato soup, brook trout, green peas, zucchini sauté, green salad, cheese, and coffee.[71] The magazine's "Talk of the Town" column later conceded that "it is true that a diet of soy beans and water will sustain life indefinitely," only to wryly comment that "Governor Dewey could live on soy beans and water until he becomes President."[72]

It was not only urban sophisticates who were skeptical of the soybean message. When Marvin Jones, the new federal War Foods administrator, suggested in late August 1943 that Americans might substitute soybeans for meat, he received numerous irate letters. A Missouri farmer, sounding a rustic note, complained that "if those experts in Washington who are trying to force the soy bean upon the American people had brains of croton oil there wouldn't be enough to physic a flea." A Brooklyn woman argued that the "propaganda that . . . soy beans are just as nutritious as a T-bone steak, while probably true, is laughable. You can't place a flock of soy beans in front of persons who are accustomed to thick steaks, and then tell them that they're deriving exactly the same nourishment out of the beans as they would from the steak." Reflecting the fact that fish and poultry were still considered substitutes as well, a New York businessman wrote, "I relatively dislike yeast, soy beans, fish, chicken, and pork in the order named, but I do love roast beef and sirloin steak."[73] By October, even the *New Yorker's* "Markets and Menus" columnist, Sheila Hibbens, seemed weary of the topic, commenting that "unless a woman is blind and deaf, she has by this time learned all there is to know about soy beans and that she can take them or leave them alone without any advice from me," before moving on to a discussion of eggplants.[74]

In the end, the wartime emergency had a limited impact on America's consumption of soy foods. Soybean sprouts never became an American staple, as Clive hoped. And as Jeanette reflected in a 1947 article, "Now that America is settling into her postwar stride, many a homemaker will find a forgotten package of some soybean product in her kitchen [and] may wonder,

*"I'm sorry, Mr. Groff, but
my family has come to prefer soybeans."*

Photo 10. "It was funny because it was unlikely." *New Yorker* cartoon from May 27, 1944. Robert J. Day/The *New Yorker* Collection/The Cartoon Bank.

'Why was there such as wartime furor over soybeans anyway?'" As the food crisis envisioned by Dewey's commission failed to materialize, "interest in soybeans gradually declined."[75] In May 1944, the *New Yorker* ran a cartoon in which a lady pushes a grocery cart past a meat counter and, in response to the butcher offering her a large cut of meat with a smile, apologizes, "I'm sorry, Mr. Groff, but my family has come to prefer soybeans" (photo 10). Her comment was both an accurate gauge of the publicity soybeans had received and something deemed laughably unlikely for someone to actually say.[76] In late 1945, another *New Yorker* cartoon showed a man at a trade show in front of a booth for "Soyzic: The Soybean Plastic," which, according to the pitch-man, could be "bored, punched, stamped, sawed, and in an emergency eaten with a light sauce."[77] At least the joke was now once again that plastic could be made from something considered food, rather than—by the evidence of Woodward's NRC study—the other way around.

Food Pills for Soldiers

It was largely for the sake of American fighting men and women that civilian food was rationed, and at military bases soldiers had great quantities of high-quality food. Male soldiers were allotted around 360 pounds of meat a year, weighted toward beef—10 ounces of beef per day, 4 ounces of pork, and 2 ounces each of bacon and chicken—at a time when American men typically consumed 125 pounds. Following nutrition guidelines and recipe books that homogenized meals around the world and among the services, soldiers consumed 5,000 calories per day in the form of "All-American" cooking: meat, potatoes, generous servings of fruits and vegetables, dessert, and cold milk, causing weight gain at some bases on the order of ten to twenty pounds per month.[78] These were provisions enabled in part by the skyrocketing production of soybeans in the Midwest, providing high-protein feed for the production of meat, milk, and eggs. It also meant that soldiers were unlikely to eat soybeans directly as a source of protein. There were important exceptions. The options for sailors at sea, while still generous, were more restricted. And army field rations, which needed to be densely nutritious and highly portable, required innovative approaches to be palatable at all.

America's enemies used soybeans more extensively to feed their armies. As the *New Yorker* informed its readers, with a peppering of wartime racism, "bean curd, which various war correspondents have told us constitutes an important item of the Japanese soldier's field ration, is simply a preparation of soy-bean flour. Good for the little rats, too, since its caloric value is twice that of beef and its waste products have less tendency to poison the system and cause fatigue."[79] The Germans, for their part, had long followed the lead of the Austrian Frederick Haberlandt in utilizing the soybean. Wartime reports indicated that the Nazis considered soybeans a strategic asset. I. G. Farben, a massive German chemical company, acquired the patent for a method developed by the Austrian Laszlo Berczeller for producing debittered, full-fat soybean flour—Edelsoja (or "pure soya") in German—and

then arranged with countries such as Romania to grow its soybean supplies.[80] Hitler also increased imports of Manchurian soybeans to stockpile
for oil and flour production.[81] As it happened, these supplies dried up when
the Soviet entry into the war blocked the land route from Manchuria.

Soybean Digest published an English translation of the Wehrmacht's
1938 manual, Speisenzusammenstellung Unter Mitverwendung Von Edelsoja
Mit Kochanweisungen ("Formulation of Menus Including Pure Soya, with
Recipes"). Since Edelsoja provided 89 grams of protein per 1,000 calories,
it was used in a wide variety of dishes to extend meat, economize on fat,
substitute for eggs and milk, make cheese spreads, enrich pasta and desserts,
and thicken sauces, gravies, and soups (including "beer soup," with the ingredients "beer, flour, soya"). Altogether, of the recipes authorized for German
army kitchens, there were around 100 that used at least a small amount of
soy flour. The idea, not unlike McCay's, was to parcel it out in small amounts
so that it went unnoticed in a host of familiar foods.[82] Soy flour was also
said to have provided the protein in the so-called Nazi Food Pill, an oblong
biscuit resembling a Scotch oatcake—but drier and less palatable—which
delivered 200 grams of carbohydrates and 100 grams each of fat and protein in each pound. These biscuits—plus water—constituted a nutritionally
complete ration during military campaigns, at least in the short run.[83] It
was here that the American armed forces moved most decisively to close the
soybean gap with the Axis powers.

The American equivalent of the Nazi Food Pill was the "Type I, Defense
Biscuit" included in the newly developed K Ration. By the end of the war,
it was simply referred to as "the K Biscuit." The K Ration, with dry food
items wrapped in cellophane and the whole thing packaged in a cardboard
box, was a lightweight alternative to the cumbersome and much-despised
C ("combat") Ration. Prior to America's entry into the war, the University
of Minnesota food scientist Ancel Keys, at the behest of the Quartermaster
Corps Subsistence Research Laboratory in Chicago, assembled the K Ration from items he found in a grocery store: dry sausage, a chocolate bar,
hard candy, and a soy-flour biscuit. As the laboratory grew in funding, personnel, and sophistication during the war, the K Ration also evolved to contain canned meat (instead of sausage), chewing gum, cigarettes, and toilet
paper.[84] According to Rohland Isker, head of the lab, the soy foods offered
in grocery stores were generally unimpressive—"poorly prepared from a

manufacturing standpoint" and "organoleptically undesirable" in flavor, odor, and appearance—compelling the lab to establish exacting quality standards for soy products. The soy flour, which constituted around 13 percent of the biscuit by weight—much higher than in bread meant to appeal to civilians—was to be carefully debittered to have a "neutral, bland" flavor and defatted to forestall rancidness. The biscuit's fat was also provided largely by soybeans in the form of shortening: hydrogenated oil kept longer.[85] Similarly, the Royal Canadian Navy formulated a "balanced concentrated food" biscuit for their life-raft rations using specially processed, debittered soybean flour.[86]

By May 1945, a review in *Soybean Digest* listed three dozen US patents issued for removing bitter tastes from soybean flour—a number to foreigners such as Berczeller—and numerous similar patents in other countries. Efforts to develop nutritionally dense foods with soy flour hinged on these processes and might founder if not enough attention was paid. For instance, in early 1943, John MacMillan Jr., heir to the grain giant Cargill in Minneapolis, invited a dog-food maker to formulate what MacMillan called "man food," ostensibly for such uses as field rations. Numerous combinations of malt powder, yeast, corn flakes, various flours, and soy grits were tried. The "objectionable taste" of the soy turned out to be a problem, despite various techniques for reducing it. MacMillan speculated that one could "start out with babies and build up their taste for soybeans" until they liked it. In the meantime, he was "afraid that the soya bean is out." The project died away after 1945.[87]

The plans of the US Navy, meanwhile, went beyond high-protein biscuits. This was largely due to Clive McCay, who continued his work on food fortification when he joined as a lieutenant commander in July 1943. In Bethesda, Maryland, he created the Mobile Nutrition Unit, consisting of himself, an enlisted man, and four WAVES (volunteers in the Women's Reserve) trained as nutritionists and home economists. Under the auspices of the Naval Medical Research Institute, they visited naval bases such as Quantico to gather samples of the meals served to sailors, using precise methods to estimate exactly how much food each one ate and, collecting samples of garbage, how much each threw away. Freezing and later chemically analyzing these samples, Clive and his "chow chemists" concluded that the typical man consumed 3,400 calories a day but that about 10 percent of the calories on each recruit's plate were discarded, mainly in the form of fat trimmed from meat. Sailors made up for this through purchases of sugar-laden candy from the commissary.[88]

Clive made recommendations for making meals more appetizing while preserving their vitamin content, but he also experimented with enriching the empty calories of the commissary sweets: "It is possible to manufacture candy bars of excellent flavor which incorporate such food items as brewer's yeast, wheat germ, milk, corn germ, soy flour, and also nuts." In a letter to Jeanette in late 1944, he noted that high-fat soy flour worked nicely in candy bars.[89] Clive also continued his work with soybean sprouts. He developed a "simple method" of sprouting soybeans with an apparatus compact enough for ships. Consisting "of a five gallon pickle jar with a half inch hole drilled in the bottom," it was capable of converting four pounds of dry beans into sprouts for 100 men, providing them with a fresh vegetable high in vitamin C.[90] It is not clear if any of these schemes, for candy bars or sprouts, ever went beyond the trial phase.

There was one notable nonfood use for soybeans in the navy, in this case enabled by the work of Percy Lavon Julian. While the sales of his Alpha protein had been sluggish before World War II, the navy requisitioned nearly all that Glidden could supply to use as a stabilizer in firefighting foam produced by National Foam Systems under the trademark Aer-O-Foam. The National Foam System patent credited soy protein for lending a "greatly increased surface rigidity to the foam bubbles," creating an "unusually tight blanket" that was also unusually adhesive when sprayed on ceilings and vertical surfaces. These properties made the foam highly effective at smothering gasoline fires on tanker ships, on occasion saving them from complete destruction.[91] The other advantage of soy protein, according to the patent, was the abundance of the nation's soybeans, making them, as in so many other instances, an affordable raw material.[92] Sailors, aware of the foam's ingredients, reportedly dubbed it "bean soup."[93] While it was the National Foam chemists, not Percy Lavon Julian, who invented the foam, the critical role played by Alpha protein was cited by the NAACP when it awarded Julian the Spingarn Medal in 1947.[94]

During the war, the use of soybeans in the military paralleled its use in civilian life. It was a key input underlying a relative abundance of meat; a generally hidden ingredient in a diverse array of foods, from soups to gravies; and a visible—indeed, publicized—component of emergency measures, in

this case field provisions, life-raft rations, and firefighting foam. There was
a final arena in which soybeans played a role, one that was at once military
and civilian, as the US Army rounded up a population consisting largely of
American citizens. At the same time that the government was trying to per-
suade the rest of the civilian population to eat more soybeans, and that the
military was compelling soldiers to do the same, Japanese Americans fought
to continue consuming them in their traditional forms.

Tofu for Internment Camps

In the spring of 1942, people of Japanese descent who lived on the West
Coast of the United States found themselves in a cruel double-bind. On
March 2, the army, authorized by President Franklin Roosevelt's Executive Order 9066, designated the western halves of California, Oregon, and
Washington as Military Area Number One, from which the Japanese were
to be removed. The army initially encouraged voluntary migration to the
eastern halves of the states, designated as Military Area Number Two, and
to points farther inland, but vocal and sometimes violent protests in the proposed receiving areas led, on March 29, to a freeze order trapping the Japanese in Area Number One. The freeze order made internment inevitable.[95]
The Japanese were first moved to "assembly centers" run by the army in Area
Number One. A wide array of structures, most notoriously the Tanforan
race track near San Francisco, were hastily retrofitted to accommodate evacuees. More than 110,000 men, women, and children—the majority of them
American citizens, although not a majority of the adults—were then gradually transferred to ten "relocation camps" run by a civilian agency, the War
Relocation Authority (WRA). Laid out like army barracks, these camps
were scattered throughout the western United States, for the most part in
isolated and inhospitable desert regions. Two were as far east as Arkansas.
They held between 10,000 and 20,000 internees each and, although run by
civilian administrators, were enclosed with barbed wire and monitored, just
outside of their perimeters, by armed military guards.[96]

By the time they disbanded three years later, all ten camps were producing their own tofu. In one sense, this was entirely natural: wherever Japanese immigrants had settled in America, tofu almost instantly appeared.

Tofu-making was a small business with low costs of entry and a reliable market. In the case of the internment camps, however, tofu production also had to align with the wartime agendas of a bureaucracy based in Washington, DC. It did so in several ways. For one thing, the camps represented an immense waste of labor when it was needed most, but the possibilities for industry were severely constrained in the camps. Internees were put to work making such things as camouflage netting and model ships, which required exacting hand labor but little capital. Such employment ran up against the Geneva Convention, however. The *Issei*, first-generation Japanese-born noncitizens who made up a majority of the adult population, were arguably prisoners of war and thus barred from military production. Even among the *Nisei*, second-generation Japanese Americans permitted to perform such work, competition over the scarce jobs became divisive.[97] In nonmilitary production, camp industries were not allowed to compete directly with commercial firms. Finally, by design the camps were geographically isolated, and, given wartime demands on transportation, they were decidedly not a priority for shipments of raw materials. Gradually, these constraints narrowed the options to industries that supplied the camp populations' own needs.

The advantage of food production was twofold: not only did it not compete with local companies, it also reduced the cost to the army of providing subsistence to inmates. Food production was also relatively simple to establish.[98] A benefit of tofu specifically was that its ample supply was unlikely to inflame the hostility of a public that frequently blamed regional food shortages on alleged hoarding at the camps. Expressing a typical sentiment, one California resident wrote to the Office of Price Administration in October 1942, "I am reliably informed that government trucks have just returned from a trip through Nevada and Arizona with six tons of ham and bacon for the Japs in Manzanar where they are interned for the duration . . . while none of us can buy it at any price. It makes one's blood boil and some of us feel like taking a tommy gun and cleaning that lot."[99] Criticisms of hoarding were also aired during congressional hearings conducted by the House Un-American Activities Committee, which considered, but ultimately rejected, transferring the camps to the War Department. This posed a direct threat to the existence of the WRA.[100] For these reasons, then, the bureaucracy had reasons to encourage tofu production.

The primary reason tofu appeared in the camps, however, was that the internees demanded it, using the limited forms of democracy permitted them. Tofu first appeared in Poston, located in Arizona, which was the largest of the internment camps and something of a special case. Situated within the Colorado River Indian Reservation, it was initially operated by the Bureau of Indian Affairs, whose head, John Collier, was a New Deal progressive. Over the previous decade, Collier had pushed for tribal self-government on reservations, and he had a similar vision for making the camp into a permanent, self-governing, economically self-sufficient, cooperatively farmed Japanese American community. This arrangement ended by the beginning of 1943, when the WRA shifted its mission to resettling internees outside of the camps.[101] In the meantime, "colonists" were involved in the planning process. The initial proposal for a tofu factory came in early June from the Department of Factory Planning, run by Harry M. Kumagai under the supervision of H. A. Mathiesen, chief of agriculture and industry.[102] In memos to Mathieson, Kumagai emphasized that "to give work to those people unable to do work that they had been trained for is a great boost to general morale." It would give everyone "an equal opportunity to demonstrate, in a very concrete way, their loyalty and willingness to serve their country." More broadly, "to keep folks busy is of paramount importance in order to sustain the morale of evacuees who have suffered mentally, spiritually, and financially" and to "instill the virtues of perseverance, initiative, industriousness, public resourcefulness, and good citizenship."[103]

Tofu production was delayed in Poston until January 1943. Construction material, in particular the firebricks required for furnaces,[104] was lacking, and necessary equipment, including copper kettles and the electric motors necessary for grinding soybeans, was difficult to obtain. Although some supplies might be available from Japanese who had run tofu shops, administrators were reluctant to authorize internees to travel to the places they had hastily stored their belongings, with no thought to shipping them, in the frenzy preceding evacuation.[105] Another challenge was that the camp's water was too hard—and was, furthermore, chlorinated—compelling the purchase of a water softener.[106] Production may also have been set back by the "opinion of [an unnamed] 'expert' who claimed that hardness of water, lack of humidity in the air, and other obstacles would cause failure of proper coagulation of bean paste particles."[107] Tofu production finally began on January 19, 1943. It never exceeded half the goal of 1,400 cakes per day set the previous June, which would have provided each of the 20,000 internees with half a cake per week,[108] but even so, the factories were deemed a success. Ben Yamaguchi, the supervisor of the camp's subsistence department, declared that "we had seemingly unsurmountable [sic] obstacles but we have conquered all of them."[109]

The news also spread to the other camps through their internee-run camp newspapers. The *Granada Pioneer* cited the "mass production of soya bean cakes" at Poston on April 17, and the *Minidoka Irrigator* reported on May 1 that "the quality of the 'tofu' [at Poston] is said to be of extra fine grade."[110] At Topaz, in Utah, construction of a tofu plant became a priority in the wake of widespread complaints about unsuitable meats served during the foods shortages of 1943—in particular organ meats such as hearts, livers, and kidneys that the Japanese considered abhorrent. The camp's Food Advisory Board, which worked with the camp administration to acquire "more palatable foods" than that "obtained by Caucasian personnel," pushed for the building of the tofu factory "not only to supplement the milk and meat supply . . . but for diet and for health."[111] Construction finally got under way in January 1944, and tofu was delivered to mess halls in April.[112] According to the camp papers, tofu was eagerly consumed by "tofu lovers" and "tofu-hungry residents," indicating that tofu, in addition to providing useful employment, was a welcome taste of home amid an alien landscape.[113] The tofu factories were supervised largely by men who had prewar experience in the trade[114] and provided work for crews ranging from eight to nineteen men. As observed by three reporters from the Manzanar *Free Press* who were "overcome by curiosity," the process of making tofu was "tedious" and required patience, although, in line with modern practice, the traditional Japanese grindstones were operated by electrically powered belts.[115]

Tofu was not the only Japanese soy food made at the camps. By mid-1943, miso production was under way at three camps. The administration at Manzanar, a camp location benefiting from high-quality water,[116] made plans to supply the entire camp system with soy sauce, with cost savings as the goal. Unlike tofu, shoyu was regularly purchased for the camps from outside suppliers.[117] Internees were encouraged to name the product through a communitywide contest. "Manza!" won, with "Manyo" and "MM" ("Made in Manzanar") taking the second and third prizes.[118] As originally formulated, however, the shoyu failed to find favor among the internees. To increase output, it was a "chemical" soy sauce that used hydrochloric acid, rather than a traditional fermentation process, to break down soy and wheat proteins into amino acids. Caramel coloring and sugar were then added.[119] The process had been pioneered in Japan during the 1920s, where the amino acids were "blended" with traditional shoyu, prompting Japanese journals to publicize methods for detecting such adulteration. Japanese Americans generally disliked chemical soy sauce, with its lack of complex flavors,[120] and Manza! was no exception. The original factory supervisor resigned, and a new batch appeared in early 1944, made using the traditional "malt method."[121] There were also proposals for making soymilk (or "tofu milk") at Poston and Topaz, but by the latter half of 1944 only 3,000 quarts, valued at less than $100, were produced at the camps, versus 172,000 cakes of tofu valued at more than $9,000.[122]

Although it is right to credit it mainly as an accomplishment of the internees themselves, camp tofu was enabled by well-meaning administrators, many of whom had transferred to the WRA from idealistic New Deal agencies such as the Bureau of Indian Affairs and the USDA's Farm Security Administration, which had helped resettle farmers impoverished by the Depression and the Dust Bowl disaster. While many in the WRA remained hostile toward internees, a good number came to view the evacuation order and the subsequent relocation as grave injustices born of vested agricultural interests and wartime hysteria. They considered their own role as one of "conserving" Japanese communities threatened by the unnatural stresses of camp life.[123] In the unusual case of Gila River, in central Arizona, it was white staff members who took the initiative to research and produce tofu, even arranging to purchase the necessary equipment during a trip to California. By January 1944, one factory in Gila was producing more than 3,500 cakes per week. A second factory struggled until it reopened under the supervision of an inmate who had made tofu at the Jerome camp.[124] Gila's camp dietician, Grace Lawson—described in the camp's newspaper as a "colorful figure" who was a "personal friend" of Eleanor Roosevelt[125]—also gained an appreciation for tofu, even as she held classes for Japanese women on American-style cooking and the principles of the government's Basic 7 Nutrition Program.[126] In July 1944, she delivered a talk at the American Women's Home Association conference in Chicago ("Tofu for the Hungry World"), and on her way home from this trip she stopped at a Pittsburgh hospital to demonstrate to a "world renowned authority on peptic ulcers" the use of tofu in curing ulcers.[127]

Well-meaning or not, WRA initiatives often compounded the initial injustice of internment. To get families out of the camps, the WRA made efforts to send them to any communities that would accept them. These were mainly in the Midwest. By the end of 1944, the WRA succeeded in resettling 35,000 internees, more than one-third of the camp populations.[128] As settlers created nuclei in these new communities, Japanese food followed: in July 1945, the Colorado Times reported that Mr. and Mrs. Toraji (Tom) Hayano, who had been confined at Heart Mountain, were setting up a tofu factory in Minneapolis to supply three Japanese restaurants, "as well as for resettlers." Prior to that, the only source of tofu was Chicago, which did not ship it during the warm summer months.[129] Ben Yamaguchi, who helped make tofu at Poston, settled in Cincinnati with his wife and started Soya Food Products Co. in 1945, which offered mung-bean sprouts and, starting in 1949, tofu made with a stone mill.[130] However, critics have argued that resettlement further undermined Japanese communities by dispersing them far from their original homes and from each other.[131]

Another hope of the resettlement program was that greater assimilation into non-Japanese communities would help moderate the venomous public hostility toward Japanese Americans. With a similar goal in mind, WRA officials pushed the army to create an all-Japanese fighting unit. The highly decorated 442nd Regimental Combat Team would ultimately help turn public opinion, but it was widely protested by camp dissidents for demanding patriotic sacrifice before the restoration of liberty, with the added insult of racial segregation. To expedite both resettlement and enlistment, the camps required internees to sign an oath of loyalty to the United States. Those who refused, many times out of outrage at the treatment they had endured, were eventually separated out and sent to the Tule Lake camp, which was redesignated a "segregation center." Self-government, which existed in a limited form in other camps, was ended altogether at Tule Lake, although even there a community co-op persisted. In November 1943, it announced that it was entering into a contract with the WRA to manufacture tofu for the camp's mess halls, an arrangement that continued until November 1945

Photo 11. Making tofu at the Tule Lake Camp, 1945. From the National Archives and Records Administration.

(photo 11).[132] By this time, many inmates had renounced their American citizenship and, in the aftermath of the war, were deported to a devastated Japan.

When other Japanese Americans were finally allowed to return to their homes on the West Coast—as even those who had earlier been released to settle in the Midwest ended up doing—the tofu makers resumed their work. A community tradition resilient enough to survive the camps was able to reassert itself, which was not the case with all food manufactories. Fortune cookies, for instance, which had their origin in Japan and had been made by Japanese companies prior to the war, were ceded to Chinese and American companies.[133] In the case of tofu, the customers returned with the producers, who reestablished their businesses or started new ones. In one case, the previous owners of Tomoye Tofu Shop in Los Angeles—Mr. Tomoe and possibly S. Okugawa, tofu supervisor at Manzanar—sold Tomoye to the Matsuda Tofu Co. in 1946, only to then found Hinode Tofu in 1947. Hinode, producing 1,500 cakes of tofu per day, would be purchased in turn by Shoan Yamauchi and his wife later in 1947.[134] Yamauchi, the son of Tsuru Yamauchi (introduced in chapter 1), was a World War II veteran who, as a native-born

Hawaiian, had avoided internment. He represented a new generation of tofu makers and would one day transform Hinode into the largest tofu producer on the West Coast.

Meanwhile, during the postwar period the soybean would become an increasingly important component of the American diet, even as it largely lost what visibility it had gained during the Depression and World War II.

CHAPTER SIX

PUSHING THE BOUNDARIES

In Hamburg in late August 1945, months after Germany's surrender, Warren Goss, a soybean researcher and newly commissioned major in the US Army, sat across a table from Conrad Mohr, managing director of Norddeutschen Olmuhlenwerke G.m.b.H. Its vegetable-oil refinery, where Goss conducted the interview, had come through the war relatively unscathed. The facilities of one of its competitors had suffered between 2,000 and 3,000 bomb hits during the last nine months of the war, reducing everything but the hydrogenation plant to "a horribly churned mixture of sandy soil and fragments of building and equipment," Goss reported.[1] At Mohr's company, in contrast, only the boiler house had been destroyed, and even this did not cripple operations: steam was available from the margarine company operated next door by Mohr's brother. Still, there was a shortage of raw inputs, so even here Goss could not observe German oilseed processing directly and had to rely instead on schematic diagrams and interviews with company officials to discover anything about German technology. Mohr provided little intelligence of value, instead boasting "at some length" about the synthetic fatty acids used to make the margarine at his brother's factory. These were edible fats produced from soap stock and other inedible sources, and Mohr claimed to like the taste of them, although he admitted that he was greatly in the minority. Goss later tasted some of the synthetic margarine himself and "found little basis for Mr. Mohr's opinion."[2]

When the topic turned to soybean oil, however, Mohr bragged that he was in possession of a valuable trade secret for combating what the Germans called *umschlag*. Goss perked up, for the problem of flavor reversion, whereby off tastes emerged that ruined refined and otherwise bland-tasting oil, was a major concern in the soybean industry. Mohr, whom Goss did not estimate to be much of a "technical man," at first described a method commonly used at other German companies, information that Goss dismissed as obviously secondhand. But then Mohr insisted that "his firm has developed an even better cure for reversion by means of which refined unhardened soybean oils can be made that will keep a year before there is any trace of reversion." Having dropped this hint, Mohr then refused to give any specifics. "It was necessary, therefore," Goss noted, "to resort to other means for obtaining the detailed information." This was likely a reference to follow-up conversations with more technically informed interview subjects, such as Herr Bull, the plant's chief engineer. But the more ominous reading of Goss's comment does give a sense of the seriousness with which he took his mission, which was after all in pursuit of something that, in the aftermath of such a devastating war, might have seemed trivial to others.

Goss's mission was in fact part of something bigger. The Combined Intelligence Objectives Subcommittee of the US and British militaries had originally been established to gather industrial intelligence that could benefit the Allied military effort, but it soon responded to pressures by trade groups to include sites on its target lists that were of purely scientific or economic interest. "Such information," one official argued, "would not only further our war effort against Japan but also help American industry to maintain its place in world trade and provide employment opportunities for discharged veterans of the war."[3] The United States created the Technical Industrial Intelligence Committee (TIIC) to coordinate the industry experts fanning across liberated Europe beginning in 1944. Their intelligence goals were determined by TIIC's nineteen subcommittees, each representing an industrial sector such as rubber, chemicals, metals and minerals, machinery, textiles, solid fuels, aeronautics, communications, and shipbuilding.[4] By the end of 1944, there were almost 200 investigators. By 1947, almost 400 had toured Germany, many of them technicians from major American companies, which continued to pay their salaries during their missions. They were "an American Industrial Who's Who," as one report put it, pursuing the ultimate goal of capturing "a modern nation's complete technology" as "the only tangible German reparations that the United States may ever receive as a result of World War II."[5]

Goss's inclusion in the TIIC campaign was due in part to the strategic importance of edible fats during wartime, but it was much more the result of the maturation of the soybean-processing industry and its support network in government and academia. There was now a generation of researchers, such as Goss himself, who had devoted themselves almost exclusively to the soybean. A graduate of the University of Washington who began his career at the US Bureau of Standards in the early 1930s, he had conducted research on the soybean at the University of Illinois beginning in 1937 as part of the US Regional Soybean Industrial Products Laboratory. By 1944, he had moved on to the USDA's Northern Regional Research Laboratory in Peoria, where he was senior chemical engineer.[6] His was one form of vested interest in the soybean, akin to the material investments processors and farmers alike had made in equipment and expertise.

Facing decreasing demand as wartime scarcities receded, the soybean industry took measures during the postwar period to protect these vested interests and to remove obstacles blocking continued expansion. When necessary, this involved transforming the genetics and chemistry of the bean and its products. Where possible, it also meant changing laws and policies. At the outset of this period, the most pressing concern was to improve the quality and flavor of soybean oil, lest its limited appeal hamper the expansion of the soybean crop overall. The outcome of this effort would be a resounding technological and economic success—but at a cost to American health.

The Struggle against *Umschlag*

Sponsored by the TIIC's Subcommittee of Food and Agriculture, Goss's charge was both broad and narrow. At its broadest, it was to discover the means by which Germans coped with wartime shortages of fats and oils. This was assumed to involve technically advanced methods to utilize unconventional raw materials, such as the synthetic fatty acids of Mohr's boasts. There were dark rumors during the war that Jewish bodies were rendered for fat—and in fact there were a small number of experiments along these lines[7]—but Goss came to a less grotesque conclusion. Germans mainly coped by doing without. The weekly ration of butter and margarine gradually decreased to 200 grams per person, then to 50 grams. In addition, German margarine, an all-purpose fat for frying, baking, and spreading on bread, was heavily diluted with water and air and, in Goss's view, would not likely "merit extensive consumer acceptance in the United States." Finally, Germany's ability to stretch supplies of fat rested on "careful planning, use of reserve stocks, subsidized production of oil crops"—mainly rapeseed—and, last on the list, "technological substitution."[8] All in all, he did not perceive many lessons for a postwar world that many feared would face global shortages of edible fats.

More narrowly, Goss's mandated was to investigate technology that could directly benefit the US soybean industry. The terrain was promising. As Goss noted, oilseed processing had long been a major German industry, and "much of the oilseed technology practiced throughout the world is of German origin."[9] This was certainly the case with Glidden, which had obtained rights to German patents. Ultimately, however, Goss was not impressed. It is true that postwar conditions limited what Goss was able to observe. In addition to damage to facilities from bombing, soybeans had not been available for a number of years, the last shipment of Manchurian soybeans having been delivered by way of Russia early in the war. Existing stores of whale, coconut, and palm-kernel oil were eventually exhausted as well, leaving only the domestic rapeseed crop as an oilseed.[10] Still, even though he was unable to witness soybean processing firsthand, he concluded with some confidence that German technology during the previous decade had come to lag behind that of the United States, mainly due to the "vastly greater quantity and quality of scientific research conducted on fats and oils" in the United States by researchers such as himself.[11]

However, there was *umschlag*. Perhaps this was an area where Germans had maintained their edge, and he was eager to find out their secrets. Although the various plant operators differed in their methods, most agreed that lecithin was the culprit. They insisted that thoroughly removing the gummy substance from the oil was key to preventing off flavors from developing. Starting with good beans was essential, most of the informants agreed, and here Americans had an advantage. One operator recalled being amazed at the high quality of oil produced from a shipment of American

soybeans that had somehow made it to Germany during the first year of
the war. American processing standards, however, fell far short of German
fastidiousness. "The Germans consider soybean oil to be one that must be
prepared and handled with the utmost care and gentleness." They insisted on
solvent extraction, which was still less prevalent in the United States. Screw
presses tended to burn the oil and cause the lecithin to "set." Even during
solvent extraction, precautions were taken against momentary overheating.
They also redoubled the degumming process, which removed lecithin and
other emulsifiers by agitating the oil with water and then separating out
the sludge with a centrifuge. US processors "washed" the oil in this fashion
once, if that. The Germans insisted on two washings. Finally, to neutralize
the traces of lecithin that remained, the Germans added 0.01 percent citric
acid to the deodorizer, which used steam to remove the volatile components
of the oil.[12]

Mohr's plant used an alternate method, the details of which Goss was
ultimately able to obtain. Whole beans were subjected to a high-pressure
steam treatment while pushed by a screw conveyor through a closed metal
trough. Ideally, this raised the moisture content of the beans by 4 percent
within 90 seconds. If it took even as long as 120 seconds to raise the moisture content, Goss was told, the method would fail to prevent reversion. The
excess moisture was removed, and the beans were then treated in the normal
manner, except that there was no need to add citric acid to the deodorizer.[13]

Goss provided details about both methods over the course of his more
than forty intelligence reports from Germany. The Commerce Department's
Office of Technical Services (OTS), which eventually housed the Technical Industrial Intelligence Division, made the reports available through its
Bibliographic and Reference Division. Each report was available separately
to all askers, but demand from the soybean industry, in particular regarding German remedies for *umschlag*, prompted Goss to compile them into a
book published in 1947.[14] In a letter to the head of OTS in late 1946, Goss
estimated that losses due to reversion cost the soybean industry $50 mil-
lion per year "under present prices" and that, once operators had invested in
the equipment required by the German methods, "the large losses occurring
because of reversion will be eliminated as a result of these discoveries."[15]
In a later letter to OTS, Goss claimed that American manufacturers, both
of soybean oil and processing equipment, were "very close-mouthed about

what they are doing with the German data" and would "probably deny using the German data if they are asked."[16]

In fact, Goss overestimated both the immediate impact of his findings and the secrecy of the companies involved in producing soybean oil. Solving the reversion problem would require decades of cooperative research involving both the government and private industry. In April 1946, the first Conference on Flavor Stability in Soybean Oil was convened at the Bismarck Hotel in Chicago by the National Soybean Processors Association (NSPA). Edward J. Dies, the NSPA's president, opened the conference with a plea for open collaboration, arguing that "any advantage to an individual or a corporation in attaining a solution before the answer [was] known generally would be of only temporary and transitory value."[17] With the end of the national emergency that had spurred soybean production, it was imperative that no soybean product lose ground, and *umschlag* threatened soybean oil's current level of use in margarine.[18] Refined, bleached, and deodorized, soybean oil was initially as bland as cottonseed oil, the gold standard for edible oils and the main oil in margarine. After mere days or weeks at room temperature—and sometimes immediately, if heated in a pan or deep fryer—it developed flavors described as "fishy" (or "mariny"), "painty," and "grassy."[19] During the war, soybean oil could be blended into margarine in relatively high amounts because of fast turnover in stores, which gave less time for bad tastes to emerge.[20] This reinforcing cycle could now run in reverse.

A key player in both the flavor stability conference and in subsequent research was the USDA Northern Regional Research Center (NRRC) in Peoria, Illinois. Its main role, aside from helping to coordinate research, was to evaluate results through "organoleptic" testing. In one trial, the NRRC evaluated German methods by presenting two samples to tasters: one was "washed-citrated" (washed two times and deodorized in the presence of citric acid), and the other was a control designated "unwashed." Both were stored at room temperature for several weeks, with samples periodically submitted to a panel of trained tasters for scoring on a scale from 1 to 10. Both samples began life at 8 or 9. By day fifteen, both hovered around 3 or 4. The decline of the washed-citrated sample was less precipitous, however, especially in the early days: on day three, it was still at 8, while the unwashed sample had fallen to 4. The panel also identified component tastes and charted their presence. "Buttery" and "bland," desirable flavors, declined at a similar rate in both samples. "Beany" peaked after a day—more dramatically in the washed-citrated sample, it turned out—and then declined. "Rancid" began a steady climb in both samples after three days. The key difference was "painty," which skyrocketed in the unwashed sample but was suppressed for a week in the washed-citrated oil. Some minor flavors, including "grassy" and "burned," were not plotted. The German method was mostly vindicated, although the key to its effectiveness remained a mystery.[21]

One of the most time-consuming tasks in conducting this research was creating a reliable taste panel.[22] As the NRRC researchers explained in a follow-up paper, two contrasting types of panels were used to perform organoleptic evaluations. One type was akin to the proverbial Peoria theater audience: designed to gauge consumer acceptance of a product, they consisted of randomly selected panelists with "normal variations in prejudices and sensitivities." The accurate and reproducible detection and measurement of reversion flavors, by contrast, called for the second type of panel where "the selection, training, sensitivity, and consistency of individuals comprising a panel" were "of paramount importance." The pool of potential members came from other labs in the NRRC. Of the thirty-five who were given preliminary acuity tests, fourteen made the cut. After a second battery of tests and consideration of less tangible factors—such as "past experience on organoleptic panels, interest in the oil problem in general, and the desire to participate"—eight made it onto the regular panel, with five others designated as alternates. During the following year, they "were given oils in many combinations, with the tasters trying to standardize their numerical and descriptive scores." They were connoisseurs of blandness.

The researchers also paid close attention to the conditions of testing. Panelists sat in individual booths, to minimize distractions and to "discourage audible comments," in a temperature-controlled laboratory kept as free as possible from foreign smells. Because odors and flavors were better detected in warm oils, the samples were presented in beakers set into a specially designed warming table. Each member was limited to testing one pair of samples, as acuity dropped off with further tasting, and water heated to body temperature was provided to rinse the mouth between swigs of oil. Under no circumstances was any oil swallowed. Afterward, the panelists were allowed to mingle and compare notes while munching on "reward" cookies that helped remove the taste of badly reverted samples. The researchers recognized that "the successful conduct of a taste panel is frequently as much a matter of human relations as it is a scientific problem," and they worked to cultivate high morale, or what they called "panel euphoria." They shared research results and plans for future experiments—the panelists were NRRC scientists themselves—and informed members how their tasting scores compared with the panel average. These averages were tracked with careful statistical methods, occasionally prompting the removal of outliers from the panel.

At the same time, the chemists hoped to find a physical property in oil that could reliably predict the appearance of reversion flavors. A high "peroxide value," a measurement of how fast a lipid oxidated, correlated well with lower taste scores, and it was used as a proxy in some routine experiments. But the researchers concluded that, although "the hope of all research workers in the field is to replace the erratic human senses with objective physical and chemical analytical methods, it must be remembered that the ultimate evaluation of flavor is subjective. As long as human beings are the final judges of flavor, organoleptic evaluation will probably be required in flavor problems." In this spirit, the NRRC participants brought three-day-old samples of unwashed and washed-citrated soybean oil to the flavor stability conference, where they assembled a taste panel that confirmed the results they had obtained in Peoria.

It required nine more flavor stability conferences and twenty more years to deal decisively with *umschlag*. In retrospect, the testing of German methods was a breakthrough, although the German theories proved to be exactly wrong. Oxidation of fatty acids was the culprit, and by 1950 experiments had established that citric acid worked by scavenging traces of "prooxidant" metals. Lecithin, it turned out, was also a metal scavenger: far from causing reversion, it delayed it. These discoveries prompted a search for the best metal scavengers, as well as the elimination of brass from processing equipment and the practice of keeping soybean oil blanketed in an inert gas such as nitrogen, especially during high-temperature processes.[23] A complementary approach was to focus on what was being oxidized, as much as what was promoting oxidation. In the early 1950s, linolenic acid was identified as the fatty acid whose oxidation most powerfully triggered *umschlag*. This was long suspected, because oils high in this acid were most prone to reversion, something as true of linseed, rapeseed, and fish oils as it was of soybean oil. A 1951 experiment confirmed the hunch. When researchers infused cottonseed oil with linolenic acid, taste panels mistook it for reverted soybean oil.[24] The question now was how to best reduce the amount of linolenic acid in soybean oil.

The key was hydrogenation. Fatty acids consist of long chains of carbon atoms with hydrogen atoms attached to them like beads. Saturated fatty acids have the maximum number of hydrogens, so that each carbon is attached to its neighbor carbon with one bond, creating a straight chain. Like sheets in a ream of paper, saturated fats are compact—and solid at room temperature. With fewer hydrogens, carbons attach to their neighbors with double bonds, forming bends in the chain. Like crumpled paper poured in a pile, the resulting unsaturated fats become fluid and are liquid at room temperature. Monounsaturated fatty acids (MUFAs) have one double carbon bond. Polyunsaturated fatty acids (PUFAs), with two or more double bonds, are even more fluid. MUFAs and PUFAs in turn come in two configurations: *cis*, where the hydrogens nearest a double bond are on the same side of the chain, and *trans*, where the hydrogens are on opposite sides. The *trans* configuration turns out to be straighter than the *cis*. The process of hydrogenation, which artificially forces hydrogens into the carbon chains and thereby saturates them, can convert fluid oils into solid fats. Partial hydrogenation, which does not result in a fully saturated fat, nevertheless pushes all of the fatty acids in a given oil toward greater stability: *cis* PUFAs become *trans* PUFAs, PUFAs become MUFAs, and MUFAs become saturated fatty acids. With fine-tuning, partial hydrogenation can result in any desired room-temperature consistency. In the case of soybean oil, it also helpfully converts linolenic acid into more flavor-stable fats.

If hydrogenated just short of becoming solid at room temperature, partially hydrogenated soybean oil might see a fall in *cis* linolenic acid content from 8 percent to 2 percent. In the postwar period, this oil was increasingly used by the growing number of chain restaurants and food processors for deep-frying. In addition to longer shelf life and flavor stability, it had the advantage of splattering less than untreated soybean oil. Its higher level of saturated fatty acids made it cloudy at room temperature, however, leading to an additional step before it could be sold directly to consumers as salad or cooking oil. The oil was cooled until crystals of the more saturated fatty acids formed, making them easy to filter out. This process was called "winterization," and the result—"hydrogenated winterized soybean oil," often abbreviated as HWSB—contained as little as 2 percent linolenic acid.[25] It was a clear liquid that did not give the outward impression of being hydrogenated at all but that also gave no hint of *umschlag*.[26] This was a major technical achievement and a substantial boon to the soy industry, assuring soy's preeminence as an edible oil. In 1949, Americans on average consumed eight pounds of soybean oil annually, less than a fifth of the total fats and oils in their diet, which also included cottonseed oil, butter, and lard. By 1969, Americans consumed an average of 30 pounds, more than all the other oils and fats combined.[27] And just about all of it, whether liquid or solid, in processed foods or on the table, was partially hydrogenated.

This was highly consequential for American health, because these products also contained substantial amounts of trans fats: up to 15 percent for HWSB oils and 18 percent for partially hydrogenated cooking oils.[28] Eventually research would reveal major cardiovascular health risks associated with trans fats, but as late as 1987 experts could proclaim that there were "no known health hazards from consumption of hydrogenated" oils.[29] The risks were certainly unknown in 1949, when a debate raged in Congress over the relative healthiness of butter and margarine, in which the antimargarine faction relied on vague notions of butter's superior wholesomeness. This debate turned out to be crucial for the more widespread incorporation of soybean oil into the American diet. If defeating *umschlag* lifted the ceiling on how much soybean oil could be included in margarine, this legislative battle expanded the amount of margarine on American tables.

The Margarine Alliance

In early March 1949, speaking before the House Agriculture Committee, Louis Bromfield made a blunt and provocative statement. Bromfield was an Ohio farmer and self-described agricultural adviser to "certain industries and banks." "If two minutes spent in the kitchen coloring some margarine has become such a great burden," Bromfield proclaimed, "all I can say is that the pioneer qualities of our ladies certainly have gone down the drain." He was testifying regarding a longstanding federal tax on the production of yellow margarine, enacted to ensure that most margarine available for purchase was an unappetizing white color. Manufacturers typically compensated by enclosing packets of yellow food coloring with their products. Alternately, some included a pellet of yellow dye with the margarine itself in an "easy-coloring bag" that could be kneaded before opening. Either way, the need to add yellow coloring by hand was a common cause for complaint among American housewives, some of whom picketed Capitol Hill that day with signs reading, "It's Time to Give Consumers a Break. REPEAL ALL FEDERAL ANTI-MARGARINE LAWS!"[30]

At the following day's hearings, Jean Whitehall of the Consumers Union amplified this sentiment. "I, for one, am not particularly anxious to be a pioneer woman and I would say that what has gone down the drain is not the pioneer qualities but probably some of that margarine which gets wasted in the bowl." She pointed to the frustrations involved even with so-called easy-coloring bags. "I will not comment at length on the hazards of possible bag breakage nor on the 2-cent premium which is levied on consumers for such a bag. I will merely mention the fact that margarine to be colored by any method must be bought hours in advance of use so that it can be allowed to soften, be colored and then refrigerated before it can be served."[31] Mary McLeod McCune likewise submitted a letter on behalf of the National Council of Negro Women that pointed to "the housewife feeding her family" as "the one who deserves to be served by this legislation."[32] When Congress eventually repealed the tax, newspapers naturally framed the story as a victory of consumers over a powerful commercial interest: the dairy industry. In fact, repeal was as much a victory of one commercial interest over another. It happened because, for the first time, the nation's margarine lobby was able to equal the political muscle and geographic breadth of the dairy lobby.

First patented in France in 1869 as a butter substitute, oleomargarine was at first a by-product of the meatpacking industry.[33] "Oleo" referred to beef fat and "margarine" to one of its constituent fatty acids, pearl-colored margaric acid. Producers took beef suet, ground it up, separated out the fats with steam, and finally churned the softer fats with milk solids, or even butter, for flavor. Dyed daffodil-yellow, it was difficult even in the 1880s to distinguish it from butter. A federal US tax imposed in 1886 funded an inspection system to verify that all margarine was properly labeled at the factory and not, it was hoped, fraudulently diverted to the butter market. Doubting the efficacy of this system, legislators added an amendment to the federal law in 1902 that levied a 10-cent tax per pound on the manufacture of yellow margarine, hoping to curb its production. Meatpackers, concentrated in cities, were in no position to counter the influence of the butter lobby, supported by dairy farmers across the nation. The situation changed somewhat as hydrogenated vegetable oils displaced beef fat as starting materials for margarine. Chief among these was cottonseed oil, which helped create a political base for margarine in the rural South.

Sometimes the margarine and butter lobbies cooperated, as in the case of the so-called cooking compounds that appeared during the 1920s. These consisted of coconut oil from the Philippines; despite having the yellow color of table fats, they were labeled as lard substitutes to skirt the margarine law. In 1929, Congress subsumed them under the margarine law over the futile protests of Filipino coconut growers. A coalition of dairy interests and cotton growers similarly aligned against margarine manufacturers when they began using palm oil from Java and Sumatra. These oils lent a yellow tint to margarine without the use of dyes, avoiding the 10-cent tax because the 1902 amendment specified the use of "artificial" coloring. Congress closed this loophole in 1931 and subjected all foreign oils to additional tariffs in 1935. This was a boon for soybean farmers, who increasingly joined with cottonseed interests to fight margarine laws. In 1940, ads in Soybean Digest placed by the National Margarine Institute sought to mobilize midwestern farmers using the language of scientific agriculture: "Soybeans cannot grow in bound soil. So consumption cannot grow in a bound market. YOUR MARKET IS BOUND!" A map of the United States, with symbols representing various kinds of state antimargarine laws, accompanied the copy, which advised farmers to write their senators.[34]

America during World War II accordingly witnessed a sea change toward repeal of antimargarine laws. On the federal level, there were hearings in both the House and Senate in 1943 and 1948, each with over sixty witnesses and transcripts running to hundreds of pages. Under House Republicans, repeal was killed in the Agriculture Committee in early 1948, but promargarine forces gathered signatures to bring up the bill for a vote by the full House, where it passed 260 to 106.[35] Then it died in the Senate, the victim not of probutter Republicans but of largely promargarine southern Democrats filibustering against President Harry Truman's civil rights agenda. Viewing the spectacle, Representative Edward A. Mitchell, Republican of

Indiana—a soybean state—voiced the hope that the Senate could eventually conduct enough business to give "the consumers at least one break by getting rid of these unfair, un-American, and silly anti-margarine laws."[36] The session ended before action was taken, setting up a repeat for 1949.

There were in fact thirty margarine bills contending with one another that year. The two chief ones were H.R. 3, a margarine-tax repeal bill sponsored by the Texas congressman William Poage, and H.R. 1703, the butter bloc's counterproposal sponsored by Minnesota's August Andresen. H.R. 1703 would eliminate the punitive tax but replace it with an outright national ban on yellow margarine. Andresen had long been a fierce defender of butter, responding to a USDA radio message promoting margarine in 1941 by decrying it on the House floor as "government sponsored propaganda," "virtually a conspiracy against the farmers," and part of the "subversive work of lavender lawyers, pink economists, and mauve home economic ladies." Poage, his antagonist even then, had risen to remind House members that there were other farmers who benefited from margarine sales, such as livestock men and soybean growers, although in 1941, as in 1949, Poage's real concern was for his cotton-growing Texas constituents,[37] in particular poor and tenant farmers whose small margin of profit often came from the sale of cottonseed for crushing.

The debate between Poage and Andresen revolved around the color yellow. Poage, and other Southerners seemingly unaware of the incongruity of their protests with their attitude toward race, decried the injustice of discriminating against margarine on the basis of color. Andresen, meanwhile, expressed outrage over the prospect of "colored" margarine passing as butter. It was not necessarily even a matter of the margarine being fraudulently passed off as butter. Yellow margarine, even when properly labeled, still misled customers because butter's natural yellow color signaled a wholesome quality that imitation products could not deliver. Margarine manufacturers could add vitamin A to match the beta-carotene that ostensibly gave butter its yellowness. But beyond that, there was "something in butter that is all of its own kind and its own nature, and none of these imitative products is a substitute for butter," as the Iowa congressman Cyrenus Cole had put it in an earlier round of hearings.[38]

Their critique of margarine was in fact civilizational and ecological in scope. Louis Bromfield argued that it was a "question of big business and tacit monopoly versus small enterprise and the small businessman." Business concentration had led to socialism and communism in Europe, he maintained, making it unwise to give any advantage to an industry where 65 percent of the output came from 5 percent of the manufacturers, whose product was "as much mass produced [as] Ford automobiles."[39] Then there was the devastation wrought by the soil-depleting crops used to make margarine. Angering southern congressmen, Bromfield asserted that "cotton agriculture has done more damage to Georgia than Sherman ever did." And he did not exempt soybeans, despite their reputation as a nitrogen-providing, soil-building crop. Describing their tendency to cause erosion when planted as a row crop, he cited Decatur, Illinois, as a place where "some years ago they put up a soybean processing plant and got all the farmers in the neighborhood to produce soybeans. I wish all you gentlemen could fly over that area today. In order to get water, they put up a dam. Within less than a generation, that dam is virtually silted up with the top soil of the farms which produced soybeans."[40]

J. W. Calland, of the National Soybean Crop Improvement Council, spent much of his testimony defending the soybean as the least soil-depleting of row crops, but this was unlikely to have persuaded congressmen who valorized the cattle-grazing that underpinned butter production. They would probably have agreed with another witness, the director of the Wisconsin Department of Agriculture, who wrote in a letter that it would do harm to the cause of preserving "the priceless heritage of soil fertility" to "change our Nation's agriculture from a grassland animal husbandry structure to a row crop soil-depleting type of agriculture that will inevitably destroy our irreplaceable topsoil."[41]

Despite these worries, the potent alliance between cotton and soybean farmers won the day, although it was not without an enormous amount of legislative wrangling. The Agriculture Committee defeated Poage's bill, favoring instead an amended version of Andresen's that achieved a compromise. Instead of barring yellow margarine, it would only bar its interstate shipment, in effect leaving the decision up to individual states, though making it impossible for yellow margarine to be shipped between two states that allowed it. Before voting on Andresen's amended bill, the Democrats on the committee swapped in an identical measure offered by Representative Walter K. Granger, a Democrat from Utah.[42] The interstate prohibition was defeated in the full House, but a new measure was added requiring margarine served in public eating places to be cut into triangular pats, with large signs posted informing patrons that they were being served margarine. The bill passed 287 to 89.[43]

A repeat of the House debate then played out in the Senate, where J. W. Fulbright of Arkansas and Guy M. Gillette of Iowa, both Democrats, adopted the respective roles of Poage and Andresen. Hugh Butler, Republican of Nebraska, warned that, after margarine gained equal status with butter, it would pave the way for "ersatz milk and cheese, such as were developed by Hitler."[44] After numerous amendments were defeated—including civil rights amendments against lynching and poll taxes, offered by William Langer of North Dakota as poison pills to southern cotton interests—the bill passed 56 to 16, with an added provision that margarine sold in stores also be cut into triangles.[45] This last provision was removed in conference, and in February 1950, margarine producers had their victory.[46] The repeal of the federal tax would sound the death knell for margarine regulations in twenty-seven states, including twenty-three that had prohibited yellow margarine altogether.

The margarine industry touted its victory as benefiting everyone, even the dairy sector, which would now be free to shift its production to higher-value uses such as milk and cheese. Repeal advocates argued that the two sectors were in fact interdependent, with dairy cows fed increasingly on soybean meal—which in turn increased the amount of available oil—while excess skim milk from butter production was included in margarine. Nonetheless, as the next decade unfolded, the butter industry's fears were largely borne out. In 1949, butter production was roughly twice that of margarine production, 1.7 billion versus 900 million pounds. By 1955 they were running even, at 1.5 and 1.4 billion pounds, respectively. By 1958, margarine production surpassed butter production, which continued a slow slide even as American consumption of table fats increased. Per capita annual consumption followed a similar trajectory: 10.5 pounds of butter versus 5.8 pounds of margarine in 1949, and 8.3 versus 9.0 pounds in 1958. By 1969, both production and consumption of margarine would be roughly double that of butter.[47] As early as 1953, Gallup found that households exclusively buying margarine surpassed those exclusively buying butter, 45 percent to 41 percent.

The blow for butter was cushioned by its continuing political influence, but this in turn created problems for Washington. Under the price support system, the federal government was obligated to buy and store millions of pounds of the dairy fat,[48] a glut that a young businessman named Dwayne Andreas would seek to sell to the Soviet Union; this glut prompted most others to call for a lower support price, which would make it more competitive with margarine. One columnist summed up the situation as a dialogue between characters from *Alice's Adventures in Wonderland*:

"Everyone loves [the price support] program," said the Mad Hatter. "Soy bean farmers have a good market for soy beans[,] for soy bean oil [and] oleo. The dairy farmers sell more milk and keep their cows longer. Cattle men are pleased because fewer cows go to slaughter. And, of course, oleo manufacturers love it most of all. They sell more oleo." "But what about butter?" The Dormouse again! "Butter, butter, why worry about butter? . . . In a few years, people will ask, 'what's that?' and it will be stored in the Smithsonian Institution."[49]

Meanwhile, as hinted by the Mad Hatter, the big winner was the soybean. Yellow margarine had broken through the legislative logjam in 1949 through an alliance of cotton and soybean growers, a year when 257 million pounds of soybean oil went into margarine versus 431 million pounds of cottonseed oil. By 1958, with advances in solving the reversion problem, and continuing government efforts to limit cotton acreage, more than a billion pounds of soybean oil went into margarine versus 145 million pounds of cottonseed oil (see figure 6.1). By 1969, the figures would be 1.3 billion and 75 million pounds, respectively. William Poage did not make a meaningful gain for his constituency, after all. When he retired as chairman of the Agriculture Committee in 1975, there would only be 261,000 acres of soybeans harvested in all of Texas, compared to 8.5 million in Illinois.[50]

Farther east, however, soybeans were becoming a southern crop, taking over land from cotton and displacing the sort of small farmer who voted for representatives like Poage. To an even greater extent, soybeans displaced tenant farmers, especially those who, by virtue of the color of their skin, had not been allowed to participate in elections at all.

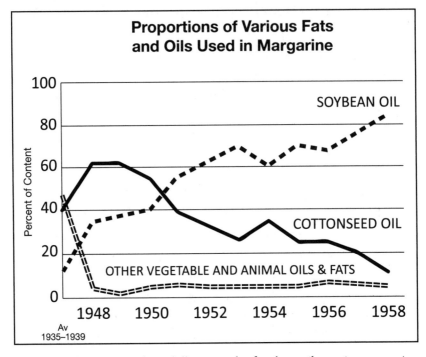

Figure 6.1. By 1958, more than a billion pounds of soybean oil went into margarine versus 145 million pounds of cottonseed oil. Source: USDA Agricultural Marketing Service.

Rise of the Confederate Cultivars

Beginning in 1948, *Soybean Digest* presented a helpful US map alongside its annual article on recommended soybean varieties, placing the names of the best-adapted, highest-producing cultivars for each state within that state's outlines. The names were densest in the Corn Belt, indicating that varietal work was most active where soybeans were most frequently grown. The map itself did not extend west beyond Texas. For the most part, there was no overarching logic in the names listed, as there had not been since the practice of designating soy cultivars with single proper names was established in 1907. It was up to the whim of individual breeders. There was a tendency in the North to name varieties after Indian tribes and American presidents: Chippewa, Blackhawk, Ottawa, Wabash, Adams, Madison, Monroe, Lincoln— as well as Lindarin, a portmanteau of Lincoln and Mandarin. But there were also names like Acme, Comet, Harosoy, Ford, Hongkong, Renville, Capital,

Clark, and Kent. Southern soybeans had names as diverse as Ogden, Dorman, Dortchsoy, Roanoke, JEW 45—based on the initials of its original cultivator—Bienville, Improved Pelican, and CNS.

Beginning in the mid-1950s, however, there were a smattering of Lee and Jackson soybeans appearing south of what had been the Missouri Compromise Line. Within a decade these had been joined by Bragg, Hampton, Hill, Hood, and Pickett, all unambiguously named after historical generals of the Confederacy (figure 6.2). Moreover, by this time, all of the former southern varieties had disappeared from the maps. The Confederate cultivars dominated the region, signaling a sea change both in the practice of soybean breeding and the course of southern agriculture. The sharecropping system that had so limited the spread of soybeans in the 1910s had finally fallen away. In the process, farming became much more of a strictly white pursuit.

The man who began naming soybeans after Confederate generals was Edgar Hartwig, a Minnesotan who received his PhD in agronomy from the University of Illinois in 1941. He then worked at the USDA under William Morse, whom he would later classify as an "agriculturalist" rather than a "soybean breeder."[51] Morse had developed new varieties by painstakingly sorting out lineages that self-pollination had made genetically uniform. Occasionally, he would discover a genetic cross that occurred naturally in the field. This approach was productive because of the amazing richness of the genetic material imported from Asia. To Hartwig, however, this was not serious breeding. He represented a new generation that sought to "artificially" breed novel soybean varieties that embodied desired sets of traits.

At the University of Illinois in the early 1930s, C. M. Woodworth had created the first chromosome maps of the soybean to better understand the genetic underpinnings of, and linkages between, given traits. When it was established in 1936, the US Regional Soybean Industrial Products Laboratory at Urbana likewise included a soybean breeding program.[52] In 1949, the soy germplasm collection, dedicated to preserving viable seeds of all surviving introductions, was established in Urbana. It had a southern counterpart in Stoneville, Mississippi, which Hartwig supervised beginning in 1951.[53] Guided by extensive tables of traits, Hartwig and his team developed a method of "backcrossing" specific genes into new soybean varieties. This involved crossing two varieties, then breeding one of the varieties with successive generations of crosses until only one trait remained from the second

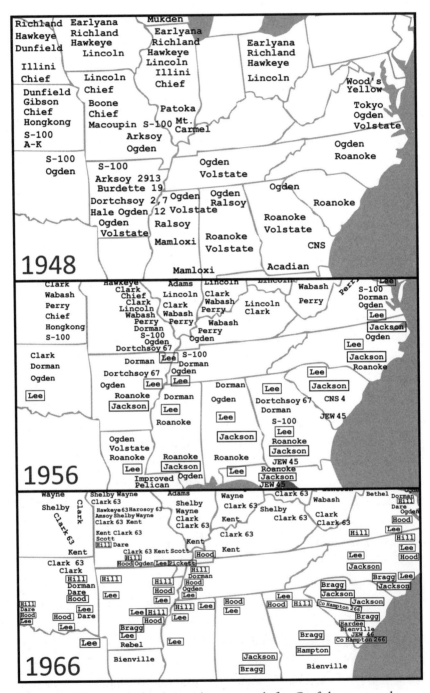

Figure 6.2. The spread of soybean cultivars named after Confederate generals, based on "Best Adapted Varieties" maps in *Soybean Digest*. Courtesy of *Corn+Soybean Digest*.

variety. The method was straightforward in principle but particularly challenging in a self-pollinating plant like the soybean.[54]

In 1948, the southern cultivars on the *Soybean Digest* map were mainly developed through observation and selection. On the coastal plain of South Carolina, John E. Wannamaker, a farmer and seed dealer who mainly bred cotton but also had an interest in soybeans, tagged any plant that looked different or promising. By this method, he discovered a variant of the Clemson variety that he named Clemson Non-Shattering, or CNS, because its pods burst less readily, saving more seed for the harvest. He also developed several varieties that he named with his own initials: JEW 45 and JEW 46.[55] But the 1948 map also included Ogden, released in 1943, a harbinger of newer methods. Created in Urbana through crossing the Tokyo variety with PI 54610, a strain gathered in 1921 in northern China,[56] it was superior to older varieties in its yield of beans and oil, although its pods were prone to shattering.[57] Because of a cooperative breeding program with agricultural experiment stations in twelve southern states—the eleven states of the former Confederacy, as it happened, plus Oklahoma—Ogden was rapidly tested and subsequently planted throughout the region as far south as Georgia and Florida. It was a small first step.

The contributions of Hartwig and his colleagues began to appear in the early 1950s. Dorman, developed by Hartwig and Leonard Williams of the University of Missouri, was released in 1952. Adapted to the heavy clay soils of the Mississippi Delta, its beans, like that of Ogden, had a high oil content, but its pods were far less given to shattering. The first variety developed by Hartwig alone, released in 1953, was Jackson. Its chief advantage, aside from a high oil content and increased disease resistance, was its height. A variety's height typically diminished the farther south it was planted. Even as far south as the Gulf Coast, however, Jackson averaged 32–34 inches, the threshold for being easily harvested with a combine.[58] Hartwig would later list Jackson among the varieties named after Confederate generals, although upon its release the source of its name was arguably ambiguous.[59] The Lincoln soybean, released a decade earlier, was the premiere variety in Illinois. Hartwig's soybean, well adapted to Georgia and the Gulf States, may have honored not the Confederate general Stonewall but rather the famously tall Andrew Jackson, who won glory in New Orleans and who, as president, removed the Cherokee people from Georgia. The name of Hartwig's next release was less ambiguous.

Both of Lee's parental strains were well-known cultivars, easily available to breeders, that had failed to live up to their anticipated commercial potential. S-100, a cross that had occurred naturally between two Manchurian varieties, was released as an oilseed variety in Missouri, but its oil content proved to be rather low, so crushers soon discouraged farmers from planting it. CNS, the variant of the Clemson variety discovered by Wannamaker, had also failed to catch on, but in addition to being nonshattering it possessed a highly desirable trait: resistance to bacterial pustule disease. In 1948, Hartwig isolated a third-generation cross of S-100 and CNS that combined resistance to bacterial pustule disease with "good agronomic qualities." After extensive testing, he handed it over to experiment stations cooperating with the Soybean Laboratory, which conducted field tests from 1951 to 1953 in forty different locations. Lee was released to commercial growers in 1954, a year after Jackson. Lee was proclaimed as "the most shatter-resistant variety developed to date," and in yield of beans and oil it was superior to Ogden. It was also less likely to lodge—that is, tip over under the weight of its pods, a trait measured on a scale from 1 (erect) to 5 (prostrate). Lee was later-maturing than Dorman or Jackson, making it well suited to the South's longer growing season. As with the two earlier varieties, being tall and straight—the very image of a southern general—permitted more efficient harvesting with a combine.[60]

After Lee, new varieties named after Confederate generals rapidly appeared over the following decades: Hood (1958), Hill (1959), Hampton (1962), Stuart (1962), Bragg (1963), Hardee (1963), Dare (1965), Pickett (1966), Davis (1966), Semmes (1966), Ransom (1970), Forrest (1973), and Tracy (1974).[61] Some cultivars were released multiple times, with years appended to their names—Lee 68, Pickett 71—as they were updated with new genes for disease resistance. When he upgraded Forrest, however, Hartwig worked backward through the name of the KKK Grand Wizard and perpetrator of the Fort Pillow Massacre: Bedford appeared in 1978 and Nathan in 1982.

The pedigrees of these cultivars were remarkably similar. Many had Dorman, Lee, and Jackson as direct forebears, and many others used Lee's sister lines. By the early 1970s, this raised concerns about the genetic uniformity of American soybeans, potentially vulnerable to being wiped out en masse by a single disease. A study released in 1972 by the National Academy of Sciences pointed out that, of the soybean introductions from overseas, a small number showed up disproportionately in the ancestry of current varieties. These included the introductions that led to Lee: Clemson, from which CNS was selected, was an ancestor to 68 percent of southern varieties, while a variety called AK, from which S-100 was selected, showed up in the ancestry of 63 percent. The fact that Lee and Bragg—Jackson × (S-100 × CNS)—together constituted 58 percent of all soybean acreage in the Delta magnified this effect. Above all, such genetic uniformity was a measure of Hartwig's success in isolating desirable traits, then backcrossing them into varieties already viable in the South.[62]

Hartwig's introductions coincided with a dramatic increase in soybean production in the South. The Mississippi Delta region was the fastest-growing region for soybeans in the country. Hartwig attributed this growth, unsurprisingly, to the improved varieties that he had introduced. While northern China and Manchuria—occupying roughly the same latitudes as Illinois—had the most productive oilseed varieties, the soybeans of southern China were lower in oil content and better suited for animal forage. Thus the economically valuable characteristics of northern varieties had to be painstakingly bred into soybeans adapted to southern day-lengths. Soybeans also suffered from a wider variety of diseases in the South, requiring breeders to seek a large number of disease-resistant genes. Enthusiasm in the South for soybeans during World War II had in fact faltered on their susceptibility to disease and insects.[63]

But while these traits undoubtedly enabled the spread of a soybean industry in the South, there were broad economic shifts that made the soybean viable as a cash crop in the 1950s where it had not been in the 1910s. One of these factors was the geography of demand. Prior to the 1950s, the Midwest was the strongest market for both the oil, used in paint and margarine manufacturing, and the meal. During the postwar period, exports became an increasingly important factor. All exports to the growing European market went through New Orleans, which became the largest soybean port in the nation. This did not necessarily give Delta planters a huge advantage—as the first leg of transportation remained the most costly—but it did level the playing field for them. At the same time, industrial production of meat—especially of broiler-type chickens, heavy with breast meat—became

significant in the South, creating local demand for the meal. The origins of
the broiler industry were in Delaware in 1923, when a farm woman named
Cecile Steele supplied meat chickens to the burgeoning Jewish community
of New York City.[64] In the post–World War II period, with the pioneering efforts of John Tyson in Arkansas and a national push in agricultural
research to find the Chicken of Tomorrow, chicken production expanded
exponentially and settled in a "broiler belt" that extended from Arkansas
into Mississippi, northern Alabama, Georgia, and North Carolina.[65] Soy
meal was part of the mixed poultry feeds that Tyson produced himself, and
proximity to soybeans traveling south to the Gulf gave the regional industry
a cost advantage, which in turn helped foster local growing of soybeans.

However, the chief value of the soybean lay not only in newfound demand for soy products but also in the need to find an alternative for the
South's traditional cash crop: cotton. Both the region and the federal government had been battling against surpluses of cotton for decades. In 1931, the
average price of cotton was lower than it had been at almost any time since
the end of the Civil War. The original Agricultural Adjustment Act of 1933
plowed under enough cotton to raise prices. When the AAA was ruled un-
constitutional, a second AAA in 1938 established a system of acreage allotments, marketing quotas, price adjustment and soil conservation payments,
and crop-storage loans. Farmers made the most of their allotments by inten-
sifying cultivation on the acres where they were permitted. During the war
years, cotton production again soared, even as labor shortages caused acreage to diminish.[66] The allotment system reappeared whenever cotton stocks
reached critical levels, as in 1950 and, following the Korean War, again in
1954. Much of the cotton cultivation shifted west, where larger farms made
use of irrigation and mechanical harvesting. In the Mississippi Delta, where
smaller farms could not as efficiently employ the new methods, cotton acreage declined from a peak of more than 1.2 million acres to less than 200,000
in 1960, while acreage in soybeans shot up.[67] The soybean did not displace
cotton singlehandedly: it was generally planted as part of a rotation with
small grains, oats, or winter wheat, with one combine able to harvest them
all.[68] But it was the soybean that was the major cash crop of the rotation, the
one that filled the void left by cotton.

The advance of the Confederate soybeans signaled more than the retreat
of cotton. It marked the adoption of mechanized agriculture in the region.

Even as productivity in harvesting cotton increased threefold, soybeans still represented a substantial savings in labor.[69] As a Louisiana State University bulletin pointed out in 1943, an acre of cotton required 183.6 hours of labor, whereas an acre of soybeans required only 9.6 hours.[70] This efficiency led to the decline of sharecropping. Pushed out of their shacks, as lower demand for their labor coincided with the need to provide clear paths for machines, share-croppers moved first to rural hamlets, staying nearby to provide labor for the remaining peak periods. Then they migrated to cities both inside and outside of the region.[71] Some managed to make the transition to independent farm-ing, but these were disproportionately white. African Americans, poorer to begin with, suffered from discriminatory practices on the part of both private and public lenders, notably the Farmers Home Administration, which sys-tematically shut out black applicants from government loans. As with whites, the nonwhites who continued to farm were more likely to own their land: the proportion of farms fully owned by their operators rose from 15 percent to 60 percent, similar to the proportion of farms owned by whites. But Afri-can Americans were on the land in far fewer numbers.[72] By 1997, the number was down to 19,000, less than 1 percent of American farm operators.[73]

The new varieties reflected these transformations. Hartwig emphasized the importance of "cultural practices"—that is, the methods of cultivating a crop—in realizing the value of the new varieties. Fertilizing with lime, potash, and phosphates was crucial in any but the richest Delta soils. Resis-tance to lodging or shattering was important only in the context of machine harvesting. As Hartwig liked to point out, shatter-prone soybeans had tradi-tionally made it easier for "Asiatic farmers" to "tramp out the seed."[74] Further-more, when other inputs limited the yield of soybeans to 15–20 bushels per acre, the improved varieties held no advantage. With more capital-intensive practices, however, a new variety could yield 45–50 bushels per acre, com-pared to 28–30 for an unimproved variety.[75] The new varieties were intended as only one element in a suite of new technologies.

Hartwig never provided a public explanation for his practice of nam-ing soybeans after Confederate generals. He perhaps intended the names to imbue soybeans with symbolism appealing to the region's white farmers as he asked them to abandon King Cotton and adopt northern-style indus-trialized agriculture. He transformed the soybean so that the South might transform itself.

This expansion of the soybean's geographical reach would prove long-lasting. In the same period, there was another, even more audacious, effort to expand soy's realm, extracting trace substances from the mass of processed soybeans and turning them into synthetic hormones to allay the pain of arthritis—but also potentially to transform America's relationship to sex and reproduction. This foray was less successful in the short term, as soy lost out to Mexican yams, but decades later the soybean would mount a victorious comeback.

Hormone Wars

Nineteen forty-nine was a banner year for Percy Lavon Julian, Glidden's African American soybean chemist, for reasons seemingly far afield from paint or paper coatings. A report in the *Afro-American* praised him for finding a solution to "the divorce cases flooding the country's courts" by synthesizing testosterone from soybeans. The cheap, widely available hormone would end male impotency, widely "understood to be one of the main reasons why so many wives have lovers,"[76] and help "weak, sissyish men" to become more masculine.[77] His synthesis of 16-methyltestosterone, an analog to testosterone, had first been announced in the more staid *Journal of the American Chemical Society*.[78] Julian made the front pages again for a method to cheaply manufacture Compound S, a substance chemically analogous to cortisone, also known as Compound E. In April, the Mayo Clinic had discovered that one or two injections of cortisone had so freed longtime sufferers of rheumatoid arthritis "that they were able to dance a jig." It would take the bile of 14,600 oxen, however, to derive enough cortisone to treat one arthritis patient for one year. Compound S, as yet untested, could be "brewed" from soybeans and promised to be available in abundance. Glidden pledged to distribute its entire supply to drug companies, clinics, and the public health service for immediate testing.[79] The story was picked up by papers across the nation, and readers of the *Chicago Sun-Times* chose Julian from among 180 candidates to be the 1949 Chicagoan of the Year.[80]

The roots of these discoveries went back a decade. By 1939, Julian had succeeded in redesigning Glidden's protein extraction process, which now churned out the high-grade protein isolate put to such good use by the US

Navy in its "bean soup" firefighting foam.[81] While grateful for his well-paid position, however, Julian was eager to return to more challenging research.[82] Glidden offered him freedom to pursue his own agenda, and a happy accident led him back to an earlier interest. Julian received a call informing him that 100,000 gallons of refined soybean oil bound for Durkee's Famous Foods had been spoiled by water leaking into the tank, a potential loss of $200,000. He found that the tank contained a mass of white sludge, which he removed from the oil by having it centrifuged. He had a suspicion. Five years earlier, while a professor at DePauw, he had seen a similar substance appear in a dish of calabar-bean oil, which upon investigation turned out to be rich in plant sterols. He then worked to derive the female sex hormone progesterone, discovered in 1934, from one of the calabar bean's sterols, stigmasterol. His interest was in part personal: his wife suffered from miscarriages, for which progesterone was thought to be a remedy. Because soybeans were more readily available than calabar beans, he had written Glidden to request a sample when he coincidentally received the phone call hiring him. Now he found that the oily mass from the tank contained 15 percent mixed sterols.[83] The accident had just handed him a method for separating out sterols without diminishing the value of the remaining oil.

This was indeed the trick of recovering any valuable by-product from soybean oil, and it was one Julian would have to repeat a number of times before he had the ultimate prize in hand. First, he had to efficiently separate the mixed sterols from the rest of the oily white sludge. Typically, this would involve making the sludge into soap, then washing out the nonsoap sterols with a solvent. Unfortunately, the gumminess of the sludge required the use of too much solvent to be cost-effective. In another chance event, Julian observed a friend mixing a batch of plaster retarder, and he noticed that the addition of quicklime made it foam up. He adapted this idea to his sterol-rich soap, puffing it up into a "porous granular mass" from which the sterols could easily be extracted by filtering through a relatively small amount of the solvent. With more tedious work than serendipity, he and his team then determined the ideal solvent to selectively wash out the sterols.[84]

The next task was to capture the stigmasterol, which was around 20 percent of the sterol mix. The other sterols were collectively known as sitosterol. This was a substantial obstacle. The sterols did not differ from each other enough to be separated by physical methods, either by distilling them or by shaking them with various organic solvents. Instead, the mixture needed to be chemically transformed until the stigmasterol fraction was slightly less soluble. This technique, first developed by German chemists in 1906, was costly and complicated. After the stigmasterol was isolated, the chemical transformations had to then be undone, with a loss of almost 60 percent of the stigmasterol.[85] Julian's team improved this low yield by adding an oxidation step using a large and very expensive ozonizer, which posed the risk of "a potentially dangerous explosive reaction"[86] but had the side benefit of converting the other sterols into useful precursors of methyltestosterone.[87] These precursors were thus valuable by-products of a by-product, the means by which Julian would later win acclaim from the *Afro-American*.

Having finally obtained pure stigmasterol, Julian synthesized progesterone through a series of steps, worked out a decade earlier by German organic chemists, that he immediately set about improving.[88] In 1940, Julian sent a one-pound package of progesterone to the Upjohn Company in Kalamazoo, Michigan, the first commercial shipment in America of an artificial sex hormone derived from plants. Valued at $63,500, it was shipped under armed guard. By one estimate, it took 3,000 pounds of soybean oil—derived from 15,000 pounds of soybeans—to end up with that one pound of progesterone, an indication of the scale of production necessary to make it feasible to recover vanishingly small fractions of the soybean.[89]

Progesterone was an immediate moneymaker for Glidden, its 1940 annual report predicting that "the production of hormones and sterols has resulted in constantly increasing sales which should add materially to our profits in the ensuing year."[90] A potential setback emerged in 1946 when the Schering Corporation, a former subsidiary of a German company that was now in the hands of the federal Alien Property Custodian, sued Glidden for patent infringement. Along with three other European-owned companies, Schering was part of a cartel that before the war had monopolized commercial synthetic sex hormones—including forms of testosterone, estrogen, and progesterone derived from animal cholesterol—setting prices and preserving their lock on the market through a shared pool of cross-licensed patents.[91] Although Julian derived his hormones from a plant source, Schering contended that converting stigmasterol to progesterone violated at least one of its patents. This was also a way to halt Glidden's development of testosterone, which was envisioned to have even greater market potential.

An exposé the following year in *The American Weekly*, a popular Sunday magazine inserted in Hearst newspapers, juxtaposed a photo of Julian—the "famed Negro chemist [who] found a way to make sex hormones out of soybeans"—with an illustration of a top-hatted plutocrat, seated among bags of money, leering at a bottle of medicine while numerous hands desperately reached for it through a transom. This prompted United States Attorney General Tom Clark, whose Department of Justice inherited Schering after the office of the Alien Property Custodian disbanded, to promise the return of the company to private hands on the condition that the new owners share its patents with all seekers in return for minimal royalties. In the midst of this, Schering and Glidden reached a settlement.[92] With Julian's synthesis of Compound S from stigmasterol in 1949—achieved after six months of working fourteen to fifteen hours every day, including Saturdays and Sundays[93]—the way seemed clear for soybeans and Glidden to become leading providers of new wonder drugs.

Within four years, however, the picture had entirely changed. Julian's Compound S was, as it happened, a clinical failure. When fed to patients with arthritis, it not only failed to relieve symptoms—it actually aggravated them.[94] Noting the abundance of naturally occurring Compound S in the adrenal gland, Julian had mistakenly theorized that the human body could easily convert his synthetic product into an active form of cortisone. It was indeed true that enzymes did exist that could convert Compound S into Compound E—as well as Compound F, or hydrocortisone, an even more powerful drug. It was just that, as researchers at the Cleveland Clinic discovered, these were enzymes present in cattle, not humans. This was actually good news for Compound S. "Manufactured in any desired quantity" from soybeans, as one newspaper suggested, Compound S could be now converted into large amounts of cortisone using the abundant enzymes of millions of slaughtered animals.[95] This is an approach that ultimately did find success—but with both the soybeans and the cattle enzymes swapped out for more cost-effective substitutes.

In a revolutionary breakthrough in 1952, scientists at Upjohn managed to ferment Compound S into hydrocortisone using microbes, which were easier to obtain than even cattle enzymes.[96] This process made chemical procedures for synthesizing cortisone instantly obsolete, including Julian's own patent, granted in 1956, the schematic diagram of which—with arrows indicating the steps by which certain four-ring sterols could be converted into others—resembled a twenty-seven-car pileup. By then the Mexican hormone industry, initiated eight years earlier by the former Penn State professor Russell Marker, was having a major impact. In the late 1930s, Marker had successfully synthesized sex hormones using plant substances called sapogenins. One of these, diosgenin, was abundant in a wild Mexican yam known locally as *barbasco*. Diosgenin could be converted into, among other things, Compound S. Between 1944 and his retirement in 1952, Marker helped establish two major hormone manufacturers in Mexico, Syntex and Diosynth, which together brought the price of progesterone from $200 per gram in 1940—when Julian sold his first pound to Upjohn—down to 30 cents per gram in 1955.[97]

Soybean stigmasterol could not compete, and in 1952 Glidden shut down sterol production, instead making Compound S from Diosynth diosgenin, a process also covered by Julian's patent.[98] Forced to compete in what the *Wall Street Journal* called a "cortisone war" characterized by dramatically falling prices, and driven to the same source of raw materials as its competitors, Glidden decided in 1953 to get out of the business altogether. "There's no money in it for us," company president Dwight P. Joyce explained to the *Journal*.[99] Julian had urged in vain for Glidden to set up its own diosgenin plant in Mexico, but Glidden seemed eager to shift focus to its core businesses: paints, varnishes, and processed foods. It licensed Julian's Compound S patent to Pfizer Laboratories, which contracted with Syntex to produce it as a starter material for hydrocortisone. In the absence of steroid research—and tasked with developing new products such as nonspattering shortening or paint that prevented icing on airplane propellers—Julian decided in 1954 to part ways with his employer of almost eighteen years. He left behind 109 patents, including his synthesis of Compound S.[100] Through his own company, Julian Laboratories, he set up a supply chain to produce diosgenin, and he eventually became a millionaire. In 1958, meanwhile, Glidden unloaded its Soya Products Division altogether. Now known as the Chemurgy Division, it was purchased by Indiana-based Central Soya, one of the pioneers of soybean crushing.

So it was that the wild barbasco yam, rather than the soybean, became the basis for the hormone industry and its crowning achievement, the birth-control pill.[101] This did not end the story, however. Julian's work with soy

sterols was carried forward by researchers at Upjohn, who had discovered
how to synthesize hydrocortisone from progesterone. Worried about their
dependence on Mexican hormones, Upjohn maintained a development program for improving the synthesis of progesterone from stigmasterol.[102] The
cost-effectiveness of this process improved dramatically when one chemist
overcame the chief obstacle limiting the use of soybean sterols, the difficulty of separating stigmasterol from sitosterol. His method, aside from
extracting high proportions of very pure stigmasterol, did so without first
chemically transforming the sterols. This saved a lot of money, and largely
as a consequence of new competition from soybeans, the price of Mexican
diosgenin-derived progesterone fell from 48 cents to 15 cents per gram by
the early 1960s.[103]

Upjohn's process did have one drawback, however. Unmodified, the sitosterol was no longer useful as a precursor of testosterone and, instead,
accumulated in metal drums on a barren patch of the company's property.
In the 1970s, Upjohn initiated sitosterol utilization research, and within
ten years its researchers successfully developed a microbial method for converting sitosterol into as effective a starting point for steroid production as
stigmasterol. In the grand tradition of chemurgy, all of those metal drums
containing a waste product became highly valuable. This hastened the decline
of the Mexican barbasco industry, already hobbled by the escalating costs of
gathering an increasingly scarce wild product.[104] Abundant soybeans became
a major though largely unheralded source of synthetic progesterone and
corticoid hormones into the twenty-first century—by which time soybean
sitosterol in its raw form had coincidentally gained favor as a cholesterol-
fighting nutraceutical.[105]

The extraction of hormones was in many ways a fulfillment of the chemurgical vision for soybeans, which would gain value through specialized by-
products created through ingenious chemistry. It was the vision displayed in
the 1949 *Fortune* magazine illustration (see the introduction of this book) that
presented the soy complex as a river delta, repeatedly dividing into smaller
streams of products. The 1960s would represent both the fulfillment and the
end of this vision. The soybean would indeed be divided and manipulated
into an array of specialized products for use by industry. But if the chemurgists imagined that most of these uses would fall outside of agriculture's

traditional domain of food, they were wrong. Rather, food production itself became more highly industrialized, demanding more specialized and arcane inputs. The value derived from soybeans, moreover, would come less from their elaboration into these inputs than from growing economies of scale as the production of its two main products—oil and meal—became concentrated in the hands of fewer companies. Chemurgists had brought attention to the soybean by adopting it as a mascot of their movement. As soy's tangible influence grew in the postwar period, however, its visibility declined. It became an obscure input in an increasingly long food chain.

CHAPTER SEVEN

THRIVING IN THE SHADE

Morton Kamerman, managing partner of the Wall Street brokerage Ira Haupt & Company, was on his way home on a Monday night in late 1963, with none but the usual worries, when he encountered an anxious group of the firm's brokers in the commodity trading room. They were discussing losses in the commodity futures market incurred by a company named Allied Crude Vegetable Oil Refining Corporation of Bayonne, New Jersey. He decided to stay, and in the course of that night Kamerman saw his firm threatened by what he had imagined was a small part of its business, something to which he gave so little thought that it was omitted from the daily financial reports he received. Before taking Allied's business earlier that year, Haupt had dealt in commodities only as a courtesy to those of its stock-market clients who wanted to dip a toe into futures trading. Now Kamerman learned that Haupt was on the hook for $14 million. "The thing came as a terrific shock to me," he later recounted, "and I'm quite convinced that every other partner, or practically every other partner, was equally in the dark on it." As Haupt's auditors pulled together an emergency balance sheet to determine whether the firm was solvent, Kamerman roamed about periodically asking, "What's going on? I'm the managing partner, somebody ought to tell me." As the audit report came in, the one piece of good news was that the $14 million in liabilities was almost completely offset by the value of warehouse receipts for stored soybean and cottonseed oil, which Allied had offered to Haupt as collateral.[1]

On Tuesday, Allied filed for bankruptcy. On Wednesday, the New York

Stock Exchange suspended Haupt for insolvency, only the second suspension of a member firm in 171 years. On Thursday, Haupt discovered that many of the warehouse receipts it had received from Allied were forged. On Friday, November 22, 1963, Stock Exchange officials met to discuss a plan to cover Haupt's obligations to its almost 21,000 clients—even as reports flashed over the news wires that President John F. Kennedy had been shot in Dallas. Over the weekend, the New York Stock Exchange liquidated Haupt and set up a fund to refund its customers. Meanwhile, investigators discovered that the oil tanks at Allied's facility in Bayonne were empty, rendering even the authentic warehouse receipts valueless. Ultimately, almost 2 billion tons of oil, most of it soy, were missing, with a stated value of $175 million.[2]

The man behind this extraordinary swindle was Anthony "Tino" De Angelis, a Bronx butcher turned self-styled Salad Oil King whose financial machinations took advantage of lax oversight of the burgeoning, but obscure, infrastructure that moved soybeans to market. At its inception, Allied was able to hide its fraud through the tremendous volume of its legitimate business, which in a circular fashion was almost certainly made possible by the fraud. De Angelis entered the soybean oil business when it was dominated by midwestern companies whose processing plants and refineries were located within the main soybean-producing regions. Mainly, the flow of oil exports went down the Mississippi River to New Orleans, rather than the more costly rail route to eastern ports. But this threatened to shut the giant, New York–based grain export companies Bunge Corporation and Continental Grain Company out of a lucrative new trade. De Angelis borrowed from these companies to buy the petroleum tank farm in Bayonne, which he refitted for edible oils. By a magic that failed to raise suspicions among his creditors, De Angelis paid higher prices than his competition for the crude oil from small midwestern crushers, then charged lower prices for the refined oil despite his higher transportation costs.[3] Eventually even larger companies—Cargill and Staley—sold through Allied.

By the late 1950s, Allied was responsible for 75 percent of the edible oils shipped overseas. Much of his business received support from the federal government, including a $42 million contract brokered with Spain in 1958 with subsidies from the Food for Peace program.[4] Evidence of fraud emerged, including falsified shipping papers in the Spain deal. Allied also used substandard cans in shipments to private relief agencies overseas paid for by the

USDA, resulting in 400 million pounds of spoiled oil. The USDA's increasing distrust of De Angelis may have compelled him to find increased profits through his sideline in fraudulent warehouse receipts.[5]

Warehousing companies, by certifying the existence of a stored commodity and issuing receipts to use as short-term collateral, helped large traders convert their large inventories into working capital. Acceptance of these receipts was limited by doubts about their trustworthiness, often with good reason. Warehouses frequently hired a client's own employees—released for this purpose—to monitor the client's inventories, creating a potential conflict of interest. De Angelis, through good luck or predatory skill, secured the services of American Express Warehousing, a struggling subsidiary so desperate for Allied's business that it was easily persuaded, through deception and possibly outright bribery, to turn a blind eye to dodgy practices. American Express's monitors took Allied's word at face value about how much oil was in the Bayonne tanks. For more rigorous inspections, Allied was able to move the same oil from tank to tank using an elaborate system of pipes. Alternately, it would fill the tanks mostly with water, with only a thin layer of oil resting on top. American Express, the parent company, was so well regarded, however, that receipts from the warehousing subsidiary were accepted far and wide—with no questions asked, for instance, by Haupt.

Commodity exchanges, by reducing risks for soybean producers and processors, greased the wheels of commerce and helped to increase trade in the crop overall. The final frenzies of De Angelis's scheming took place at the Chicago Board of Trade and the New York Produce Exchange, key futures markets for soybean oil and cottonseed oil, respectively. De Angelis bought massive numbers of futures contracts on both exchanges, at first it seems in anticipation of a massive overseas sale that never came to fruition. Then he found himself in a trap, as any substantial drop in the futures prices he had succeeded in inflating would be fatal to the scheme. Although he purchased the futures on margin—with Haupt fronting the cash for the 10 percent down payment in return for the bogus warehouse receipts—he was required to fully cover his losses when prices fell. His ongoing purchases, coming near the close of business each day, were designed to sustain futures prices, which exchange rules did not allow to fall more than a certain amount in one day's trading. His behavior prompted the suspicion that he was trying to corner the market on soybean oil, although he never controlled enough of the physical supply to run a successful corner. Despite the many red flags—and previous run-ins with the Chicago Board of Trade—nobody at the board or its federal overseer, the Commodity Exchange Authority, took any action. When De Angelis could no longer afford to keep batting up the futures prices each day, he went into the financial death spiral that sucked in Haupt along with him.

As the dust settled on the biggest business story of 1963, the major institutions involved survived with their reputations more or less intact and, after some protracted legal wrangling with the smaller victims, settled back to business as usual. For the public, the window again closed on a realm that Morton Kamerman was not alone in ignoring even as it grew in scope and importance. American farmers were increasingly aware of soybeans, of course, but farmers made up a decreasing portion of the US population, only 8 percent in 1960, on their way to 5 percent a decade later. (They had constituted almost 40 percent in 1900.) And as crops made their way from the farm, soybeans' identity as soybeans dropped away before they reached consumers. They became the meat of cattle who consumed soybean meal, or the small-type ingredient in processed food, or in the partially hydrogenated frying oil used in the growing number of fast-food restaurants. By 1960, more than a third of the fats Americans consumed derived from soybean oil, a figure that would grow to 60 percent in 1970,[6] but it was largely in the form of generic salad oil, margarine, and shortening. Even the De Angelis scandal, which mostly involved soybean oil, would become known as the Great Salad Oil Swindle. Whereas soybeans had enjoyed a fair amount of publicity in the heyday of Henry Ford, their visibility had long since lagged behind their actual presence in American life.

This paradox was embodied less by De Angelis, however, than by a man who rose to prominence as a businessman in tandem with the growth of the soybean industry, someone who quietly influenced the nation's politics but remained largely unknown to the larger public.

Growth of an Industry

In 1955, while delivering a talk ("Commodity Markets and the Processor") to a group of professors from business schools and agricultural colleges,

Dwayne Andreas commented that "it is very difficult for a business man to find himself surrounded by a group of experts." The occasion was the Chicago Board of Trade's Symposium on Commodity Markets, held each year in September at the Union League Club with the goal of educating educators about the workings of the market, and its benefit to the public at large, to prevent misunderstanding about an institution that often felt itself to be widely misunderstood.[7] Andreas's difficulty was not that he was cowed by expertise, but rather it was the opposite: he felt "the urge to expound on personal economic theories" to an audience that might appreciate them. For the time being, he pledged to avoid theory in order to relay practical knowledge: "a description of just how, at the working level, the merchandising operations of a modern soybean crushing plant are managed."

Practically speaking, no matter how many things soybeans might eventually become—in an earlier speech, Andreas had lightly mocked the chemurgical notion of turning them into everything from "houses to diapers"—the crusher was concerned with only two products: oil and meal. Andreas argued that only the oil truly left the farm "in the economic sense." Though it did not literally remain on the farm, the meal eventually returned in the form of livestock feed. The crusher served "as the conduit through which soybeans move in their natural journey from farm to farm."[8] The crusher was, in essence, a middleman between farmers and themselves—and in an era when farmers had become vastly more dependent on intermediaries for inputs, technology, and marketing, Andreas could imagine no better role for himself than to be the consummate middleman.

Andreas was born to farming. His parents were strict Mennonites whose families were part of a migration from Prussia to the American Midwest in the 1870s.[9] They themselves moved from Minnesota to a sixty-acre farm in Lisbon, Iowa, in 1922. The family lived frugally, canning its own vegetables and growing its own oats, hay, and corn to feed livestock. But his father, Reuben Andreas, had ambitions beyond self-sufficiency. In 1927, he took over a bankrupt grain, coal, and seed business in Lisbon, and soon R. P. Andreas & Son expanded to operating the town's grain elevator. Reuben became an all-purpose middleman to farmers.[10] He expanded again to provide an input that was growing rapidly in popularity: mixed, or formulated, feeds. This sector had grown from almost nothing three decades earlier into a $400 million industry, comprising 750 firms, by 1929. By 1956, spurred by the increasing meat production and the advances in formulation achieved by Clive McCay and his colleagues, it was a $2 billion industry in which 6,000 feed manufacturers, and countless feed stores, produced 33 million tons annually.[11]

Like most of these operations, Andy's Feeds started off on a small scale. Reuben mixed the feeds by hand as his sons shoveled the ingredients—corns, oats, molasses, alfalfa, and soybean meal—into bins. But his business grew, prompting him in 1934 to purchase a feed-mixing machine that could handle 10 tons of ingredients every hour.[12] This was also the year that Dwayne and his older brothers Osborn and Glenn joined his father and brother Albert in the business, prompting a name change to R. P. Andreas & Sons. In 1936, it moved its operations to Cedar Rapids and became Honeymead, a name chosen at the family dinner table.[13] The company installed three machines in an old storehouse to manufacture different sizes of the sort of hard-pellet feeds pioneered by Staley, preferred by customers over powdered feeds easily blown around by the wind. In August 1937, the company's net worth was appraised at $24,200, and the Iowa Securities Commission authorized a public stock offering.

In 1938, Dwayne was Honeymead's most aggressive salesman, and he was eager to branch out into new ventures. That year, he traveled to Decatur, Illinois, to buy 8,000 tons of ground soybean meal for the feed operation. As he was completing his business, Gus Staley himself—the son of the company's legendary founder—buttonholed him. Over lunch, Staley predicted that Iowa farmers would increasingly plant soybeans in the coming years and, as his company had no plans to move beyond Illinois, he suggested that Honeymead make the most of a profitable opportunity by entering the crushing business. For financing, Staley suggested Allis-Chalmers, an equipment manufacturer based in Milwaukee that was then developing a new solvent-extraction system for oilseeds. After Andreas consulted with his father and brothers—and donned a hat to look more mature than his twenty years—he sped off to Wisconsin and obtained the loan.[14] By the end of the year, Honeymead was in the soybean business, processing 100 tons per day using an innovative extractor built inside what had been a grain elevator.[15]

In 1945, anticipating that he might soon be drafted, Andreas sold the Cedar Rapids plant and a controlling share of Honeymead stock to Cargill, a Minneapolis-based exporter of grain. The deal worked out well for him. His personal share of the proceeds was $1.5 million,[16] and Cargill even arranged a three-month draft deferment for him. When the war ended (less than three months later), he joined the Minneapolis company as vice president in charge of the Vegetable Oils Division. He stayed for seven years, absorbing the wisdom of Julius Hendel, the leading commodities trader at Cargill.[17] Hendel trained Andreas in the subtle art of hedging.[18] Academic economists often viewed hedging as merely a way to insure against short-term price risks—so that, for example, if the price of soybeans were to decline suddenly right before a warehouse operator sold them, the loss would be countered by an equal and opposite gain in the futures market. Businessmen like Hendel, however, had long known that hedging could be much more: the key for making a profit in trading or processing grain or, as one writer in 1899 put it, for furnishing "to the trader his reward as middleman."[19] This was an insight that academics cyclically lost and rediscovered.

Andreas, after a decade of tutelage under Hendel, explained the nuts and bolts in his 1955 talk to the audience of economists gathered for the Board of Trade symposium. The "merchandising department of a modern soybean operation includes four basic functions which usually are represented by four individuals," he began. First was the bean buyer who purchased soybeans "day by day as the country appears willing to sell," keeping one eye on prices in relation to the futures prices in Chicago, but making sure above all "that there is an adequate supply of beans ahead of the plant to keep it running at capacity at all times" and that the company's warehousing capacity was utilized as profitably as possible. Second, there was the oil salesman who tried "to be prepared to quote a competitive price every day, regardless of the crushing margin"—the premium for converting beans to oil and meal—so "that the entire production of the plant can be shipped regularly." Then there was the meal salesman, who likewise endeavored to quote a "competitive price at all times, even when the crushing margin is unsatisfactory," with a special concern for saving on freight charges, as the meal was far bulkier than the oil. As Andreas stressed, these three individuals faced separate competitive pressures that forced them to disregard the crushing margin. Indeed, in cash terms a plant typically crushed at a loss.[20]

Lastly, there was the merchandising supervisor, the job Andreas himself often performed. The supervisor's job, in addition to looking over the shoulders of the other three, was "fixing the margin between the beans and the products at a time most favorable, in his opinion, to his operation." Fixing the margin was something achieved through the futures market. For a warehouse operator—whose profits derived from buying beans when they were plentiful during the harvest, and then storing them until steady demand pushed up prices for a diminishing supply—this was a relatively straightforward process. Whenever they purchased physical beans, they would sell the same amount of "future" beans at a higher price—representing the market's best guess of the value of storing the beans until the delivery date—and pocket the difference. When they later sold the physical beans, they would "lift the hedge" by buying the same quantity of futures contracts—and, given that the futures price was still likely higher than the cash price—they would now be out the difference. If cash and futures prices tracked each other precisely, so that the difference between them, known as the "basis," remained the same, the hedger would end up making no profit at all. Cash and futures prices typically converged in a predictable way, however, and the basis was by definition zero on the delivery date, so that the hedger who waited until that day kept the entire profit. Thus the system allowed the hedger to lock in a predictable profit, while speculators could place bets on the less predictable ups and downs of the futures price alone.

For a processing plant's merchandising supervisor, things were much more complicated. There were three futures markets to follow. By 1955, the Chicago Board of Trade offered futures contracts not only for whole soybeans but also separate contracts for soybean oil and soybean meal, established in 1950 and 1951, respectively. Earlier, processors customarily hedged with cottonseed oil futures on the New York Produce Exchange and cottonseed meal futures on the Memphis market, but these were inexact proxies for soy products.[21] The supervisor had to pinpoint the exact moments when the three markets aligned to lock in the crushing margin. In this way, the futures market enabled the processor to disconnect profitmaking from the flow of actual beans through the plant. Lest this "sound too simple," Andreas emphasized that adequate crushing margins "existed only for a few days at a time during the year. Thus, an alert merchandising supervisor might conceivably do a very large share of his year's business in a very short time, in spite of the fact that the cash purchases of beans and the sale of meal and oil are scattered throughout the year."[22] Some complained that the opportunities for profiting were becoming ever more rare—perhaps the fault of the futures market itself, as speculators such as Tino De Angelis drove the price of

beans above their real worth, then used strong-arm methods to work a corner—but Andreas saw it differently. Offloading risk onto speculators may
have meant smaller profit margins, but more predictable returns enabled
mills to safely make capital investments, ultimately earning more revenue
through greater volume.[23]

Andreas did note, however, that some processors went beyond hedging into forms of speculation. In one practice that Andreas described as a
"strange phenomenon," a processor might make "a good share if not all of
their earnings" through a form of virtual crushing. When the price-spread
in the futures market between soybeans and its products was less than the
cost of converting real soybeans into oil and meal, a processor would sell
soybean futures and buy meal and oil futures. This was essentially a bet
that the spread would increase, at which point the processor would reverse
the transaction—buying bean futures and selling oil and meal futures—and
make a profit. This practice "in effect gave them additional crushing capacity
at less than it would cost to own a plant and operate the capacity." Andreas
expected pure speculators to join in, as they were just as able as processors
to operate this kind of purely financial "crushing capacity."[24] While successful
speculation provided an additional stream of revenue, which in theory might
enable processors to lower their prices to once again increase their volume, it
risked being a distraction. Andreas's mentor was generally opposed to hedgers engaging in this kind of thing: "If a trader is speculating, his mind will not
be on business," Hendel would write in an instructional pamphlet.[25]

Andreas, for his part, kept his mind on business. He pursued new markets, in fact, with an aggressiveness that put him at odds with other executives in the buttoned-up corporate culture of Cargill. In 1952, at the height
of McCarthyism, he decided to attend a trade conference in Moscow. He
was to accompany a French group, having obtained a visa in Washington
on the condition of keeping a low profile. Still, Cargill management feared
that banks would cut off credit when the news got out, and Hendel himself
forbade him to go. Andreas sensed a market opportunity, however, and no
ideological or geopolitical considerations would deter him. Upon his return,
he was forced to resign from Cargill, at a gain of $400,000 in redeemed
common stock.[26]

Taking up the reins of his family's remaining Honeymead interests, he
was still determined to sell to the Soviets. Soybean oil might have been a

logical commodity for Andreas to trade, but he focused instead on the nation's growing stock of surplus butter. The choice was largely strategic: as
no less an adviser than then Vice President Richard Nixon noted, the anti-
communist crusader Joe McCarthy, being a Wisconsinite, would not object
to the deal. The secretary of commerce, however, refused to issue the export license,[27] and in the meantime Andreas's defiance of Cold War norms
earned him a fair amount of notoriety. He received one letter simply addressed to "the son of a bitch who wants to sell butter to the Russians." Andreas shrugged off the hate mail and instructed his traders in Rotterdam to
fulfill the Russian deal with cottonseed and linseed oil however they might
obtain it.[28]

Andreas had by now extended his deal-making into politics. His first
friend in office was the Democrat Hubert Humphrey, to whose 1948 re-
election campaign for mayor of Minneapolis he gave an unsolicited $1,000
donation. At the same time, in 1953 he met and became fast friends with the
failed Republican presidential nominee Thomas Dewey. On the strength of
Dewey's promotion of soybeans while governor of New York, Andreas arranged for him to become special counsel to the National Soybean Processors Association. The two became traveling, fishing, and golfing companions,
often joined by Humphrey, now a US senator. Andreas insisted that Dewey
and Humphrey, their party affiliations notwithstanding, actually had "a lot in
common" when discussing policy.[29] Andreas himself straddled the political
spectrum, on the one hand being a proponent of free markets, and on the
other—especially in the years prior to the rise of the New Right—a pragma-
tist, realizing that, for better or worse, government policy structured agricultural markets. As he advised a group of investment bankers many years later,
"Get along with the government whether you like it or not, [or] you're going
to get rolled over, as if you were a pig in a manger with its mother sow. When
she rolls over, either you get a teat in your mouth or you get squashed."[30]

From this standpoint, Andreas's most notable political success was Humphrey's introduction of the Agricultural Trade Development and Assistance
Act of 1954, also known as Public Law 480 (PL 480) and, in a later incarnation, the Food for Peace Program. Andreas would later claim some credit
for suggesting the concept to Humphrey.[31] The heart of PL 480, which also
provided direct food aid on a small scale, was a loan program to foreign governments, who were allotted credits to buy certain American commodities.

The recipients made arrangements with private exporters—middlemen like Andreas—whom the US government paid in dollars. Recipient governments repaid these loans in their own currencies, providing funds for US overseas programs to use locally. The chief beneficiaries of the system were wheat exporters, but the soybean industry benefited as well. With demand for meal driving the growth of the soybean crop, soybean oil was produced in excess of domestic demand, even with the repeal of the margarine tax. The value of soybean oil was indirectly buoyed by government price support for its chief competitor, cottonseed oil—when Humphrey blocked a USDA plan to lower this support, Andreas wrote to say how pleased he was[32]—but PL 480 had the biggest impact. In 1959, the program financed four out of every five dollars' worth of wheat exports—and nine out of every ten dollars' worth of soybean oil exports.[33] It was precisely the business resulting from PL 480 that provided Tino De Angelis the seed money for his epic fraud.

Even as the glut of soybean oil was siphoned off, a glut of soft currencies accumulated overseas in US government accounts. This was earmarked in part for programs promoting American farm products. PL 480 money funded both the Japanese American Soybean Institute—which coordinated the export of soybeans for Asian food purposes—and the Soybean Council of America, which fostered soybean use in dozens of the sixty countries eligible for soybean credits. One effort sought to spread broiler chicken operations, which intensively raised chickens for meat using high-protein feed, to Iran.[34] The council's main focus was to push Mediterranean countries to adopt soybean oil in place of, or at least blended with, olive oil for domestic purposes. The council argued that countries like Spain could then export its more valuable olive oil for hard currency.[35] The US government agreed and extended credits under PL 480 to Francisco Franco's regime in Spain. At the end of 1957, Honeymead was the first Minnesota company to ship soybean oil to Spain, as a train of eighty tank cars left its plant in Mankato, Minnesota, to fulfill the first installment of an 8,000-metric-ton order. In a news account, Andreas pointed out how local farmers would benefit: "Our sales of this processed product means we can pay the farmer more for his beans, and in turn sell him back the meal at the lowest possible prices."[36]

When the Kennedy administration retooled PL 480 as the Food for Peace Program, Humphrey and Andreas pushed to have George McGovern appointed director of the program. With Humphrey's help, Andreas himself

later joined the Food for Peace Council that advised McGovern.[37] Nevertheless, Andreas continued to criticize domestic farm policies. In one speech,
he assailed the "ignoble goals" and "hysteria about surpluses" surrounding
the USDA's continued attempts to cut back farm production. It was a "crop-
cutting orgy" implemented by "statisticians who would substitute lead-
penciled calculations for the judgment of farmers and the needs of hu-
manity."[38] Outraged, Secretary of Agriculture Orville Freeman denounced
Andreas by name in a report to now–President Lyndon Johnson as "someone who has benefitted from the actions of this administration" but then
turned on it with "a vicious attack." Humphrey wrote to Freeman to remind
him that Andreas had "helped substantially"—presumably in the financial
sense—such senators as McGovern, Gaylord Nelson, Bill Proxmire, Gale
McGee, Lee Metcalf, and Ted Moss, "all good Administration votes."[39] Andreas's conflict with the administration revealed consistency in his attitude
toward government: he applauded it when it worked to increase demand
for farm products but lambasted it when it sought to restrict supply. He
depicted himself as an ally to farmers, but whereas farm quotas might help
their bottom line, only expansion helped his own.

After leaving Cargill, Andreas remained in Minneapolis to oversee, with
his younger brother Lowell, what remained of Honeymead. Its central operation was a 1,000-ton soybean processing plant in Mankato, made profitable
by a special freight rate negotiated with the Chicago and North Western
Railway. Through Humphrey, Andreas met Myron W. "Bill" Thatcher, the
secretary general of the Farmers Union Grain Terminal Association (GTA),
one of the Democratic Party's most powerful backers in Minnesota. Andreas
generally lauded farm cooperatives like the GTA, arguing that farmers ought
to "organize to protect themselves from the vagaries of the market place."
In 1960, GTA bought out the Andreas family's remaining Honeymead interests for $10 million, and Dwayne and Lowell Andreas took over as the
cooperative's vice president and executive vice president.[40] GTA gained a
reliable outlet for its member farmers, while the Andreases moved into
banking when their holding company, Interoceanic Corporation, founded
the National City Bank of Minneapolis. Meanwhile, Dwayne and Lowell
maneuvered to once again control a major soybean processor.

In 1966, Lowell was elected as a director of Archer-Daniels Midland,
a comparatively small grain export company also based in Minneapolis at

the time. ADM was a pioneer in soybean processing, operating the nation's first solvent-extraction plant in 1934. By the mid-1960s, it had diversified, Glidden-like, into a wide portfolio of enterprises, including industrial chemicals. With profits slipping, it began to shed these sidelines, focus on its core business, and court the Andreas brothers to help improve its fortunes. In 1967, Lowell became executive vice president, effectively taking the reins from the nominal president, John H. Daniels. Dwayne became a director. By 1968, Lowell was president of the ADM board. In 1969, ADM acquired Interoceanic Corporation—and thereby the soybean-processing plant in Decatur, Illinois, that ADM had been leasing from Interoceanic—in a swap of company stock that gave the Andreas brothers control of 14 percent of ADM shares. In 1970, Dwayne became the company's CEO.

To signal the company's renewed focus on soybeans, Dwayne Andreas moved ADM's headquarters from Minneapolis to Decatur.[41] The move took place in the context of greater consolidation of the soybean processing industry. The number of plants had been dropping for years, from 193 in 1951 to a low of 123 in 1959, as many expeller plants were shuttered. By the early 1970s, the number ticked up to 131. At the same time, the overall capacity of the industry more than doubled, from 350 million bushels in 1951 to around 770 million bushels in 1970.[42] The shift to capital-intensive solvent extraction encouraged these economies of scale (see figure 7.1). Certain geographical locations—Decatur being a prime example—were favored by a longstanding policy of railroads known as "transit privilege," which for the purpose of freight discounts treated two separate journeys—of soybeans from grain terminal to processing plant, and of meal from processing plant to market—as one. This helped make it economical for plants to locate farther from the sources of beans and thus encouraged consolidation.[43] But the move also allowed Andreas to operate the company with a freer hand, as Decatur became increasingly an ADM company town. In 1989, his son, Michael, having been brought into the business, described it as "a kind of fraternity. It's important to keep things secret. . . . All our trading is done on the phone, and your word is your bond. When people come here for the first time and ask for instructions, I simply tell them to sit back, keep their eyes and ears open, and learn the Indian trails."[44]

ADM would ultimately seek to dominate the vast middle of the soybean supply chain, which converted raw beans into an ever-growing menu

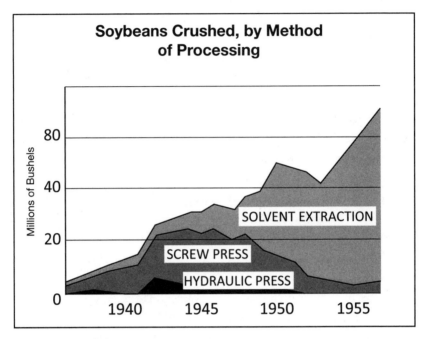

Figure 7.1. The shift to capital-intensive solvent extraction encouraged economies of scale. Source: USDA Agricultural Marketing Service.

of specialty protein and oil products and derivatives, as well as mixed feeds. Generally, these were commercial ingredients to be included in other foods, not retail products that called attention to themselves in supermarket aisles. There was one area, however, where Andreas made a concerted effort to raise the soybean's profile: a campaign to convince Americans to eat soy protein directly, as a substitute for meat, rather than indirectly through eating that same meat—to, in other words, convert soy from a feed into a food. The outcome from this effort only seemed to cement the fact, however, that soy was fated to remain in obscurity.

The Fabrication of Meat

By the time PL 480 became the Food for Peace Program, its chief rationale was no longer to dispose of surplus American commodities but instead to address world hunger. Both Hubert Humphrey and Dwayne Andreas argued that increasing America's agricultural output was necessary to address the problem. But whereas PL 480 focused on soybean oil, the problem of world hunger was increasingly posed not as a deficiency of calories—which oil could well address—but specifically as a deficiency of protein. Indeed, for the United Nations Food and Agriculture Organization (FAO), the 1960s would be the "protein decade."[45] One target was kwashiorkor, a fatal childhood disease in impoverished regions of Africa and Latin America, thought to be triggered by early weaning (*kwashiorkor* was a West African word meaning "the deposed child").[46] Medical researchers had determined that kwashiorkor could be successfully treated with skim milk, but this was in short supply in many of the worst-affected regions, compelling the FAO's Committee on Nutrition to call in 1955 for greater efforts to take locally available "protein-rich foods now used for animal feeding only" and convert them into viable foods for children.[47] This reflected a sense among nutritionists, dating back to the turn of the century, that supplies of animal protein could not keep up with population growth indefinitely; because "meat is vegetation at one remove," as one treatise from 1962 put it, "it should be possible in a scientific age to produce protein from plants, in assimilable, concentrated form, without the intervention of animals."[48]

Between 1955 and 1975, the Protein Advisory Group of FAO/UNICEF explored such options as "fish flour" or "fish protein concentrate" in places like Chile, whose fish-meal exports supplied much of the world's livestock feed. There were also experiments with producing "single-cell proteins" from yeasts, bacteria, and fungi.[49] Most of the Protein Advisory Group's efforts, however, focused on plant protein derived from oilseeds such as peanuts, cottonseed, and soybeans. India's government and commercial companies in Nigeria produced weaning foods from peanut flour, although there was an ongoing problem of carcinogenic aflatoxins secreted by fungi growing on improperly dried nuts. The Institute for Nutrition in Central America and Panama developed a cottonseed-based powder called Incaparina (based on its acronym, INCAP), which was marketed for several years in a number of Latin American countries. Soybean grits and flour, meanwhile, were the basis for Pronutro—which was developed in South Africa for low-income Bantu children but rose in price and fell in Bantu esteem when whites reportedly began buying it for their dogs—and Fortifex in Brazil, which consumers rejected as tasting too beany.[50]

There was a parallel push for the domestic American market by Adventist-run operations that had experimented for decades with meat analogs for vegetarians, as well as by large food-processing corporations betting that rising meat costs would create demand for lower-cost alternatives. Developing these alternatives had the additional attraction of offering a higher-value outlet for oilseed meal, much as margarine was a cheap but profitable outlet for the oil. As with soybean oil, there were efforts to eliminate bad tastes. Two products, in particular, seemed to promise a bland, pure protein that could be flavored and textured to a close approximation of meat: edible spun soy-protein isolate and extruded soy flour.

Both innovations had their origins with researchers formerly employed by Henry Ford. Robert A. Boyer, the wunderkind who created Ford's suit of soybean wool, realized as early as 1942 that, if the process were adjusted to keep it soft, the wool would resemble muscle fiber. Following Ford's death, Boyer left the soybean division, which was sold to the Drackett Company and subsequently to ADM. He obtained a patent for spun soy protein in 1949, and a broader one, including other vegetable proteins, in 1954. Swift employed him for a time, albeit in secrecy so as not to alarm livestock producers. At another company he produced meatless pork chops using corn gluten, the strong flavor of which ultimately hobbled the project. He also worked with Unilever to incorporate peanut-protein isolate in sausage. In 1956, he was hired by Worthington Foods, an Adventist company based in Ohio. Having acquired and consolidated the assets and patents of Madison Foods, Kellogg's Battle Creek Food Company, and Harry Miller's non-soymilk business, Worthington effectively split the Adventist food business with California-based Loma Linda Foods.[51] Worthington licensed Boyer's patent, enlisting large processors such as Ralston Purina, General Mills, and Nabisco to manufacture the protein for Worthington products. In 1962, Boyer joined Purina to create Textured Edi Pro, which Worthington incorporated into its Soyameat line of canned products such as Fried Chicken, Sliced Chicken, Diced Beef, and Salisbury Steak.[52] In 1965, General Mills test marketed Bac-o's, imitation bacon bits made from spun soy-protein isolate, which by 1969 had become the first soy-based meat analog to find broad commercial success.[53]

Bac-o's would eventually swap spun protein for a competing product, one originally developed by Boyer's colleague at Ford. William Atkinson had remained with the soybean division as it wended its way to ADM. Something like the plastic in Ford's famous soybean car, Atkinson's "thermoplastic" protein began with soy flour, mixed it with water under high pressure and temperature—producing a "plastic mass"—and then, in the words of ADM's patent, forced it through "flow-restricting orifices into a medium of lower pressure and temperature" so that the water would evaporate as steam. Unlike Boyer's spun product, this was not a true protein isolate, but when crumbled it could be rehydrated into something resembling ground meat.[54]

When he and his brother took control, Dwayne Andreas pushed ADM to market this "textured vegetable protein," which was later sold under the trademark TVP.[55] In the fall of 1967, guests at a dinner honoring the new president of the Chicago Board of Trade learned to their surprise that the "beef" stroganoff they "had savored so appreciatively" was actually TVP. Weeks later, at the Cologne Food Fair, ADM's manager of soybean specialties, James Sellner, prophesied that within two years it would be as successful a product as margarine.[56] Two years later, a story in the *Wall Street Journal* indicated, however, that soy meat might take longer to catch on. A housewife in Chicago complained that the flavor of analog fried chicken tasted "like it was painted on," while "underneath was that soybean taste." A "matron" in Fort Wayne, Indiana, meanwhile, reported that after a couple of bites of meatless bacon "my husband and I looked at each other and wrinkled our noses. Then I got up and threw the rest of the package out."[57]

The quest for fake meat continued despite the setbacks. A 1973 Reuters dispatch, coinciding with the release of the film *Soylent Green*, reflected the gee-whiz enthusiasm of food technologists: "Steak a la test tube, chicken a la laboratory—the science fiction menu is coming nearer." Reuters noted that twenty-five firms in the United States were producing artificial meat, "mostly from soya-bean flour," and that in Britain "a major textile group has begun marketing a synthetic meat made from bean protein—the fibrous texture makes it much more realistic and enjoyable than the American product." In this case, Courtaulds Ltd. imitated Boyer's work to produce Kesp (a phonetic acronym for Courtaulds's Edible Spun Protein), using fava beans rather than soybeans. On the more exotic end of the spectrum, an experimental plant set up by an unnamed "British combine" produced two tons a week of "golden fungus" A3-5, a "yellowish-brown substance contain[ing] twice as much high quality protein as good beef steak." In a nod to the movie, the article proclaimed that fungus A3-5 "could just as easily be colored GREEN!" And indeed, the impetus for this accelerating research and marketing was "meat prices rising everywhere."[58] Production of textured soy protein—spun and extruded combined—grew from almost nothing in 1967 to 30 million pounds in 1970, and then to more than 100 million pounds in 1973, causing one analyst to project that the figure would be 188 million pounds in 1975 and around 2 billion pounds by 1980.[59]

The market for soy meat fell short of expectations, however. In Britain, Kesp was pronounced such a fiasco by 1977 that, even though it did not use soybeans, its notoriety was blamed for giving TVP a bad name.[60] In the United States, Miles Laboratories (makers of Alka-Seltzer) acquired Worthington Foods and test-marketed a new line of meat analogs in 1972, launching the Morningstar Farms label in 1974 with a national advertising campaign. Its Breakfast Links, Breakfast Patties, and Breakfast Slices—later it would introduce Leanies, Grillers, and Luncheon Slices as well—were the first meat analogs beyond Bac-o's to reach supermarkets nationwide. Although an estimated 10 million American families tried the breakfast foods in the first year and a half, sales were disappointing, with Miles taking a pretax loss of $33 million on its meat substitutes.[61] Robert Boyer, when interviewed in 1980, attributed these failures in part to poor quality as manufacturers made compromises in equipment and processing to keep down costs. The marketed products were inferior in taste and texture to what researchers were able to achieve working by hand in the lab.[62] The other problem was that few of these substitutes were significantly cheaper than the products they imitated, especially as meat prices came down. With these failures, production of textured soy protein remained at around 100 million pounds in 1982,[63] much of it going into pet food.[64]

One bright spot was the use of TVP as an extender in soy-beef blends, which captured around 30 percent of the ground beef/hamburger market at the peak of beef prices in 1973. By March 1974, however, the share fell to 20 percent.[65] In general, this use of textured soy was sustained by the federal School Lunch Program, which changed its guidelines in 1970 to allow the use of extended meats with up to 30 percent TVP.[66] The program, serving a captive market and under tight budgetary constraints, would come to use 40 million pounds of textured protein a year.[67] This was largely a hidden ingredient, although the University of Massachusetts Cooperative Extension

Figure 7.2. Illustration of meat fabrication from 1975 brochure for schoolchildren, *Introducing Sammy Soy Bean.*

Service, for one, made an effort to familiarize children with the soybean. It issued a booklet, *Introducing Sammy Soy Bean*, that featured a cartoon bean ("Sammy Soy Bean," sporting a cowboy hat and cane) explaining the various uses of the soybean, with an emphasis on textured soy protein as "an important part of your food experience," as "it has been estimated that by 1980 extenders . . . will replace a significant amount of meat in our diets" (figure 7.2). There was no reference to tofu or other Asian soy foods apart from an image of one of Sammy's forebears wearing a conical hat. Despite the effort to appeal to Western sensibilities—"With a name like Sammy I felt I'd be more like one of your friends and not just a bean"—Sammy Soy Bean never caught on as a mascot for soy protein.[68]

The Soybean Embargo

One leg up for meat extenders in early 1973 was the increasing cost of food. Prices had gone up slowly but markedly in 1972. According to the Bureau of Labor Statistics, which computed the Consumer Price Index, food prices overall went up 5 percent in 1972, which included a 14 percent increase in the price of meat. In January 1973, however, food prices jumped 2.3 percent, the steepest one-month rise in twenty-two years, followed by a 2.4 percent rise in February and a 3.1 percent rise in March. James Trager, in *Amber Waves of Grain* (1973), recounted a typical scene on Lincoln's Birthday in 1973 at a Pathmark supermarket in Long Island. Meat and poultry prices, which had been inching up a few cents per week throughout 1972, had suddenly jumped by 10 or 20 cents per pound. A crowd of housewives gathered at the meat department. "They were indignant," recounted Trager. "They were scream-ing." A store manager, briefed by Pathmark headquarters, arrived to mollify the crowd. "It's the Russians," he explained.[69]

The manager was alluding to what would become known as the Great American Grain Robbery: the sale of $750 million of American wheat, corn, and other grains to the Soviet Union in July 1972 at government-subsidized prices, a tremendous windfall as well for grain exporters such as Cargill, Bunge Corporation, Continental Grain Company, Garnac Grain Company, and Cook Industries.[70] These were companies accustomed to keeping their secrets—some had been entangled in the Great Salad Oil Swindle a decade earlier, which was enabled by a similar lack of transparency—ensuring that the full extent of Russian purchases was unclear until ships carrying an esti-mated one-quarter of the US wheat harvest were departing from American shores.[71]

Soybeans were involved as well. One goal of the Russian buying spree was to allay public dissatisfaction in the Soviet Union by increasing the availability of meat to consumers.[72] This required feed crops. Ned Cook of Memphis-based Cook Industries managed to sell the Russians a mil-lion tons of soybeans in August 1972. In reports that Cook denied, he was said to have promised the Russians technical help in processing soybeans into feed.[73] The disappearance of soybeans into Russia was not the primary reason for a subsequent rise in prices. Overall exports of soybeans in 1971–1972 were, in fact, slightly down compared to the previous year.[74] But rising international demand more generally was a culprit. Consumers in Europe and Japan were buying more meat, pushing up sales of American feed crops, just as the Japanese American Soybean Institute would wish. Meanwhile, an El Niño weather pattern caused a shortfall in the catch of Peruvian anchovies, a major international source of fish meal fed to cattle.[75] Soybean exports went up from 11.3 million tons to 13 million tons in the 1972–1973 crop year,[76] along with a simultaneous rise in the price of meal. By the spring of 1973, the price of soybean meal had more than doubled from the previous year. The price of feed required to produce a pound of beef rose from 20 cents to as high as 28 cents.[77]

If the purchases by the Soviet Union were not solely to blame, they were the most visible cause, prompting what would later be considered a disastrous overreaction. Now the US president, Richard M. Nixon put the fight against inflation front and center in August 1971 when he announced his New Economic Policy. He declared a ninety-day freeze on prices and wages. This was paired with a devaluation of the dollar that turned out to be the beginning of the end for the postwar Bretton Woods system of fixed international exchange rates. These measures succeeded in stabilizing prices until the rapid rise of food prices in 1972—something that the devaluation of the dollar might have actually exacerbated by lowering the cost of American farm products on international markets. In response to consumer protests—and threats of boycotts—the Nixon administration imposed price ceilings on beef, lamb, and pork at the end of March, followed by a sixty-day freeze on all prices in June, during which time the government hoped to develop a new strategy for fighting inflation in America.

The Nixon administration's price freeze exempted basic agricultural inputs, which included feed grains and soybeans. This shifted the pain of rising prices from the consumer to ranchers and meat producers, who in turn threatened to minimize feed costs by drastically culling breeding stock, a decision that would only exacerbate meat shortages later on. It was in this context that the administration put in place a new reporting system to track overseas grain sales, mandating that American traders issue weekly announcements on their deals. This was seen as a first step in instituting stricter export controls. The shadowy world of international soybean-trading was now more visible to the White House, but the weekly snapshots it received turned out to be highly misleading. It appeared that the volume

of sales exceeded available supplies of soybeans: specifically, there were com-
mitments to export 1.8 million tons of soybeans from July 15 to August 30,
double the 0.9 million tons deemed available after domestic needs were
taken into account. What the White House missed was that many of these
deals were speculative, with the amount actually traded likely to go down
substantially after the usual cancellations and delays.[78] The government did
not yet realize this on June 27, however, when it imposed an export embargo
on soybeans—an unprecedented peacetime restriction on an American farm
commodity.[79]

This ban on soybean exports, which also encompassed cottonseed and
its products, lasted one week. A series of gradually loosening export controls then took its place, until all controls were removed on October 1. In
the meantime, the pain was again shifted upward in the chain of commerce,
this time from ranchers and meat producers to brokers and traders. Cash
soybean prices, which had begun the year around $5 per bushel, and which
peaked at over $12 per bushel early in June, now fell dramatically, to around
$6 per bushel.[80] Trade in Chicago ground to a standstill.[81] The ban was also
greeted with outrage by the nations cut off from expected supplies of soybeans. As the secretary general of the Japan Oilseed Processors Association
(JOPA) put it, "We are really angry at Nixon-san."[82] This outcome might not
have come at a big political cost to Nixon, except that the American Soybean
Association had been working with JOPA for a decade to increase Japanese consumption of fats and soybean-fed beef. American soybean farmers rightly worried about the long-term damage the embargo might cause.
Indeed, the embargo was later seen as a turning point in the international
soybean trade, as purchasing nations looked to other sources, such as Brazil,
after the United States proved to be an unreliable trading partner. At the
time, newspaper editorials were certainly unkind to the embargo, with the
Washington Post calling it a "staggering confession of incompetence"[83] and
pointing to the harm it might do to negotiations over farm prices with the
European Common Market.[84]

Whether Nixon ended up paying any political price for the embargo
of US soybean exports is uncertain. He faced bigger problems, not least of
which was the *Post* doggedly pursuing a trail that linked him to a break-in at
the Democratic National Committee headquarters. A key piece of evidence
in the Watergate scandal was a cashier's check for $25,000 made out to the

Nixon campaign. It was discovered in the bank account of Bernard Baker, one of the seven "plumbers" who conspired in the break-in. The source of the check was Dwayne Andreas, who was politically flexible enough to donate to the nemesis of his good friend Hubert Humphrey, at least during the presidential primary campaign season.[85] For the rest of his career, Andreas gave generously to both parties, but increasingly to the Republicans, with whom he arguably had a natural affinity, which would only grow when Ronald Reagan took office in 1981. Contributing as well to Nixon's troubles was an embargo imposed on the United States just as its soybean embargo was lifted. In October, the Organization of Petroleum Exporting Countries, or OPEC, proclaimed an oil embargo in retaliation for the US role in supplying weapons to Israel during the Yom Kippur War. If high food prices had not fully succeeded in instilling a sense of dystopian scarcity, long lines at the gas pump created a mood of crisis among American consumers.

It was in this context, with the counterculture message of living within the limits of nature gaining traction, that the American soybean rose to prominence in an entirely new way: not as a farm commodity mired in swindle and scandal, nor as a sign of a degraded standard of living, but as a healthy means to achieving a simpler, more natural lifestyle.

CHAPTER EIGHT

RISING INTO VIEW

Soylent Green, released in April 1973, is not really about soybeans. The term "soylent" was taken from the film's source material, Harry Harrison's 1966 book, *Make Room! Make Room!*, which imagined an overcrowded New York City on the brink of the year 2000. Having done extensive background re-search on the ways society might make do in a world of more people and scarcer resources, he featured soybean-lentil steaks in one scene as a plausi-ble and—at least to a young man raised on seaweed crackers and oatmeal—delicious fabricated meat. In the movie adaptation, Soylent became instead the plausible name of an evil, monopolistic corporation that offers an array of color-coded famine wafers. "Quick energy yellow soylent" is revealed, in a blink-or-you'll-miss-it shot of an outdoor marketplace, to be made of "genu-ine soybean." The soylent green product is said to be derived from pressed ocean plankton. As Thorn (Charlton Heston), the police detective at the center of the story, eventually discovers, however, the real source of soylent green is somewhat higher up on the food chain. As he shouts out in his dy-ing moments to a seemingly indifferent crowd, "Soylent green is . . . people!" Even as it veers away from actual soybeans, however, *Soylent Green* provides some clue of attitudes at the time toward the sort of fabricated food that Dwayne Andreas was eager to promote—and which Americans seemed re-luctant to incorporate into their daily lives.

Released three years after the relative optimism of the first Earth Day, *Soylent Green* depicts a population crisis that spells the end of nature and the worst imaginable dehumanization of people, all of which is conveyed by the horrific artificiality of the film's food. In one sequence, Thorn's aged roommate, Sol (Edward G. Robinson), exclaims "Beef!" at the sight of real meat, before breaking down and weeping, "Oh my God! How did we come to this?" Thorn and Sol then spend an evening slowly dining on authentic food, with an accompanying soundtrack of chamber music. This parallels Sol's death at a euthanasia center, where volunteers are treated to scenes of forests, deer, and sunsets, set to Beethoven's Symphony No. 6 ("Pastoral"), as they die. Witnessing the images from a viewing area, Thorn weeps in turn, "How could I know? How could I ever imagine?" He then tracks Sol's body to the soylent green factory, where there is nothing resembling nature. Rather, there is a system of pipes, vats, and conveyor belts—not unlike the array of devices that crush, deodorize, and process soybeans into protein isolate—that transform Sol into a batch of the eponymous green wafers. The film evokes the Holocaust, in part through Sol's Jewishness, but implies that such horrors would now be the outcome not of racial hatred but of modern efficiency. While Dwayne Andreas might have cheerfully imagined American technological ingenuity seamlessly providing meat substitutes as real meat inevitably became scarce, *Soylent Green* indicates that people might just as easily link this prospect with a declining standard of living, alienation from nature, and general dehumanization.

If these were indeed Americans' mental associations with soy-based foods—to the extent that people were aware of them at all—the future looked dim. It was at this moment, however, when an alternate vision of soybeans was gaining prominence, in which they were not a symptom of modernity's malaise but rather a remedy. Much as the soybean was a symbol of a different kind of industrialization for the chemurgy movement, the 1960s counterculture embraced traditional Asian soy foods as a way to express solidarity with the victimized peasants of Vietnam, to reject the inherent and interrelated violence of warfare and meat production, and to recapture a sense of craftwork in an age of mass production. The soy foods movement began in small pockets of the counterculture, notably the Tennessee commune named simply The Farm, but by the mid-1970s a vegetarian revival helped it gain momentum and even popular awareness through books such as *The Book of Tofu*. By the end of the decade, the movement was grappling with its own success, as it began accommodating itself to capitalist realities—at the same moment, it turned out, that soybean capitalism in its purest form, the trading floor of the Chicago Board of Trade, was reaching its historic peak.

Hippies

In 1974, the 600 residents of The Farm distributed a recruitment magazine, *Hey Beatnik! This Is the Farm Book*, describing life on the 1,700 acres near Summertown, Tennessee, where they had founded their utopian experiment. One section, "Foodage," was devoted to promoting vegetarian nutrition. Much of the information was derived from the World Health Organization, including a chart listing dozens of foods and how much of each of the twelve essential amino acids they each contained, with a quote from the *Proceedings of the Sixth Annual International Congress of Nutrition* explaining that "it is known today that the relative concentration of amino acids, particularly the essential ones, is the most important factor determining the biological value of protein." Soybeans, along with soy flour and soymilk, topped the list. As explained in a section titled "Yay, Soybeans!" since "soybeans have such high-quality protein, and so much of it, they should be your main staple. Eat them three times a week, as well as soymilk, soy cheese, and soy yogurt."

Soybean advocates had been pointing to its high-quality protein for decades, arguing that it was a cheap alternative to increasingly scarce meat, but the booklet noted an additional benefit of becoming a "complete vegetarian"—that is, vegan—once enabled to do so by the adoption of soy foods. "Since we can get everything we need from vegetable foodage, and since one can't get very telepathic or high eating those who are so close"—a reference to animals, close to us in the great chain of being—"it seems obvious that being a complete vegetarian is the kind and Holy way to make it."[1] Adventism had long mixed religion and nutrition in its arguments for soy foods, but this was something new. The hippies had discovered the soybean.

The story of The Farm began in San Francisco a decade earlier. The Bay Area was not the only source of the hippie movement. The Beat movement began in New York City, and the LSD experiments of Timothy Leary took place in Cambridge, Massachusetts. Zen Buddhism, which became a fad in the late 1950s and steadily attracted American adherents, likewise had bases on both coasts, in New York, Cambridge, and Los Angeles in addition to San

Francisco. The civil rights and antiwar movements, as well as the Baby Boom generation that energized them, were national in scope. But the Bay Area, in particular the Haight-Ashbury neighborhood of San Francisco, with its cheap Victorian housing, saw a unique confluence of Buddhism, drugs, protest, and psychedelic rock that, fed by media exposure, culminated in the Summer of Love of 1967. And it was from this milieu that Stephen Gaskin, founder of The Farm, emerged as a movement leader.

Like many leaders of the 1960s counterculture, Gaskin was older than many of his followers. Born in 1935, he had served with the Marines in the Korean War. In 1962, he was an instructor in English at San Francisco State College. He noticed students dropping out and followed them to Haight-Ashbury.[2] While smoking a variety of marijuana called Acapulco Gold, he discovered that he could become telepathic with others, creating a group high. He worked his way through LSD—which Ken Kesey had experienced as a volunteer for psychological experiments in 1959, then introduced to the wider Bay Area[3]—as well as peyote, psilocybin mushrooms, and numerous pharmaceuticals. While drugs were only one of a complex array of factors producing a counterculture, they were the catalyst for Gaskin. His philosophy evolved through voracious reading—science fiction, "books on weird mind disciplines," Zen writings, *The Tibetan Book of the Dead*, the Bible—while continuing to teach at San Francisco State. He was also influenced by Shunryu Suzuki, a *roshi* (or Zen priest) who welcomed non–Japanese Americans—many of whom had wandered from the Haight, seeking a grounding to their drug experiences—to the Soto Zen Mission in San Francisco.[4] Suzuki taught that the essence of Zen was its practice, and that to practice was simply to sit *zazen* in the traditional cross-legged pose and approach the world with a "beginner's mind." As Gaskin paraphrased it, enlightenment "is to live each moment afresh."[5]

Gaskin gradually developed a distinctive lingo, using "stoned" and "high" to refer to spiritual attainment, regardless of the assistance of drugs.[6] To truly get high meant to get beyond the "trips," rooted in unaddressed subconscious blockages, that could bring the whole group down. In 1966, in the wake of protests, students and some faculty there founded the Experimental College, an ongoing teach-in, and Gaskin signed on to teach a class during a vacant Monday slot. Dedicated to exploring the culture's spiritual awakening, he at first called the course "Group Experiments in Unified Field

Theory," then "Magic, Einstein, and God," then "North American White Witchcraft"—and, finally, simply "Monday Night Class." Six students attended the first semester, but Gaskin gradually gained a following of 2,000 spiritual seekers each week. Classes became wide-ranging sessions devoted, above all, to maintaining the group high—"we can all be really stoned in here together"—and creating a positive vibe in the moment. When the Haight-Ashbury scene turned sour, as an influx of newcomers and harder drugs overwhelmed the neighborhood, Gaskin decided to embark on a national speaking tour. More than 200 of his followers accompanied him, driving thirty old school buses in a four-month odyssey they called the caravan. The challenges of the road bonded them into a communal group that made their return to San Francisco in January 1971 a letdown. Thus, one Sunday morning in Sutro Park—Sunday Services had supplanted Monday Night Class—Gaskin announced that the caravan was going to Tennessee to find a farm.

Gaskin and others had publicly discussed a "farm thing" as early as December. Counterculture communes had in fact boomed during the previous four years, fed in part by disillusionment with the cities that had made the gathering together of like minds possible. "Whatever you put your attention on you get more of," Gaskin told his followers that Sunday morning. "I can't put my attention into a city scene anymore. Because the worst thing happening on the planet is the cities. Like the cities are the major cause of warfare, poverty, totalitarian police state, whatnot. All those things are functions of being crowded up in cities." He announced, "After services the caravan's going to take off to Tennessee and get a farm. Because what you put your attention into you get more of, and I need more trees, more grass, more wheat, more soybeans, more healthy babies, more good-looking sane people, people that can work. That's what I really want to see a lot more of and that's what I'm going to put my attention into."[7]

It is not clear exactly when soybeans became something Gaskin poured his attention into. Jerry Sealund, a close friend who ran a natural foods store, Far-Fetched Foods, in the Haight, later recalled that as early as 1964 Gaskin had "a great and powerful psychedelic vision of the soybean, in which he saw it as a great provider for all humankind."[8] By the time of the caravan, he was a vegan, explaining to an audience at Princeton that "there's a place where you get so high that you say, 'Okay, we're all one.' But if you're eating meat, you hang up there. Like how straight are you with something you're eating? . . . As far as the karma of it goes, I've been to animal killings and I've been to rice boilings and rice boilings got better vibes." He added, "I don't do dairy products because I feel that's just part of the meat system on another level. I don't do chicken or fish because they're just like cows except they live in different places." He mentioned that, as an alternative, "we've been into a lot of soybeans, soybeans are good for protein."[9] One member of The Farm later recalled that, during the summer of 1971, when the reconstituted caravan camped as guests on an abandoned farm before purchasing their own land, they spent "a ridiculous amount of money" on health-food groceries, including Soyagen milk, which Gaskin had enjoyed in California.[10] This was an Adventist product made by Loma Linda Foods from Harry Miller's formula.

When it came to actually growing soybeans, neighboring Tennessee farmers provided the essential know-how. The group's first conception of farming involved plowing with Belgian mares purchased from the local Amish, but they soon acquired a combine and a tractor.[11] Michael of the Farming Crew recounted in *Hey Beatnik!* that "learning mechanics and how the tractors run and how to plant straight rows and plow and disc ten-acre fields expanded our consciousness, because it took more real attention than we were used to putting out." They also made peace with some use of chemical fertilizer, even as they worked to build up the organic matter in the soil. Most of their garden and field crops, including sweet potatoes, okra, peas, and green beans, "were just what the neighbors grow. We've found out that if they don't grow it, it probably doesn't grow so well." Fortunately, soybeans were "grown all over, and most anywhere you move away from the city there'll be a half-dozen neighbors who grow soybeans and will tell you exactly how to do it."[12] This was a recent development, of course, especially in Tennessee and other southern states. It is an indication of how much the counterculture adoption of the soybean relied on the previous work of the USDA, agricultural experiment stations, and private growers.

For Gaskin and The Farm, soybeans were key to becoming "voluntary peasants."[13] The goal, which echoed Henry Ford's Village Enterprises, was to adapt and downscale modern technology in order to upgrade rural life. The hippies of The Farm communicated through CB radios, as well as an old-style phone exchange, and they used passive solar-heating features in their housing, eventually branching out to photovoltaics. Similarly, they assembled a diverse array of equipment to create what they termed their "soy dairy." After grinding soybeans into grits, they boiled them in a propane-fueled double-boiler made from a restaurant-sized coffee urn—purchased for $15 at an army auction—then separated the milk from the okara in a centrifuge jury-rigged from the spinning basket and basin of an old front-loading washing machine, held upright with a stand of two-by-fours. Aside from the addition of some vitamins and a little salt, there was no evident effort to improve the taste or quality of the milk. The milk was distributed throughout the community in cans and milk bottles at an estimated cost of 30 cents per gallon; it was also used to make yogurt, cheese, and ice cream. By 1974, their operation produced 60 gallons of soymilk per day.[14]

The need for soymilk was made more urgent by the numerous children born on The Farm. Gaskin taught against abortion or chemical contraception, which he felt "cheapened human life."[15] *Hey Beatnik!* put out a call: "Hey Ladies! Don't have an abortion, come to the Farm and we'll deliver your baby and take care of it, and if you decide you ever want it back, you can have it." Half of the babies born on The Farm, in fact, were to outsiders. Gaskin's wife led a group of certified midwives who delivered babies without anesthesia.[16] As the author of *Spiritual Midwifery* (1977), Ina May Gaskin has been widely regarded as the mother of the modern midwifery movement. The Farm encouraged breastfeeding, but the sheer abundance of babies created the need for a weaning food. Luckily, the midwives found that "babies love soymilk," although they counseled sterilizing it for younger babies, who had not yet developed "hearty stomachs," with an extra thirty minutes of boiling. This may have also made the milk more palatable and digestible.

It was to learn all he could about the use of soymilk as a weaning food that Alexander Lyon, a commune member with a PhD in biochemistry, ventured to libraries in upstate New York and stumbled, in the process, on what would become a notable focus of The Farm's soybean work.[17] He discovered work done in the 1960s on an Indonesian soy food, tempeh, by microbiologists at Cornell and the USDA Northern Regional Research Center in Peoria. Tempeh consists of dehulled soybeans, lightly cooked and then fermented into solid cakes using a white mold, *Rhizopus oligosporus*, which lends it a meaty taste and texture. In 1972, Lyon ordered starter mold from Cornell—a special strain, NRRL 2710, cultured from a pulverized sample of tempeh brought in by an Indonesian member of the research team[18]—and used it to make tempeh from okara, the soy pulp left over from milk production. In 1974, Gaskin visited Holland, which had ruled Indonesia as a colonial power, and tasted whole-bean tempeh, which he encouraged the soy dairy to produce. Lyon had by this time transferred to the Motor Pool, but his partner in tempeh-making, Cynthia Bates, set up a laboratory to make powdered, pure-culture tempeh starter. The food became a favorite on the commune, and the starter was widely distributed elsewhere through the mail. The first commercial tempeh shops in the United States were developed, in fact, by those who learned how to make it at The Farm, and by 1984 the Tempeh Lab would supply more than half of all the starter used in the United States.[19]

Bates oversaw an expansion of the soy dairy as it moved into the community's canning and freezing building. She helped develop *Yay Soybeans*, a fourteen-page booklet of recipes that included okara "soysage," soy cheese (fermented tofu), tofu cheesecake, soy ice cream ("Ice Bean"), soymilk mayonnaise, and okara granola. Many of these, along with tempeh recipes, were included in *The Farm Vegetarian Cookbook*, published by The Book Publishing Company in 1975, which became a staple, along with *The Tassajara Bread Book* (1970) and *Diet for a Small Planet* (1971), on the shelves of vegetarians and natural foods enthusiasts. By 1978, the soy dairy had expanded commercially as Farm Foods, which offered not only tempeh kits but also bags of whole soybeans and soy flour, nigari, and Ice Bean. It also offered Good for Ya Textured Vegetable Protein, which it could not market as TVP because of ADM's trademark.[20] As different as the two organizations were, The Farm shared ADM's confidence that soy foods would ultimately prevail because of inescapable constraints on the expansion of meat. As *Hey Beatnik!* put it: "Here's a spiritual reason for being a vegetarian: You can get ten times as much protein growing soybeans than raising beef cattle. If everyone was vegetarian, there would already be enough to go around, and no one would be hungry."[21] It was not long before The Farm put the theory into practice in a dramatic way.

In 1974, The Farm founded Plenty, a nonprofit corporation, whose charter stated that its mission was "to help share out the world's food, resources, materials, and knowledge equitably for the benefit of all."[22] Plenty began by providing food and other help in the wake of tornadoes and hurricanes in the United States. The 1976 earthquake in Guatemala, killing 23,000 and leaving hundreds of thousands homeless, compelled Plenty to delve into international disaster relief. Two volunteers, one of whom spoke Spanish and had worked in the Farm Clinic, flew down to Guatemala City to distribute several large shipments of medicine and medical equipment gleaned through a network of sister communities and urban contacts. The Guatemalan army, treated the Plenty volunteers like foreign dignitaries and drove them around the highlands in military trucks to deliver food and supplies, but the Plenty emissaries protested when their hosts insisted on diverting a shipment to a military, rather than a civilian, hospital. They returned to The Farm "completely mind-blown," both by the destruction and poverty they had witnessed and by the grace of the Mayan people whom, stunningly attired in rainbow-colored fabrics, they considered "long-lost psychedelic cousins."[23]

Alerted to the dire need for housing in the wake of the earthquake, The Farm sent three of its best carpenters, who were soon hired by the Canadian embassy to make use of 700 tons of building materials. Over the next four years, rotations of some 200 Plenty volunteers, with the generous support of the Canadian government, built 1,200 homes, twelve schools, and a number of clinics, water systems, and CB base stations in two Guatemalan villages, as well as a two-story *municipalidad indigenes* community center that included an FM radio station that broadcast in Cakchiquel Mayan.[24] Soon there were plans for a soy dairy.

One of the Plenty volunteers, Darryl Jordan, felt that "The Noble Bean" could greatly benefit villagers forced to cultivate marginal land (photo 12). There were also numerous malnourished babies, some of whom volunteers were able to nourish back to health with The Farm's soy-based infant formula.[25] Jordan faced the challenge, however, of finding a variety that could thrive in the highland tropics, whose climate combined short days and cool temperatures. He obtained the seeds of more than twenty varieties from INTSOY, based at the National Soybean Research Laboratory at the University of Illinois. Having conducted soybean trials in the tropics since 1973, INTSOY computed the yields of Jordan's trials. A variety named Improved Pelican had already shown promise on the coast of Guatemala, but it did not yield well at high elevations. Many of the varieties that Jordan planted had been developed by Hartwig and his colleagues for the American South, including a number of the Confederate cultivars: Davis, Forrest, Ransom, and Bragg. Davis and Forrest ranked among the top four in terms of yield. The

Photo 12. Plenty agricultural technician Darryl Jordan talks to Mayan farmers in their soybean field in the late 1970s. Photograph by David Frohman, reprinted courtesy of Plenty International.

delegation of hippies, knowingly or not, recommended that Mayans plant a soybean named after a Grand Wizard of the Ku Klux Klan.[26]

The ultimate value of the beans would rest on whether the indigenous people were willing to eat them, so Plenty did extension work as part of what became its Integrated Soy Project. Suzy Jenkins, a "soy utilization technician," taught four women at a time in the Itzapan home of a Mayan apprentice, Becilia, who translated from Spanish to Cakchiquel. Students learned simple techniques for making soymilk and tofu using readily available utensils. After soaking overnight, soybeans were boiled over an open fire and ground, if a mill or blender were not available, on the same stone *metate* used to grind corn for tortillas. The puree was then boiled again and strained into a bowl, which could then be consumed as soymilk. To make tofu, the demonstrators used vinegar as a curdling agent and simply strained the curds through cheesecloth. The result was a mound of soft tofu, rather than a compressed cube. Sliced, it resembled local farmer's cheese in appearance, though not in taste. The tofu was then scrambled in a pan with sautéed onions, tomatoes, and salt or eaten plain with a little salt on tortillas or bread. The "soy pulp," or okara, could also be fried with onions and vegetables. Students were sent home with cheesecloth and a small bag of soybeans, initially from a 1,500-pound supply donated by UNICEF. Suzy and Becilia taught hundreds of women this way, then trained eighteen Mayans to carry on the work. By 1980, more than a thousand men and women in seventy-four villages had been taught how to make soymilk and tofu. Two hundred of these grew small plots of soybeans.[27]

The program culminated in the construction of a soy dairy for the village of San Bartolo in the summer and fall of 1979. With the help of the Canadian International Development Agency, Plenty enlisted local masons to complete the 22-by-44-foot cinder-block building, designed as a split-level so that the strained soymilk could be gravity-fed to the lower floor where it was turned into tofu. The Farm supplied equipment—stainless-steel cooking kettles, industrial blenders, and a soft-serve ice-cream maker—while the grinding mill was supplied locally. The cauldrons were fueled by sawdust waste from local sawmills. After an inauguration attended by several hundred people, La Lecheria produced 200 pounds of tofu and 35 gallons of Ice Bean daily, with some of the ice cream handed out free to school lunch programs.[28] The dairy was eventually managed by locals and remained in operation. One of the volunteers who helped build the plant commented twenty years later that it continued to "pump out high-protein food," and you could "see the difference in the kids around the village. They are bigger, stronger, more energetic, and bright-eyed."[29]

La Lecheria was a legacy that outlasted Plenty's presence in Guatemala. With the 1980 election of Ronald Reagan in the United States, the Guatemalan government's war against guerrilla fighters intensified. There were more soldiers in the streets, roadblocks at the entrances to towns, helicopters flying over Plenty's camp in search of guerrilla fighters operating in the mountains, and killings by death squads. The local people that Plenty worked with began to receive threats. Plenty helped some to relocate elsewhere in Guatemala, or even up to Tennessee on student visas, but worried about drawing further attention from the death squads. In 1981, Plenty left Guatemala behind.[30] The next decade would also see the end of The Farm as a communal experiment. Although the land continued to be held in trust, members were responsible for their own incomes and finances, and the population dropped from a peak of 1,500 to around 250. Although a mounting communal debt was due largely to the altruism of ventures like Plenty—unlike some gurus of the 1970s, Gaskin continued to live in the same conditions of his followers—Farm residents began to question their leader's role in setting the spiritual and material direction of the community.

Mostly, they grew tired of living in third world conditions rather than the promised, upgraded version of traditional village life. As one member later reflected, "I think that if at that time we had been able to build the town and been able to live within the graceful standard of living that we had envisioned as 'voluntary peasants,' a lot of us would not have left. We were so close yet so far."[31]

Popularizers

The Farm was a small social experiment whose engagement with the soybean depended on many prior decades of work by university researchers, agricultural extension agents, and American farmers. The fact that it could reach a broader public with some of its offerings was testament to its participation in a broader movement popularizing soy foods. This in turn followed the emergence of the environmental movement and the resulting experimentation of many Americans with vegetarianism. This involved a two-step of fear and hope. Paul Ehrlich's *The Population Bomb* was a best-seller in 1968, warning of famine and environmental degradation linked to the inexorable rise in global population. It came out too late to help the initial sales of Harry Harrison's *Make Room! Make Room!*, but Ehrlich wrote the introduction to the 1973 edition that accompanied the release of *Soylent Green*. In line with Harrison's book, Ehrlich noted in particular the likely rise in urban populations and the consequent decline in the standard of living to what he not-so-subtly characterized as Asiatic: "Tokyo Bay is frantically being filled with garbage in order to obtain land for expansion of a city already so crowded that there is a two-year wait for middle class apartments. Calcutta today has hundreds of thousands of people living homeless in the streets. . . . By 2023 everyone would live in an urban area, and by 2044 everyone would live in cities with a million or more population."[32] Harrison's book portrayed a future plagued by kwashiorkor, the often deadly childhood disease attributed at the time to severe protein deficiency.

The hope came in the form of Frances Moore Lappé's vegetarian polemic and cookbook *Diet for a Small Planet*, first published in 1971 and then, with even broader impact, as a Ballantine paperback in 1975. Lappé argued that there was plenty of protein to go around, even at current levels of agricultural production, if only people stopped consuming so much of it secondhand from meat. She noted that a cow consumed 21 pounds of protein for every pound of protein it provided as food, a "protein factory in reverse."[33] This argument might be irrelevant if humans were simply not able to eat enough plant food in a single day to meet protein requirements, but Lappé emphasized that getting enough protein was in fact easy, especially with "protein combination," the practice of consuming, for instance, grains and legumes in one meal to obtain a full complement of essential amino acids. Soy foods did not figure prominently, however. Lappé lauded tofu for the high quality of its protein, which more closely matched the requirements of the human body than the protein of most other beans or bean products, and she included a number of recipes that contained bean curd as an ingredient. She noted, however, that while it could be purchased in "many parts of the country," tofu was not universally available—and that her own "single attempt" to make it had failed.[34] The overall thrust of her argument, in any case, was that sufficient protein could be obtained from combinations of common foods, no exotic miracle food required.

Vegetarianism had other popularizers, notably the comedian and activist Dick Gregory in the African American community. He published *Dick Gregory's Natural Diet for Folks Who Eat: Cookin' with Mother Nature* in 1973, guided by Alvenia Fulton, who had opened the Fultonia Health Center on Chicago's South Side in 1966. She was trained in naturopathy, which shared many of Adventism's food traditions, and was photographed as early as 1969 helping Gregory end an extended protest fast with, among other things, "soybean chicken" fashioned to look like a drumstick.[35] Beyond a recipe for soymilk that might have come from *Back to Eden*, Gregory as well was not too interested in soybeans. At the same time, interest in exotic foods was on the rise in America, which included global ethnic foods generally and, following Nixon's opening of China, authentic Chinese food specifically. It was an opportune time to publish a Lappé-style book on traditional soy foods, and William Shurtleff and Akiko Aoyagi did just that in 1975 with *The Book of Tofu*.

William Shurtleff took a winding path to his eventual fame as a popularizer of tofu. He came from a leading California family with roots extending back in America to the Puritans of New England. His grandfather Roy graduated from the University of California in 1912—the future chief justice Earl Warren was a classmate—and went on to help found the San Francisco brokerage firm Blyth, Witter & Co. Both he and Shurtleff's father became millionaires.[36] Shurtleff gained a love of wilderness at the family's summer cabin on Echo Lake, in the Sierra Nevada Mountains. He attended Stanford University, where in 1963 he earned degrees in industrial engineering and honors humanities, and spent six months near Stuttgart at Stanford's Overseas Campus.[37] As a Peace Corps volunteer in Nigeria, he spent six weeks in Gabon visiting the compound of Albert Schweitzer, someone whose writings he had long admired and whose love and care of animals influenced his decision to become a vegetarian (even as he was clear-eyed about Schweitzer's evident callousness toward Africans).[38] After a second year in the Peace Corps, Shurtleff returned to Stanford to pursue an MA in education. His idealism having gradually become more radical, he joined Palo Alto's Peace and Liberation Commune. Within the commune, he became part of what one member recalled as a group of "aspiring Buddhists, with diets of brown rice, meditation as a regular ritual, and various other attempts to fine-tune their karma."[39]

Shurtleff took a course in Japanese art in the spring of 1967, traveling to Japan that summer and subsequently directing a branch of the Esalen Institute, a center of East-West awareness and the human-potential movement, at Stanford. After hosting Michio Kushi, a Japanese teacher of macrobiotics, he committed to becoming a vegetarian.[40] In 1968, he entered the Tassajara Zen Mountain Center as a student of Shunryu Suzuki, whose

Zen Center in San Francisco introduced Japanese Buddhist philosophy to
many Americans, including Stephen Gaskin. The 1970 publication of *The
Tassajara Bread Book*, by Edward Espe Brown, popularized the monastery's
simple fare. With his interest in food and macrobiotics, Shurtleff worked in
the kitchen as well. In 1969, he wrote and distributed a photocopied book
to friends at Christmas called "The Tassajara Food Trip," which included
four recipes that called for tofu, as well as those that used miso and whole
soybeans.[41] Tofu was not, however, the focus of Tassajara cuisine. The macrobiotic system, developed by the Japanese philosopher and self-taught nutritionist George Ohsawa and predicated on a balanced diet of yin and yang
foods, moreover considered tofu overly yin—and not a true "whole food,"
due to the removal of the okara.[42]

Where Buddhism and macrobiotics failed to lead Shurtleff to tofu, a
stint as a poor student in Japan succeeded. In 1971, he attended Tokyo's
Christian University to study Japanese, with the ultimate aim of assisting
Suzuki in establishing a retreat in Japan similar to Tassajara. Tofu—cheap,
nourishing, and easily procured—became a mainstay of his diet. When Suzuki died suddenly, Shurtleff was left to search for a new mission. Akiko
Aoyagi, a Japanese woman nine years his junior, was similarly at loose ends.
An illustrator and clothing designer starting out in the Tokyo fashion world,
she was dissatisfied with her career. As she later explained to *Mother Earth*
magazine, "I was always looking for more meaning in my life. I was looking
for a way to serve my fellow man." She contemplated traveling to Africa as
an international aid worker and was therefore intrigued by Shurtleff's Peace
Corps experiences when her sister, who attended Christian University, introduced the two.[43] One evening, they enjoyed a meal at a renowned haute-
cuisine restaurant in which each of twelve artistically presented small dishes
featured tofu in a different guise. The total bill was the equivalent of $2.75
per person. That was the night, as Shurtleff later recounted, that *The Book
of Tofu* was born.[44]

Tofu appealed to both the Buddhist and the engineer in Shurtleff. In
Tokyo, it was frequently a temple food: silky soft and of purest white, protein at its most rarified, a rebuke to the bloodiness of meat. Shurtleff was
equally impressed by the many forms that tofu could take, as indicated by
his experience at the restaurant, but equally on display in even small shops:
soft tofu custards, grilled tofu steaks, as many as three different kinds of

deep-fried tofu alone.[45] It was a cheap and nutritionally dense raw material for creating an endless variety of foods, an engineer's delight. Shurtleff was not interested in simply eating tofu as a spiritual practice, or even in promoting it as a food beneficial for humankind. He wanted to delve into the technical details of how it worked, from its creation to its elaboration into its diverse end products.

Following their restaurant meal, Shurtleff and Aoyagi visited their neighborhood tofu shop at the owner's invitation. It was the craft involved, even more than the product, that impressed them, the precise and graceful movements that "flowed like a dance" in a compact space at most 12 by 15 feet in size. The tools were "simple and energy non-intensive." After repeated visits, Shurtleff asked to become a disciple and apprentice and subsequently spent more than a year learning the traditional techniques. His master urged him to "record the methodology and, if possible, the spirit of his art both for Westerners seeking meaningful work and for future generations of Japanese who might someday wish to rediscover the rewards of fine craftsmanship presently obscured by modern industrial values and the 'economic miracle.'"[46] He also visited other tofu makers, including modern factories, to glean as much information as possible, and in the warm months he and Aoyagi would hitchhike the length of Japan. There were still 38,000 small tofu shops in Japan, where it was made using traditional tools, and they were grateful to observe methods that tofu artisans had traditionally shrouded in secrecy.

In the spring of 1973, they set out to discover the origins of the craft: farmhouse tofu, the kind that Tsuru Yamauchi presumably made as a young girl in Okinawa at the turn of the century. By the 1970s, it was the stuff of nostalgic legend among tofu makers. So firm that you could tie it into a bundle with rice-straw rope, it was said to have a deeply satisfying flavor. To find it, even in remote villages, was nearly impossible. Shurtleff and Aoyagi donned backpacks and hitchhiked to the picturesque mountain village of Shirakawa-go, where the closest they could get to the traditional food was the temple's attic museum; an energetic old woman showed them the traditional tools and explained how they were used. Nobody under seventy had actually made it, and women over seventy, finding the heavy grindstones increasingly difficult to turn and the ingredients increasingly hard to obtain, now bought their tofu from a shop that had opened in the neighboring village.

Finally, the couple arrived in one village at just the right moment to watch two women making a batch of tofu to commemorate a dead friend. The beans were ground into gô, sprinkled with rice bran to settle the foam as it cooked, then transferred to a pressing sack set on a rack made from tree limbs. The resulting milk was curdled with store-bought nigari and pressed in a settling box weighted by a large rock. Then, without soaking it in water, the tofu-maker cut it into small pieces for tasting. The flavor "was graced with the faintest aftertaste of woodsmoke," and it possessed "a firmness and slight coarseness of texture quite unlike the soft, smooth tofu common to the cities," as well as a beige color and a smell that preserved "a fine edge of bouquet." The outcome of authentic craft, it embodied and shared "completely in the total configuration out of which it had been born. The wine-sweet morning air, the water drawn from the deep farmhouse well, the pleasure of communal down-home craftsmanship all participated in its essence."[47]

The Book of Tofu took three years to complete. In addition to documenting how tofu was produced as an ingredient, the pair stood at the elbow of chefs at Japanese restaurants and, through trial and frequent error, replicated recipes at home. They ultimately prepared 1,200 different dishes, including 500 recipes "suited to Western tastes."[48] Aoyagi, a talented cook, eventually developed Western-style dishes: dips, dressings, casseroles, barbequed tofu, and deep-fried tofu burgers. Their recipes made use not just of various types of tofu itself—silken, grilled, frozen—but of all of the intermediary foods leading up to tofu: soybeans themselves ("Soybeans in Tortillas"), gô ("Thick Onion Soup with Gô"), okara ("Okara Croquettes"), soymilk ("Soymilk Mayonnaise Dressing"), and curds ("Warm Soymilk Curds").[49] In addition to recipes, Aoyagi provided illustrations that subtly evoked Japanese wood prints: black-and-white line drawings of shops, tools, and craftspeople that were highly detailed yet simple and clean, fitting complements to Shurtleff's precise prose.

Released at the end of 1975 by Autumn Press, a small publisher of Zen and macrobiotic books, *The Book of Tofu* was a hit. During its first year in print, it sold 40,000 copies and did almost as well during its second year. Ballantine later released it as a mass-market paperback.[50] Shurtleff and Aoyagi soon completed a second book, *The Book of Miso*. To promote both volumes, in September 1976 they hit the road on a four-month, cross-country tour of the burgeoning vegetarian and natural-foods circuit, traveling in a

Photo 13. William Shurtleff and Akiko Aoyagi embarking on the Tofu and Miso Tour, 1976. Courtesy of Soyinfo Center.

white Dodge van with "Tofu & Miso America Tour 1976–77" painted on its side (photo 13).[51] They envisioned their mission as "trying to do for soyfoods what Johnny Appleseed did for apples." They delivered seventy lectures and cooking demonstrations to more than 3,500 people in thirty-two states. Their largest audience, 300 people, was at the Wedge Food Co-op in Minneapolis. In addition to their books, they offered a home tofu-making kit based on designs from *The Book of Tofu*: a mahogany forming box, a muslin pressing sack, cloths, a packet of natural nigari, and an instruction booklet, all for $11.95.[52] Shurtleff stopped over at The Farm for two weeks. A speaking event there went rather badly, with him noting cryptically in his log that there was "heavy confrontation with Farm folks about how they didn't like my way," but he was able to work with Cynthia Bates on a four-page pamphlet titled "What Is Tempeh?" This was the seed for a later book, *The Book of Tempeh* (1979).

In an interview with *Mother Earth News*, Shurtleff drew the connection between their work and the issue of world hunger. He recounted traveling in Taiwan, where the population had not yet adopted a Western-style diet of meat, eggs, milk, McDonald's, and Kentucky Fried Chicken. "Everyone in Taiwan bases his or her diet on tofu and soy milk," Shurtleff noted. "And

even though there are twice as many people per cultivated acre of land in
Taiwan as per cultivated acre in Bangladesh, everyone in Taiwan is well fed."
Up to that time, Shurtleff "had been thinking more in terms of bringing the
Zen of tofu making to the United States," but now he "suddenly realized—
click!—this is relevant to everyone." He was inspired to begin the book with
a section titled "Tofu: Food for Mankind," in which he argued that there was
no population or food crisis. He blamed world hunger not on scarcity but on
surplus. Agribusiness in the United States had promoted resource-intensive
foods such as meat precisely to absorb a glut of grain and soybeans, a model
that was then internationalized through the Green Revolution. Like The
Farm, he looked to soybeans as a way to achieve abundance without recourse
to industrial agriculture and its "rape of the planet."[53]

With this broad outlook, Shurtleff was willing to forgive the saddening
displacement of traditional tofu shops in Japan by large factories that mass-
produced tofu with stainless-steel, automated machinery. The output was
not "as good as the tofu made fresh each morning in the little shops," but he
did not judge the Japanese for proudly embracing the new technology. "How
can I criticize the Japanese for using factories to produce so much of the tofu
that they now consume? At least they're eating mostly tofu instead of meat
. . . which means they're getting almost all their protein eight or ten times
more efficiently than we're getting ours. How can I criticize a people that still
has so much to teach us?"[54]

As they toured the country, Shurtleff and Aoyagi worked on a rough
draft of The Book of Tofu's lesser known follow-up, Tofu and Soymilk Production (1979), which indicated the couple's evolving vision of tofu production.
They still extolled the traditional Japanese shop as the source of "the most
delicious tofu" and the exemplar of "the most beautiful feeling of craftsmanship" but noted that it was only viable when a large number of nearby customers ate tofu regularly, permitting the tofu to be retailed directly from
the store.[55] While offering detailed advice and schematics for all scales of
production, including "village" shops appropriate mainly for communes, the
book argued that the best model for medium-sized commercial operations
was the "Pressure-Cooker Plant," which had come to represent almost half
of the tofu producers in Japan itself.[56] Able to turn out up to 3,700 pounds
of tofu each day, pressure-cooker plants used stainless-steal equipment either imported from Japan or, more commonly, improvised from American

equipment normally intended for other uses.⁵⁷ The Rietz Stainless Disintegrator, for example, typically used for pulping fruits and vegetables, was suitable for grinding beans, and the Brown No. 2203 Extractor could just as effectively separate soymilk from okara as fruit juice from pulp.⁵⁸ Aoyagi took great care to render complicated arrays of modern equipment, such as "carousel curding machines," in elegant black-and-white drawings. Larger machinery was used at the next two scales of operation: the "Soy Dairy" and "Modern Factory."

Tofu and Soymilk Production accommodated its outlook to the realities of American capitalism. The first chapter was devoted to sound business practices, such things as how to choose "a good location and area and estimating the market potential," how to deal with "health inspectors, sanitation, safety, and standards," and advice for "choosing a business name or logo" (examples of good choices were The Cow of China, The Soy Plant, and The Joy of Soy). A section titled "Starting a Business and Right Livelihood"—which cautioned that six out of ten new businesses failed within five years, with the potential "loss of all one's savings, home, and even personal possessions"—made peace with the profit motive. "We view money as a form of energy which, like other forms of energy[,] should be treated with due respect and used creatively to accomplish worthwhile objectives. Profits are often the most accurate measurement of a business' success in accomplishing its objectives." This perhaps represented a rapprochement on Shurtleff's part to the outlook of his capitalist father and grandfather. Right livelihood could be practiced by businesspeople running large enterprises, as well as small-scale craftspeople. In either case, the book emphasized that "when the master becomes selfless, the tofu makes itself."⁵⁹

During their tour, Shurtleff and Aoyagi visited and inspired Richard and Kathy Leviton, the owners of the Corncreek Bakery in South Deerfield, Massachusetts. The Levitons, with two other partners, rented a 1,000-square-foot shop in nearby Millers Creek to make tofu. While using stainless-steel equipment where necessary, they soaked the beans in cedar barrels typically used for lobsters and extracted the soymilk with a solid-oak cider press, giving the factory a rustic New England feel. Originally named the Laughing Grasshopper Tofu Shop, it started producing up to 1,000 pounds of tofu per week beginning in January 1977. The wooden equipment tended to warp and absorb some of the curd, which then rotted, and it took a superhuman effort

to hoist the pressing sacks into the cider press. The town library, located in
the same building, complained of the smell. "Only willpower and dedication
kept us going," one of the managers later remarked.[60] Nevertheless, with
demand strong, the company was producing 7,000 pounds of tofu per week
by the beginning of 1978. By this time, they had incorporated under a new
name, the New England Soy Dairy, and had moved to a new location where
they installed a pressure-cooker system purchased from Japan. They upgraded the equipment again in the early 1980s and by 1982 produced almost
40,000 pounds of tofu per week. If this expansion belied strict adherence
to their originally stated goal of producing "high-quality natural nigari tofu
in the traditional Japanese way using small-is-beautiful technology,"[61] it signaled the maturation of a new soyfood industry.

Variously called "soycrafters" or, following The Farm's lead, "soy dairies,"
these new, Caucasian-run plants outnumbered Asian tofu manufacturers in
North America by the middle of 1978, although the latter still produced
the lion's share of tofu by volume. In 1975, by contrast, there had been only
fifty-five tofu makers in the United States, all Asian.[62] In 1978, the Shurtleff-
Aoyagis and Levitons joined others to found the Soycrafters Association of
North America (SANA), which espoused a distinctive set of values.[63] Unlike most Asian tofu makers, who used calcium sulfate as a curdling agent,
soycrafters used traditional nigari, which they argued retained more protein
in the tofu.[64] Soycrafters were also critical of modern meat analogs. They
opposed the use of solvent extraction to separate the oil from the meal, not
trusting assurances that the toxic hexane could be thoroughly removed from
the meal. Above all, they objected to soybeans being hidden as "functional
ingredients or extenders to be used in other products." Soycrafters wanted
the soybean to be out and proud. They saw no point in pretending "you are
eating meat, poultry, or fish, when soyfoods taste so much better."[65] Finally,
as much as their operations might shift to larger machinery, they remained
committed to the use of "appropriate technology" that was less energy-
intensive and more people-centered and key to improving conditions in the
third world.[66] Commitment to such principles would set the stage for tensions—between holism and commercialism, craft and industrial production—as the industry sought to grow.

In early 1977, circling back toward home on their Tofu and Miso Tour,
Shurtleff and Aoyagi became aware for the first time of the extent of the

nation's existing Japanese American tofu industry. In Los Angeles, Shurtleff had dinner one evening with Shoan Yamauchi, the son of Tsuru Yamauchi. In 1940, Tsuru and her husband had taken over a small tofu and noodle shop in Honolulu, Aala Tofu, which provided them a good living during the meat and food shortages of World War II—when Japanese Americans in Hawaii avoided the fate of those interned on the mainland—and which Tsuru largely ran herself after the war with the help of her sons, including Shoan, a returning veteran.[67] It was Shoan's brother, Shojin, however, who largely took over the business in Hawaii, while Shoan and his wife moved to California in 1946. They purchased the Hinode Tofu Co. in Los Angeles, introducing products common in Hawaii but as yet unfamiliar on the mainland: Chinese-style tofu, silken tofu, and deep-fried tofu pouches.[68]

In 1958, Shoan innovated further by packaging tofu cakes individually in plastic bags filled with water and sealed with a heat sealer, then placed in the white cartons with wire handles that during World War II had become widely used for Chinese takeout.[69] This step was spurred by a new regulation in Los Angeles requiring tofu to be sold in individual containers. It also enabled Hinode to sell its product in Boy's Market, the first supermarket chain to offer tofu. Yamauchi approached the Sealright Company to devise a waterproof plastic tray for his tofu deep enough to hold 28 ounces and capable of being made by high-speed machines that met the challenge of heat-sealing containers brimming with water. The result, debuted in 1966, proved enduring and eventually iconic, despite drawbacks—printing was possible only on the top flap of the packaging—and even as competing forms of packaging later tried to edge them out.[70] In 1963, Hinode had bought out a competitor to become Matsuda-Hinode, the largest tofu manufacturer on the mainland.

Partly as a result of Shoan Yamauchi's aggressive marketing and innovative packaging, tofu gained a following among non-Asians several years before *The Book of Tofu*. In a 1968 newspaper article, which reported that "although tofu is far from becoming an American household word, the number of Americans eating the product appears to be increasing, at least in the Los Angeles area," Yamauchi testified that "about 10 years ago, 95 per cent of our users were Japanese, with all purchases made in neighborhood stores. Now only about 50 per cent of all tofu customers are Oriental, and most chain stores sell it in their delicatessen sections." This resulted in sales of more than

1 million packages of tofu, a 15 percent increase over the previous year. Low
cost was cited as one reason for its crossover appeal, its "high protein content
and digestibility" being another, leading to its use in two area hospitals as a
meat substitute for heart patients.[71] Los Angeles was also a center of Adventist food production, including tofu-like offerings. Despite his early advantage in the mainstream market, however, Yamauchi was keenly aware that
the new wave of interest in tofu among whites during the mid-1970s would
revolutionize his business, even as most of his Japanese American colleagues
remained indifferent or hostile to the soy-dairy movement.

Yamauchi was so taken with Shurtleff's mission, in fact, that, in a parking
lot after dinner one evening, he handed him an envelope full of cash, containing perhaps several hundred dollars, Yamauchi's "way of saying thank you for
the work" he and Aoyagi "were doing on behalf of tofu."[72] Thus did the son
of a picture bride become a patron of the descendent of seventeenth-century
New England Puritans. This small exchange marked the moment when tofu
and other Asian soy foods crossed over into American culture, in a way that
they had failed to do when largely confined to an ethnic subculture. And
Yamauchi was not wrong: in the end, Japanese American tofu makers would
be among the chief beneficiaries of the food's high profile.

Market Movers

Even as the soy dairy movement gained momentum, its use of soybeans represented a small fraction of US production. As Shurtleff and others were
keenly aware, soybean protein was still overwhelmingly consumed by way
of its inefficient conversion into animal protein, and soybeans were less the
underpinnings of a new utopia than of the capitalist wheeling and dealing
of commodity exchanges. At the same time, exchanges such as the Chicago
Board of Trade responded to the same global trends that soy promoters
found both troubling and hopeful: there was an increase in the global demand
for protein, as a result of rising population and in some areas rising affluence,
and therefore the prospect of potential shortages. The soyfoods movement
might suggest that direct consumption of soybean protein might ease the
situation, but the market response instead was to increase production of

feed grains. And while this maintained the invisibility of soybeans in the food chain, it enhanced their visibility in the financial world.

Of all American crops, the soybean was the one most governed by the whims of the free market, with low government-support prices leaving it up to the Chicago Board of Trade and other exchanges to set international prices, and thus was the most sensitive to changing conditions around the world. Complicating this picture was the rise of the Brazilian soybean industry after the Nixon administration's 1973 embargo prompted the Japanese to increase purchases from Brazil and to invest directly in expanding its soybean-crushing capacity. Brazilian competition, especially in soybean meal, was sufficient to undermine the US position as a near-monopoly supplier. The overall effect in the late 1970s was not simply an expansion of trade but also a marked rise in price volatility, as weather in Brazil—and to a lesser extent Argentina—now mattered as much as the weather in Illinois. As one portrayal of the Chicago Board of Trade put it, the "bean market suffers the exchanges' most mercurial outbursts, neurotic flights and dips."[73] At the Board of Trade, the octagonal bean pit thus became, in the 1970s and into the early 1980s, the arena of greatest risk and excitement, especially when compared to corn, described as a "dependable brown-bagger, coming to work every day, on time, doing a job free of temperamental extremes." In an era before the board of trade expanded into more exotic derivatives, such as currency markets, soybean trading was the center of flashy, capitalist excess, attracting the group that one author would dub the "New Gatsbys." Soybeans, despite their own lack of glamour, were the glamour crop of the commodity markets.

All the same, the most successful trader of the era, who spent most of his time in the bean pit, was decidedly low-key and pointedly frumpy. Richard Dennis, even as he was dubbed the "Prince of the Pit," in fact shared a fair number of personality traits with members of the soy counterculture, including the attempt at Zen-like detachment in the face of market volatility. Balding with thick glasses, he eschewed ostentatious displays of wealth, unlike the typical trader, choosing instead to dwell "in a kind of pecuniary purgatory, preferring the more ascetic life," as one account put it.[74] Even as he amassed millions—"his money tends to pile up, unused," according to a profile in the New York Times—he lived with his parents on Chicago's

South Side, drove "an old, inexpensive car," and dressed "in clothes of cheap knit."[75]

In the bean pit itself, this sense of detachment became his trading ethic. He traded, as he put it, "at the edge," anticipating the next fraction-of-a-penny move in futures prices just before it happened, then reaping the rewards as the rest of the floor followed him. On successful days, this allowed him to buy contracts at their lowest point, then sell them as prices moved upward. He believed in the importance of understanding mob psychology and working against one's own impulse to "go wherever the mob takes you. You have to separate yourself from it in this business." And again, he thought it crucial to understand people's tendency to self-destruct: "I think it's far more important to know what Freud thinks about death wishes than what Milton Friedman thinks about deficit spending." He did not trade on the fundamentals—that is, by paying attention to natural and economic factors—but on a disinterested sense of where the collective mind of the market was headed next. He preferred to enter the pit with a "lingering cold or a mild depression," or even the rare hangover, in order to dampen his own emotional responses. The volatile bean pit was an obvious place to deploy this strategy, a trading focus that was reinforced as his stature on the exchange grew, for the simple reason that his unexpected appearance in the wheat pit, for instance, would in and of itself move the market.[76]

He increasingly did his trading from home, where he could deal in wheat and silver over the phone without spooking other traders, even though this restricted his view of the floor action. By the early 1980s, when he was worth an estimated $50 million, he worked from an office nineteen stories above the trading floor. A $150,000 mainframe computer crunched data through the night to assist him in his "technical" pricing formulas, based on the theory that "certain cycles and patterns repeat themselves." He still dismissed fundamentals, like the amount of rain in Iowa, as "fluff"—and he still drove a "beat up 1977 Mercedes" and hiked "his polyester pants over his substantial waist."[77] He used his money to fund side projects, including a liberal Washington think tank to study policy issues and, closer to home, a project to teach neophyte students, whom he called his "turtles," his trend-following system, mainly to prove that it could be taught.[78] His turtles reportedly made an aggregate profit of $175 million by the time the five-year

experiment ended. Dennis himself retired from trading, however, after in-
curring heavy losses in the 1987 Wall Street crash.

The prospect of high returns for gambling on soybeans also attracted
more typically flamboyant characters. Ned Cook was the brash scion of
Cook Industries, the Memphis-based cotton-trading company his father
had built.[79] He took over the company at a time when the South was in transition away from cotton, toward corn and soybeans—a shift enabled by the
Confederate cultivars developed by Edgar Hartwig and his colleagues at the
USDA's Agricultural Research Service. It was Cook who, during the Soviets'
1972 grain-buying spree, managed to sell them a million tons of soybeans,
at the same time making his fortune by going "long" on soybeans—buying
soybean futures at the same time he was buying soybeans—a double bet on
rising prices for which he had good reason to be confident. Unlike Dennis,
Cook had no compunction about flaunting his wealth, traveling the world
on his Lockheed JetStar. At the same time, he had moved from the parochial
and, by its own lights, gentlemanly world of cotton trading to the cloak-
and-dagger realm of the international grain trade. In 1976, Cook Industries
was indicted for its part in an industrywide underloading scandal—in which
cargoes of grains and soybeans loaded in New Orleans were systematically
skimmed, in particular when bound for ports in developing countries—
although the commodity adviser who had arranged the scheme in 1970, Phil
McCaull, had left the company by 1972. It was also in 1976 that the staff who
Cook had hired to replace McCaull, whom he called his "whiz kids," decided
to go "short" on soybeans the following year, betting on a glut that would
drive down prices.

The senior vice president in charge of daily trading, Willard Sparks,
was like Dennis in that his decisions were data-driven and often contrar-
ian, based on detecting when short-term moves of the market were out of
step with long-term trends. Unlike Dennis, however, he did not attempt to
anticipate the volatile ups and downs of the market just before they happened; instead he stuck doggedly in the spring of 1977 to his sense that
soybeans were overpriced. Brazil played a part in confounding Sparks's predictions, as its farmers unexpectedly withheld their bumper crop of beans
from the market. In previous years, they had released their beans during the
Northern Hemisphere spring—near the time of the harvest in the Southern

Hemisphere—only to see prices rise through July, prior to the new US harvest. In 1977, Brazilian farmers instead decided to wait at just the wrong time for Cook and Sparks and, as it turned out, to their own detriment: in 1977, soybean prices peaked in the spring and fell throughout the summer.[80] Cook's whiz kids suspected that the Brazilian government was taking a long position in the futures market to artificially prop up international soybean prices, but he became aware too late that the threat came from a place much closer to home. Bunker Hunt, an heir to a Texas oil fortune who was an even brasher and more flamboyant gambler than Ned Cook, was buying up soybean futures even as he amassed physical soybeans, an apparent attempt to corner the market. Hunt evaded the 3-billion-bushel limit placed on speculators by the Chicago Board of Trade by enlisting other members of his extended family to amass 21 billion bushels in all.

Even after Cook, tipped off to Hunt's activities, reported this activity to the US Commodity Futures Trading Commission (CFTC)—the successor to the largely ineffective Commodity Exchange Authority—and even after the CFTC announced during a press conference that the Hunts held more than 20 billion bushels of beans in defiance of the speculative limit, there was no rush to sell soybean futures. The Hunts refused to sell their contracts without a fight in court, and the rest of the market bet on their success. The price of soybean futures remained high. In the meantime, Cook was required to deposit the full amount of his paper losses with the board of trade as the price moved against him—the same requirement that had brought down Tino De Angelis in 1963. By May 1977, Cook had exhausted hundreds of millions of dollars' worth of credit at fifty banks, and in June he suspended the trading of Cook Industries stock. Within a year, the company was dismantled, a process completed in June 1978 when Mitsui & Co. bought eight grain elevators for $53 million, giving the Japanese company the secure foothold it sought in its upstream supply of grain and soybeans.[81] Even as Shurtleff and Aoyagi sought to emulate the Japanese in their tofu consumption, the Japanese were pursuing soybeans in part to feed a growing number of cattle.[82]

As the 1980s began, the rise of the Brazilian soybean industry, which had its origins with one US embargo, blunted the effects of another. This time it was a broader grain embargo put in place by President Jimmy Carter in 1980 against the Soviet Union in response to the Soviet invasion of

Photo 14. Tote board at Chicago Board of Trade, showing soybean prices down during Soviet embargo, 1980. Bettman/Contributor/Getty Images.

Afghanistan (photo 14). Unlike Nixon's embargo, Carter's was wholly political. Unlike Nixon, he initially gained political support, even from farm states—he handily won the Iowa caucuses that year—as the public deferred to the commander in chief during a sense of national emergency that had less to do with the Soviet incursion than the Iranian hostage crisis. There is no indication that the embargo had its intended effect, however, as other countries undermined its impact by selling grain to the Soviets. In the case of soybeans, Brazil diverted much of its harvest to the Soviets, while Americans sold to the overseas customers who would normally have purchased beans from Brazil. It ended up being an elaborate game of musical chairs, with enough chairs to go around. Meanwhile, the political goodwill toward Carter did not last the year.[83] If the embargo did not ultimately harm American exports, the decade that it kicked off would nonetheless be a difficult one for American soy. A combination of domestic recession and debt crises overseas, as well as government supports for other crops that would make planting soybeans less profitable in comparison,[84] led to a prolonged dip in the acreage devoted to soybeans. This was unprecedented in the postwar era. Meanwhile, just as commodity soybeans were entering a slump, the utopian soy movement showed signs of becoming big business.

CHAPTER NINE

CRESTING THE PEAK

In 1981, around eight months into the Reagan presidency, the administration's penchant for slashing budgets provoked outrage in an unlikely way when it seemingly proposed including ketchup as a vegetable for the purposes of public school lunches. It was a display of Orwellian language. It was the heartless theft of wholesome food from children. It evoked Oliver Twist and Marie Antoinette. And, like many things that spark angry public reactions, it did not exactly happen that way. Facing a billion-dollar budget cut to the National School Lunch Program, the USDA's Food and Nutrition Service convened a task force to consider greater flexibility in standards to allow schools to either shrink servings or to meet nutritional requirements with a greater variety of foods. Ketchup, used as an ingredient, was briefly considered for eligibility as a vegetable portion, but it did not make the final cut, which was released in early September 1981. A lawyer, however, unwisely added clarifying language to the rules stating that schools "could credit a condiment such as pickle relish as a vegetable."[1] An advocacy group, the Food Research and Action Center, then formulated a nightmare offering—a small hamburger on half a roll, with nine grapes, a glass of milk, and six French fries smothered in ketchup—that, it argued, fulfilled the requirements for two vegetables under the new standard. The point was as much about reduced portions as it was about substitutions, but the image of ketchup took hold, giving the impression that President Reagan himself did not understand, or care about, the nutritional difference between a fresh tomato and a packet of Heinz.[2]

While the ketchup scandal would be cited for decades to come, it has been largely forgotten that this was also a controversy about tofu. Among the input that the task force received from school-lunch administrators was a request, reportedly from a district with a significant Asian presence, that soybean curd be eligible as a meat. It was duly added to a list that included peanut butter, cottage cheese, yogurt, nuts, and other high-protein foods deemed the equivalent of some portion of the meat allotment. In the mockery that followed, however, tofu was coequal to ketchup. "WHEN IS KETCHUP A VEGETABLE?" the *Washington Post* asked in one headline. "WHEN TOFU IS MEAT." A follow-up editorial criticized Reagan's "nouvelle cuisine for kids" for allowing tofu to qualify as meat, daring readers to "try that on your second grader."[3] A number of readers defended the proposal, arguing in letters to the editor that "including items such as tofu, peanuts and yogurt, viable and nutritious sources of protein, does not lead to unhealthy diets as hinted in the article" and that such foods "should not be labeled as 'meat substitutes,' but as protein suppliers in and of themselves." A Virginia couple confessed bemusement at being "radical health-food-vegetarian-hippies" who agreed with a Reagan policy.[4] A later *Post* editorial even acknowledged that "tofu has lots of protein," its main defect being that "it sounds funny to most people."[5] The irony, of course, was that the meat to be replaced by tofu itself contained a fair amount of soy in the form of textured vegetable protein—just ask Sammy Soy Bean.

The new standards were ignominiously scuttled, a warning to future bureaucrats. Regarding tofu, however, exceptions were carved out for Hawaii, where tofu was said to be "as common as peanut butter," as well as for forty schools included in a New York City pilot program to offer "meatless meats."[6] USDA officials did not dare to propose loosening requirements to allow tofu until 1999, when the justification was to provide healthier options, not to cut costs.[7] The schools that adopted the new framework had mixed experiences. Organic produce and stir-fried tofu failed to entice students at a high school in, of all places, Berkeley, California, whereas a student in Bridgehampton, New York, "found himself eating tofu regularly."[8] A food-service director in a Mesa, Arizona, school likely voiced the consensus viewpoint when she stated: "I can't see putting tofu on a student's plate and having a good acceptance. I can see taking a product that's familiar with the students and enhancing it with a larger amount of soy and having it be acceptable."[9] After twenty years, and on the brink of a new millennium, it seemed a matter of *plus ça change, plus c'est la même chose.*

In the intervening decades, however, much had changed for the soybean. Despite the knee-jerk disdain voiced by the *Washington Post*, tofu emerged from the 1970s with a reputation as a valuable health food. In the 1980s, tofu enthusiasts had high hopes that it might be diversified into a range of foods that would successfully appeal to a broader public. Whether tofu could truly become a health-food success on par with yogurt was up for debate, but its fame did provide an opening for soy more generally in the marketplace. By the 1990s, with news about possible added health benefits, "soy" started appearing on the front of labels, not just hidden on the back in ingredient lists. But even as soy gained public approval, there were signs of a backlash late in the century, rooted at first in fears of genetically modified crops. Would 1999 represent peak soy?

The Next Yogurt

With the soy-dairy boom of the 1970s came the need—as it had several times before in the history of the American soybean—for an overarching organization. In 1920 it was the American Soybean Association, in 1930 the National Soybean Processors Association. In the postwar era, there were the ad hoc meetings of government and industry scientists to address flavor reversion in soybean oil. In the case of the fledgling "soyfoods" industry—a term coined in 1976 by Surata Soyfoods in Eugene, Oregon, and eventually adopted by other tofu, miso, and tempeh makers—the moment arrived during the summer of 1978 in Ann Arbor, Michigan. At the invitation of The Soy Plant, seventy-five people attended the first conference of the Soycrafters Association of North America. Included among the attendees were twenty tofu-shop owners, of which only two were Asian. The lecture and discussion sessions were largely impromptu, the vegetarian meals were informal, and the organizational goals established were basic: to facilitate communication, to compile statistics and a library of resources, and to provide information to the public and media. The next summer, a larger and more ambitious follow-up conference ("Producing and Marketing Soyfoods") took place in Amherst, Massachusetts, where more than 200 participants shared a strong sense that soyfoods would break free of its niche status in the next decade.[10] It was a common refrain, as it would be throughout the 1980s, that tofu in particular was poised to become the "next yogurt," a health food that had recently gone mainstream in a big way. Soycrafters, it seemed, were ready to make the transition from hippie to yuppie.

In his address to the conference, William Shurtleff urged that the nascent industry organize itself effectively to face challenges and marketing opportunities. He likened its position to Hobbits in a world of dark forces that could overwhelm them: possible FDA restrictions on the use of nigari or the production of tofu; media coverage that might overhype and then promptly forget about soyfoods; and big corporations poised to steal their profitable ideas. The solution, he urged, was a strong association able to play a role analogous to the Milk Council: shaping the image of its products over decades, promoting their virtues in public schools, and influencing legislation. As a counterexample, he held up the Japanese National Tofu Association, "thirty-eight thousand individual tofu producers who have never gotten their heads together" or disseminated information beyond a "funky newsletter." When new restrictions on fishing in international waters suddenly reduced the supply of fish in Japan, he pointed out, there were no television ads proclaiming "now that you have no more fish to eat, return to your really good protein source, tofu"—because there was no effective trade organization to take advantage of the situation.[11]

Nevertheless, and despite emerging from a counterculture that embraced cooperation and spiritual solidarity, there was some reluctance in the audience to band together to pursue joint interests. During a roundtable discussion on the topic of competition and cooperation, Steve Demos, of WhiteWave Foods (now DanoneWave) near Boulder, Colorado, while praising the "spirit of exchange," was uncomfortable with the idea of sitting "beside someone you're competing with and actually handing him information you know will help his business grow," insisting instead that "you must maintain certain things in your business that you have proprietary interest over." Implicit in Demos's discomfort was a recognition that the tofu market in America was unlikely to ever resemble the 38,000 tofu shops in Japan, which another panelist embraced as the "gas-station-on-every-corner, tofu-shop" ideal.[12] Rather, Demos projected future growth to be located in supermarkets—and, beyond that, in institutions such as schools, hospitals, and "old peoples' homes"—where competition for market share would favor the most efficient producers. In a later interview with *Soyfoods* magazine, Demos pointed out that "if you reach only 1 percent of the clientele of a supermarket," it is a far larger customer base than "a market penetration of 15 percent of the natural foods community." One Denver-area supermarket alone moved 2,000 pounds of tofu out of the 7,500 pounds that White Wave produced each week. With more aggressive marketing, Demos hoped to increase production to 20,000 pounds a week.[13]

Demos and other tofu promoters were not the only ones bullish on the prospects of tofu as a supermarket staple. In May 1981, the New York marketing firm FIND/SVP issued a 139-page report, "The Tofu Market: Overview of a High-Potential Industry," which drew an explicit parallel to the history of yogurt. Yogurt, it noted, had been sold in the United States for decades, but production only took off in the early 1970s, growing from 50 million pounds in 1955 to around 580 million pounds in 1978. Similarly, it projected that the tofu market could grow from $50 million in 1981 to $200 million in 1986.[14] Like yogurt, tofu appealed to increasingly health-conscious consumers.[15] Another advantage was tofu's low cost, $1.10 per pound, compared to $1.50 for hamburger, $3.00 for fish, or 71 cents for chicken (including bones)—one reason for its attractiveness, as one news source noted, to the USDA school lunch task force.[16] One sign that Americans might begin treating tofu as a supermarket staple—like eggs, ground beef, chicken, or milk—was the proliferation of new tofu cookbooks. These included *The Tofu Cookbook*, for gourmet cooks wishing to incorporate tofu into "international-style" dishes, and *The Great American Tofu Cookbook*, which sought to Americanize tofu by using it in familiar recipes, in the same way that earlier generations had sought to Americanize the soybean itself. Tellingly, while *The Tofu Cookbook* included instructions for making tofu, *The Great American Tofu Cookbook* did not, instead assuming its availability in nearby grocery stores.[17]

However, as FIND/SVP recounted, the key moment in the rise of yogurt had occurred in 1968 with the addition of sweetened fruit flavors. In 1981, even as sales were buoyed by rising interest in healthy and natural foods, yogurt was eaten "mainly for its taste."[18] One of the selling points of tofu as an ingredient, by contrast, was that its taste was supremely bland.

Yogurt also benefited from the American lifestyle becoming "faster paced." There were more households in which two parents worked, and those who worked were putting in longer hours, taking time away from food preparation and the leisurely enjoyment of meals at home. Yogurt was convenient and portable, a wholesome snack or, in a pinch, meal. Tofu was unlikely to duplicate any of these features unless it was transformed into what the soy-foods industry dubbed "second-generation products," packaged ready-to-eat foods that used tofu as their main ingredient. Or, as Larry Needham of Bean Machines in Bodega, California, put it during the 1981 conference, soycrafters should "consider tofu as a raw material," not market it primarily as a finished product: "Tofu is just a starting point."[19] Tofu was an interchangeable commodity, while second-generation products were likely what Demos had in mind when he spoke of his proprietary interests. Anyone who established a first-mover advantage with a hot new dip, spread, or frozen dessert could win market share for years to come.

The proving ground for second-generation products was the soy deli (photo 15). Many of these delis, cafés, and restaurants evolved from, or alongside, soy dairies in the late 1970s. Some changed their names to reflect a new marketing strategy.[20] The Tofu Shop of Telluride, Colorado, became Far Pavilions. The Tofu Shop of Rochester, New York, became the Lotus Café. Steve Demos changed The Cow of China to The Good Belly Deli, which promised to supplant fast food with "real food, real fast." It offered soy versions of familiar offerings: Dairyless Tofu Pizza, Tofuna (mock tuna), Tofu "Meatball" Sandwiches, Tofu Turnovers, Soy Coconut Creme Pie, Tofu-Fruit Pies, Tofu Cinnamon Rolls, and Tempeh Sloppy Joe.[21] Likewise, the Lotus Café, which grew into a forty-seat restaurant serving 200 people daily by 1981, featured moussaka, manicotti, enchiladas, and stroganoff, all made with tofu or tempeh—as well as Creamy Tofu Dips, Tofu Burgers, Tempeh Reubens, Tofu Spinach Pies, Tofu Carob Mint Pie, Okara Peanut Butter Cookies, and more. By the end of 1981, there were nineteen soy delis, cafés, and restaurants in North America, including three in Canada, with combined yearly retail sales of around $1.5 million.[22] By mid-decade, there were new additions, including Soul Vegetarian East on the South Side of Chicago, operated by the vegan religious group African Hebrew Israelites of Jerusalem, offering healthy versions of traditional soul foods made with an

Photo 15. Northern Soy Deli, 1979. Copies of *The Book of Tofu* are for sale at the counter. Courtesy of Soyinfo Center.

array of soy ingredients.[23] By and large, however, the hope was not simply to run a successful deli but also to create new products that might break through to supermarket shelves.

As it happened, the breakout second-generation product of the decade came from a kosher deli. In the early 1970s, David Mintz, owner of Mintz's Buffet in New York City, sought to make beef stroganoff without sour cream to avoid the prohibition under Jewish law against mixing meat and milk. As he later enjoyed recounting, "everything I tried tasted just awful" until he read about tofu in a health magazine. Like other soyfood pioneers before him, he ventured to Chinatown, "picked up a pail of tofu and started experimenting." These experiments yielded a palatable tofu sour cream—at least when included in highly spiced recipes such as stroganoff—followed by tofu lasagna, tofu pancakes, tofu bran muffins, tofu Caesar salad, tofu cheese dips, and tofu quiche. "Discovering tofu was like discovering America; it opened a whole new world." Some of his more devout customers suspected him of violating dietary laws, so he tacked up a flyer to his wall, "WHAT IS TOFU?" He also spread the word at a Weight Watchers meeting he attended, promoting a dairy-free, tofu-based lifestyle as good in its own right: cholesterol-free and low in fat and calories.[24]

The greatest challenge came in creating a dairy-like dessert that successfully counteracted the beany taste and firm texture of tofu. Like Harry Miller before him, he became an obsessive tinkerer, leaping out of bed in the middle of the night to pursue a sudden idea. Like Harry Miller, he also emphasized the unprecedented nature of his eventual product, citing a university food technologist who told him soy desserts had been tried and never worked. In fact, tofu ice cream in America had a lineage stretching back to a patent in 1922, filed by a Chinese American, for "Frozen Confection and Process of Making Same." Adventists, including Miller, had been experimenting with soybean ice cream since the 1930s, the decade when Henry Ford offered his soy ice cream at the 1934 World's Fair. The Farm produced Ice Bean by the late 1970s, and Mintz's fellow kosher caterers, who had offered nondairy water ice since the 1920s, had introduced nondairy ice creams using soy protein as early as the 1950s. New York State established a standard in 1969 for what it called "parevine," a portmanteau of "pareve"—a term for foods deemed kosher by virtue of not being made with either milk or meat—and "margarine."[25]

Mintz was determined, however, to outdo other kosher frozen desserts in his product's taste and overall hedonic appeal. He finally achieved this through tricks like adding apple juice to enhance the taste of strawberries and counter that of tofu. Soon he was selling his tofu Ice Kreme in packages out of a separate freezer in his deli. In 1981, he came up with the more upscale name, Tofutti, aimed to appeal to yuppies avidly consuming Häagen-Dazs. Then, at age fifty, he decided to sell his deli and pursue Tofutti full time, at first supplying health-food stores and Mt. Sinai Hospital. His big break came with an order from Bloomingdale's. By 1986, with Häagen-Dazs itself selling Tofutti at its 28,000 parlors nationwide, Mintz had moved operations from Brooklyn to Rahway, New Jersey, and was pulling in $17 million per year in revenues.[26] While it generally raised the profile of tofu, with Mintz regularly featured in newspaper and magazine articles about soyfoods, the crossover success of Tofutti also seemed to fulfill the misgivings of those who, at the 1981 Soycrafters Conference, nervously eyed representatives in attendance from Kraft, Land O'Lakes, Dannon, and Beatrice. Would mainstream success mean, as it so often did in the 1980s, that some would grow big while others went bust? Would it require sacrificing integrity and authenticity?

Mark Medoff, writing for *Whole Life Times*, soon exposed that Tofutti in fact contained little or no tofu.[27] As he scaled up production, Mintz had found it easier instead to work with isolated soy protein, which had made its way into food products more generally by that time. Isolated protein did not have tofu's beany taste and was less perishable. In the absence of any FDA standard for tofu, it was not only Tofutti but also some of its imitators—including LeTofu, a California brand, and Gloria Vanderbilt's Glacé, from a partnership between the celebrity jeans designer and the New Jersey company Frusen Glädjé—that used protein isolates instead. Gary Barat, president of the American Soyfoods Association, complained that companies wanted "to say that they're using tofu when they're not because it's a terrific marketing angle." Tofu makers found themselves in the position of the butter industry in the 1940s during its fight against yellow margarine: they objected to imitation products piggybacking on the healthy image of tofu. Nonetheless, fearful that stringent regulation would hinder all attempts to more widely market tofu, the American Soyfoods Association hoped that the industry could police itself. Mintz ultimately agreed to add small amounts of real tofu back into his product, although he denied that the decision was a response to outside pressure. It was listed as the fourth or fifth ingredient, depending on the flavor, after water, high-fructose corn sweeteners, and corn oil but before protein isolates.[28]

Despite the controversy, Tofutti found lasting success. This was not true of the decade's most straightforward attempt to emulate yogurt's success. In 1982, the legendary Dannon executive Juan Metzger, the person most responsible for the rise of yogurt itself, joined the board of the New England Soy Dairy, now renamed Tomsun Foods, to unfurl plans for a revolutionary new product: Jofu, custardy tofu mixed with fruit, to be sold in single-serving yogurt containers. In 1986, Tomsun test-marketed Jofu in New England, raised cash through a public stock offering, and prepared to launch Jofu in the New York City metropolitan area. In the subsequent marketing blitz, it followed Tofutti's lead. In addition to linking the product to tofu through its name—its main competitor at the time was Soygurt—the ads emphasized Jofu's hedonic appeal with the tagline "LUSCIOUS. CREAMY.

AND LOADED WITH FRUIT." It balanced this with a negative-nutrition message about everything it was not. It was "lower in calories" with "absolutely no cholesterol." Also lower in sodium and saturated fats, while high in calcium and protein, it had "less of what you don't want, and more of what you do." It was "BEYOND YOGURT" (photo 16). If anything, the campaign was too effective, as more orders from stores poured in than Tomsun was equipped to fulfill. The company lost $2 million in 1987 even as its sales rose to $3.6 million. With the focus on its second-generation blockbuster, it also largely ceded its bread-and-butter tofu business in New England to its competitor, Nasoya. In 1988, it declared bankruptcy.[29]

Meanwhile, competition to supply supermarkets with basic tofu heated up, with the most efficient companies having the edge. Chief among these, especially on the West Coast, were Japanese American tofu companies, along with companies based in Japan itself. By 1984, Hinode Tofu in Los Angeles was processing 180 bushels of soybeans each day, a volume that allowed it to invest in pasteurizing its product to prevent souring.[30] Hinode, owned by Shoan Yamauchi—whose gratuity to Shurtleff in 1977 seemed increasingly justified—had recently merged with the Japanese-owned House Food Industrial Company, Ltd.[31] Addressing a growing non-Asian customer base, Hinode sought to Americanize tofu, presenting recipes for such things as Tofu Lambless Stew in its advertising.[32] Morinaga Nutritional Foods Inc. of Los Angeles, a subsidiary of Morinaga Milk Industry Company, Ltd., of Japan, bested Hinode's pasteurization in 1986 by introducing its Mori-Nu brand *ultra*-pasteurized tofu. This came in an aseptic Tetra Brik carton, of the type used for Parmalat and many brands of soymilk, with a shelf life of ten months "without preservation, irradiation, or refrigeration."[33] Morinaga's marketing campaign turned vicious in 1989 when it ran an ad in health-food and produce trade magazines labeling the now-traditional tubs of tofu "Water Hazards" and its own packaging a "Life Preserver." Art Mio, Morinaga's national sales manager, wrote to health inspectors and the FDA, encouraging them to crack down on spoiled tofu in produce aisles, perhaps hoping to force supermarkets to transfer the tubs to better-refrigerated dairy cases where customers were not used to finding them.[34]

The competition was intense in part because the market for tofu was showing signs of saturation. In 1984, the *Chain Marketing & Management* newsletter had predicted that tofu sales would grow from $50 million in 1982

IT'S TIME TO GO BEYOND YOGURT.

Jofu™ is here. Luscious. Creamy. And loaded with fruit.

Jofu is made from tofu, so it's lower in calories, yet more filling. And, unlike yogurt, it has absolutely no cholesterol, no lactose (it's dairy-free), and no sour, yogurt taste. You'll love it from your first, fruit-filled spoonful.

Jofu is also lower in sodium and saturated fats, but high in calcium, protein, iron and vitamins.

It's got less of what you don't want, and more of what you do.

Jofu. In 9 great fruit flavors. You'll find it in the dairy section. Just beyond yogurt.

ONLY 165 CALORIES

STRAWBERRY
LACTOSE FREE   CHOLESTEROL FREE

© Tomsun Foods, Inc 1986

℗ PARVE

MANUFACTURER'S COUPON/EXP. DATE. Dec. 31. 1987

BUY ONE, GET ONE FREE.

TO THE DEALER: For each coupon you accept as our authorized agent, we will pay you the shelf price of this product plus 8¢ handling allowance, provided you and your customer have complied with the terms of this offer. Any other application constitutes fraud. Invoices showing your purchase of sufficient stock to cover all coupons must be shown upon request. Void if prohibited, taxed or restricted. Cash value 1/20 of 1 cent. This coupon may be redeemed by mailing to: JOFU Coupons, Box 1050, Greenfield, MA 01302. LIMIT: One coupon per purchase.

BUY ONE, GET ONE FREE.

Jofu ®

LUSCIOUS
TOFU AND FRUIT
BEYOND YOGURT

NYT4/29

Photo 16. Jofu ad in the *New York Times*, 1987.

to $200 million in 1988—"comparable to the growth yogurt experienced a number of years ago"—but by 1988 sales had in fact reached only $71 million.[35] By the early 1990s, industry insiders would describe the rise in tofu consumption, from 60 million pounds in 1985 to 84 million pounds in 1992 (worth $100 million), as "not a meteoric, flash-in-the-pan increase" but a "steady 5 percent to 10 percent rise" each year.[36] Between 1983 and 1988, the number of tofu manufacturers decreased from 191 to 150, with only four producers—all Japanese or Japanese American—producing more than 100,000 pounds weekly. The next tier, which included WhiteWave and Island Spring, topped out at 30,000 pounds.[37] Growth was thus less than hoped for and consolidation less than feared. Aseptic packaging, which had promised to bring dynamism to tofu by offering a greater array of spiced and flavored tofu, never succeeded in entirely displacing the water-filled tofu tubs in the produce aisle. In 1987, some newspaper articles still included predictions that tofu would be the next yogurt over an ever-receding ten-year horizon. While second-generation products continued to be the most promising way to achieve that growth, there were also indications that some were looking to diversify along an entirely different line.

In August 1987, the *New York Times* profiled Elizabeth Appel, whose Ambrosia Soy Company produced SweetSoy, a drink available in "plain, honey-vanilla, carob, [and] cha-cha cherry." She had been a senior accountant with a large consulting firm, serving mostly manufacturing clients, when she decided to leave the financial industry. She felt the time was ripe for the soyfood business, as "Americans are very health-conscious right now," but she wanted to explore a "different niche" than tofu. "The tofu market is flat," she commented. Less ambivalent about capitalism than the soycrafters of 1981, she pursued similar business strategies. Even as she introduced an array of soymilk flavors, she had plans to branch out into second-generation products: soy pudding, vegetarian entrées, and, sold out of a small retail shop, soy ice cream. While SweetSoy was sold at the time in health-food stores, her target was to be sold in major supermarkets in New England and the New York area. "I can see myself outgrowing this place in no time," she commented.[38] As it happened, Ambrosia Soy did not last into the next decade. Nonetheless, it was a harbinger of things to come. Soymilk would indeed be the high-growth soy product of the 1990s, with "soy" coming into its own as a marketing hook, no longer required to hide behind the mystique of tofu.

Finally, the sales pitch would no longer simply be the negative-nutrition message that soy was low in cholesterol and saturated fat. Rather, a positive message would emerge positioning soy as what was variously called a "functional food" or "nutraceutical." At one point, Appel expressed bewilderment that, although she expected to attract the "yuppie market," the highest enthusiasm for her products came from women in their forties and fifties who wanted "to know about the product or already have a lot of knowledge about soy products." She had unknowingly caught the very beginning of a wave that would crest ten years later.

Hormonal Appeal

During the summer of 1990, the National Institutes of Health hosted a two-day conference, "The Role of Soy Products in Cancer Prevention." The event was organized by Mark Messina, a nutritionist with the Diet and Cancer Branch of the National Cancer Institute, charged with identifying promising areas of research for increased government funding. Messina brought in a vegetarian chef to prepare a soy luncheon—continuing the long tradition of such meals, from the founding meeting of the American Soybean Association on—because many of the visiting scientists who studied soybeans had never knowingly tasted them.[39] Messina was not, at that point, a fully converted soybean proponent. His own doctorate had dealt with the effects of cruciferous vegetables (e.g., cauliflower, broccoli) on colon cancer, but he was aware of the investigations into soybean phytochemicals that had been mounting over the 1980s. Phytochemicals are plant compounds— *phyton* being Greek for "plant"—that perform varied functions for the plants themselves and that remain biologically active when ingested by animals or humans. Soybean phytochemicals were a mixed bag. Some were nuisances that interfered with digestion. But some were suspected to have potential benefits for human health.

On the negative side, one class of phytochemicals, protease inhibitors, had long been known to stunt the growth of livestock by interfering with protein digestion. Heat treatment, whether by "toasting" soy flour or boiling soymilk, substantially eliminated this effect. Likewise, phytate (aka inositol hexaphosphate) was a form of phosphorus known to bind with calcium and iron, making these minerals harder to absorb by the intestine. Relatively abundant in soybeans, phytate was a harder problem for food technologists to solve: boiling or toasting defatted soy flour diminished phytate's mineral-binding capacity, but not entirely, and other methods had undesirable side effects.[40] Even these disagreeable phytochemicals might have their uses, however: researchers at the conference reported that protease inhibitors in amounts too low to affect animal growth halted the development of colon, lung, and other cancers experimentally induced in mice. Phytate likewise inhibited colon cancer, perhaps by limiting some of the harmful effects of iron. Some potentially beneficial phytochemicals were removed inadvertently by processing. The amount of phytosterols, of the sort that Percy Lavon Julian used as the raw material for synthetic hormones, dropped markedly in soybean oil as it was refined and hydrogenated. Along with another class of phytochemicals, saponins, phytosterols were thought to bind with cholesterol and thus lower its levels in the blood. One researcher at the conference reported that diets supplemented with sitosterol inhibited colon cancer in mice, while saponins were toxic to certain types of cancer cells.

The class of phytochemicals that caused the greatest excitement at the 1990 conference—as would be the case more broadly during the decade to come—had documented effects on animals that, on the face of it, were quite alarming. Isoflavones are a class of phytoestrogens, plant compounds that mimic animal estrogens. The leading expert on them at the conference was Kenneth Setchell, a British biochemist based at Cincinnati Children's Hospital. His doctoral research during the early 1980s used mass spectrometry to track the ups and downs of steroidal hormones during the menstrual cycle, and in the process he and his colleagues discovered tiny amounts of plant estrogens in the urine they analyzed. Curious, he fed monkeys and rats on various diets until he established that the source of the phytoestrogens was soybeans. He and his labmates even analyzed their own urine after ingesting a large amount of soy protein. Sure enough, their phytoestrogen levels went up 5,000 times. Isoflavone research henceforth became a sideline for Setchell, as he considered whether the lower rates in Asia of some hormone-dependent diseases—breast cancer chief among them—was due to higher soy consumption.[41]

At the conference, Setchell noted that 300 plants were known to produce estrogenic effects, sometimes strongly enough to induce estrus in animals or, alternately, to interfere with fertility. Isoflavones in clover, for instance, were pinpointed in a 1946 Australian case as the culprits disrupting the fertility of sheep. In 1986, Setchell himself had helped investigate an unusually high incidence of liver disease and infertility among cheetahs at the Cincinnati Zoo, which was ultimately linked to their food, a commercial preparation consisting mostly of horse meat but that also included substantial amounts of soy meal.[42] The conjectured upside to ingesting isoflavones was that they would interfere with hormone-dependent cancers as much as they did with cheetah reproduction, and for the same reason: as weak estrogens, they would bind to estrogen receptors in tissues without sending the signals the body's own stronger estrogen would. They would fit in the lock but not turn it.[43] Setchell and his collaborators had indeed found that soy protein, in various forms, seemed to have an anti-estrogenic effect on breast cancer tumors induced in mice. At the same time, the levels of soyfoods consumed by Asian women did not cause any noticeable cheetah-like problems with reproduction.[44]

As in the case of phytate and protease inhibitors, assessing the benefits and harms of isoflavones rested on numerous contextual details. Different isoflavones, of which daidzein and genistein are most abundant in soybeans, differ in their strength. Depending on how they are prepared or processed, or from which soybean variety they were made, different sources of soy protein differ in their isoflavone content. Different tissues in the body respond differently to isoflavones, and people are different from test animals, rodents being susceptible to cancer in ways that human bodies are not. The degree to which gut bacteria convert the other isoflavones into equol, a relatively strong estrogen, varies from species to species, and even person to person, further complicating the impacts of ingesting soy products. These subtleties would occupy researchers into the next century, and all of the results in 1990 were therefore delivered with numerous caveats pointing to unsettled questions. In the end, the leads were strong enough to compel the National Cancer Institute to fund a $3 million research program on soybeans and cancer.[45]

In the years following the 1990 conference, Messina became notably less cautious about his embrace of the soybean's potential to prevent cancer. In 1992, he left the National Cancer Institute, where he headed a new Designer Foods Program that sought to develop anticarcinogenic foods for use in research, to devote more of his time to promoting soy.[46] He contributed a regular column to *The Soy Connection* newsletter, and in 1994 he coauthored *The Simple Soybean and Your Health* with his wife, Virginia, a registered dietician, and Setchell. Aimed at a popular audience, the book was in part a compendium of scientific research that tended to downplay the uncertainties and caveats that emerged in 1990, and in part an advice book that provided fourteen days' worth of sample menus for a soy-rich "optimal diet." For the book's epigraph, the Messinas chose a poem written in 1956 by a soybean enthusiast. It included the lines, "I am very good to eat, / I am cheese and milk and meat / I am soap to wash your dishes / I am oil to fry your fishes." They added a new stanza, "But if all of this hasn't captured your attention, / Wait until you see my role in cancer prevention!"[47] By the late 1990s, the Messinas had become committed vegans and were hired by the Adventist Loma Linda University as professors. While not Adventists themselves, they contributed devotionals about the soybean to Adventist publications, including "The Miracle Bean," which listed soybeans among God's gifts that provided a "miraculous sign of His great love for us."[48] At the same time, Mark Messina remained deeply immersed in the hard science, organizing a quadrennial series ("International Symposia on the Role of Soy in Preventing and Treating Chronic Disease") beginning in 1994.[49]

By then, the popular media were beginning to gain an interest in soy phytoestrogens as well. The eventual focus of coverage was on a topic that had been touched upon only briefly during the 1990 conference, when researcher Donna Baird described an experiment to gauge the estrogenic—rather than anti-estrogenic—effects of isoflavones. Her subjects, all postmenopausal women, consumed soy products daily over four weeks. At the conclusion, they had gained "superficial cells of the vaginal epithelium" compared to the control group, which indicated an estrogenic response.[50] In 1992, *Lancet* reported high levels of "isoflavonoid phyto-estrogens" in postmenopausal Japanese women—on the order of 100–1,000 times higher than in women eating Western diets—which they linked to the low frequency in that population of menopausal symptoms such as hot flashes.[51]

This research appeared at a time when the women of the Baby Boom generation were entering the menopausal years, prompting greater discussion of menopausal symptoms in the media and by the government, as well as the more widespread prescription of hormone-replacement therapy (HRT) by physicians.[52] By the late 1990s, some women were questioning the advisability of treating menopause with estrogen drugs, which were linked to an increase in breast cancer, and instead opted for what seemed to be a gentler, more natural alternative.[53] For some, this meant incorporating Asian foods into their diet, while others turned to the growing number of herbal supplements on the market. One product in particular seemed to benefit, however. A reader of the *New York Times* responding favorably to a 1997 op-ed critical of HRT commented that "the only thing missing were some recipes to keep hormone levels up through diet." She concluded, "Soy milk, anyone?"[54]

During tofu's heyday in the 1980s, there were a number of factors simultaneously boosting the market for soymilk. Disenchantment with dairy products, in particular with dairy fat, had contributed to a decline in consumption of cow's milk since the 1940s, although a large part of the slack was taken up by soft drinks. Beginning in the late 1960s, there was also a growing realization that lactose intolerance—a sharp reduction in the ability to digest milk sugars past infancy—was the rule among the world's population rather than the exception. Up to 30 million Americans were estimated to be lactose intolerant to some degree in 1984.[55] In addition to Asian immigrants, this included a large portion of the African American community, with the *New York Amsterdam News* describing milk in 1977 as "white poison for young blacks."[56] All told, sales of soymilk amounted to 2.7 million gallons in 1984.[57] According to statistics published by William Shurtleff in 1984, the existing American soymilk market was dominated by Adventist companies, which sold products such as Soyagen and Soyamel to Adventists, vegetarians, and health-food consumers. Roughly a quarter of American soymilk was imported from Asia, where brands such as Vitasoy, based in Hong Kong, were popular soft drinks served in bottles. The exports to the West, however, came in aseptic Tetra Brik cartons that could be sold from grocery shelves. Even though it was a precursor to tofu, and seemingly a natural offering for soy dairies or kosher soy delis, less than 10 percent of American soymilk was manufactured by tofu makers.[58]

A decade later, soymilk sales had risen to $108 million, or approximately 13.5 million gallons, a steady expansion of 15–20 percent per year. The volume enabled natural food companies that had begun by importing soymilk from Japan in the 1980s to establish factories of their own. Eden set up a plant in Saline, Michigan—near the site, as it happened, of one of Henry

Ford's soybean-processing mills—as early as 1986.[59] Between 1997 and 2000, as drinking Vanilla Edensoy became a proverbial rite of passage for women entering menopause, sales of soymilk further quadrupled.[60] This was also due in part to savvy marketing, in particular on the part of WhiteWave— the Boulder-based company that had originated as a soy deli—which introduced its Silk brand of soymilk in 1996, packaged in gable-top milk cartons for placement in supermarket dairy cases. By 1999, when the major dairy producer Dean Foods acquired a 25 percent stake in WhiteWave, it was sold in more than 6,000 supermarkets and chain stores nationwide.[61] In a separate marketing niche, soy-based infant formulas were also increasingly popular. Even in 1984, 32 million gallons of soymilk were sold as infant formula. Geared to babies with dairy allergies—a separate condition from lactose intolerance—it was produced largely by Mead Johnson and other companies that made dairy-based infant formulas. The exception was Loma Linda, the Adventist maker of Soyalac, which was based on Harry Miller's patent. By 1999, soy-based formulas constituted up to 25 percent of sales in some areas, well beyond the population that needed it because of allergic reactions to dairy milk.[62]

The growing reputation of soy protein also propelled an entirely new market in energy bars, which had jumped into the mainstream in 1997 and whose sales equaled that of soymilk by 2000.[63] Further establishing 1997 as a turning point in soy products, it was the year that Amerifit Brands released Estroven, a supplement containing soy isoflavones and other plant estrogens. Advertising heavily in health magazines and during television programs such as *Live! with Regis and Kathie Lee*, Estroven was billed as an alternative to hormone-replacement drugs, a help during menopause "as natural as the process you're going through."[64] While the success of supplements might have arguably undermined the market for soyfoods proper, these foods received a major boost at the tail end of the decade.

In October 1999, the FDA authorized foods to carry a label stating that soybean protein helped reduce the risk for heart disease. This was based on research indicating that, beyond the fact that soyfoods were often low-fat and cholesterol-free, they contained compounds that lowered blood cholesterol. The claim could appear on packages of tofu, tempeh, soy-based beverages such as Ensure and Sustacal, and ersatz meat products.[65] At the "Third International Symposium on the Role of Soy in Preventing and Treating

Chronic Disease," which got under way in Washington, DC, five days later, the FDA announcement was greeted with papers further establishing soy protein's "hypocholesterolemic effects," although there was an active debate on exactly which compounds were responsible for it. As reported by Mark Messina, there was also a fair measure of caution about the burgeoning health claims for soy and some concern about the risks of taking too many isoflavone supplements. Overall, however, there was a positive sense that "the image of soy foods has come a long way since the early 1970s, when most Americans were either unfamiliar with these foods or believed them to be unappealing products consumed only by vegetarians." Now, as large food and pharmaceutical companies joined the soy market, surveys suggested that Americans were ever more willing to "incorporate soy products into their diet."[66] Indeed, after decades working its way out of the shadows, soy was out in the open by the turn of the millennium. Starbucks was offering Soy Lattes, and even green soybeans—long the focus of William Morse's promotional ambitions—were the new rage in supermarket produce sections.[67]

There was one ongoing news story that tarnished the soybean's reputation, however, one that extended public awareness beyond the benefits of its consumption to the methods of its breeding and cultivation. A full century after the USDA set the stage for the soybean's American success by importing thousands of varieties from Asia, the latest advance in genetic manipulation threatened to create lasting controversy.

Brave New Crop

As the reporter Daniel Charles recounts in his lively account of the rise of the biotech industry, *Lords of the Harvest*, it was not until 1996 that the St. Louis–based Monsanto Company hit upon a business strategy to cash in on its Roundup Ready Soybeans.[68] The research leading up to the company's revolutionary reshaping of the soybean genome stretched back to the early 1970s, when Monsanto was a chemical company that happened to market agricultural herbicides. At the time, the key to success in such products was selectivity—that is to say, a chemical property that harmed the target weeds but not the farmer's crop. One Monsanto researcher, Ernest Jaworski, wondered if the opposite strategy would work: using a broad-spectrum herbicide that crops could be bred to selectively resist. Most of his chemistry-oriented colleagues scoffed at his idea—as is so often the case in the origin myths of groundbreaking technologies—but he had enough support from management to create a laboratory to explore the genetic engineering of plants. The lab operated for several years without any immediate payoff in sight. Many of the researchers Jaworski hired from academia were more interested in basic research or in the myriad possible benefits from genetic engineering. Old hands in the agricultural division urged Jaworski's team to return to his original vision and hurry up to produce soybean cultivars tolerant to glyphosate, Monsanto's broad-spectrum herbicide sold under the brand name Roundup. To this, one of Jaworski's researchers retorted that if all biotechnology was good for was "to sell more damned herbicide, we shouldn't be in this business."[69]

Tolerance of open-ended research ended abruptly in 1985 when, under new leadership and facing a financial crunch, Monsanto concentrated its biotech resources on producing blockbuster products. In practice, this meant focusing on corn and soybeans, the crops one Monsanto researcher once characterized as "the elephants of the crop world," pointing out that if "you're collecting manure, you follow elephants, not sparrows."[70] With corn, the pursuit was to insert a gene that produced Bt toxin, a natural pesticide secreted by the bacterium *Bacillus thuringiensis* and widely used as a natural alternative to synthetic insecticides. For soybeans, it was glyphosate resistance. The technical challenges alone were daunting. First there was finding a gene that would enable a plant to survive exposure to glyphosate. By 1980, it was understood that the chemical worked by disabling a plant enzyme necessary for producing essential amino acids. The first strategy was to reverse-engineer a gene that would either produce substantially more of the necessary enzyme—thus overwhelming glyphosate's effect—or produce an enzyme with a slightly different shape that resisted glyphosate but performed the same duties in plant cells. The results were disappointing, but it turned out that natural selection had already solved the problem. Samples of mud from waste ponds adjacent to a Monsanto factory near New Orleans, collected regularly by the waste-cleanup division, contained bacteria that had evolved an entirely novel enzyme to sidestep Roundup.[71] Genetic engineers could thus leverage the bacterial talent for speedy evolution to further their work transforming relatively slowly evolving members of the plant kingdom.

When it came to inserting the gene into soybeans, however, a usually reliable bacterial strategy failed. In a technique partly developed by Monsanto, *Agrobacterium tumefaciens* transported both the desired gene and a gene for antibiotic resistance into plant-cell cultures. Dousing the culture with antibiotics then killed off the untransformed cells, while the others were coaxed into growing into full plants. In the case of soybeans, however, the cells killed by the antibiotic released a poison that in turn killed the genetically transformed cells. This "necrotic response" was eventually dealt with, so that *A. tumefaciens* became a common tool for genetically altering soybeans after 2000,[72] but in the late 1980s it prompted a search for a new technique entirely. This came in the form of "microprojectile bombardment" using a tool popularly known as a "gene gun." This was developed at Cornell starting in 1983 by a plant breeder named John Sanford and initially involved literally shooting a gun full of tungsten powder—which could be impregnated with DNA—into onions. This technique was met with hearty laughter until collaboration with researchers at the Pioneer Hi-Bred company successfully refined it to create transgenic maize. In the meantime, Sanford's concept inspired a researcher at a small biotech company in Madison, Wisconsin, to use an electrically generated shockwave to shoot a strip of Mylar, covered with DNA-coated microbeads, against a metal screen, thereby propelling the beads through the screen and into the target plant cells (figure 9.1).[73] This was the method eventually used to bombard Roundup-resistant genes into soybean somatic embryos, small clusters of cells that could regenerate into entire plants.[74]

Putting all the pieces together required an agreement in 1989 among three companies: Agracetus, which had developed the gene gun; Asgrow, a leading producer of soybean seeds; and Monsanto, which possessed the Roundup-resistant gene itself.[75] The precision of biotechnology, and its ability to introduce novel genes from unrelated species as far afield as bacteria, promised to accelerate genetic innovation. Some steps remained slow and painstaking, however. To transfer the glyphosate-resistance trait from a transformed soybean variety into other cultivars required the same backcrossing techniques Edgar Hartwig had perfected decades earlier. And it still then took years

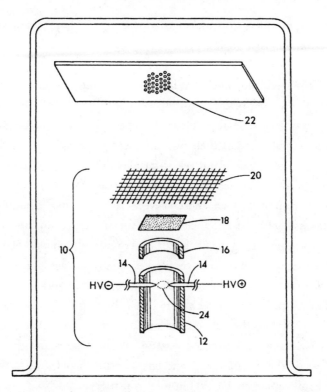

Figure 9.1. Diagram of a variant of the "gene gun," in which an electric charge blasts a piece of foil (18) covered in DNA-coated particles against a screen (20), thereby propelling the particles into the target plant cells (22). From US Patent 5,015,580, filed by Agracetus in May 1988.

to multiply the seed in sufficient quantities for the market. It was not until 1995 that Asgrow was able to set up demonstration projects on farms across the Midwest, inviting farmers to spray Roundup on fields from which they would later witness soybean plants emerge. By early 1996, Asgrow had sold enough Roundup Ready Soybean seed to cover a million acres.[76]

This was good business for Asgrow, but the challenge remained for Monsanto to recover the value of its investment. It might have simply sought to "sell more damned herbicide," using the crop itself as a loss leader. Some in Monsanto's herbicide division supported this approach, to the point of having pushed the company in 1992 to sell Pioneer Hi-Bred the rights to use the Roundup gene in its soybeans in perpetuity for the bargain-basement price of a half-million dollars.[77] The biotech faction at Monsanto had the opposite idea. They wanted to use the ever-cheaper price of Roundup in comparison to competing products to lure farmers into paying a higher price for resistant seed. If Roundup cost $15 less per acre than other herbicides, the reasoning went, farmers would be willing to pay up to $15 more per acre for the seed— at least if the seed companies that licensed the Roundup gene were willing and able to raise their prices accordingly.[78]

This was the perennial problem of the seed business: its products, by their nature, multiplied of their own accord. By one estimate, in the mid-1980s, the annual rate of "plantback"—farmers cleaning part of their harvest to provide seed for the next year—was 70 percent for oats, 60 percent for wheat, 50 percent for cotton, and 40 percent for soybeans.[79] That the plant-back rate was not higher was due mostly to the cost, especially for cotton and soybeans, of maintaining the quality of seed to ensure high rates of germination. This meant that most seed companies were run as agricultural services rather than as breeding operations. Until the 1970s, that work was left largely to the USDA and breeders such as Hartwig. With the exception of hybrid corn—which did not breed true, compelling farmers to buy new seed each season—farmers paid for crop innovation through taxes, not through the price of seed. The situation began to change after the passage of the Plant Variety Protection Act (PVPA) in 1971, which extended patent protection to novel plants in order to entice more commercial seed companies into varietal development.[80] Indeed, by the 1980s there was a dramatic increase in the work done by commercial breeders, while the USDA's Agricultural Research Service largely abandoned the development of finished cultivars.[81] One sign of this was that, by 2000, the era of proper names for soybeans—in honor of Confederate generals and otherwise—was at an end. Instead, new varieties had designations like AG2702 and 5344STS.[82]

The PVPA did not bar farmers from replanting seeds or even from selling a limited number of seeds to their neighbors, although this became a subject of legal contention that reached all the way to the United States Supreme Court. The case involved Asgrow, which had released its highly productive A3127 soybean in the 1970s, and an Iowa farm couple who sold seed to a man they thought was a farmer but who turned out to be working undercover for Upjohn, Asgrow's parent company. They insisted that this was just a "brown-bag" sale, neighbor to neighbor, but Asgrow charged that they were in fact operating a competing seed business.[83] The 1995 decision in favor of Asgrow rested on the PVPA's prohibition on "marketing" patented seeds, a term the majority read to mean selling any amount beyond what would have been needed to replant a farmer's own crop. A dissenting opinion distinguished between "marketing" and simply "selling" and argued that farmers were entitled to sell up to half of their crop before they should be considered in the seed business rather than the grain business.[84]

Neither standard suited Monsanto's ambitions, of course, and Roundup Ready Soybeans were covered in any case under a 1980 ruling that living organisms can be patented when they are a "product of human ingenuity."[85] The problem for Monsanto was not legal but rather a matter of the willingness of seed companies to charge a substantially higher price for seed in defiance of longstanding tradition—and in the face of farmers' outrage. This nervousness turned out to be the key to the business strategy that Monsanto improvised on the fly in 1996.

The Delta and Pine Land Company of Mississippi hesitated to raise the price of its genetically engineered cotton, which included Monsanto's Bt gene, from $30 to $120 per bag. It was instead considering a separate $32-per-acre fee for the insecticidal gene, allowing it to charge the same price it always had for the seed itself. Monsanto executives, who had long sought to position the company as the Microsoft of agriculture—designing the software inside the hardware of seeds—immediately embraced the idea. They would license out their genes directly to farmers rather than to seed companies, charging individual farmers a "technology fee" and requiring them to sign contracts that would prohibit them from planting part of their harvests the following year—achieving through a legal contract what the brute force of biology had achieved for corn. The only question that remained was whether farmers really would sign on the dotted line, agreeing not to replant Roundup Ready Soybeans, or else face "a claim for liquidated damages which will be based on 120 times the applicable Technology Fee."[86] The answer soon came: farmers grumbled, but they signed. The Roundup Ready Soybean became by some estimations the "most rapidly adopted agricultural technology in history." By 2000, it was grown on more than half of all soybean acreage, projected to soon grow on three-quarters.[87] Seed companies hurriedly backcrossed the Roundup Ready trait into numerous cultivars, so that by 1998 the University of Wisconsin extension service reported that of the 256 new varieties it tested that year, 125 were glyphosate-resistant.[88]

This turned out to be perfect timing for Monsanto, which caught the elephant in the midst of a growth spurt. Recessions and farm crises had hurt soybeans during the 1980s. At the same time, spurred in part by the soybean embargo of 1973 and to a lesser extent by the grain embargo against the Soviet Union in 1980, Brazil and Argentina expanded their soybean crops to supply Japan and other world markets.[89] If this was a downside of globalization for the American soybean, the upside appeared in the early 1990s, when China roared to life as an industrial giant and became a substantial net importer of beans. Exports were bolstered by the establishment in 1990 of a national soybean check-off program, which automatically assessed a small percentage of each farmer's sales and directed the money to research and promotion. In 1996, moreover, American farmers were given extra incentive to meet this demand with the passage of the Federal Agriculture Improvement and Reform Act, also known as the Freedom to Farm Act. Farmers were allowed to plant their fields entirely in one crop, and many made the choice to go with soybeans due to the strong export market. As it happened, they overshot demand. Beginning in 1998 and into the twenty-first century, soybean prices fell, which triggered price supports included in the 1996 legislation.[90] Total government subsidies for soybeans jumped from $143 million in 1997 to more than $4.5 billion in 2001.[91] This helped spark a debate about farm legislation but was in no way a problem for Monsanto's bottom line.

For its part, the American buying public, apart from antibiotech groups that had been protesting the technology since the early 1980s, did not show much concern about transgenic soybeans. It was difficult to raise the alarm about the Roundup Ready Soybean's environmental or public health impacts, in part because it arguably provided environmental benefits. For decades, a major concern about soybeans was that they exacerbated soil erosion, pushing some famers to adopt no-till methods that prevented weeds through herbicides rather than plowing. While some considered this a tradeoff between two evils, Roundup was commonly used for this purpose, even before the advent of glyphosate-tolerant soybeans, because it quickly degraded in the soil, a trait that allowed farmers to use it to prepare fields before planting.[92] With Roundup Ready Soybeans, these practices could extend to later stages of growth. Roundup's low environmental impact, in fact, raised the concern that its more widespread use—not to mention the risk of the resistant gene migrating to wild plants—would increase the prevalence of glyphosate-resistant weeds, thereby compelling a shift to less benign herbicides. Still, the tangible environmental benefits were arguably significant: one researcher in 2000 projected that the resulting increase in no-till farming would save 37 million metric tons of soil from erosion by 2020, as well as spare the atmosphere 40,000 metric tons of carbon dioxide through fuel savings.[93]

The impact on human health of transgenic soybeans was likewise not an obvious cause for concern. The Roundup Ready trait entailed the alteration of a soybean protein, and most soy protein was not destined for direct human consumption. Animals did not seem to respond any differently to feed made with Roundup Ready Soybeans.[94] The FDA, for its part, had declared the soybeans safe for humans in 1994, although critics pointed out that this was based on a comparatively cursory review of data voluntarily provided by Monsanto, not on the kind of full-scale safety review that it had earlier performed on the Flavr Savr Tomato.[95] Just as the popularity of soyfoods was peaking out of enthusiasm for soy isoflavones, one study in 1999 presented potentially damning data suggesting that levels of two phytoestrogens were lower in Roundup Ready than conventional soybeans.[96] As supporters of transgenic soybeans pointed out, however, the varieties in the study were not "true near-isogenic lines"—that is, they were not backcrossed to differ from conventional cultivars only in the Roundup Ready gene—because such lines did not yet exist for research purposes. The American Soybean Association pointed out that the differences in phytoestrogen levels were moreover in line with the variability among conventional soybean varieties.[97]

Meanwhile, some genetic engineers explored the possibility of using their techniques to improve the health profile of soybeans. One of these efforts hit a snag. Pioneer Hi-Bred sought to create a high-methionine soybean, using a gene from Brazil nuts to increase the amount of what was otherwise the limiting amino acid of soy protein, but found that the highly allergenic properties of Brazil-nut protein was also transferred to the soybean. This experimental cultivar was never released to the public.[98] Of greater potential impact were attempts to increase the oleic fatty-acid content of soybeans, which would simultaneously lower the saturated-fat content and diminish the use of hydrogenation to stabilize soybean oil, thereby reducing the prevalence of trans fats in the American diet.[99]

Opposition to transgenic crops was, in any case, slow to build in the United States. Consumer reaction was notably more intense and immediate in Europe, where environmental parties held greater sway. As early as

1996, Germans were said to be in a "furor" over genetically modified organisms (GMOs).[100] Popular outrage over biotechnology culminated in a 1999 decision by the European Commission to allow members to decide on the issue, with twelve of the fifteen governments then announcing that they would suspend imports of all foods with genetically modified ingredients until they could be tracked and appropriately labeled. This was an enormous headache for exporters, such as ADM, who now faced the job of keeping transgenic and conventional soybeans separate from each other. In the short term, ADM addressed the problem by sourcing exports to Europe from parts of the country where Roundup Ready Soybeans were not yet prevalent. It also partnered with DuPont to sell varieties of soybeans transformed through chemical mutagenesis, not genetic engineering, to tolerate DuPont's herbicide, Synchrony. Mutagenesis, in which soybean tissue was soaked in chemicals to induce mutation, providing greater variability for selection, was not barred by Europe's anti-GMO rules.[101] Events in Europe ultimately catalyzed the anti-GMO movement in the United States, which by the end of 1999 had raised the issue into a major plank in the anti–World Trade Organization activism in Seattle. The movement also mounted a class-action lawsuit against Monsanto involving six farmers, charging that Monsanto had not sufficiently guaranteed the safety or marketability of genetically modified crops.[102] The labeling requirements in Europe, meanwhile, laid the basis for companies in the United States to track and label their products as "GMO-free."[103]

Coming at literally the tail end of the twentieth century, it is hard to say that the antibiotech movement did much damage to the reputation of the soybean. It maintained its status as a healthy food. Many of the brands that sold soyfoods, such as Tofurky, already sourced their beans from organic farms, and organic producers were largely eschewing transgenic crops as spreading "genetic pollution." But in many ways 1999 represented a high-water mark for enthusiasm for the soybean, and the debate over biotechnology that continued with growing intensity into the new millennium was an early sign of popular disaffection with the crop, in part because it highlighted the ubiquity of soy in the US food supply. Monsanto had prioritized the soybean precisely because it was now an elephant among American crops, but this also had the appearance of an end run around public deliberations over biotechnology and, as the lawsuit against Monsanto emphasized, its many unknowns. If people imagined that genetically modified foods would enter the market one by one, following the model of the ill-fated Flavr Savr To-mato, so that each case could be judged on its individual merits—pros versus cons, costs weighed against benefits—Roundup Ready Soybeans meant that in one fell swoop biotechnology was suddenly, like soybeans themselves after their century-long journey from the outskirts of American life, everywhere and in everything.

EPILOGUE: HERE TO STAY?

Over the course of the twentieth century, America transformed the soybean. It began the century sorting the soybean's genetic heritage into standard varieties; it ended the century by contributing wholly novel genes. It grew the soybean in rows and harvested it with combines. It split the soybean into oil and meal on an unprecedented scale and, in turn, split the oil and meal into an array of new products. Even as it used the meal to spur meat and dairy production, it spun and extruded soybean protein into imitations of meat and treated and flavored soymilk into a closer approximation of cow's milk. It put tofu into plastic tubs and marketed soy in everything from energy bars to isoflavone supplements. Soybeans had long been a commodity, in the form of oil or soy sauce, but America made them one of the world's leading farm commodities. The soybean thus provides a valuable case study in how America has gone about transforming the material world, but any appraisal of the historical significance of all of this should also flip the question: How has the soybean, in its turn, transformed America? Were certain developments possible only because the soybean was there to be conscripted into use? On balance, was the influence of the soybean on American life harmful or beneficial? These questions are an occasion for historical reflection. As it happens, they also provide an excuse to continue the historical narrative into the twenty-first century. This was when America, having become aware of its close relationship with soy, increasingly wondered out loud whether it was a good thing.

One consistent outcome of this line of thinking was a distinction between "good soy" and "bad soy," although with an increasing tendency for the bad reputation of some soybeans to taint them all. This pattern was established by the ongoing controversy over genetically modified organisms such as Roundup Ready Soybeans. In some respects, this debate seemed to be more an international than a domestic dispute: the European public, expressing deep opposition to genetically altered foods through their Green and environmental parties, succeeded in banning GMO soybeans entirely from the continent until a 2004 ruling by the World Trade Organization forced Europe to end its moratorium. It was a pyrrhic victory, however, as new traceability and labeling requirements alerted hostile European consumers to the presence of GMO ingredients. Meanwhile, the Cartagena Protocol on Biosafety, under the auspices of the United Nations, went into effect in 2003, obliging exporters to alert concerned countries whenever their shipments might contain GMOs.[1] Calls for mandatory labeling of foods with GMO ingredients in the United States have so far not been successful, with most large food corporations opposed, but international pressures have reshaped soybean marketing channels: there is now a need for the "identity preservation" of non-GMO soybeans, making them a distinct stream available for domestic companies that wish to promote their products as GMO-free.

Since the 1980s, the US government has held that genetic engineering does not require a separate set of safety standards and that each GMO food should be assessed according to its specific characteristics, just like any other food or product. This framework helped give the biotech industry a leg up in America and was consistent with business-friendly policies in general. Whether federal policy reflects greater comfort with GMOs on the part of the American public, in contrast to the hostility of Europeans, is not entirely clear. In a survey published in 2003, 26 percent of respondents did not know whether they had ever eaten genetically modified foods, and 50 percent were unaware that they were already on supermarket shelves.[2] In a Pew survey in 2006, 60 percent of respondents were certain that they had not eaten GMO foods.[3] Even though soybean cultivation and varietal development had received unprecedented attention because of the issue, it appeared that, for many consumers, GMO soybean ingredients were still hidden in plain view. As for opinions on the matter—whether or not people realized that it applied to food they themselves had consumed—45 percent of respondents in 2006 felt that GMO foods were safe versus 29 percent who felt they were unsafe.[4] In a Pew study in 2015, those who felt GMO foods were safe dropped to 37 percent, while 57 percent now felt they were unsafe.[5] In a different phrasing of the question in 2016, 39 percent of respondents felt that GMO foods were "worse for health" than non-GMO foods, while 48 percent felt they were "neither better nor worse for health."[6]

Whether the opinion of a majority or simply a substantial minority of the public, mistrust of genetically modified foods has been widespread—and, within the environmental movement, increasingly entrenched.[7] Monsanto has remained a target as a symbol for the corporate takeover of the food supply, an image problem not necessarily helped by its legal victories. In 2012, a federal judge dismissed a class-action lawsuit by the Organic Seed Growers and Trade Association that sought to invalidate Monsanto's patents, fearing that member farmers could be sued if Monsanto's strains appeared by accident in their fields. The hearings attracted hundreds of farmers and environmental advocates in a mass protest, but the judge denied that the group had standing to sue and was creating "a controversy where none exits."[8] In an even higher-profile case, the United States Supreme Court ruled in 2013 against an Indiana farmer who had planted soybeans purchased from a grain elevator, arguing that Monsanto's license agreement did not extend to soybeans sold as grain.[9] By 2010, 93 percent of soybeans planted in the United States were genetically modified, with rising seed prices fueling anger at Monsanto by farmers and an antitrust probe by the Justice Department—a probe that was ended with no action in 2012.[10]

If public opposition did not result in legal setbacks, it did reinforce the need of growers and processors to separate GMO from non-GMO soybeans, a requirement that first arose from the European moratorium on GMOs. Mandatory labeling has been proposed in several American states but is not US law. Although most food companies staunchly oppose requirements to label foods with GMO ingredients—the Campbell Soup Company is a notable, and recent, exception[11]—many have proudly displayed "GMO-FREE" on "NON-GMO" on their packaging. This is true of most soy-based manufactured products, such as Tofurky and Silk Soymilk, which in any event have traditionally sourced from organic growers. Indeed, it is a matter of debate among economists whether the "identity preservation" of non-GMO soybeans has imposed a net cost on the industry or has provided a profitable opportunity for market segmentation.[12] Organic growers certainly seem to have benefited from the presumption that their crops are GMO-free: organic soybean acreage tripled between 1995 and 2001, from 50,000 to 175,000 acres, largely on the strength of the price premium enjoyed by organic soybeans.[13] Nonetheless, the mental association of soybeans with genetic modification has risked tarnishing soy in general. Recently, for example, Post reformulated its venerable health cereal, Grape-Nuts, to include isolated soy protein. Facing a consumer backlash, mostly for having slipped a GMO into the ingredients, Post restored the original recipe and for a time emblazoned the front of its Grape-Nuts boxes with a prominent "SOY FREE" label—since removed, although boxes retain a graphic proclaiming the cereal verified by the Non-GMO Project.[14]

Among the Americans who mistrust GMOs, one group has been notably absent: scientists. At least among members of the American Association for the Advancement of Science surveyed by the Pew Research Center, 88 percent responded that it was "safe to eat genetically modified foods," as opposed to 37 percent among the general public.[15] Numerous scientific studies in fact have found GMO soybeans to be as safe and nutritious as their non-GMO counterparts. The specific protein that disables glyphosate has not been found to be allergenic, and rates of allergic reactions were the same in GMO and non-GMO soybeans. Feed studies found that neither transgenic DNA nor transgenic protein survived the digestive tract to end up in the muscle of pigs, the milk of cows, or the eggs of hens. Experiments in humans likewise indicated that neither the protein nor the DNA made it through the digestive tract. In rat-feeding experiments, the nutritional quality of GMO soybeans was found to be equivalent to that of non-GMO soybeans. Governmental reviews in North America and Europe have come to similar conclusions, although not all of their data were made public. There was a headline-making study, however, that reported adverse effects on liver aging in rats from GMO soybeans, but its outcomes were not replicated by other researchers. Finally, in 2015 the World Health Organization cited glyphosate itself as a possible carcinogen, but this was countered by a group of European researchers. In any case, this would be more of an issue for farmers than for consumers: residues of Roundup have been detected in samples of GMO soybeans, but at very low levels.[16]

Yet early fears about environmental impacts were well founded. The glyphosate-resistant gene was derived from bacteria—the speed champions of evolution through natural selection—drawn from glyphosate-contaminated mud near a Roundup factory. Monsanto researchers, who labored so mightily to transfer glyphosate resistance to soybeans, never dreamed that weeds in the field could match the evolutionary performance of bacteria, even as farmers increasingly drenched their fields in Roundup.[17] Nature did not take long to prove them wrong. In 2000, Roundup-resistant horseweed, also known as marestail, appeared in Delaware. By 2003, water hemp was also showing resistance, and by 2010 at least ten species of glyphosate-resistant weeds plagued millions of acres in twenty-two states. The use of Roundup enabled low-till and no-till farming, with herbicides killing the weeds instead of plowing, which in turn lowered the amount of soil erosion and farm run-off into nearby waters. With the advent of glyphosate-resistant weeds, however, some farmers returned to plowing or were forced to use other, stronger herbicides in conjunction with Roundup.[18] In 2017 one of these herbicides, dicamba, sold in conjunction with Monsanto-engineered dicamba-resistant soybeans, wreaked havoc on neighboring fields of nonresistant soybeans, as well as other plants.[19] At the same time, there were some concerns about the effects of Roundup itself when used in massive amounts. As indicated by the bacteria in glyphosate-contaminated mud, Roundup could alter the makeup of a field's microbes—the "soil microbiome"—just as antibiotics altered the human gut microbiome. It was also feared that Roundup's breakdown products bound up key soil nutrients such as calcium and manganese.[20]

Whatever the exact constellation of health and environmental benefits and harms turns out to be, it is one particular to Roundup Ready Soybeans rather than GMOs in general. Glyphosate resistance was designed to have an impact in farm fields, not in human bodies. Health impacts may come to the fore, however, as soybeans are redesigned for specific nutritional benefits. So far, most prominent among this sort of effort has been the creation of a high-oleic soybean. The potential value of this is tied to another public controversy involving soybeans: the presence of trans fats in hydrogenated and partially hydrogenated soybean oil.

For many decades, and increasingly during the fat-phobic era of the 1970s through the 1990s, vegetable oils, even when hydrogenated, were thought to be healthier than saturated animal fats and even highly saturated vegetable oils such as palm and coconut. By the 1990s, as fast-food restaurants such as McDonald's switched from tallow to partially hydrogenated soybean oil for deep-frying, it was estimated that the average per capita consumption of trans fats in developed countries was 7–8 grams per day, or 6 percent of total fatty acid intake. Meanwhile, in 1993 an article in *Lancet* shocked everyone by revealing that, in a study of more than 85,000 nurses, eating four or more teaspoons of margarine a day resulted in a higher risk of heart attacks. Human bodies, it turns out, are well adapted to *cis* fats, whereas trans fats result in higher levels of low-density lipoprotein ("bad cholesterol") and lower levels of high-density lipoprotein ("good cholesterol"), making it far worse than saturated fat has been considered to be.[21] Soybean oil was the major source of trans fats: by 2005, 15.5 billion pounds of it were consumed—or roughly 12 kilograms per person per year, up sixfold from the 1960s—half of which was partially hydrogenated.[22]

As public awareness of the dangers of trans fats increased, the food industry took measures to eliminate them. Margarine manufacturers reverted to an older technique of blending hard, fully hydrogenated oils with liquid unhydrogenated oils to achieve the desired consistency. Sometimes the previously maligned palm oil was substituted for hydrogenated soybean oil. The FDA, meanwhile, mandated that processed foods display the amount of trans fats on nutrition labels by 2006, causing many to scramble for acceptable substitutes. When it came to the use of trans fats in restaurants, more drastic action was taken, with partially hydrogenated soybean oil specifically highlighted in public discussions as a health villain. McDonald's, having vowed to eliminate trans fats by 2003, was sued in 2005 for its continuing use of partially hydrogenated soybean oil, and other fast-food restaurants were similarly reluctant to switch from what was—given soybean oil's abundance—a low-cost ingredient.[23] In 2006, New York City forced restaurants' hands by instituting a wholesale ban on trans fats, to go fully into effect in 2008. There was widespread public approval (which would elude Mayor Michael Bloomberg's later efforts against sugary drinks), and California passed its own trans fat ban in 2008. National chains such as Starbucks soon fell into line.[24] Daily per capita consumption of trans fat fell from 4.6 grams in 2003 to 1 gram in 2013, while the FDA took measures to eliminate all artificial trans fats from processed foods, estimating that it would result in a further annual reduction of 20,000 heart attacks—some indication, perhaps, of the toll that cheap soybean oil, and the mistaken belief that it was heart-healthy, exacted over the second half of the twentieth century.[25]

Another strategy for eliminating trans fats was the bioengineering route. Beginning in the early 1990s, two separate efforts by Monsanto and DuPont, which had acquired Pioneer Hi-Bred, sought to create high-oleic soybeans. Oleic acid is a MUFA (monounsaturated fat) with a reputation for health-fulness, especially during the peak of advocacy for the so-called Mediterranean diet's high consumption of olive oil, of which it is a major component. From the food technologist's point of view, however, the chief advantage of MUFAs is their oxidative stability, requiring less hydrogenation or other techniques to prevent rancidity or to remove off tastes. This promised to reduce processing costs, but particularly after the 1993 *Lancet* report, the more urgent need was to eliminate trans fats. This urgency increased after the FDA required labeling and cities such as New York instituted their bans. By 2005, business giants such as the Kellogg Company were pledging to use the new soybean oil to cut down on trans fats, even though they faced a shortage of the oil as demand rose faster than cultivation and supply of the soybeans.[26] In 2013, as the FDA was working to implement a complete ban, the situation was much the same: DuPont expected at most 300,000 acres of its Plenish soybean to be planted, a tiny percentage of the soy crop, although the United Soybean Board stated a goal of 18 million acres by 2023.[27] Proponents of GMOs pointed out that high-oleic soybeans provided a direct benefit to consumers, rather than just a cost saving for farmers, boosting biotech's image—although manipulating the nutritional content of soybeans raised the specter for GMO opponents of other, unintended changes.

By 2013, moreover, enthusiasm for MUFAs as the most healthful of fats had waned in favor of PUFAs (polyunsaturated fats), or at least one class of PUFAs. The key distinction, according to this theory, is between omega-3 and omega-6 fatty acids: that is, PUFAs whose last double carbon bond is three carbons from the end of the molecule versus six carbons from the end, respectively.[28] Since the 1980s, an extremely long omega-3 fatty acid, docosahexaenoic acid (DHA), found mainly in fish oils, has been known to be important and beneficial as a constituent of nerve-cell membranes. It has been added to infant formula, for instance, to promote eye and brain development.[29] At the same time, there are much shorter omega-3s in vegetable oils, chief among them linoleic acid (LA). This is found largely in leaves as an aid to photosynthesis, but it is also abundant in some seeds and is thought to be assembled into longer-chain omega-3s such as DHA and eicosapentaenoic acid when direct intake of these is low. In contrast, short-chain omega-6s such as alpha linolenic acid are assembled into less beneficial fatty acids. Since 1900, the ratio of short-chain omega-6s to omega-3s in the diet has shifted dramatically, by one recent estimate from 6.4:1 in 1909 to 10:1 in 1999. This was largely attributable to massive increase in the use of refined soybean oil.[30]

The irony is that soybean oil is actually quite rich in omega-3s, which constitute around 8 percent of its total fats. Its omega-6 to omega-3 ratio is roughly 7:1, substantially higher than that of the omega-3 champions, flax-seed (1:5) and canola oil (2:1), but far lower than cottonseed oil (266:1), sun-flower oil (131:1), and peanut oil (76:1).[31] It is the omega-3s, however, that are processed out of soybean oil as it is refined. The reason is that omega-3s are far more reactive than omega-6s and thus oxidize more readily. This is why they are so useful in nerve-cell membranes and leaves performing photosyn-thesis. They are more plentiful in seeds such as soybeans that are primed for germination precisely because these seeds benefit from having omega-3s at the ready for photosynthesis. Seeds designed for long-term dormancy favor the more stable omega-6s, which store energy for the long haul. Fast oxida-tion is also why flaxseed oil, which is incredibly rich in omega-3s, is fast-drying and good for paint; why soybean oil develops off flavors, described as "fishy" or "painty," so readily; and why researchers spent decades learning how to remove or stabilize the volatile omega-3s to refine soybean oil into salad oil. Finally, it is why partial hydrogenation is so effective at solving the flavor stability problem in soybean oil: the omega-3s are the first to take up hydrogens. In any case, the shift to omega-6s at the expense of omega-3s has been theorized by some to be a key risk factor for heart disease, high blood pressure, and inflammation.

None of this, however, is settled science. The purported harm of the widening omega-6 to omega-3 ratio—which posits that omega-3s are preferentially taken up into tissues to perform their specialized functions unless crowded out by an overwhelming number of the inferior omega-6s—remains controversial.[32] Even when it comes to the value of long-chain, marine-derived omega-3s like DHA, one meta-analysis of randomized clini-cal trials found no link at all to a lower risk of mortality, cardiac death, sudden death, myocardial infarction, or stroke—at least among at-risk patients who actively supplemented their diets with omega-3 PUFAs.[33] Another study has moreover established a link between the intake of the omega-6 fatty acid LA and a lowered risk of coronary heart disease.[34] Such was the endless quest to discover a bright line separating good fats from bad fats: only artificial trans fats maintained their standing as unequivocal dietary villains. Meanwhile, these debates both harmed consumption of soybean oil, which fell to 12.3 billion pounds by 2013, and raised the profile of soy as a harmful, rather than a virtuous, component of food. All the same, exposés of trans or omega-6 fats did not necessarily pin the blame on the soybean. Rather it was the use that the industrial food system had made of soybeans that was at fault, as it processed what was otherwise a healthful oil to suit its own purposes. In the absence of abundant soybeans, it might very well have conscripted other oils to meet these ends. Soybean oil was more sinned against than sinning.

In any case, the main argument in favor of soyfoods had long rested on the high quality of soy protein. By the early 2000s, however, soy protein was in the crosshairs of an avowedly antisoy movement in such books as Kaayla Daniel's 2005 *The Whole Soy Story: The Dark Side of America's Favorite Health Food*. Daniel is associated with the Weston A. Price Foundation, named for a dentist who toured the world in the 1920s and 1930s to document traditional diets and the vibrant health of the peoples who continued to eat them. The Price Foundation challenges the health benefits not only of processed foods but also of vegetarian diets, advocating that people consume substantial quantities of meat—including beef and pork—raw milk, eggs, and dairy fat. Soy protein—in particular, the solvent-extracted, extruded textured vegetable protein or spun isolated soy protein that is concentrated into veggie burgers and energy bars—is, in their view, a toxic substitute for animal protein, much the way that hydrogenated vegetable fat ultimately proved to be more harmful than saturated butterfat. In *The Whole Soy Story*, Daniel in fact praises what she calls the "good old soys"—tofu, miso, and tempeh—as embedded in culinary traditions that have discovered ways to mitigate the more harmful properties of soy protein, most effectively through fermentation. But for the most part, the Price Foundation and its vegetarian opponents, such as the vegan food writer John Robbins, continue a polemical battle with roots going back at least a century that now finds expression through countless websites and blogs.[35]

The central concern about soy protein had been its biggest selling point during the 1990s: isoflavones. In part, the image of these estrogenic compounds tracked that of estrogen itself. This took a major hit in 2002 when a major, federally funded clinical trial of hormone-replacement therapy was halted due to safety concerns. The Women's Health Initiative (WHI) study revealed elevated levels of breast cancer among women on HRT, as well as increased risks of blood clots, heart attacks, and strokes.[36] Scientists expressed concerns as early as 2000 about the increased popularity of soy isoflavone supplement pills, which provided roughly ten times the daily dose of isoflavones than the Japanese gained eating traditional soy foods. A study in 1998 had identified increased breast-cell proliferation—a risk factor for eventual cancer—in women given soy supplements.[37] In the wake of the WHI report, however, a toggle suddenly flipped, causing women who may have previously embraced soy as a gentler alternative to HRT to view it with caution as a possible cause of breast cancer. Given the level of concern, the Agency for Healthcare Research and Quality, part of the Department of Health and Human Services, published a meta-analysis of soy research in 2005 that overall threw cold water on hype and panic alike, as meta-analyses tend to do.[38] Mostly, it highlighted the areas of uncertainty: it showed moderately positive effects on cholesterol and menopause symptoms, but with a wide variation among studies of varying quality. Likewise, it cited evidence that soy isoflavones promote the growth of estrogen-dependent mammary tumors in laboratory rodents, but it also noted that human studies focused on intermediate biomarkers thought to be associated with breast cancer but that were not established risk factors—and even here results were mixed.[39]

There were also increasing concerns about the estrogenic effects of soy isoflavones on men, consistent with growing worries about environmental exposure to synthetic chemicals that mimicked the effects of estrogen in the male body. Some studies linked soy to lower levels of testosterone, a putatively positive effect when it came to the risk for prostate cancer,[40] which Kaayla Daniel (among others) linked to tofu's popularity in Asian monasteries as an "aid to spiritual development and sexual abstinence."[41] Some on the internet went further, with the evangelical writer Jim Rutz proclaiming that "Soy Is Making Kids 'Gay'" through the feminizing effects of soy-based infant formula, which "commonly leads to a decrease in the size of the penis, sexual confusion and homosexuality" and which therefore bore most of the "medical (not socio-spiritual) blame for today's rise in homosexuality."[42] There was reputable research linking soy to "an unusual case of gynecomastia"—swelling of breast tissue in men—and lower testosterone levels, but Mark Messina concluded in a 2010 review of the "totality of evidence" that feminization concerns were unwarranted.[43] Critics also identified soy as a likely culprit for what appears to be a real decline in sperm count among men in the industrialized world—although there has not been a corresponding decline in the sperm count of farm animals, which consume the vast majority of soy protein.[44] With the science constantly evolving, however, the failure of studies in the past to detect major long-term effects of soy formula is not definitive proof of their absence.[45]

By 2017, the idea that soy was responsible for a generation of gender-confused men—whether gay, transgender, or simply enervated and docile from a lack of testosterone—migrated to the blogs and YouTube videos of the burgeoning alt-right movement. They generally cite the same studies that Rutz had a decade earlier, while pointing misleadingly to the ubiquity of soy in supermarket products as meaning high exposure to soy isoflavones.[46] "Soy boy," a pejorative meant to describe "males who completely and utterly lack all necessary masculine qualities . . . through an over-indulgence [in] emasculating products and/or ideologies," joined the ranks of far-right epithets.[47] This is consistent with a general anxiety about masculinity and its pollution among such figures as Alex Jones—and not unlike worries from a century earlier, on the part of figures in the eugenics movement such as John Harvey Kellogg, about "race suicide" through practices that undermined sexual health.

From a medical standpoint, perhaps of greater worry was a 2000 study linking midlife tofu consumption among men participating in the Honolulu-Asia Aging Study with increased cognitive impairment and faster brain atrophy decades later, possibly due to the weak estrogens of soy blocking the action of stronger estrogens in the repair of brain tissue.[48] This study depended on somewhat inconsistent self-reports of dietary intakes separated by decades from the evaluation of cognitive function, raising methodological concerns. An Indonesian study similarly found a negative effect on memory from tofu, but not from tempeh, perhaps the result of the use of formaldehyde in Indonesia's cottage tofu industry. Other experimental studies, meanwhile, discovered favorable effects of a high-soy diet on the cognitive abilities of college-age students; or no effect at all on women over sixty-five; or some reasons for optimism for the cognitive impacts of isoflavones, though usually in studies of postmenopausal women.[49] As with so many other issues surrounding isoflavones, the research was too preliminary to be conclusive.

The other great fear associated with soy protein surrounds allergic reactions. Since the 1990s, the UN Food and Agriculture Organization has listed soybeans among its Big Eight food allergens, along with milk, eggs, fish, crustacean shellfish, wheat, peanuts, and tree nuts. At least sixteen potential soy-protein allergens have been identified, but the actual prevalence of allergic reactions to soy and the severity of these reactions are difficult to pin down. Soy advocates argue that both are relatively low. A widely agreed-upon figure is 0.4 percent of children, most of whom outgrow the allergy by age ten—compared to 0.6 percent for peanuts with only 20 percent outgrowing the allergy.[50] Estimates based on skin-prick tests or serum screening for soy-specific antibodies may overestimate the actual prevalence of clinical reactions; in some studies, only 10 percent of those with the antibodies actually had an adverse reaction to eating soy.[51] Likewise, in one study, while 13 percent of children with symptoms of allergy responded to the skin-prick test, only 1.8 percent was soy-positive in a "double-blinded, placebo-controlled food challenge."[52] A 2007 survey tallying up self-reports of food allergies among adults found that 1 percent of those with allergies reported a soy allergy, representing 0.05 percent of those surveyed.[53] If the allergy is not ubiquitous, however, soy is. Since 2005, the FDA has required food labels to clearly highlight the presence of, or possible contamination by, the Big Eight allergens, giving consumers the impression of a widespread allergy epidemic. For those inclined to view allergic reactions among some as a sign of less acute, long-term detrimental health impacts for all, soy has now become highly suspect.

As far as severity, at least one study determined that the dose safe for 90 percent of soy allergy sufferers was 400 milligrams, many times larger than the safe dose for peanuts (0.1 milligram).[54] However, Kaayla Daniel and other soy opponents cite a Swedish study from the 1990s that identified four soy-related deaths from anaphylaxis among young people not known to have been allergic to soy (although they all had severe peanut allergies), with the authors concluding that soy is an underestimated cause of fatal allergic reactions.[55] Daniel argues that soy has gone unnoticed as a component of foods causing fatal allergic reactions, resulting in a gross underestimate of its true harm. Indeed, periodic stories about the true makeup of fast-food meat serve as a repeated reminder of how much soy is hidden in plain sight: a DNA analysis of the chicken served at Subway, to take a recent example, found that only 50 percent of it was actually chicken, with the other half being soy.[56] By the same token, however, soy advocates point to the longtime use of soy-based infant formula, as well the inclusion of soy protein in numerous foods, as evidence that there is no widespread problem. Whatever the true hazard, it represents another case where biotechnology seemed to offer a solution—a low-allergy soybean developed in 2002—only to go by the wayside as baby formula companies shied away from GMO ingredients.[57]

By 2010, in any case, the reputation of soy had suffered a number of hits, even if not as many as soybean opponents might desire. Even its biggest advocates had become much more measured and cautious in their claims. In September 2009, nearly twenty years after he convened the first of what became at least ten major symposia on the health effects of soy, Mark Messina presented a paper to the Soy Summit at Columbia University that reflected on what had been learned in the meantime. Conceding that "the role of soy-foods in an overall healthy diet has become somewhat of a confusing and contentious issue," one that had generated hundreds of papers and studies, he emphasized digging down to the effects of specific foods on specific populations. Earlier that year, for instance, a separate conference had explored the role of equol, a metabolite of soy isoflavones produced by gut bacteria present in some people but not others, as the source of many of soy's health benefits. Amid the numerous unclear or conflicting results, Messina found encouraging signs that soy decreased hot flashes in menopausal and increased bone density in postmenopausal women; that it lowered cholesterol and blood pressure; and that it decreased the risks of breast and prostate cancer. He cautioned that "no food should play too large a role in the diet" and that, in the interests of dietary diversity and moderation, people might limit their isoflavone intake to no more than they would get from around two servings of traditional soyfoods per day (representing 15–20 grams of protein and 50–75 milligrams of isoflavones).[58]

Indeed, it seems that the controversies did not end up hurting sales of soyfoods. According to the Soyfoods Association of North America, annual sales in all categories expanded from just over $1 billion in 1996 to just under

$3 billion in 2000, then to $4 billion in 2007 and over $5 billion in 2008, with a dip back to $4.5 billion by 2013. In addition to strong growth in soymilk and protein bars, the "other products" category grew along with consumer enthusiasm for edamame, soy cereals, condiments, and various snack foods. Meanwhile, the proportion of Americans consuming soyfoods or beverages at least once per week increased from 24 percent to 31 percent between 2010 and 2014, and more than 75 percent of consumers reportedly perceived soyfoods as healthy.[59] Thinking more broadly, however, if the future envisioned by vegans ever came to pass, only a fraction of the soybean crop currently channeled into meat and dairy production would be required for the direct provision of soy protein. Soy has had the first-mover advantage in meat and dairy analogs, but the same time, the space in supermarkets initially staked out by soy has become crowded with alternatives—rice and almond milks, or Quorn veggie burgers made from fungal protein—raising the possibility that even this outlet for soybeans might decline. In fact, a number of recent bids to become the future of food draw upon the legacy of soy while at the same time largely bypassing it as a raw material.

Soylent is a postmodern take on the modernist dream of a complete food in the lineage of Ford's soy biscuit or Cargill's "man food." Developed as a life hack by coders too busy to procure actual food, it is a combination of powdered ingredients and oil purchased online into what has been described as a very dense, filling pancake batter—or, alternately, "one step better than what you drink before a colonoscopy."[60] The ultimate meal replacement, it is meant to reserve the pleasures of dining for special occasions, not everyday eating. The name, of course, ironically refers to *Soylent Green*—one more remove from the original concept of a soybean-lentil analog steak—and demonstrates the hacker's fearlessness in reducing the world to its elements and recombining them to suit oneself. This DIY sensibility belies the fears of the 1970s that such a capability would enable powerful oligarchies to compel people to eat literally anything. In terms of ingredients, aside from soy lecithin, it contains no substantial quantity of soy: the protein comes mainly from oat powder, the fat from grapeseed oil.[61]

On the other end of the spectrum of what food scientists call organoleptic appeal is the Impossible Burger, designed to be a truly mouthwatering, nearly indistinguishable imitation of hamburger meat. Just as Soylent is the hacker's update of man food, the Impossible Burger is Silicon Valley's update of Morningstar Grillers. It aims for the taste, chew, and even the bloodiness of real meat and draws upon the soybean in a novel way. The iron-rich hemoglobin of blood, which transports oxygen throughout the body, has a sister in the root nodules of legumes. Leghemoglobin's job is to intercept oxygen and then release it slowly to the bacteria at the center of the nodules, whose ability to fix nitrogen from air is scuttled by an excess of oxygen.[62] Leghemoglobin is thus the key to the ability of legumes to enrich soil, and heme molecules from soybean roots are the key to the Impossible Burger's verisimilitude. Lest one imagine that this involves pulping and filtering nodules, however, Impossible Foods has instead genetically engineered yeast to pump out heme. Or, as the company describes it, "We discovered how to take heme from plants and produce it using fermentation—similar to the method that's been used to make Belgian beer for nearly a thousand years," a wily deflection for those who oppose GMOs. Meanwhile, the protein is mainly from wheat, with the addition of some soy-protein isolate; the fat comes from coconut oil, which melts something like animal fat.[63] Its chief rival is the Beyond Burger, which uses an improved technique to extrude pea protein into an imitation of muscle. Its bloodiness comes from beet juice; unlike the Impossible Burger, it is proudly free of GMOs and wheat gluten and soy, a selling point indicating that allergy warnings and worries about genetic engineering have indeed hurt soy's reputation and long-term prospects.[64]

Even if soy is sidelined from the future of food, it may yet fulfill the chemurgical dreams of the 1930s, as its industrial uses have been revived in an era of green manufacturing. Soy ink has made a comeback. The Ford Company, carrying on the work of its founder, has touted its car-seat foam made partly from soy—resulting in the strangely specific figure of 31,251 soybeans used in each vehicle.[65] The chemurgy movement also foretold the use of soy as fuel, with one report from the 1935 Dearborn conference noting that a farmer who extracted his own soybean oil and used it to run a diesel tractor would "be ahead of the game all around."[66] This became a reality decades later when Midwest Biofuels introduced SoyDiesel in 1991 as a clean-burning, sulfur-free alternative to diesel made from petroleum. Once again, their ready availability put soybeans at the leading edge of a new development: biodiesel made from rapeseed and palm oil would follow. By 2016, American biodiesel production exceeded 1.8 billion gallons, with proponents touting its potential to reduce greenhouse gas emissions.[67] Biofuels remain controversial, with critics questioning whether claims of environmental benefits hold up in the face of a full accounting of the inputs required to produce the fuels. Above all, replacing a substantial portion of conventional diesel with biodiesel would require a tremendous amount of land. By one estimate, the land required to meet the needs of the world's maritime fleet, if powered by biodiesel derived from temperate oil crops, would surpass the current global total of all cultivated land.[68]

That would arguably be a boon for the soybean, ensuring its future in America, although it would raise the perennial issue of the meal—the oil's joint product in the soybean complex—becoming too plentiful, dragging down not only the soybean's commodity price but also its claim to be an energy-efficient fuel source. Given what is arguably biodiesel's lack of viability as a major fuel substitute, people may ultimately look elsewhere entirely.[69] For the time being, however, it is all but assured that Americans will continue to find new uses for soybeans. Their current abundance makes them a cheap resource, to be sure, but it is more than that. The American soybean represents a century of investment, not only in the physical capital to grow and process it but also in the deep knowledge of its biology and the steep learning curve of manipulating its genetics and chemistry. Whatever the soybean's intrinsic virtues, it is this legacy of human involvement with its fate that remains the key to its ongoing magic. For better or worse, it has become a thoroughly American crop with deep roots in our soil.

Notes

Introduction: Destined to Succeed?

1. W. J. Morse and J. L. Cartter, "Improvement in Soybeans," in *U.S. Dept. of Agriculture Yearbook 1937* (Washington, DC: US Government Printing Office, 1937), 1156.

2. US Bureau of the Census, "Chapter XII: Individual Crops," in *Fourteenth Census of the United States Taken in the Year 1920*, vol. 5, *Agriculture* (Washington, DC: US Government Printing Office, 1922), 777. Other evidence indicates that there may have been soybeans grown by Asian Americans that the census missed in California and other western American states, but this is not certain.

3. National Agricultural Statistics Service (NASS), Agricultural Statistics Board, US Department of Agriculture, "Acreage," released 30 June 2000, 14, usda.mannlib .cornell.edu/usda/nass/Acre//2000s/2000/Acre-06-30-2000.pdf.

4. Steven T. Sonka, Karen L. Bender, and Donna K. Fisher, "Economics and Marketing," in *Soybeans: Improvement, Production, and Uses*, 3rd ed., ed. H. Rogers Boerma and James E. Specht (Madison, WI: American Society of Agronomy, 2004), 922–924.

5. Arturo Warman, *Corn and Capitalism: How a Botanical Bastard Grew to Global Dominance*, trans. Nancy L. Westrate (Chapel Hill: University of North Carolina Press, 2003), 100, 105, 111.

6. Judith A. Carney, *Black Rice: The African Origins of Rice Cultivation in the Americas* (Cambridge: Harvard University Press, 2001).

7. H. H. Hadley and T. Hymowitz, "Speciation and Cytogenetics," in *Soybeans: Improvement, Production, and Uses*, ed. B. E. Caldwell (Madison, WI: American Society of Agronomy, 1973), 102.

8. Ping-Ti Ho, "The Loess and the Origin of Chinese Agriculture," *American Historical Review* 75 (October 1969): 29.

9. US Department of Agriculture, *Human Food from an Acre of Staple Farm Products*, by Morton O. Cooper and W. J. Spillman (Washington, DC: US Government Printing Office, 1917).

10. M. S. Kaldy, "Protein Yields of Various Crops as Related to Protein Value," *Economic Botany* 26 (April–June 1972): 143.

11. William Shurtleff and Akiko Aoyagi, *The Book of Tofu: Protein Source of the Future . . . Now!* (Berkeley: Ten Speed Press, 1983), 15.

12. Theodore Hymowitz and J. R. Harlan, "Introduction of the Soybean to North America by Samuel Bowen in 1765," *Economic Botany* 37 (December 1983): 373–374, 377.

13. Ibid., 375.

14. Theodore Hymowitz, "Introduction of the Soybean to Illinois," *Economic Botany* 41:1 (1987): 30–31. Hymowitz cites "The Japan Pea," *Moore's Rural New Yorker* 4:7 (12 February 1853): 54.

15. Ibid., 30–31.

16. William Shurtleff and Akiko Aoyagi, *Friedrich Haberlandt—History of His Work with Soybeans and Soyfoods (1876–2008): Extensively Annotated Bibliography and Sourcebook* (Lafayette, CA: Soyinfo Center, 2008), 35–36.

17. Ibid., 82; Soyinfo Center, "History of Soybeans in North Carolina, A Special Exhibit—The History of Soy Pioneers around the World—Unpublished Manuscript by William Shurtleff and Akiko Aoyagi," last modified 2004, www.soyinfocenter.com /HSS/north_carolina.php.

18. Morse and Cartter, "Improvement in Soybeans," 1155.

19. US Department of Agriculture, *The Soy Bean as a Forage Crop*, by Thomas A. Williams, with appendix, "Soy Beans as Food for Man," by C. F. Langworthy, Farmers' Bulletin No. 58 (Washington, DC: U.S. Government Printing Office, 1899), 23.

20. W. O. Atwater, "American and European Dietaries and Dietary Standards," *Fourth Annual Report of the Storrs School Agricultural Experiment Station, Storrs, Conn.* (Middletown, CN: Pelton & King, 1892), 160.

21. US Department of Agriculture, *Use Soy-Bean Flour to Save Wheat, Meat and Fat*, contributions from the States Relations Service, A. C. True, Director, Circular No. 113 (Washington, DC: U.S. Government Printing Office, 1918), 3.

22. Marcel Mazoyer and Laurence Boudart, *A History of World Agriculture: From the Neolithic Age to the Current Crisis*, trans. James H. Membrez (New York: Monthly Review Press, 2006), 300–302.

23. See Steven Stoll, *Larding the Lean Earth: Soil and Society in Nineteenth-Century America* (New York: Hill and Wang, 2002).

24. See Benjamin Cohen, *Notes from the Ground: Science, Soil, and Society in the American Countryside* (New Haven: Yale University Press, 2009); and Peter McClelland, *Sowing Modernity: America's First Agricultural Revolution* (Ithaca: Cornell University Press, 1997).

25. Shurtleff and Aoyagi, *Book of Tofu*, 16.

Chapter 1. Crossing Oceans

1. Tsuru Yamauchi, interview by Michiko Kodama, in *Uchinanchu: A History of Okinawans in Hawaii*, ed. Marie Hara, trans. Sandra Iha and Robin Fukijawa (Honolulu:

Ethnic Studies Oral History Project, Ethnic Studies Program, University of Hawaii, 1981), 488–489. Hereafter Yamauchi Oral History.

2. Ibid., 494.

3. Ibid., 493.

4. Naomiche Ishige, *The History and Culture of Japanese Food* (London: Kegan Paul, 2001), 138–139.

5. Yamauchi Oral History, 492.

6. This was the custom in Japan, at least; Yamauchi later recalled that Okinawans squeezed out the okara without having first boiled the gô. Yamauchi Oral History, 504.

7. William Shurtleff and Akiko Aoyagi, *The Book of Tofu: Protein Source of the Future . . . Now!* Volume I (Berkeley: Ten Speed Press, 1983), 284.

8. Ibid., 71, 286.

9. Shurtleff and Aoyagi, *Book of Tofu*, 271.

10. US Department of Agriculture, Office of Experiment Stations, *A Description of Some Chinese Vegetable Food Materials*, by Walter C. Blasdale (Washington, DC: US Government Printing Office, 1899), 33, 35; Joseph Burtt-Davy, "Lily-Bulbs and Other Chinese Foods," *The Gardeners' Chronicle: A Weekly Illustrated Journal* 22, Third Series (25 September 1897): 213; "Vegetable Cheese," *The Dietetic and Hygienic Gazette*, June 1900, 340–41; M. L. Holbrook, "The Science of Health: Vegetable Cheese," *Phrenological Journal and Science of Health*, September 1900, 88–89.

11. Alice A. Harrison, "Chinese Food and Restaurants," *Overland Monthly*, June 1917, 532.

12. William Shurtleff and Akiko Aoyagi, *How Japanese and Japanese-Americans Brought Soyfoods to the United States and the Hawaiian Islands—A History (1851–2011): Extensively Annotated Bibliography and Sourcebook* (Lafayette, CA: Soyinfo Center, 2011), 48.

13. Ibid., 7. These directories were reprinted in Tokyo in 2001 by Nihon Tosho Senta as part of their series *Nikkei Imin Shiryôshû. Dai 1-kai* [Collected Documents on Japanese Emigration. No. 1], then translated and compiled by William Shurtleff with the aid of Akiko Aoyagi and, at the Asian Division of the Library of Congress, Eiichi Ito, Dr. Ming Sun Poon, Dr. Jeffrey Wang, Kiyoyo Pipher, and Hiromi Shimamoto. Ibid., 21, 6.

14. Shurtleff and Aoyagi, *How Japanese . . . Brought Soyfoods*, 7. A tofu shop still in business in the 1990s may have been founded as early as 1903 in New York City, one of the few East Coast cities to see significant Japanese immigration during this period. Ibid., 18.

15. Alan Takeo Moriyama, *Imingaisha: Japanese Emigration Companies and Hawaii, 1894–1908* (Honolulu: University of Hawaii Press, 1985), 29.

16. Ibid., 51.

17. Ibid., 134.

18. Yukiko Kimura, "Social-Historical Background of the Okinawans in Hawaii," in

Uchinanchu: A History of Okinawans in Hawaii (Honolulu: Ethnic Studies Oral History Project, Ethnic Studies Program, University of Hawaii, 1981), 57.

19. Shurtleff and Aoyagi, *How Japanese Brought Soyfoods*, 44.

20. Kimura, "Social-Historical Background," 58.

21. Shurtleff and Aoyagi, *How Japanese Brought Soyfoods*, 51.

22. Chester H. Rowell, "Editorial Comment from Fresno *Republican*: A Calamity" (Fresno, CA) *Republican*, 30 May 1910; quoted in Eliot Mears, *Resident Orientals on the American Pacific Coast* (Chicago: University of Chicago, 1928; reprint New York: Arno Press, 1978), 446–448; James Augustin Brown, *The Japanese Crisis* (New York: Frederick A. Stokes, ca. 1916).

23. Shurtleff and Aoyagi, *How Japanese Brought Soyfoods*, 78.

24. Ibid., 74.

25. Ibid., 67.

26. Ibid., 48, 77, 117.

27. By a back-of-the-envelope calculation, this works out to be one for every 2,300 Japanese people in the region. By comparison, in 1965 Japan, before the thoroughgoing modernization of tofu production, there was one tofu shop for every 2,000 people. Soyinfo Center, "History of Tofu: A Chapter from the Unpublished Manuscript, History of Soybeans and Soyfoods: 1100 b.c. to the 1980s by William Shurtleff and Akiko Aoyagi," last modified 2007, 3.

28. Kimura, Social-Historical Background," 66.

29. Shurtleff and Aoyagi, *How Japanese Brought Soyfoods*, 9; Yamauchi Oral History, 494.

30. Shurtleff and Aoyagi, *How Japanese Brought Soyfoods*, 39.

31. Hawaii Agricultural Experiment Station, *Leguminous Crops for Hawaii*, by F. G. Krauss, Bulletin No. 23 (Washington, DC: US Government Printing Office, 1911), 23–24. Piper and Morse also note that the Otootan variety was introduced from Hawaii in 1911; ultimately traceable to Formosa, it is unclear how long it had been grown in Hawaii. Charles V. Piper and William J. Morse, *The Soybean* (New York: McGraw-Hill, 1923; reprint, New York: Peter Smith, 1943), 168.

32. Burtt-Davy, "Lily-Bulbs," 213.

33. Harry W. Miller, typewritten memoir transcribed from voice recordings, ca. 1958, Department of Archives and Special Collections, Del E. Webb Memorial Library, Loma Linda University, Loma Linda, CA, 52–53.

34. Ibid., 250.

35. Ibid., 54.

36. Harry W. Miller, *The Story of Soya Milk* (Mt. Vernon, OH: International Nutrition Laboratory, 1941), 6–7.

37. Ronald L. Numbers, *Prophetess of Health: Ellen G. White and the Origins of Seventh-day Adventist Health Reform* (Knoxville: University of Tennessee Press, 1992), 81.

38. Gerald Carson, *Cornflake Crusade* (New York: Rinehart & Company, 1957), 142;

and J. H. Kellogg, *The Living Temple* (Battle Creek, MI: Good Health Publishing Company, 1903), 23.

39. Carson, *Cornflake Crusade*, 136.

40. Ibid., 136.

41. Harry W. Miller, "A Legacy of Long Life," unpublished manuscript, n.d., Archives of the E. G. White Estate Branch Office, Loma Linda University, Loma Linda, CA, 1.

42. Numbers, *Prophetess of Health*, 171–72, 174.

43. Karen Iacobbo and Michael Iacobbo, *Vegetarian America: A History* (Westport, CT: Praeger, 2004), 128.

44. John H. Kellogg, "Vegetable-Food Compound," US Patent 670283, 19 March 1901 (filed 3 June 1899), 1.

45. Soyinfo Center, "Dr. John Harvey Kellogg and Battle Creek Foods: Work with Soy, a Special Exhibit—The History of Soy Pioneers around the World—Unpublished Manuscript by William Shurtleff and Akiko Aoyagi," last modified 2004, www.soyinfo center.com/HSS/john_kellogg_and_battle_creek_foods.php.

46. Kellogg, "Vegetable-Food Compound," 120.

47. Ibid., 158–59.

48. US Department of Agriculture, *The Soy Bean as a Forage Crop*, by Thomas A. Williams, with an appendix, "Soy Beans as Food for Man," by C. F. Langworthy, Farmers' Bulletin No. 58 (Washington, DC: U.S. Government Printing Office, 1899), 21.

49. Ibid., 21–22.

50. Ibid., 23.

51. US Department of Agriculture, Office of Experiment Stations, *A Digest of Metabolism Experiments in Which the Balance of Income and Outgo Was Determined*, by W. O. Atwater and C. F. Langworthy, Bulletin No. 45 (Washington, DC: US Government Printing Office, 1898), 79–80.

52. M. L. Holbrook, "The Science of Health: Vegetable Cheese," *Phrenological Journal and Science of Health*, September 1900, 88–89; "Vegetable Cheese," *Dietetic and Hygienic Gazette*, June 1900, 340–341; Langworthy, "Soy Beans as Food for Man," 21–23.

53. Daniel Carpenter, *The Forging of Bureaucratic Autonomy: Reputations, Networks, and Policy Innovation in Executive Agencies, 1862–1928* (Princeton: Princeton University Press, 2001), 183.

54. David Fairchild, assisted by Elizabeth and Alfred Kay, *The World Was My Garden: Travels of a Plant Explorer* (New York: Charles Scribner's Sons, 1938), 106–107.

55. Ibid., 105.

56. US Department of Agriculture, Division of Forestry, *Systematic Plant Introduction: Its Purposes and Methods*, by David Fairchild (Washington, DC: US Government Printing Office, 1898), 17.

57. Ibid., 15.

58. Ibid., 13.

59. Fairchild, *World*, 202.

60. USDA, *Systematic Plant Introduction*, 13.

61. Isabel Shipley Cunningham, *Frank N. Meyer: Plant Hunter in Asia* (Ames: Iowa State University Press, 1984), 6. Also see F. H. King, *Farmers of Forty Centuries or Permanent Agriculture in China, Korea and Japan* (New York: Harcourt, Brace & Company, 1911).

62. USDA, *Systematic Plant Introduction*, 19.

63. Cunningham, *Frank N. Meyer*, 18–20.

64. Fairchild, *World*, 315.

65. Cunningham, *Frank N. Meyer*, 35.

66. Ibid., 41, 45.

67. Ibid., 76, 68.

68. Ibid., 45.

69. Ibid., 72.

70. "The People Who Stand for Plus: Frank N. Meyer, Scientific Explorer for the United States Government in China and Russia," *The Outing Magazine* 53:1 (October 1908): 73–74.

71. Jerry Israel, *Progressivism and the Open Door: America and China, 1905–1921* (Pittsburgh: University of Pittsburgh Press, 1971), xi.

72. William J. Morse estimated that there were at most eight, a figure that has become canonical. See US Department of Agriculture, Office of Forage Crops, Bureau of Plant Industry, *Soy Beans: Culture and Varieties*, by W. J. Morse, Farmers' Bulletin 1520 (Washington, DC: US Government Printing Office, 1927), 2.

73. US Department of Agriculture, Division of Botany, *Inventory No. 1: Foreign Seeds and Plants Imported by the Section of Seed and Plant Introduction. Numbers 1–1000* (Washington, DC: US Government Printing Office, 1898), 53.

74. Fairchild, *World*, 196, 259.

75. This is calculated on the basis of the USDA's inventories of *Seeds and Plants Imported, Numbers 1–11*, which cover the period February 1898 through December 1905 and inventory numbers 1 through 16796.

76. This is calculated on the basis of the USDA's inventories of *Seeds and Plants Imported, Numbers 12–15*, which cover the period January 1906 through June 1908 and inventory numbers 16797 through 23322. Meyer's total number of plant (and some entomological) introductions during this period was 1,108.

77. Ibid.

78. Letter from Meyer to Fairchild, 8 January 1908, quoted in William Shurtleff and Akiko Aoyagi, *William J. Morse—History of His Work with Soybeans and Soyfoods (1884–1959): Extensively Annotated Bibliography and Sourcebook* (Lafayette, CA: Soyinfo Center, 2011), 25.

79. US Department of Agriculture, Bureau of Plant Industry, *Seeds and Plants Imported during the Period from December, 1905, to July, 1906: Inventory No. 12; Nos. 16797 to 19057* (Washington, DC: US Government Printing Office, 1907), 56, 72.

80. Cunningham, *Frank N. Meyer*, 42. As it happened, chop suey, which included water chestnuts and sprouts, was something of a craze in the United States at the time.

81. US Department of Agriculture, Bureau of Plant Industry, *Seeds and Plants Imported during the Period from July, 1906, to December 31, 1907: Inventory No. 13; Nos. 19058 to 21730* (Washington, DC: US Government Printing Office, 1908), 7; Cunningham, *Frank N. Meyer*, 41.

82. USDA, *Seeds and Plants Imported . . . No. 13*, 16.

83. Ibid., 92–93.

84. Shurtleff and Aoyagi, *Morse*, 25.

85. Ibid., 22.

86. Letter from Meyer to Fairchild, 18 December 1907, quoted in Shurtleff and Aoyagi, *Morse*, 25.

87. Letter from Meyer to Fairchild, 8 January 1908, quoted in ibid., 25.

88. Cunningham, *Frank N. Meyer*, 67.

89. Ibid., 81.

90. US Department of Agriculture, Bureau of Plant Industry, *Seeds and Plants Imported during the Period from December, 1905, to July, 1906: Inventory No. 12; Nos. 16797 to 19057* (Washington, DC: US Government Printing Office, 1907), 54–55. The use of "delicatessen" as a plural for specialty foods was common English usage at the time.

91. Cunningham, *Frank N. Meyer*, 33.

92. Alan L. Olmstead and Paul W. Rhode, *Creating Abundance: Biological Innovation and American Agricultural Development* (New York: Cambridge University Press, 2008), 271–272.

93. L. W. Kephart, "Charles Vancouver Piper," typed manuscript prepared for *Wallace's Farmer*, 1926, Folder: MorsPipe, Record: Keph-1926, Soyinfo Center, Lafayette, CA, 5.

94. Ibid., 3–4.

95. US Department of Agriculture, Bureau of Plant Industry, "The Search for New Leguminous Forage Crops," by C. V. Piper, in *Yearbook of the U.S. Department of Agriculture: 1908* (Washington, DC: US Government Printing Office, 1909), 489.

96. US Department of Agriculture, Bureau of Plant Industry, *Soybean Varieties*, by Carleton R. Ball, Bulletin No. 98 (Washington, DC: US Government Printing Office, 1907), 3.

97. Ibid., 8.

98. Langworthy, "Soy Beans as Food for Man," 6.

99. USDA, *Soybean Varieties*, 14.

100. Ibid., 3.

101. Ibid., 8.

102. Ibid., 20.

103. US Department of Agriculture, Bureau of Plant Industry, *The Soy Bean: History, Varieties, and Field Studies*, by C. V. Piper and W. J. Morse, Bulletin No. 197 (Washington, DC: US Government Printing Office, 1910), 37, 39–74.

104. These were "field selections": the following spring, they began sorting newly introduced seeds even before planting them, so-called seed selections. Ibid., 25.

105. Morse and other breeders did note, and separate out, natural crosses when they occurred. Even at Arlington Farm, where so many distinct varieties were grown in contiguous rows, only one out of every two hundred plants was a natural cross. Ibid., 23.

106. All of the varieties were given distinct SPI numbers. Ibid., 39–74.

107. 17852 B through 17852 R, although E through M are not listed in Piper and Morse's 1910 bulletin; 17852 A was the Meyer variety. Ibid., 48–49.

108. Ibid., 48–49.

109. US Department of Agriculture, Bureau of Plant Industry, *The Arlington Experiment Farm: A Handbook of Information for Visitors*, compiled by Edwina V. A. Avery (Washington, DC: US Government Printing Office, 1928), 3. As an indication of the burgeoning volume of plant material arriving from around the world, this superseded by only a year Congress's allotment of seventy-five acres in DC itself.

110. US Department of Agriculture, *Soy Beans*, by C. V. Piper and H. T. Nielsen, Farmers' Bulletin No. 372 (Washington, DC: U.S. Government Printing Office, 1909); US Department of Agriculture, Bureau of Plant Industry, *Seeds and Plants Imported during the Period from January 1 to March 31, 1909: Inventory No. 18; Nos. 24430 to 25191* (Washington, DC: US Government Printing Office, 1909), 36.

111. Edward Jerome Dies, *Soybeans: Gold from the Soil* (New York: Macmillan Company, 1942), 2.

Chapter 2. Jumping the Gun

1. US Department of Agriculture, Bureau of Plant Industry, *The Soy Bean: Its Uses and Culture*, by W. J. Morse, Farmers' Bulletin No. 973 (Washington, DC: US Government Printing Office, 1918), 5.

2. W. J. Morse, Biloxi, MS, to C. V. Piper, Washington, DC, 22 October 1920, Division of Forage Crops and Diseases, Series: General Correspondence, 1905–29, Boxes 92–93: Morgan-Morse to Morse-Napier, National Archives II, College Park, MD (hereafter Morse Correspondence).

3. Charles S. Plumb, "A Substitute for Coffee," in *Purdue University: Seventh Annual Report of the Agricultural Experiment Station, Lafayette, Indiana, 1894* (Indianapolis: Wm. B. Buford, 1895), 45–47.

4. *Report of the Secretary of Agriculture, Executive Documents of the House of Representatives for the Second Session of the Fifty-Third Congress, 1893–1894* (Washington, DC: US Government Printing Office, 1895), 378.

5. G. H. Alford, *Southern I.H.C. Demonstration Farms* (Chicago: International Harvester Company of New Jersey, ca. 1914), 20.

6. N. E. Winters, "Soil and Crop Improvement under Boll Weevil Conditions," *Atlanta Constitution*, 4 January 1920, 2F.

7. Fabian Lange, Alan L. Olmstead, and Paul W. Rhode, "The Impact of the Boll Weevil, 1892–1932," *Journal of Economic History* 69 (September 2009): 687.

8. US Department of Agriculture, Bureau of Plant Industry, *The Soy Bean, with Special Reference to Its Utilization for Oil, Cake, and Other Products*, Bulletin No. 439, by C. V. Piper and W. J. Morse (Washington, DC: US Government Printing Office, 1916), 18.

9. G. H. Alford, *How to Prosper in Boll Weevil Territory* (Chicago: International Harvester Company of New Jersey, ca. 1914), 26.

10. USDA, "Search for New Leguminous Forage Crops," 245, 249–250. For a recent overview of how the boll weevil affected southern agriculture and to what degree it brought about "material change," see James C. Giesen, *Boll Weevil Blues: Cotton, Myth, and Power in the American South* (Chicago: University of Chicago Press, 2011).

11. USDA, *Soy Beans* [1909], 5.

12. Department of Commerce and Labor, Bureau of Manufactures, *Soya Beans and Products*, Special Consular Reports, vol. 40 (Washington, DC: US Government Printing Office, 1909), 29.

13. USDA, *Soy Beans* [1909], 2.

14. USDA, *Soy Bean* [Bull. 439], 7.

15. Ibid., 8. The area "less certain of profitable production" edged up into southern Illinois, well south of where the soybean oil industry would actually emerge the following decade. A note on the first page of the bulletin explained: "This bulletin is intended for general distribution in the Southern States, where it will be of special interest to farmers and cotton-oil millmen."

16. W. J. Morse, Washington, DC, to C. V. Piper, Washington, DC, 4 December 1914, Morse Correspondence. A Seattle mill had crushed imported soybeans as early as 1911, but this was the first recorded use of American soybeans for producing oil. Soyinfo Center, "History of Soybeans in North Carolina, a Special Exhibit—The History of Soy Pioneers around the World—Unpublished Manuscript by William Shurtleff and Akiko Aoyagi," last modified 2004, www.soyinfocenter.com/HSS/north_carolina.php.

17. Or possibly as early as 1870, when legend has it they were brought to the state by an old sea captain who had obtained them in the Orient. Soyinfo Center, "History of Soybeans in North Carolina."

18. E. E. Hartwig and W. L. Nelson. "Soybeans in North Carolina," *Soybean Digest*, November 1947, 11.

19. W. J. Morse, Beaumont, TX, to C. V. Piper, Washington, DC, 19 August 1917, Morse Correspondence.

20. Soyinfo Center, "North Carolina."

21. Woody Upchurch, "Soybean Industry Builds on Foundation Laid by Tar Heel Farmers, Businessmen," [Lumberton, NC] *Robesonian*, 23 December 1967, 5.

22. Soyinfo Center, "North Carolina."

23. W. J. Morse, "The Soy-Bean Industry in the United States," *Yearbook of the Department of Agriculture 1917* (Washington, DC: US Government Printing Office, 1918), 104; and Charles V. Piper and William J. Morse, *The Soybean* (New York: McGraw-Hill, 1923; reprint New York: Peter Smith, 1943), 22, table 13.

24. R. A. Oakley, Washington, DC, to W. J. Morse, Arlington Farm, Virginia, 10 September 1910, and Morse Correspondence. He had correspondents in at least fifteen other states.

25. Walter O. Scott, "Cooperative Extension Efforts in Soybeans," in *50 Years with Soybeans*, ed. R. W. Judd (Urbana, IL: National Soybean Crop Improvement Council, 1979), 64.

26. Soyinfo Center, "North Carolina."

27. Morse, "Soy-Bean Industry," 104.

28. Soyinfo Center, "North Carolina"; and W. J. Morse, "Soy-Bean Output Increasing in United States," *Yearbook of the Department of Agriculture 1926* (Washington, DC: US Government Printing Office, 1927), 671.

29. Approximately 78 square miles, or slightly bigger than two American townships.

30. Ibid., 671.

31. W. J. Morse and J. L. Cartter, "Improvement in Soybeans," in *U.S. Dept. of Agriculture Yearbook 1937* (Washington, DC: US Government Printing Office, 1937), 1155; Morse, "Soy-Bean Output," 671; and Bruce L. Gardner, *American Agriculture in the Twentieth Century: How It Flourished and What It Cost* (Cambridge, MA: Harvard University Press, 2002), 19.

32. Maximilian Toch, *The Chemistry and Technology of Paints* (New York: D. Van Nostrand Company, 1916), 195.

33. R. A. Oakley, Washington, DC, to W. J. Morse, Arlington Farm, VA, 23 May 1911, Morse Correspondence.

34. Linda O. McMurry, *George Washington Carver: Scientist and Symbol* (New York: Oxford University Press paperback, 1982), 91.

35. North Carolina Agricultural Extension Service, *The Commercial Use of the Soybean*, extracts of letters to C. B. Williams, Extension Circular No. 29 (Raleigh, NC: Agricultural Extension Service, 1916).

36. Theodore F. Bradley, "Nonedible Soybean Oil Products," in *Soybeans and Soybean Products*, vol. 2, ed. Klare S. Markley, Fats and Oils: A Series of Monographs (New York: Interscience 1951), 854.

37. Giesen, *Boll Weevil Blues*, 127–141.

38. Lange, Olmsted, and Rhode, "Impact," 715.

39. Ibid., 704, 709.

40. Ibid., 688.

41. J. B. Killebrew and William H. Glasson, "Tobacco—Discussion," *Publications of the American Economic Association, 3rd Series* 5 (February 1904): 138.

42. Soyinfo Center, "North Carolina."

43. Parnell W. Picklesimer, "The New Bright Tobacco Belt of North Carolina," *Economic Geography* 20 (January 1944): 14.

44. John Fraser Hart and Ennis L. Chestang, "Turmoil in Tobaccoland," *Geographical Review* 86 (October 1996): 554.

45. David Manber, *Wizard of Tuskegee: The Life of George Washington Carver* (New York: Crowell-Collier Press, 1967), 117.

46. Andrew F. Smith, *Peanuts: The Illustrious History of the Goober Pea* (Urbana: University of Illinois Press, 2002): roasted, 22–27; salted 48–54; peanut butter, 30–39; Cracker Jack, 74.

47. The culmination of his work was the Victor Cowpea, so named because Piper, always a stickler in matters of language, thought that naming things "Victory" had become "rather overworked" during the war. C. V. Piper, Washington, DC, to W. J. Morse, 7 April 1919, Morse Correspondence.

48. M. J. Rosenau, *The Milk Question* (Boston: Houghton Mifflin Company, 1912), 6.

49. Ibid., 2.

50. William J. Melhuish, "Process for the Manufacture of Artificial Milk, and Treatment of Its Residues," US Patent 1210667, 2 January 1917 (filed 22 October 1915).

51. Yu Ying Li, "Method of Manufacturing Products from Soja," US Patent 1064841, 17 June 1913 (filed 10 October 1911).

52. Louis J. Monahan and Charles J. Pope, "Process of Making Soy-Milk," US Patent 1165199, 21 December 1915 (filed 10 April 1913).

53. "To Make Synthetic Milk," *Washington Post*, 24 November 1912, M4.

54. Yu Ling Li, "Products from Soja."

55. Monahan and Pope, "Process of Making Soy-Milk."

56. Gaston D. Thévenot, "Process of Manufacturing Milk and Cream Substitutes," US Patent 1359633, 23 November 1920 (filed 24 January 1919); Gaston D. Thévenot, "Process of Making Vegetable Milk," US Patent 1541006, 9 June 1925 (filed 11 June 1923); and Gaston D. Thévenot, "Process of Making Vegetable Milk," US Patent 1556977, 23 October 1925 (filed 8 December 1923).

57. William J. Melhuish, "Manufacture of Vegetable Milk and Its Derivatives," US Patent 1175467, 14 March 1916 (filed 1 June 1914); and Melhuish, "Manufacture of Artificial Milk."

58. Margery Currey, "World's First Patriotic Food Show Starts," *Chicago Daily Tribune*, 6 January 1918, 5; Mrs. Lynden Evans, "A Call for Kitchen Patriotism," *Chicago Daily Tribune*, 12 January 1918, 5; and "Learning How to Win the War," *Chicago Daily Tribune*, 6 January 1918, 5.

59. Evans, "A Call for Kitchen Patriotism," 5.

60. Mary Swain Routzahn, *The Chicago Patriotic Food Show: A Brief Review of Its Main Features* (New York: Russell Sage Foundation, 1918), 3–4.

61. Ring Lardner, "In the Wake of the News: War Eats," *Chicago Daily Tribune*, 9 January 1918, 11.

62. Evans, "A Call for Kitchen Patriotism," 5.

63. *Official Recipe Book: Containing All Demonstrations Given During Patriotic Food Show, Chicago, January 5–13, 1918* (Chicago: Illinois State Council of Defense: 1918), 25.

64. *Official Recipe Book*, 59–72. The Bean Spice Cake, however, used no wheat flour at all.

65. Lardner, "War Eats," 11. Oney Fred Sweet was a *Tribune* features writer. Lardner's "Luncheon" included, in references now equally obscure to today's readers, "SWEETS. Rosie O'Grady and Annie Rooney, with soy beans. FATS. Filet of Bob Lee, with soy beans."

66. "Learning How to Win the War," 5. A photo in this article shows Hattie Don Sang in front of a table with a sign reading "BEAN BREAD"; Eddington did not identify it by that name. Nor did she give the name of the young women staffing the booth; see Currey, "World's First Patriotic Food Show Starts," 5.

67. Jane Eddington, "Tribune Cook Book: Soy Bean Products, Etc.," *Chicago Daily Tribune*, 8 January 1918, 14.

68. Jane Eddington, "Tribune Cook Book: Soy Beans as Human Food," *Chicago Daily Tribune*, 12 January 1919, B4.

69. Piper and Morse, *The Soybean*, 273. The Chicago Bean Bread Company was incorporated shortly after the food show and had its plant in Chicago's Chinatown. There is no definitive indication that this was the same group that mounted the food show booth, but it seems likely. "Trade Items," *The National Baker*, 15 May 1918, 70.

70. USDA, *Soy Bean as a Forage Crop*, 21.

71. "Wonderful Soya Bean," *Los Angeles Times*, 16 July 1911, II11.

72. Jane Eddington, "Economical Housekeeping: Soy Beans," *Chicago Daily Tribune*, 11 February 1914, 11; and Jane Eddington, "Economical Housekeeping: More About Soy Beans," *Chicago Daily Tribune*, 4 February 1914, 16.

73. Jane Eddington, "Tribune Cook Book: Baked Soy Beans," *Chicago Daily Tribune*, 13 December 1917, 18.

74. William Shurtleff and Akiko Aoyagi, *History of Edamame, Green Vegetable Soybeans, and Vegetable-Type Soybeans (1275–2009): Extensively Annotated Bibliography and Sourcebook* (Lafayette, CA: Soyinfo Center, 2009), 117; and US Department of Agriculture, Bureau of Plant Industry, *Inventory of Seeds and Plants Imported by the Office of Foreign Seed and Plant Introduction during the Period from January 1 to March 31, 1915: Inventory No. 30; Nos. 39682 to 40388* (Washington, DC: US Government Printing Office, 1918), 69. *Hato-koroshi-daizu:* "Daizu" means "large bean," a common suffix for the large-seeded soybeans used as green vegetables; "Hato-koroshi" means "dove killer," perhaps also a reference to the bean's size.

75. Shurtleff and Aoyagi, *Edamame*, 121.

76. Ibid., 117.

77. Eddington, "Economical Housekeeping: Soy Beans," 11.

78. Morse, "Soy Bean Industry," 107.

79. Jane Eddington, "Tribune Cook Book: Pinto Beans," *Chicago Daily Tribune*, 29 December 1917, 10; and R. A. Oakley, Washington, DC, to Carl L. Alsberg, Washington, DC, 25 May 1917, Record Group 88, Records of the Food and Drug Administration, Subgroup: Records of the Bureau of Chemistry 1877–1943, Series: World War I Project File 1917–19, National Archives II, College Park, MD (henceforth Records of the Bureau of Chemistry).

80. Jane Eddington, "Tribune Cook Book: Baked Pinto Beans," *Chicago Daily Tribune*, 2 April 1918, 14.

81. Soyinfo Center, "History of Soy Flour, Grits, Flakes, and Cereal-Soy Blends—A Special Report on the History of Soy Oil, Soybean Meal, and Modern Soy Protein Products: A Chapter from the Unpublished Manuscript, History of Soybeans and Soyfoods: 1100 B.C. to the 1980s by William Shurtleff and Akiko Aoyagi," last modified 2007, www .soyinfocenter.com/HSS/flour3.php, 1.

82. Ibid., 3; and *Soy Bean* [Bull. 439], 1.

83. US Department of Agriculture, *Use Soy-Bean Flour to Save Wheat, Meat and Fat*, contributions from the States Relations Service, A. C. True, director, No. 113 (Washington, DC: US Government Printing Office, 1918), 3.

84. Ibid., 4.

85. Helen B. Wolcott, Lexington, KY, to Hannah L. Wessling, Washington, DC, 9 May 1917; and H. L. Wessling, Washington, DC, to Helen B. Wolcott, Lexington, KY, 23 May 1917, Records of the Bureau of Chemistry.

86. Jane Eddington, "Tribune Cook Book: Soy Bean Flour," *Chicago Daily Tribune*, 21 March 1917, 12; and Eddington, "Soy Beans as Human Food," B4.

87. Robert E. Speer, "The Man and His Work: From an Occidental Viewpoint," in *A Missionary Pioneer in the Far East: A Memorial of Divie Bethune McCartee*, ed. Robert E. Speer (New York: Fleming R. Revell Company, 1922), 9; and James Kay MacGregor, "Yamei Kin and Her Mission to the Chinese People," *The Craftsman*, 1 November 1905, 244.

88. "Among the Recent Graduates," *Iowa State Reporter* [Waterloo], 13 October 1887, 1; "Miss May King," *Sumner* [Iowa] *Gazette*, 11 June 1885, 1; and All-China Women's Federation, "Women in History: First Woman Overseas Student of Modern China and Legend in Her Own Time," last modified July 4, 2010, www.womenofchina.cn/html /report/106099–1.htm.

89. An American citizen, he was killed in Europe during World War I. Gerald Jacobson, comp., *History of the 107th Infantry U.S.A.* (New York: Seventh Regiment Armory, 1920), 208.

90. All-China Women's Federation, "A Chinese Woman Physician, Dr. Yamei Kin," *Outlook*, 16 May 1917, 108; "Their Day of Rest," *Los Angeles Times*, 14 July 1897, 6; and "Brevities," *Los Angeles Times*, 10 January 1903, 1.

91. "Woman's World: Around the World with Women," [Winnipeg] *Free Press*, 15 April 1911; All-China Women's Federation.

92. "China's Foremost Woman Physician," [Frederick, MD] *Evening-Post*, 25 January 1911, 1.

93. "Woman off to China as Government Agent to Study Soy Bean," *New York Times*, 10 June 1917, 65.

94. "Emperor Forgot China," *Peace River* [Alberta, Canada] *Record*, June 1917.

95. "Bandits of Shantung," *North-China Herald*, 25 August 1917, 428; and American Legation, Peking, to Secretary of State, Washington, DC, 15 September 1917, Record Group 59, Textual Records from the Department of State, M329, Roll 183, 893.61321/6a and 893.61321/7, National Archives II, College Park, MD.

96. "Makes New Kind of Meat," [Monticello, Iowa] *Express*, 25 July 1918, 3.

97. "Testing Food Stuffs at Appraiser's Stores," *New York Times*, 18 September 1904, SM7.

98. Kin later told McDougal that the dessert was made with "a little red bean," which probably referred to the adzuki bean, not the soybean.

99. B. R. Hart, San Francisco, CA, to Chief, Bureau of Chemistry, Washington, DC, 22 May 1917, Records of the Bureau of Chemistry.

100. "A New Meat Substitute," *New York Times*, 21 July 1918, 18.

101. Walter T. Swingle, "Our Agricultural Debt to Asia," in *The Asian Legacy and American Life*, ed. Arthur E. Christy (New York: Asia Press, 1945), 91.

102. "Use of Soy Beans as Fat Substitute Urged by Chinese Expert," *Oil, Paint and Drug Reporter*, 17 December 1917, 25.

103. Daniel J. Sweeney, comp., *History of Buffalo and Erie County, 1914–1919* (Buffalo, NY: Committee of One Hundred, 1919), 434. This may be a garbled recollection, as she, like others, probably used soybean flour, not tofu, in bread.

104. "Food Value of Soy Bean: Chinese Expert Rates It High," *Evening Capital and Maryland Gazette*, 2 October 1918.

105. *Official Recipe Book*, 14.

106. US Department of Agriculture, *Program of Work of the United States Department of Agriculture for the Fiscal Year 1919* (Washington, DC: US Government Printing Office, 1918), 300.

107. Piper and Morse, *The Soybean*, 273.

108. William Henry Adolph, "How China Uses the Soy Bean as Food," *Journal of Home Economics* 14 (February 1922): 69.

109. W. J. Morse, Washington, DC, to R. A. Oakley, Washington, DC, 18 November 1918, Morse Correspondence.

110. Soyinfo Center, "Madison College and Madison Foods, a Special Exhibit—The History of Soy Pioneers around the World—Unpublished Manuscript by William Shurtleff and Akiko Aoyagi," last modified 2004, www.soyinfocenter.com/HSS/madison_college_and_foods.php.

111. William Shurtleff and Akiko Aoyagi, "Harry W. Miller," in *History of Soybeans*

and Soyfoods, Past, Present, and Future, unpublished manuscript (Lafayette, CA: Soy-foods Center, ca. 1999).

112. William Shurtleff and Akiko Aoyagi, *History of Seventh-Day Adventist Work with Soyfoods, Vegetarianism, Meat Alternatives, Wheat Gluten, Dietary Fiber, and Peanut Butter (1863–2013): Extensively Annotated Bibliography and Sourcebook* (Lafayette, CA: Soyinfo Center, 2014), 151, 162, 463.

113. J. H. Kellogg, *The New Method in Diabetes* (Battle Creek, MI: Good Health Publishing Company, 1917), 64.

114. Carson, *Cornflake Crusade,* 223.

115. John Leonard Kellogg, "Manufacture of a Food Product," US Patent 1189128, 27 June 1916 (filed 19 November 1915).

116. John Harvey Kellogg, *The New Dietetics: What to Eat and How* (Battle Creek, MI: Modern Medicine Publishing Company, 1921), 299.

117. Ibid., 302.

Chapter 3. Taking Root

1. W. A. Ostrander, "It's Fun to Remember," *Soybean Digest* 4 (September 1944), 16–17; and Record Group 54, Subgroup: Division of Forage Crops and Diseases, Series: Correspondence with State Agricultural Experiment Stations, 1899–1928, Box 12: Illinois-Indiana, National Archives II, College Park, MD. (Henceforth Indiana Correspondence.)

2. *Proceedings of the American Soybean Association,* vol. 1: 1925, 1926, 1927 (n.p.: American Soybean Association, 1928), 39–40.

3. Taylor Fouts, "Putting Soybeans on the Hoof," in *Proceedings of the American Soybean Association,* vol. 1: 1925, 1926, 1927 (n.p.: American Soybean Association, 1928), 125.

4. *Proceedings of the ASA,* vol. 1, 42.

5. W. J. Morse, Champaign, IL, to C. V. Piper, Washington, DC, 31 August 1930, Record Group 54, Subgroup: Division of Forage Crops and Diseases, Series: General Correspondence, 1905–29, Boxes 92–93: Morgan-Morse to Morse-Napier, National Archives II, College Park, MD.

6. Ostrander, "It's Fun to Remember"; and Indiana Correspondence.

7. The Hacklemans, "Memorial to Prof. J. C. Hackleman" (presented to the Urbana-Champaign Faculty Senate on 14 December 1970 by a committee of the University of Illinois Department of Agriculture, W. O. Scott, Chairman), thehacklemans.com/id121.htm.

8. Samuel O. Rice, "Missouri's War Rations: The 'Show-Me' State Is Showing the Nation How to Grow More Food," *The Country Gentleman,* 10 August 1918, 13.

9. His lack of a doctorate notwithstanding, he became a full professor in 1923 and served as a crops extension specialist in the department until his retirement in 1956. "Memorial to Hackleman."

10. Robert W. Stark, Urbana, IL, to C. V. Piper, 11 March 1918, Illinois Correspondence.

11. Deborah Fitzgerald, *The Business of Breeding: Hybrid Corn in Illinois, 1890–1940* (Ithaca: Cornell University Press, 1990), 117–123.

12. Gladys Baker, *The County Agent*, Studies in Public Administration, vol. 11 (Chicago: University of Chicago Press, 1939), 25–32.

13. Ibid., 33.

14. Ibid., 37–41; and M. C. Burritt, *The County Agent and the Farm Bureau* (New York: Harcourt, Brace, 1922), 208–209.

15. Baker, *The County Agent*, xiv.

16. Ibid., 46–47.

17. Hackleman to Morse, 25 November 1919, Illinois Correspondence.

18. F. B. Mumford, *Work and Progress of the Agricultural Experiment Station for the Year Ended June 30, 1915*, University of Missouri Agricultural Experiment Station Bulletin No. 141 (Columbia: University of Missouri, 1916), 30, 53.

19. Hackleman to Morse, 9 January 1920; and Morse to Hackleman, 13 January 1920, Illinois Correspondence.

20. Hackleman to Morse, 14 February 1920; Morse to Hackleman, 10 March 1920; and Hackleman to Morse, 18 March 1920, Illinois Correspondence.

21. Hackleman to Piper, 12 June 1920; Piper to Hackleman, 16 June 1920; Morse to Hackleman, 30 June 1920; and Hackleman to Morse, 6 July 1920, Illinois Correspondence.

22. Hackleman to Morse, 22 April 1921; Hackleman to Morse, 3 March 1922; Hackleman to Morse, 25 April 1922; Hackleman to Morse, 9 July 1923; and University of Illinois Department of Agronomy, "Project: Soybean Varieties," typewritten report, enclosed with Hackleman to Piper, 17 July 1923, Illinois Correspondence. There are 102 counties in Illinois.

23. Hackleman to Morse, 25 April 1922, Illinois Correspondence.

24. *Proceedings of the ASA*, vol. 1, 3–4. In other years, demonstrating its national scope, the ASA met in Clarksdale, Mississippi; Washington; North Carolina; and Columbia, Missouri.

25. Hackleman to Morse, 16 April 1920; and Morse to Hackleman, 26 April 1920, Illinois Correspondence.

26. Frank Sumner Bash, ed., *History of Huntington County, Indiana*, vol. 2 (Chicago: Lewis Publishing Company, 1914), 650–651.

27. Quoted in William Shurtleff and Akiko Aoyagi, *Early History of Soybeans and Soyfoods Worldwide (1900–1923): Extensively Annotated Bibliography and Sourcebook* (Lafayette, CA: Soyinfo Center, 2012), 1134.

28. Hopkins to Morse, 9 December 1916, Illinois Correspondence.

29. W. L. Burlison, Urbana, IL, to W. J. "Moore," 27 February 1917, Illinois Correspondence.

30. J. C. Hackleman, "The Future of the Soybean as a Forage Crop," typewritten manuscript enclosed with Hacklelman to Piper, 7 December 1923, Illinois Correspondence, 3. Corn prices recovered after 1920 from 60 to 81 cents per bushel in 1923, but this was still far below the wartime high.

31. Ibid., 2–3.

32. W. J. Spillman, "Changes in Type of Farming," *Yearbook of the Department of Agriculture 1926* (Washington, DC: US Government Printing Office, 1927), 206; John C. Hudson, *Making the Corn Belt: A Geographical History of Middle-Western Agriculture* (Bloomington: Indiana University Press, 1994), 158; and Historical Statistics of the United States: Millennial Edition Online, "Table Da693–706—Corn, Barley, and Flaxseed—Acreage, Production, Price, and Corn Stocks: 1866–1999," last updated 2006, hsus.cambridge.org.

33. W. L. Burlison, "Soybeans Gain Popularity: They Make Good in Illinois," *Orange Judd Farmer* 66 (1 March 1919): 349. Burlison did not officially take charge until 1920; in the meantime Hopkins continued to be listed on the letterhead as head of the department, but with an asterisk indicating that he was deceased. Hackleman to Morse, 25 November 1919, Illinois Correspondence; and Hackleman to Forage Crops Investigation Office (in Morse's absence), 21 August 1920, Illinois Correspondence.

34. "Dr. William Leonidas Burlison: Your Friends Say," Transcript of the Burlison Banquet, Illini Union Ballroom, University of Illinois, Urbana, 26 June 1951. William L. Burlison Papers, 1888–1968, Series 8/6/22, University of Illinois Archives, Urbana, IL, no page.

35. Hudson, *Making the Corn Belt*, 69–70, 156.

36. Frank Ridgway, "Corn and Soy Beans," *Chicago Tribune*, 10 August 1920, 14.

37. Ibid.

38. Hackleman, "The Future of the Soybean," 3. In an address to the ASA in 1925, Hackleman offered a different, and even more dramatic, set of numbers: from 25,000 acres in five Corn Belt states in 1919 to 1,189,000 acres in 1924. *Proceedings of the ASA*, vol. 1, 83.

39. Hackleman, "The Future of the Soybean," 3.

40. *Proceedings of the ASA*, vol. 1, 94; and Andrew F. Smith, *Peanuts: The Illustrious History of the Goober Pea* (Urbana: University of Illinois Press, 2002), 66; Alonzo E. Taylor, *Corn and Hog Surplus of the Corn Belt* (Stanford University: Food Research Institute, 1932), 562; and George H. Primmer, "United States Soybean Industry," *Economic Geography* 15 (April 1939): 210.

41. The reason why it could grow where red clover failed was because it required less limestone per acre, as red clover grew more densely. Hackleman, "The Future of the Soybean," 5.

42. Ibid., 3–5.

43. Ibid., 8.

44. "Soybean Special to Carry Experts," *The Decatur* [Illinois] *Review*, 11 March 1927, 30.

45. Dan J. Forrestal, *The Kernel and the Bean: The 75-Year Story of the Staley Company* (New York: Simon and Schuster, 1982), 65.

46. Baker, *The County Agent*, 7.

47. US Department of Agriculture, *Motion Pictures of the United States Department of Agriculture*, Misc. Circular 86 (Washington, DC: US Government Printing Office, 1926), 10.

48. Forrestal, *The Kernel*, 9; and Soyinfo Center, "A. E. Staley Manufacturing Company (1922–1980s): Work with Soy, a Special Exhibit—The History of Soy Pioneers around the World—Unpublished Manuscript by William Shurtleff and Akiko Aoyagi," last modified 2004, www.soyinfocenter.com/HSS/ae_staley_manufacturing.php. He did not grow up, however, in what would become soybean country in North Carolina: Elizabeth, on the coast, was quite distant from Greensboro.

49. US Department of Agriculture, Division of Plant Industry, *The Production and Utilization of Corn Oil in the United States*, by A. F. Sievers (Washington, DC: US Government Printing Office, 1920), 4.

50. William Shurtleff and Akiko Aoyagi, *History of Cooperative Soybean Processing in the United States (1923–2008): Extensively Annotated Bibliography and Sourcebook* (Lafayette, CA: Soyinfo Center, 2008), 18.

51. Edward Jerome Dies, *Soybeans: Gold from the Soil* (New York: Macmillan, 1942), 16; Helen M. Cavanaugh, *Seed, Soil and Science: The Story of Eugene D. Funk* (Chicago: Lakeside Press, 1959), 348; and Shurtleff and Aoyagi, *Cooperative Soybean Processing*, 19.

52. Dies, *Gold from the Soil*, 16–17.

53. Staley's life story and business travails are recounted in Forrestal, *Kernel*.

54. Forrestal, *Kernel*, 60–61.

55. Hackleman to Morse, 7 December 1920, Illinois Correspondence.

56. Forrestal, *Kernel*, 60–61, 56; and F. A. Wand, "Relation between the Soybean Grower and the Oil Mill," in *Proceedings of the American Soybean Association*, vol. 1: *1925, 1926, 1927* (n.p.: American Soybean Association, 1928), 105. A bushel of corn is 56 pounds, a bushel of soybeans 60 pounds.

57. "Monticello Is to Have Soybean Mill," *Decatur [Illinois] Review*, 11 March 1922, 2.

58. Hackleman to Morse, 18 November 1922, Illinois Correspondence.

59. Morse to Hackleman, 6 January 1922, Illinois Correspondence.

60. Fitzgerald, *Business of Breeding*, 117.

61. Hackleman to Morse, 23 February 1923, Illinois Correspondence.

62. Shurtleff and Aoyagi, *Cooperative Soybean Processing*, 14, 20.

63. Klare S. Markley and Warren H. Goss, *Soybean Chemistry and Technology* (Brooklyn, NY: Chemical Publishing Company, Inc., 1944), 138–139.

64. Forrestal, *Kernel*, 63; and Hackleman to Morse, 23 April 1923, Illinois Correspondence.

65. Wand, "Relation between Grower and Mills," 105; Dies, *Gold from the Soil*, 26; and Forrestal, *Kernel*, 63.

66. Wand, "Relation between Grower and Mills," 104–105.

67. Ibid., 105; and Forrestal, *Kernel*, 63.

68. Frederick A. Wand, "Commercial Outlet for Soybeans," in *Proceedings of the American Soybean Association*, vol. 2: *1928, 1929* (n.p.: American Soybean Association, 1930), 35.

69. University of Illinois Agricultural Experiment Station, *Soybean Production in Illinois*, by J. C. Hackleman, O. H. Sears, and W. L. Burlison, Bulletin No. 310 (Urbana: University of Illinois, 1928), 492–493.

70. E. C. Young, "The Proper Place for Soybeans in the System of Farming," in *Proceedings of the American Soybean Association*, vol. 2: *1928, 1929* (n.p.: American Soybean Association, 1930), 20.

71. Wand, "Commercial Prospects of Soybeans," 28.

72. Dies, *Gold from the Soil*, 26.

73. Wand, "Commercial Prospects of Soybeans," 30–31.

74. W. E. Reigel, "Protecting the American Soybean Market," in *Proceedings of the Sixteenth Annual Meeting of the American Soybean Association* (n.p.: American Soybean Association, 1936), 49.

75. Wand, "Commercial Outlet for Soybeans," 35; L. B. Breedlove, "Soybean—The Magic Plant, Article XIX: Trading in Futures Next Development in Perfecting Market Facilities," *Chicago Journal of Commerce and La Salle Street Journal*, 16 July 1936, 12; Cavanaugh, *Seed, Soil and Science*, 353.

76. Forrestal, *Kernel*, 66–67.

77. R. C. Ross, "Cost of Growing and Harvesting Soybeans in Illinois," in *Proceedings of the American Soybean Association*, vol. 3: *1930* (n.p.: American Soybean Association, 1931), 50; and University of Illinois Agricultural Experiment Station, *Supply and Marketing of Soybeans and Soybean Products*, by C. L. Stewart, W. L. Burlison, L. J. Norton, and O. L. Whalin, Bulletin No. 386 (Urbana: University of Illinois, 1932), 440.

78. Ibid., 445.

79. I. D. Mayer, "Harvesting Soybeans with the Combine," in *Proceedings of the American Soybean Association*, vol. 2: *1928, 1929* (n.p.: American Soybean Association, 1930), 21; and *Supply and Marketing of Soybeans*, 451.

80. *Proceedings of the American Soybean Association*, vol. 2: *1928, 1929* (n.p.: American Soybean Association, 1930), 110.

81. David Wesson, "Contributions of the Chemist to the Cottonseed Oil Industry," *Journal of Industrial and Engineering Chemistry* 7 (April 1915): 277.

82. M. M. Durkee, "Soybean Oil in the Food Industry," *Industrial and Engineering Chemistry* 28 (August 1936): 899.

83. Ibid.

84. University of Illinois College of Agriculture, Agricultural Experiment Station and Extension Service in Agriculture and Home Economics, *Recent Developments in the Utilization of Soybean Oil in Paint*, by W. L. Burlison, Circular 438 (Urbana: University of Illinois, 1935).

85. J. E. Barr, "The Development of Quality Standards for Soybeans," in *Proceedings*

of the American Soybean Association, vol. 1: *1925, 1926, 1927* (n.p.: American Soybean Association, 1928), 78–79; and L. B. Breedlove, "Soybean—The Magic Plant, Article XVIII: Crop Movements, Grade Requirements and Federal Inspection," *Chicago Journal of Commerce and La Salle Street Journal*, 14 July 1936, 12.

86. US Department of Agriculture, *Plant Material Introduced by the Office of Foreign Plant Introduction, Bureau of Plant Industry, during the Period from Oct. 1 to Dec. 31, 1925: Inventory No. 85; S.P.I. Nos. 65048 to 65707* (Washington, DC: US Government Printing Office, 1928), 15; "Explorers Send Plants Home for Trial," *Los Angeles Times*, 3 April 1927, J20; Morse to Hackleman, 16 April 1926, Illinois Correspondence.

87. Morse to Hackleman, 28 February 1927, Illinois Correspondence.

88. Theodore Hymowitz, "Dorsett-Morse Soybean Collection Trip to East Asia: 50 Year Retrospective," *Economic Botany* 38 (October–December 1984): 385.

89. Ibid., 382; Morse and P. H. Dorsett, Tokyo, to Knowles A. Ryerson, Washington, DC, 5 March 1930, Morse Correspondence.

90. Cavanaugh, *Seed, Soil and Science*, 365.

Chapter 4. Exploring All Avenues

1. David L. Lewis, *The Public Image of Henry Ford: An American Folk Hero and His Company* (Detroit: Wayne State University, 1976), 297; and Cheryl R. Ganz, *The 1933 Chicago World's Fair: A Century of Progress* (Urbana: University of Illinois Press, 2008), 79–80.

2. Lewis, *Public Image*, 298–299; Lisa D. Schrenk, *Building a Century of Progress: The Architecture of Chicago's 1933–34 World's Fair* (Minneapolis: University of Minnesota Press, 2007), 112; Roland Marchand, "The Designers Go to the Fair: Walter Dorwin Teague and the Professionalization of Corporate Industrial Exhibits, 1933–1940," *Design Issues* 8 (Autumn 1991): 4; and *Official Guide Book of the World's Fair of 1934* (Chicago: A Century of Progress International Exposition, 1934), 137–138.

3. James Sweinhart, *The Industrialized American Barn: A Glimpse of the Farm of the Future* (Dearborn, MI: Ford Motor Company, 1934), 15–16.

4. Ibid., 5.

5. Earl Mullin, "Ford Will Push His Farm Ideas in Fair Exhibit," *Chicago Daily Tribune*, 4 April 1934, 14.

6. Sweinhart, *Industrialized American Barn*, 15.

7. "Ford Barn at Fair Burned," *New York Times*, 10 August 1934, 15.

8. Lewis, *Public Image*, 286.

9. "Declaration of Dependence upon the Soil and the Right to Self-Maintenance," 30–35, in *Proceedings of the Dearborn Conference of Agriculture, Industry and Science, Dearborn, Michigan, May 7 and 8, 1935* (New York: Chemical Foundation, 1935), 30.

10. "Industry, Farm Chiefs Lay Own Revival Plans," *Chicago Daily Tribune*, 8 May 1935, 31.

11. William J. Hale, "Farming Must Become a Chemical Industry," *Dearborn Independent*, 2 October 1926, 4–5, 24–26.

12. Anne B. W. Effland, "'New Riches from the Soil': The Chemurgic Ideas of Wheeler McMillen," *Agricultural History* 69 (Spring 1995): 292.

13. Schrenk, *Building*, 151.

14. Hale, "Farming," 25.

15. Soyinfo Center, "Henry Ford and His Employees: Work with Soy—A Special Exhibit—The History of Soy Pioneers around the World—Unpublished Manuscript by William Shurtleff and Akiko Aoyagi," last modified 2004, www.soyinfocenter.com /HSS/henry_ford_and_employees.php; Steven Watts, *The People's Tycoon: Henry Ford and the American Century* (New York: Alfred A. Knopf, 2005), 483.

16. Soyinfo Center, "Ford and His Employees."

17. Some of the oil was used in the production of the resins themselves. R. H. Mc-Carroll, "Increasing the Use of Agricultural Products in the Automobile Industry," in *Proceedings of the Dearborn Conference*, 60; and William Shurtleff and Akiko Aoyagi, *Henry Ford and His Researchers—History of Their Work with Soybeans, Soyfoods and Chemurgy (1928–2011): Extensively Annotated Bibliography and Sourcebook* (Lafayette, CA: Soyinfo Center, 2011), 31.

18. "Golden Grain," *Los Angeles Times*, 12 December 1932, A4.

19. McCarroll, "Increasing," 60; L. B. Breedlove, "Soybean—The Magic Plant, Article XIV: Industrial Uses Already Manifold with More in Prospect," *Chicago Journal of Commerce and La Salle Street Journal*, 2 July 1936, 12.

20. Brian Ralston, "Soy Protein Plastics: Material Formulation, Processing and Properties" (PhD diss., University of Wisconsin–Madison, 2008), 16.

21. Ibid., 17; R. S. Burnett, "Soybean Protein Industrial Products," in *Soybeans and Soybean Products*, ed. Klare S. Markley, vol. 2, Fats and Oils: A Series of Monographs (New York: Interscience Publishers Ltd., 1951), 1035.

22. McCarroll, "Increasing," 61.

23. Shurtleff and Aoyagi, *Ford and His Researchers*, 58; Burnett, "Soybean Protein," 17.

24. University of Illinois College of Agriculture, Agricultural Experiment Station and Extension Service in Agriculture and Home Economics, *Recent Developments in the Utlization of Soybean Oil in Paint*, by W. L. Burlison, Circular 438 (Urbana: University of Illinois, 1935), 4; and E. E. Ware, "Role of Soy Bean Oil in Paint Formulation," in *Proceedings: Second Dearborn Conference, May 12, 13, 14* (Dearborn, MI: Farm Chemurgic Council, 1936), 250.

25. Rudolf A. Clemen, *By-Products in the Packing Industry* (Chicago: University of Chicago Press, 1927), 6.

26. Ibid., 311; and "The House That Joyce Built," *Fortune*, May 1949, 95.

27. "The House," 96.

28. Ibid., 99.

29. Ibid., 95.

30. Ibid., 99.

31. Christy Borth, *Pioneers of Plenty: Modern Chemists and Their Work*, new enlarged ed. (New York: The New Home Library, 1943), 259–261.

32. Hugh Farrell, *What Price Progress? The Stake of the Investor in the Discoveries of Science* (New York: G. P. Putnam's Sons, 1926), 197; Charles N. Cone and Earl D. Brown, "Protein Product and Process of Making," US Patent 1955375, 17 April 1934 (filed 5 March 1930), 1.

33. W. J. O'Brien, "Soy Bean Proteins," in *Proceedings: Second Dearborn Conference, May 12, 13, 14* (Dearborn, MI: Farm Chemurgic Council, 1936), 258.

34. Ibid., 256.

35. Ibid., 255; Percy L. Julian and Andrew G. Engstrom, "Process for Production of a Derived Vegetable Protein," US Patent 2238329, 15 April 1941 (filed 3 December 1937), 1.

36. Cone and Brown, "Protein Product," 1–2.

37. O'Brien, "Soy Bean Proteins," 258; "Glidden Company to Make Soya Bean Oil and Meal," *Oil, Paint, and Drug Reporter* vol. 126 (November 1934): 52.

38. Arthur Evans, "Lusty Industry Born in Chicago from Soy Bean," *Chicago Daily Tribune*, 29 March 1935, 4; and "Probe Factory Blast Fatal to Six; 43 Injured," *Chicago Daily Tribune*, 8 October 1935, 1.

39. "Science: Bean Blast," *Time*, 21 October 1935, 34; and David J. Price and Hylton R. Brown, *Quarterly of the National Fire Protection Association* 29 (January 1936).

40. O'Brien, "Soy Bean Proteins," 256.

41. "Probe Factory Blast."

42. "Four More Bodies Are Taken from Ruins of Plant," *Chicago Daily Tribune*, 11 October 1935, 14.

43. "Probe Factory Blast"; "Dig in Wreckage for 5 Men Still Missing in Blast," *Chicago Daily Tribune*, 9 October 1935, 11.

44. "Soy Bean Plant Owner Killed in Blast on 1st Day," *Chicago Daily Tribune*, 23 October 1935, 8; and David J. Price, "A Rural Soybean Plant Explosion," *Quarterly of the National Fire Protection Association* 29 (January 1936): 241–243.

45. Price and Brown, "Glidden Soybean Plant Explosion," 239.

46. "Glidden to Erect Soy Bean Plant, Office Building," *Chicago Daily Tribune*, 1 November 1935, 33; "Glidden Sales up, but Profits Slip behind Last Year," *Wall Street Journal*, 17 April 1936, 6; and Soyinfo Center, "History of the Glidden Company's Soya Products / Chemurgy Division, a Special Exhibit—The History of Soy Pioneers around the World—Unpublished Manuscript by William Shurtleff and Akiko Aoyagi," last modified 2004, www.soyinfocenter.com/HSS/glidden.php.

47. Ibid.

48. Carol Willis, *Form Follows Finance: Skyscrapers and Skylines in New York and Chicago* (New York: Princeton Architectural Press, 1995), 121–123.

49. William D. Falloon, *Market Maker: A Sesquicentennial Look at the Chicago Board of Trade* (Chicago: Board of Trade of the City of Chicago, 1998), 184–186.

50. The following discussion of futures is drawn from Gail L. Cramer and Wal-

ter G. Heid Jr., *Grain Marketing Economics* (New York: John Wiley & Sons, 1983), 171–212.

51. Roland McHenry, Chicago, to J. C. Murray, Chicago Board of Trade, 25 September 1931, Correspondence Re. Soybean Futures 1931, Archives of the Chicago Board of Trade, Box II.1.128, Folder 3091, Daley Library Special Collections, University of Illinois at Chicago (henceforth Soybean Futures Correspondence 1931).

52. University of Illinois Agricultural Experiment Station, *Supply and Marketing of Soybeans and Soybean Products*, by C. L. Stewart, W. L. Burlison, L. J. Norton, and O. L. Whalin, Bulletin 386 (Urbana: University of Illinois, 1932), 529.

53. Fred Clutton, Chicago, to John E. Brennan, Chicago, 1 October 1931, and responses, 5 and 18 November 1931, Soybean Futures Correspondence 1931; Chicago Board of Trade Directors Meeting Minutes, 17 November 1931, Directors Meeting Minutes 1931–1935, Archives of the Chicago Board of Trade, Box II.1.128, Folder 3091, Daley Library Special Collections, University of Illinois at Chicago (henceforth Directors Meeting Minutes).

54. H. E. Robinson, "The Economic Significance of Soybean Oil Flavor Stability," in *Proceedings of the Conference on Flavor Stability in Soybean Oil* (Chicago: National Soybean Processors Association, 22 April 1946), 9.

55. US Department of Agriculture, Bureau of Agricultural Economics, *Soybeans in American Farming*, by Edwin G. Strand, Technical Bulletin No. 966 (Washington, DC: US Government Printing Office, November 1948), 2, 5.

56. Edwin G. Nourse, Joseph S. Davis, and John D. Black, *Three Years of the Agricultural Adjustment Administration* (Washington, DC: Brookings Institution, 1937), 86, 89; Strand, *Soybeans in American Farming*, 5.

57. Dean Dorhees, Fairbury, IL, to C. S. Beach, Chicago, 13 March 1935, Soybean Committee Materials 1935–1936, Archives of the Chicago Board of Trade, Box III.937, Folder 5, Daley Library Special Collections, University of Illinois at Chicago (henceforth Soybean Committee Materials 1935–1936).

58. L. B. Breedlove, "Soybean—The Magic Plant, Article I: Picturing Its Multiple Industrial and Economic Possibilities," *Chicago Journal of Commerce and La Salle Street Journal*, 2 June 1936, 12.

59. Frank Ridgway, "Corn-Hog Plan Is Helped by Chinch Bug," *Chicago Daily Tribune*, 3 April 1935, 15; Primmer, "United States Soybean Industry," 205; Mabel P. Crompton, "The Soybean Crop of Illinois," *Journal of Geography* 39 (April 1940): 143; Dorhees to Beach, 13 March 1935, Soybean Committee Materials 1935–1936.

60. Paul Potter, "A 'Baby' Combine for Medium Size Farms Is Shown," *Chicago Daily Tribune*, 25 July 1933, 16.

61. "Active Thresher Sales Expected by Leading Farm Tool Makers," *Wall Street Journal*, 14 June 1935, 2.

62. "Farm Machine Output Up," *New York Times*, 5 April 1937, 28.

63. US Department of Agriculture, Bureau of Agricultural Economics, *Soybean Pro-*

duction in War and Peace, by Edwin G. Strand (Washington, DC: US Government Printing Office, September 1943), 33.

64. Primmer, "United States Soybean Industry," 206. Combined soybeans were, for the same reason, more soil-conserving than soybeans harvested for hay, unless the manure of hay-fed animals was conscientiously returned to the land. The Agricultural Adjustment Act of 1936, however, added soybean hay as a soil-conserving crop but not soybeans harvested for beans. Strand, *Soybeans in American Farming*, 5.

65. M. M. Durkee, "Soybean Oil in the Food Industry," *Industrial and Engineering Chemistry* 28 (August 1936): 901.

66. Arthur Evans, "Processing Tax Sought by Dixie on Foreign Oils," *Chicago Daily Tribune*, 29 October 1933, 9; and "Hearing on Oleo Is Attended by Groups of the Farm Interest," *Oshkosh* [Wisconsin] *Northwestern*, 16 May 1935, 3.

67. George F. Deasy, "Geography of the United States Cottonseed Oil Industry," *Economic Geography* 17 (October 1941): 351; and Ruth Dupré, "'If It's Yellow, It Must Be Butter': Margarine Regulation in North America since 1886," *Journal of Economic History* 59 (June 1999): 360–361.

68. Soybean Committee Report, 15 March 1935, Exhibit 3: Soybean Production Tables, Soybean Committee Materials 1935–1936.

69. George F. Deasy, "Geography of the United States Soybean-Oil Industry," *Journal of Geography* 40 (January 1941): 2.

70. L. B. Breedlove, "Soybean—The Magic Plant, Article XIX: Trading in Futures Next Development in Perfecting Market Facilities," *Chicago Journal of Commerce and La Salle Street Journal*, 16 July 1936, 12.

71. Chicago Board of Trade Directors Meeting Minutes, 4 December 1934, Directors Meeting Minutes.

72. Soybean Committee Report, 15 March 1935, Soybean Committee Materials 1935–1936.

73. E. H. G., Pontiac, IL, to Beach, Wickham & Co., Chicago, Soybean Committee Materials 1935–1936.

74. Crompton, "Soybean Crop of Illinois," 142.

75. Deasy, "Geography," 2.

76. Approval of Soybean Committee, 28 January 1936, Soybean Committee Materials 1935–1936.

77. Second Draft of Report, 18 August 1936, Soybean Committee Records 1936, Archives of the Chicago Board of Trade, Box IV.16.599, Folders 1–3, Daley Library Special Collections, University of Illinois at Chicago (henceforth Soybean Committee Records 1936).

78. Ibid.

79. Ibid.

80. Breedlove, "Soybean—The Magic Plant, Article I."

81. Second Draft of Report, 18 August 1936, Soybean Committee Records 1936.

82. Amendment to Rule 1823, 21–23 September 1936, Archives of the Chicago Board of Trade, Box II.2.139, Folder 3337, Daley Library Special Collections, University of Illinois at Chicago.

83. Proposed Amendment to Rules, 2 July 1936, Archives of the Chicago Board of Trade, Box I.1.18, Folder 16/26, Daley Library Special Collections, University of Illinois at Chicago.

84. Forest Glen Warren, "Economic Significance of the Futures Market for Soybeans" (PhD diss., University of Illinois, 1945), 85.

85. Max Tishler, "Percy L. Julian, the Scientist," *The Chemist* 42 (March 1965): 109.

86. "The House That Joyce Built," *Fortune*, May 1949, 99; Tishler, "Percy L. Julian," 109. The name of the first director of research for the Soya Products Division, Eric Wahlforss, appeared on a Glidden patent application as late as August 1936. Eric Wahlforss, "Soya Bean Product," US Patent 2284700, 2 June 1942 (filed 6 August 1936).

87. William F. McDermott, "Slavery's Grandchildren," *Coronet*, January 1948, 123–127; NOVA, "Transcripts: Forgotten Genius. PBS Airdate: February 6, 2007," last modified 2007, www.pbs.org/wgbh/nova/transcripts/3402_julian.html; and Paul de Kruif, "The Man Who Wouldn't Give Up," *Reader's Digest*, August 1946, 113–118; Tishler, "Percy L. Julian"; and "Dr. Julian Makes Good at Depauw, Ind., University," *Afro-American*, 14 July 1934, 14.

88. Until 1947, it seems, when he was compared to his fellow Spingarn Medal winner. Drew Pearson, "Drew Pearson on the Washington Merry-Go-Round," *Florence* [South Carolina] *Morning News*, 29 June 1947, 4. Also Albert Barnett, "Dr. Carver or Dr. Julian: Which Would You Choose?" *Chicago Defender (National Edition)*, 15 October 1949, 7.

89. De Kruif, "Man Who Wouldn't Give Up," 116.

90. Percy L. Julian and Andrew G. Engstrom, "Process for Production of a Derived Vegetable Protein," US Patent 2238329, 15 April 1941 (filed 3 December 1937), 1.

91. Ibid., 2.

92. Ibid., 3.

93. Arthur A. Levinson and James L. Dickinson, "Method of Preparing Feed Material," US Patent 2162729, 20 June 1939 (filed 8 June 1938); and Soyinfo Center, "History of the Glidden Company's Soya Products/Chemurgy Division, a Special Exhibit—The History of Soy Pioneers around the World—Unpublished Manuscript by William Shurtleff and Akiko Aoyagi," last modified 2004, www.soyinfocenter.com/HSS/glidden.php.

94. Tishler, "Percy L. Julian," 109.

95. Percy L. Julian and Andrew G. Engstrom, "Preparation of Vegetable Phosphatides," US Patent 2249002, 15 July 1941 (filed 8 June 1938); and Soyinfo Center, "History of Soy Lecithin—A Special Report on the History of Soy Oil, Soybean Meal & Modern Soy Protein Products: A Chapter from the Unpublished Manuscript, History of Soybeans and Soyfoods: 1100 b.c. to the 1980s by William Shurtleff and Akiko Aoyagi," last modified 2007, www.soyinfocenter.com/HSS/lecithin2.php.

96. Tishler, "Percy L. Julian," 110.

97. Soyinfo Center, "History of Glidden's Soya Products Division."

98. Shurtleff and Aoyagi, "Ford and His Researchers," 98–99.

99. R. A. Boyer, "How Soybeans Help Make Ford," in *Proceedings, Eighteenth Annual Meeting of the American Soybean Association*, 12–14 September 1938 at Wooster and Columbus, Ohio, 9.

100. Robert A. Boyer, William T. Atkinson, and Charles F. Robinette, "Artificial Fibers and Manufacture Thereof," US Patent 2377854, 12 June 1945 (filed 7 June 1941), 1.

101. Soyinfo Center, "Ford and His Employees."

102. Shurtleff and Aoyagi, "Ford and His Researchers," 313; Lewis, *Public Image*, 285.

103. Soyinfo Center, "Ford and His Employees."

104. Watts, *The People's Tycoon*, 483.

105. Borth, *Pioneers of Plenty*, 363–365.

106. Shurtleff and Aoyagi, "Ford and His Researchers," 82.

107. Soyinfo Center, "Ford and His Employees."

108. The last quote was from the *Decatur* [Illinois] *Herald Review*, which obviously had a vested interest in soybean use. Watts, *The People's Tycoon*, 283.

109. Howard P. Segal, *Recasting the Machine Age: Henry Ford's Village Industries* (Boston: University of Massachusetts Press, 2005), 4.

110. Ibid., 164. He had previously established a similar plant in the Rouge complex itself.

111. David E. Wright, "Alcohol Wrecks a Marriage: The Farm Chemurgic Movement and the USDA in the Alcohol Fuels Campaign in the Spring of 1933," *Agricultural History* 67 (Winter 1993): 65.

112. L. B. Breedlove, "Soybean—The Magic Plant, Article XV: Industrial Uses Already Manifold with More in Prospect," *Chicago Journal of Commerce and La Salle Street Journal*, 7 July 1936, 12; and Crompton, "Soybean Crop of Illinois."

113. Lewis, *Public Image*, 284.

114. Charles V. Piper and William J. Morse, *The Soybean* (New York: McGraw-Hill, 1923; reprint, New York: Peter Smith, 1943), 238–257.

115. Ibid., 273–279.

116. Ibid., 236.

117. William J. Morse, "Letter from Dr. Morse," in *Proceedings of the American Soybean Association*, vol. 2: *1928, 1929* (n.p.: American Soybean Association, 1930), 51–52.

118. William Shurtleff and Akiko Aoyagi, *William J. Morse—History of His Work with Soybeans and Soyfoods (1884–1959): Extensively Annotated Bibliography and Sourcebook* (Lafayette, CA: Soyinfo Center, 2011), 255.

119. Ibid. He sent a can of Almen for the chronically ill Oakley to try. Morse, Keijo, to Oakley, 3 November 1929; Morse, Tokyo, to Pieters, 30 January 1930, Morse Correspondence.

120. Morse, Sapporo, Hokkaido, to Oakley, 28 September 1929, Morse Correspondence.

121. Morse, Tokyo, to Pieters, 15 February 1930, Morse Correspondence.

122. Morse, "Letter from Dr. Morse," 51.

123. Shurtleff and Aoyagi, "William J. Morse—History of His Work," 380.

124. Soyinfo Center, "Madison College and Madison Foods, a Special Exhibit— The History of Soy Pioneers around the World—Unpublished Manuscript by William Shurtleff and Akiko Aoyagi," last modified 2004, www.soyinfocenter.com/HSS/madi son_college_and_foods.php.

125. William Shurtleff and Akiko Aoyagi, *History of Seventh-Day Adventist Work with Soyfoods, Vegetarianism, Meat Alternatives, Wheat Gluten, Dietary Fiber and Peanut Butter (1863–2013): Extensively Annotated Bibliography and Sourcebook* (Lafayette, CA: Soyinfo Center, 2014), 185–186.

126. William Shurtleff and Akiko Aoyagi, *Mildred Lager—History of Her Work with Soyfoods and Natural Foods in Los Angeles (1900–1960): Extensively Annotated Bibliography and Sourcebook* (Lafayette, CA: Soyinfo Center, 2009), 30.

127. Gordon Kennedy, ed., *Children of the Sun: A Pictorial Anthology; From Germany to California, 1883–1949* (Ojai, CA: Nivaria Press, 1998), 7–10.

128. Shurtleff and Aoyagi, *Mildred Lager*, 30.

129. "For Your Health's Sake Use Jones Fresh Ground Soy Bean Flour!" [Ad] *Los Angeles Times*, 3 April 1932, J21; "The May Company Modern Market: Savory Wednesday" [Ad], *Los Angeles Times*, 2 May 1934, A6.

130. Mildred Lager, *The Useful Soybean: A Plus Factor in Modern Living* (New York: McGraw-Hill, 1945), 125.

131. Jethro Kloss, *Back to Eden: A Human Interest Story of Health and Restoration to Be Found in Herb, Root, and Bark* (Coalmont, TN: Longview Publishing House, 1939), 160, 269.

132. Elmer Vernon McCollum, *A History of Nutrition: The Sequences of Ideas in Nutrition Investigation* (Cambridge, MA: Riverside Press, 1957), 158, 167.

133. J. H. Kellogg, "Be Sure to Chew Your Milk," *Washington Post*, 8 October 1916, ES4.

134. John Harvey Kellogg, "Method of Making Acidophilus Milk," US Patent 1982994, 4 December 1934 (filed 14 June 1933); and Soyinfo Center, "Dr. John Harvey Kellogg and Battle Creek Foods: Work with Soy—A Special Exhibit—The History of Soy Pioneers Around the World—Unpublished Manuscript by William Shurtleff and Akiko Aoyagi," last modified 2004, www.soyinfocenter.com/HSS/john_kellogg_and _battle_creek_foods.php.

135. William Shurtleff and Akiko Aoyagi, *History of Soy Yogurt, Soy Acidophilus Milk, and Other Cultured Soymilks (1918–2012): Extensively Annotated Bibliography and Sourcebook* (Lafayette, CA: Soyinfo Center, 2012), 6.

136. "No Intestinal Poisoning Here!" [Ad for Theradophilus], *Los Angeles Times*, 17 June 1934, J21.

137. Harry W. Miller, typewritten memoir transcribed from voice recordings, ca. 1958, Department of Archives and Special Collections, Del E. Webb Memorial Library, Loma Linda University, Loma Linda, CA, 252 (hereafter Miller Memoir).

138. Soyinfo Center, "History of Soymilk and Dairy-like Soymilk Products—A Special Report on the History of Traditional Non-fermented Soyfoods—A Chapter from the Unpublished Manuscript, History of Soybeans and Soyfoods: 1100 B.C. to the 1980s by William Shurtleff and Akiko Aoyagi," last modified 2007, www.soyinfocenter.com/HSS/soymilk1.php.

139. Kloss, 611.

140. Miller Memoir, 164–166.

141. Harry W. Miller, *The Story of Soya Milk* (Mt. Vernon, OH: International Nutrition Laboratory, 1941), 20.

142. William Shurtleff, "Dr. Harry Miller: Taking Soymilk around the World," *Soyfoods* 1 (Winter 1981): 30.

143. Miller Memoir, 256.

144. Miller, *Story of Soya Milk*, 22.

145. Harry Willis Miller, "Process of Making Vegetable Milk," US Patent 2078962, 4 May 1937 (filed 3 December 1935), 1.

146. Miller Memoir, 254; Pierce Mason Travis, "Dispersion Mill," US Patent 1851071, 29 March 1932 (filed 30 June 1923); and Miller, "Process of Making Vegetable Milk."

147. Miller, *Story of Soya Milk*, 25.

148. Miller Memoir, 257; Miller, *Story of Soya Milk*, 24; Shurtleff, "Miller," 30.

149. Miller, *Story of Soya Milk*, 26.

150. Miller Memoir, 258–259.

151. Shurtleff, "Miller: Taking Soymilk," 32–33.

152. Shurtleff and Aoyagi, "Henry Ford and His Researchers," 8.

153. Ronald Deutsch, *The Nuts among the Berries*, rev. ed. (New York: Ballantine Books, 1967), 135–136.

154. Lewis, *Public Image*, 229.

155. Ibid., 229; and Watts, *The People's Tycoon*, 328.

156. Reynold Wik, *Henry Ford and Grass-roots America* (Ann Arbor: University of Michigan Press, 1972), 152.

157. Shurtleff and Aoyagi, "Ford and His Researchers," 191.

158. Ibid., 191; and Soyinfo Center, "Ford and His Employees."

159. As Willemse and others recalled in the 1980s, though there is no mention of him in reports from the 1930s. Shurtleff and Aoyagi, "Ford and His Researchers," 37, 300–301, 306.

160. Ibid., 37; and Soyinfo Center, "Ford and His Employees."

161. Shurtleff and Aoyagi, "Ford and His Researchers," 36.

162. Soyinfo Center, "Ford and His Employees."

163. Lewis, *Public Image*, 285.

Chapter 5. Answering the Call

1. "Governor Is Host at Soy Bean Lunch," *New York Times*, 15 June 1943, 24.

2. Richard N. Smith, *Thomas E. Dewey and His Times* (New York: Simon and Schuster, 1982), 367–368.

3. H. E. Babcock, "Report of State Food Commission," *New York Times*, 11 June 1943, 8.

4. Harvey Levenstein, *Paradox of Plenty: A Social History of Eating in America*, rev. ed. (New York: Oxford University Press, 1993; Berkeley: University of California Press, 2003), 83.

5. "Soybeans: Governor Dewey Sponsors Them as Partial Solution to Food Crisis," *Life*, 19 July 1943, 45–47.

6. US Department of Agriculture, Bureau of Agricultural Economics, *Soybean Production in War and Peace*, by Edwin G. Strand (Washington, DC: US Government Printing Office, September 1943), 24; and "Brazil Tests Tung Groves to Replace Idle Acres of Old Coffee Plantations," *Soybean Digest*, April 1941, 12.

7. D. J. Bunnell, "Soybean Oil in the War Time Economy," *Soybean Digest*, October 1942, 4.

8. *Soybean Digest*, April 1941, 6; and Strand, *Soybean Production*, 15.

9. "USDA Urges Soybean Increase," *Soybean Digest*, June 1941, 1.

10. "Million More Acres, Says A.A.A.," *Soybean Digest*, October 1941, 3.

11. "Eight Million Acres in 1942," *Soybean Digest*, January 1942, 2.

12. "Battle of the Soybean," *Soybean Digest*, March 1942, 2–3.

13. D. J. Bunnell, "Problems of the Soybean Processor," *Soybean Digest*, April 1943, 6, 9.

14. "The CCC Purchase Program," *Soybean Digest*, November 1942, 1–2. By comparison, the average US price for soybeans in 1941 was $1.55, up from 90 cents in 1940. Strand, *Soybeans in American Farming*.

15. "Telling the Straight Story," *Soybean Digest*, April 1942, 1.

16. "Battle of the Soybean IV," *Soybean Digest*, June 1942, 8.

17. Strand, *Soybean Production*, 15.

18. L. R. Combs, "Let's Solve Soybean Erosion Problem," *Soybean Digest*, April 1942, 6–7, 12.

19. G. G. McIlroy, "Problems of the Soybean Grower," *Soybean Digest*, April 1943, 5.

20. Walter W. McLaughlin, "Soybean Industry as Seen by a Grower," *Soybean Digest*, September 1943, 10.

21. Bunnell, "Problems."

22. "The Soybean Storage Problem," *Soybean Digest*, July 1942, 6–7.

23. "Battle of the Soybean," *Soybean Digest*, March 1942, 2–3.

24. US Department of Agriculture, Bureau of Agricultural Economics, *Soybeans in American Farming*, by Edwin G. Strand, Technical Bulletin No. 966 (Washington, DC: US Government Printing Office, November 1948), 57.

25. "Educating the Public to Feed More Protein," *Soybean Digest*, October 1942, 3.

26. "The Meal Situation," *Soybean Digest*, November 1942, 1–2.

27. Earl O. Heady, "The Meal Situation," *Soybean Digest*, December 1942, 5, 9; "Too Much Feeding of Whole Beans," *Soybean Digest*, November 1943, 12; and D. J. Bunnell, "Problems of the Soybean Processor."

28. O. D. Klein, "The 1943 Soybean Meal Distribution Program," *Soybean Digest*, September 1943, 12, 44.

29. "Those 1943 Bean Goals," *Soybean Digest*, January 1943, 6.

30. Klein, "1943"; and "WFA Order Limits Proteins, Effective January 1," *Soybean Digest*, December 1943, 9–10.

31. "Declare War on These Weasels [Ad]," *Soybean Digest*, June 1943, inside front cover.

32. "Everybody Is Short," *Soybean Digest*, February 1944, 1.

33. "Expand Processing Output: New Mills Going Up," *Soybean Digest*, November 1943, 13.

34. Strand, *Soybean Production*, 20.

35. Porter M. Hedge, "Washington Digest: Protein Supplies," *Soybean Digest*, October 1944, 19; and Walter S. Berger, "The Feed Situation: No Time to Relax," *Soybean Digest*, December 1944, 9, 14.

36. Historical Statistics of the United States: Millennial Edition Online, "Table Da995–1019—Beef, veal, pork and lamb—slaughtering, production, and price: 1899–1999," last updated 2006, hsus.cambridge.org; Historical Statistics of the United States: Millennial Edition Online, "Table Da1039–1058—Chicken, turkeys, and eggs—number, production, price, sales, and value per head: 1909–1999," last updated 2006, hsus.cambridge.org; and Strand, *Soybean Production*, 22, 27.

37. C. R. Weber, "Lincoln: A New Variety High in Yield and Oil Content," *Soybean Digest*, March 1944, 6–7.

38. Levenstein, *Paradox of Plenty*, 83–84.

39. Ibid., 87.

40. Jethro Kloss, *Back to Eden: A Human Interest Story of Health and Restoration to Be Found in Herb, Root and Bark* (Coalmont, TN: Longview Publishing House, 1939), 584.

41. Donald S. Payne, "Soybeans in Lend-Lease," *Soybean Digest*, September 1942, 8.

42. Soyinfo Center, "History of Soy Flour, Grits, Flakes, and Cereal-Soy Blends—A Special Report on the History of Soy Oil, Soybean Meal, & Modern Soy Protein Products: A Chapter from the Unpublished Manuscript, History of Soybeans and Soyfoods: 1100 B.C. to the 1980s by William Shurtleff and Akiko Aoyagi," last modified 2007, www.soyinfocenter.com/HSS/flour3.php.

43. Jeanette McCay, *Clive McCay*, 332.

44. William Shurtleff and Akiko Aoyagi, *Clive M. McCay and Jeanette B. McCay— History of Work with Soyfoods, the New York State Emergency Food Commission, Improved Bread, and Extension of Lifespan (1927–2009): Extensively Annotated Bibliography and Sourcebook* (Lafayette, CA: Soyinfo Center, 2009), 7; and Cornell University Cooperative Extension, *Soybeans: An Old Food in a New World*, Cornell Extension Bulletin 668 (Ithaca: Cornell University, 1945), 2.

45. Soybean Committee of the New York State Emergency Food Commission, Report to H. E. Babcock and L. A. Maynard, 20 December 1943, Table: "Soybean Letters Received," no page, in Clive McCay Papers 1920–1967, Box 3, Division of Rare and Manuscript Collections, Carl A. Kroch Library, Cornell University, Ithaca, NY (henceforth McCay Box 3.).

46. Ibid., 1; and Shurtleff and Aoyagi, *McCay: Work with Soyfoods*, 28.

47. Ibid., 28; and Jeanette McCay, *The Miracle Bean* (Ithaca: New York State Emergency Food Commission, n.d.), Clive McCay Papers 1920–1967, Box 1, Division of Rare and Manuscript Collections, Carl A. Kroch Library, Cornell University, Ithaca, NY (henceforth McCay Box 1).

48. Jeanette McCay, *Clive McCay, Nutrition Pioneer: Biographical Memoirs by His Wife* (Charlotte Harbor, FL: Tabby House, 1994), 375; and C. M. McCay, *Sprouted Soy Beans* (Ithaca: New York State Emergency Food Commission, n.d.) in McCay Box 1.

49. McCay, *Clive McCay*, 376.

50. McCay, *Clive McCay*, xvi, 143, 488; C. M. McCay and Mary F. Crowell, "Prolonging the Life Span," *Scientific Monthly* 39 (November 1934): 406–407, 412; Hyung Wook Park, "Longevity, Aging and Caloric Restriction: Clive Maine McCay and the Construction of a Multidisciplinary Research Program," *Historical Studies in the Natural Sciences* 40 (Winter 2010): 88–90; Roger B. McDonald and Jon J. Ramsey, "Honoring Clive McCay and 75 Years of Calorie Restriction Research," *Journal of Nutrition* 140 (July 2010): 1205; C. M. McCay, "Effect of Restricted Feeding upon Aging and Chronic Diseases in Rats and Dogs," *American Journal of Public Health* 37 (May 1947): 525; and Ida Jean Kain, "Full Calories Boost Health with Nutrients," *New York Times*, 24 January 1952, B5.

51. Clive M. McCay, *Nutrition of the Dog* (Ithaca: Comstock, 1943), 84.

52. "Housewife Urged to Buy Best Food," *New York Times*, 12 November 1942, 28.

53. Ibid., 28.

54. Shurtleff and Aoyagi, *McCay: Work with Soyfoods*, 29; Cornell University Cooperative Extension, *Soybeans: An Old Food*, 44–45; and "Open Formula Bread," food label, n.d., in McCay Box 1.

55. McCay, *Clive McCay*, xx; and "Open Formula Bread," McCay Box 1.

56. "Governor Is Host at Soy Bean Lunch."

57. "Open Formula Bread," McCay Box 1.

58. "Meat Substitute," *Science News Letter* 43 (22 May 1943): 326.

59. McCay, *Clive McCay*, 332; Cornell University Cooperative Extension, *Soybeans: An Old Food*, 29.

60. McCay, *Clive McCay*, 332.

61. "Meat Substitute."

62. "Governor Dewey Sponsors Soybeans," 45.

63. C. M. McCay, *Sprouted Soy Beans*.

64. Patricia Woodward, "A Practical Study in Nutrition Education," *Journal of Home Economics* 37 (January 1945): 19–22.

65. Soya Food Research Council Organoleptic Committee, *Report on Tests of Continued Flavor Acceptance of Soy Flour in Bread* (Chicago: Soya Food Research Council, 1944), 4.

66. James L. Doig, "White Bread: The Big Market for Soy," *Soybean Digest*, November 1943, 5.

67. "It's Time to Act," *Soybean Digest*, September 1943, 3.

68. Porter M. Hedge, "Washington Digest: Soya Food Is Here to Stay," *Soybean Digest*, April 1944, 19.

69. Mildred Lager, *The Useful Soybean: A Plus Factor in Modern Living* (New York: McGraw-Hill, 1945), 175.

70. Lager, *The Useful Soybean*, 80, 175.

71. Russell Maloney, "The Food Crisis," *New Yorker*, 10 July 1943, 58–59; and "Governor Dewey Sponsors Soybeans."

72. Eugene Kinkaid and Russell Maloney, "Talk of the Town: Meat without Bones," *New Yorker*, 31 July 1943, 14–15.

73. Quoted in Levenstein, *Paradox of Plenty*, 84–85.

74. Sheila Hibbens, "Markets and Menus: Substitutes and Other Things," *New Yorker*, 76–79.

75. Jeanette B. McCay, "Soybeans Are Here to Stay," *Journal of Home Economics* 39 (December 1947): 629.

76. *New Yorker*, 27 May 1944, 26.

77. *New Yorker*, 15 September 1945, 31.

78. Levenstein, *Paradox of Plenty*, 90–93.

79. Kinkaid and Maloney, "Meat without Bones."

80. Martin V. H. Prinz, "The Dramatic Story of Soy Flour: It Began in Vienna," *Soybean Digest*, March 1944, 4.

81. Bunnell, "Soybean Oil in the War Time Economy."

82. "German Army Soya Cookbook," *Soybean Digest*, December 1941, 2–3.

83. Prinz, "The Dramatic Story."

84. Anastacia Marx De Salcedo, *Combat-Ready Kitchen: How the U.S. Military Shapes the Way You Eat* (New York: Current, an Imprint of Penguin Random House, 2015), 70.

85. "Soybeans . . . and People," *Soybean Digest*, March 1942, 10; and Rohland S. Isker, "Soybeans in the Army Ration," *Soybean Digest*, September 1942, 11.

86. James L. Doig, "Life Raft Ration: Canadian Navy Adopts Soy," *Soybean Digest*, March 1943, 6, 14.

87. Wayne G. Broehl Jr., *Cargill: Trading the World's Grain* (Hanover, NH: University Press of New England, 1992), 664–665.

88. McCay, *McCay*, 361–366.

89. Ibid., 365, 358.

90. C. M. McCay to Captain D. G. Hakansson, 5 January 1944 in McCay Box 3.

91. Wm. H. Adams, "Now! It Can Be Told! Soy Saves Ships," *Soybean Digest*, July 1944, 8.

92. George Gordon Urquhart, "Fire Extinguishing Composition," US Patent 2269958, 1 January 1942 (filed 26 July 1938).

93. Soyinfo Center, "History of the Glidden Company's Soya Products/Chemurgy Division, a Special Exhibit—The History of Soy Pioneers around the World—Unpublished Manuscript by William Shurtleff and Akiko Aoyagi," last modified 2004, www.soyinfocenter.com/HSS/glidden.php.

94. "The House That Joyce Built," *Fortune*, May 1949, 99.

95. US Department of the Interior, War Relocation Authority, *WRA: A Story of Human Conservation* (Washington, DC: US Government Printing Office, 1946), 25–30; Greg Robinson, *A Tragedy of Democracy: Japanese Confinement in North America* (New York: Columbia University Press, 2009), 93.

96. War Relocation Authority, *WRA*, xiv-xv, 22.

97. Ibid., 97–100.

98. "Minutes of the Meeting of Advisory Board of Industry," 28 September 1942, Camouflage Net Factory, Reels 256–257, *Japanese-American Evacuation and Resettlement Records, 1930–1974 (bulk 1942–1946)*, BANC MSS 67/14 c, Bancroft Library, University of California, Berkeley, available online at content.cdlib.org/view?docId=ft6j49n9ck&brand=calisphere&doc.

99. War Relocation Authority, *WRA*, 100.

100. Ibid., 111–112; "Member of Dies Committee Raps Majority Report," *Minidoka Irrigator*, 28 August 1943, 1; "Denver Post Article Censured by WRA," *Manzanar Free Press*, 5 June 1943, 1.

101. Robinson, *A Tragedy of Democracy*, 154–155.

102. Harry M. Kumagai, memos to H. A. Mathiesen, 10 June 1942 and 12 June 1942, Record Group 210, Records of the War Relocation Authority, Records of Relocation Centers, Subject-Classified General Files 1942–1946, Colorado River, Box 114, National Archives, Washington, DC (henceforth Colorado River Box 114); Harry M. Kumagai and H. A. Mathiesen, memo to Wade Head, 30 June 1942, Record Group 210, Records of the War Relocation Authority, Records of Relocation Centers, Subject-Classified General Files 1942–1946, Colorado River, Box 106, National Archives, Washington, DC (henceforth Colorado River Box 106).

103. Harry M. Kumagai, "Organization Plan and Policies of the Department of Factory," report to John Evans, 16 September 1942, Colorado River Box 106; Industry

Department, Poston III, to H. A. Mathiesen, 10 November 1942, Colorado River Box 114.

104. "Unit II Tofu Industry Delayed by Lack of Construction Material," *Poston Chronicle*, 22 December 1942, 7.

105. Harry M. Kumagai and H. A. Mathiesen, memo to Wade Head, 30 June 1942 in Colorado River Box 114; Harry M. Kumagai, memos to H. A. Mathiesen, 10 June 1942 and 12 June 1942, in Colorado River Box 114.

106. "Indy. Dept. Expected Tofu Production within Fortnight," *Poston Chronicle*, 16 January 1943, 3.

107. "Production of Tofu Starts in Unit I," *Poston Chronicle*, 14 April 1943, 1.

108. Report of the Poston Community Enterprise Department of Factory Planning, 12 June 1942, 2, in Colorado River Box 114; "Daily Output of 500 Tofu Planned for Poston III," *Poston Chronicle*, 2 October 1942, 1; "Indy. Dept. Expected Tofu"; "Tofu Production to Be Doubled Soon," *Poston Chronicle*, 2 February 1943, 5; "Production of Tofu Starts in Unit I"; and "Tofu Production," *Poston Chronicle*, 18 April 1943, 4.

109. "First Tofu Produced by Poston III Industry," *Poston Chronicle*, 19 January 1943, 1.

110. "Poston Starts Tofu Factory," *Granada Pioneer*, 17 April 1943, 3; and "Mass Production of 'Tofu' Begun by Poston Factory," *Minidoka Irrigator*, 1 May 1943, 2.

111. "Community Government Closing Report," 1945, Topaz Final Reports, Folder 9 of 15, Reels 14–17, *Records of the War Relocation Authority, 1942–1946: Field Basic Documentation*, BANC FILM 1932, Bancroft Library, University of California, Berkeley, available online at content.cdlib.org/view?docId=ft9b69p234&brand=calisphere&doc.

112. "To Manufacture Soy Bean Cakes for Topazans," *Topaz Times*, 16 February 1943, 2; "Construction of Tofu Plant Begins," *Topaz Times*, 4 January 1944, 1; and "1800 Cakes of Tofu Distributed to Mess Halls," *Topaz Times*, 12 April 1944, 3.

113. "'Tofu' Lovers!" *Manzanar Free Press*, 15 May 1943, 1; "Large Scale Production of Tofu to Start," *Granada Pioneer*, 20 November 1943, 1.

114. For example, Tomoji Wada and Masayoshi Yamaguchi at Poston ("Indy. Dept. Expected Tofu Production," *Poston Chronicle*, 16 January 1943, 3, and "Production of Tofu Starts in Unit I," *Poston Chronicle*, 14 April 1943, 1); S. Okugawa at Manzanar ("'Tofu' Manufacture Given Approval," *Manzanar Free Press*, 5 June 1943, 3); Kichizo Umeno at Heart Mountain ("Tofu Factory in Operation," *Heart Mountain Sentinel*, 8 January 1944, 8); and Gonshiro Harada at Denson ("Manufacturing of 'Tofu' to Start Here Soon," *Denson Tribune*, 30 March 1943, 4); and William Shurtleff and Akiko Aoyagi, *How Japanese and Japanese-Americans Brought Soyfoods to the United States and the Hawaiian Islands—A History (1851–2011): Extensively Annotated Bibliography and Sourcebook* (Lafayette, CA: Soyinfo Center, 2011), 140).

115. "Reporters Learn Process in Tofu Making Tedious," *Manzanar Free Press*, 16 October 1943, 4; "1,500 Tofu Cakes to be Made Daily," *Minidoka Irrigator*, 20 January 1945, 1; and "These Fellows Know Their 'Soybeans,'" *Denson Tribune*, 29 June 1943, 3.

116. "Shoyu Project Ready," *Manzanar Free Press*, 10 October 1942, 1. Manzanar was located in Owens Valley, from which Los Angeles famously obtained its drinking water.

117. "Shoyu, Rice Arrive," *Manzanar Free Press*, 22 April 1942, 2.

118. "Name Selected for Local Shoyu," *Manzanar Free Press*, 3 December 1942, 1.

119. "Record Output of Shoyu Made," *Manzanar Free Press*, 21 November 1942, 1.

120. William Shurtleff and Akiko Aoyagi, *History of Soy Sauce (160 c.e. to 2012): Extensively Annotated Bibliography and Sourcebook* (Lafayette, CA: Soyinfo Center, 2012), 865, 896, 927, 1088.

121. "Malt Method Used in Shoyu," *Manzanar Free Press*, 23 February 1944, 6.

122. "Semi-Annual Report, July 1–Dec. 31, 1943: Industry Section," Record Group 210, Records of the War Relocation Authority, Washington Office Records, Washington Document, Box 5, National Archives, Washington, DC; "Poston May Get Soybean Milk," *Poston Chronicle*, 22 October 1943, 3; War Relocation Authority, *Human Conservation*, 96; "Semi-Annual Report, July 1-Dec. 31, 1944: Industry Section," Record Group 210, Records of the War Relocation Authority, Washington Office Records, Documentary Files, Semi-Annual Reports, Box 5, National Archives, Washington, DC.

123. War Relocation Authority, *Human Conservation*, 1.

124. "Tofu Manufacture Contemplated Here," *Gila News-Courier*, 23 March 1943, 3; "Tofu for Rivers a Possibility," *Gila News-Courier*, 24 June 1943, 1; "'Tofu' Manufacture in Rivers Soon," *Gila News-Courier*, 13 November 1943, 1; "Mess 45 to Be Turned into Tofu Factory," *Gila News-Courier*, 20 November 1943, 5; "Tofu a Dream No More," *Gila News-Courier*, 23 November 1943, 3; "Keadle Gets Facts on Tofu Delivery," *Gila News-Courier*, 2 December 1943, 4; "Tofu Factory Shifts to High," *Gila News-Courier*, 15 January 1944, 1; and "Tofu Factory to Open Again," *Gila News-Courier*, 5 August 1944, 3.

125. "Lawson Joins Hospital Staff," *Gila News-Courier*, 19 August 1943, 5. This description, along with the frequent items in the paper about Lawson, may have been provided by Lawson herself.

126. Grace Lawson, "The Dietary Department," 15 August 1945, Gila River Final Reports, Folder 22 of 31, Reels 40–43, *Records of the War Relocation Authority, 1942–1946: Field Basic Documentation*, BANC FILM 1932, Bancroft Library, University of California, Berkeley, 9. It is not clear whether the cookbook contained American or Japanese style recipes or a combination of both.

127. "Dr. Lawson: Tofu for Peptic Ulcers," *Gila News-Courier*, 11 July 1944, 5.

128. War Relocation Authority, *Human Conservation*, xiv.

129. "Tofu Factory Set Up in Minn.," *Colorado Times*, 19 July 1945, 1.

130. Shurtleff and Aoyagi, *How Japanese and Japanese-Americans*, 182, 191.

131. Robinson, *A Tragedy of Democracy*, 256.

132. "Co-op Plans to Make Tofu," *Tule Lake Cooperator*, 6 November 1943; "Tofu Making Discontinued on Nov. 30," *Tule Lake Cooperator*, 10 November 1945.

133. Jennifer 8. Lee, *The Fortune Cookie Chronicles: Adventures in the World of Chinese Food* (New York: Twelve, 2008), 264.

134. Shurtleff and Aoyagi, *How Japanese and Japanese-Americans*, 86, 168.

Chapter 6. Pushing the Boundaries

1. W. H. Goss, *The German Oilseed Industry* (Washington, DC: Hobart Publishing Company, 1947), 17.

2. Ibid., 56.

3. John Gimbel, *Science, Technology, and Reparations: Exploitation and Plunder in Postwar Germany* (Stanford: Stanford University Press, 1990), 5.

4. Ibid., 7.

5. Office of Technical Services, Technical Industrial Intelligence Division, "Purpose and Activity Summary," January 1947, Records of the Office of Technical Services, Series: Industrial Research and Development Division Subject File, 1944–1948, Box 65, National Archives II, College Park, MD.

6. Allie Shah, "Obituary: Warren H. Goss, 86, Noted Pillsbury Co. Scientist," *Minneapolis-St. Paul Star-Tribune*, 16 July 1998; and Goss, *German Oilseed Industry*, no page.

7. Michael Shermer and Alex Grobman, *Denying History: Who Says the Holocaust Never Happened and Why Do They Say It?* (Berkeley: University of California Press, 2002), 114–117; and Nuremberg Trial Proceedings Vol. 7, Sixty-Second Day, 19 February 1946, Morning Session, avalon.law.yale.edu/imt/02-19-46.asp.

8. Goss, *German Oilseed Industry*, 3.

9. Ibid., 3.

10. Ibid., 10.

11. Ibid., 14.

12. W. H. Goss, "Processing Oilseeds and Oils in Germany," *Oil & Soap* 23 (August 1946): 244.

13. Goss, *German Oilseed Industry*, 56.

14. Ibid., no page.

15. US House of Representatives, *Department of Commerce Appropriation Bill for 1948: Hearings before the Subcommittee of the Committee on Appropriations*, H.R., 80th Congress, First Session, February 1947 (Washington, DC: US Government Printing Office, 1947), 131.

16. Gimbel, *Science*, 98.

17. Edward Dies, "Introductory Remarks," in *Proceedings of the Conference on Flavor Stability in Soybean Oil* (Chicago: National Soybean Processors Association, 22 April 1946), 3.

18. H. E. Robinson, "The Economic Significance of Soybean Oil Flavor Stability," in

Proceedings of the Conference on Flavor Stability in Soybean Oil (Chicago: National Soybean Processors Association, 22 April 1946), 1; and O. H. Alderks, "Soybean Oil," *Oil & Soap* 21 (September 1945): 233.

19. H. J. Dutton, "History of the Development of Soy Oil for Edible Use," *Journal of the American Oil Chemists' Society* 58 (1981): 235.

20. Alderks, "Soybean Oil," 233.

21. Herbert J. Dutton, Helen A. Moser, and John C. Cowan, "The Flavor Problem of Soybean Oil I: A Test of the Water-Washing Citric Acid Refining Technique," *Journal of the American Oil Chemists' Society* 24 (August 1947): 261–264.

22. Helen A. Moser, Carol M. Jaeger, J. C. Cowan and H. J. Dutton, "The Flavor Problem of Soybean Oil II: Organoleptic Evaluation," *Journal of the American Oil Chemists' Society* 24 (September 1947): 291–296.

23. Herbert J. Dutton, Arthur W. Schwab, Helen A. Moser, and John C. Cowan, "The Flavor Problem of Soybean Oil IV: Structure of Compounds Counteracting the Effect of Prooxidant Metals," *Journal of the American Oil Chemists' Society* 25 (November 1948): 385–388; and Dutton, "History of the Development of Soy Oil," 235.

24. H. J. Dutton, Catherine R. Lancaster, C. D. Evans, and J. C. Cowan, "The Flavor Problem of Soybean Oil VIII: Linolenic Acid," *Journal of the American Oil Chemists' Society* 28 (March 1951): 115–118.

25. W. J. Wolf and J. C. Cowan, *Soybeans as a Food Source* (Cleveland: CRC Press, 1971), 28; Dutton, "History of the Development of Soy Oil."

26. J. C. Cowan, "Key Factors and Recent Advances in the Flavor Stability of Soybean Oil," *Journal of the American Oil Chemists' Society* 43 (July 1966): 300A.

27. J. P. Houch, "Domestic Markets," in *Soybeans: Improvement, Production, and Uses,* ed. B. E. Caldwell (Madison, WI: American Society of Agronomy, 1973), 606.

28. Wolf and Cowan, *Soybeans as a Food Source,* 28.

29. Harry Snyder and T. W. Kwon, *Soybean Utilization* (New York: Van Nostrand Reinhold Company, 1987), 214.

30. "Bromfield Arouses Ire in Oleo Fight," *Washington Post,* 4 March 1949, 25.

31. House of Representatives, *Oleomargarine: Hearings before the Committee on Agriculture, March 1–5, 1949,* 81st Congress, First Session (Washington, DC: Government Printing Office, 1949), 228.

32. House of Representatives, *Oleomargarine Hearings* (1949), 260–261.

33. The history of margarine and its legislative travails is often told: See William H. Nicolls, "Some Economic Aspects of the Margarine Industry," *Journal of Political Economy* 54 (June 1946): 221–42; S. F. Riepma, *The Story of Margarine* (Washington, DC: Public Affairs, 1970); Ruth Dupré, "'If It's Yellow, It Must Be Butter': Margarine Regulation in North America since 1886," *Journal of Economic History* 59 (June 1999): 353–371; and Bee Wilson, "Pink Margarine and Pure Ketchup," 152–212 in Bee Wilson, *Swindled: The Dark History of Food Fraud, from Poisoned Candy to Counterfeit Coffee* (Princeton, NJ: Princeton University Press, 2008).

34. "Your Market Is Bound," *Soybean Digest* 1 (August 1941): 11.

35. John Ball, "House Oleo Battle Only a Starter," *Washington Post*, 4 April 1948, B8; and "Housewives' Victory," *New York Times*, 29 April 1948, 22.

36. Samuel A. Towers, "Senate GOP Maps Final Move to End South's Filibuster," *New York Times*, 2 August 1948, 1.

37. Sigrid Arne, "Washington Daybook," *Corsicana* [Texas] *Daily Sun*, 13 September 1941, 6.

38. House of Representatives, *Oleomargarine Hearings* (1949), 17.

39. House of Representatives, *Oleomargarine Hearings* (1949), 148–149.

40. "Bromfield Arouses Ire in Oleo Fight"; and *Oleomargarine: Hearings before the Committee on Agriculture*, 148–149.

41. House of Representatives, *Oleomargarine Hearings* (1949), 308.

42. John W. Ball, "House Group Votes Repeal of Oleo Tax," *Washington Post*, 10 March 1949, 1.

43. John W. Ball, "House Passes Bill to Remove All Taxes on Oleomargarine," *Washington Post*, 2 April 1949, 1.

44. John W. Ball, "'Ersatz' Food Threat Seen in Oleo Bill," *Washington Post*, 11 January 1950, 5.

45. John W. Ball, "'Senate Votes to End Oleo Taxes, 56–16," *Washington Post*, 19 January 1950, 1. Though Langer was genuinely in favor of civil rights, this move was motivated by his opposition to the margarine bill, not a tactic to get civil rights legislation through; the NAACP voiced opposition to his amendments.

46. John W. Ball, "'Oleo Issues Are Settled at Meeting," *Washington Post*, 22 February 1950, 15.

47. Riepma, *The Story of Margarine*, 148–151.

48. George Gallup, "The Gallup Poll: Half of Families Would Use Butter at 45c Lb," *Washington Post*, 15 May 1953, 19.

49. J. A. Livingston, "Mad Hatter Picks Smithsonian as Storage Place for Butter," *Washington Post*, 5 March 1953, 20.

50. A. H. Probst and R. W. Judd, "Origin, U.S. History and Development, and World Distribution," in *Soybeans: Improvement, Production, and Uses*, ed. B. E. Caldwell (Madison, WI: American Society of Agronomy, 1973), 10.

51. William Shurtleff and Akiko Aoyagi, *William J. Morse—History of His Work with Soybeans and Soyfoods (1884–1959): Extensively Annotated Bibliography and Sourcebook* (Lafayette, CA: Soyinfo Center, 2011), 390.

52. Edgar E. Hartwig, "Soybean Varietal Development 1928–1978," in *Fifty Years with Soybeans*, a compilation of invited papers presented during the Advisory Board meeting of the National Soybean Crop Improvement Council, Hilton Head, South Carolina, 26–28 August 1979, 2; and Shurtleff and Aoyagi, *Morse*, 366.

53. Edgar E. Hartwig, "Varietal Development," in *Soybeans: Improvement, Production,*

and Uses, ed. B. E. Caldwell (Madison, WI: American Society of Agronomy, 1973), 193; and Shurtleff and Aoyagi, *Morse*, 409.

54. "Hartwig to Get Award," *Delta Democrat-Times*, 9 October 1975, 8; and N. W. Simmonds and J. Smartt, *Principles of Crop Improvement* (London: Blackwell Science, 1979), 159.

55. Shurtleff and Aoyagi, *Morse*, 362–363.

56. USDA Agricultural Research Service, "Germplasm Resource Information Network (GRIN): National Plant Germplasm System (NPGS)," www.ars-grin.gov/npgs :PI548477.

57. Edgar E. Hartwig, "The New Varieties for the Southern States," *Soybean Digest* 14 (October 1954): 8.

58. "Farmers Given Warning upon Soybean Fraud," *Sarasota Herald-Times*, 29 January 1954, 7; and Hartwig, "New Varieties," 9.

59. E. E. Hartwig, "Hill, a New Early Maturing Soybean for the South," *Soybean Digest* 19 (August 1959): 21.

60. Edgar E. Hartwig, "Lee—A Superior Soybean for the Midsouth," *Soybean Digest* 14 (June 1954): 14–15.

61. Hartwig, "Varietal Development," 201; and USDA, "Germplasm Resource Information Network."

62. National Academy of Sciences, National Research Council, Division of Biology and Agriculture, *Genetic Vulnerability of Major Crops* (Washington, DC: National Academy of Sciences, 1972), 211–213.

63. Harry D. Fornari, "The Big Change: Cotton to Soybeans," *Agricultural History* 53 (January 1979): 251.

64. Roger Horowitz, *Putting Meat on the American Table: Taste, Technology, Transformation* (Baltimore: Johns Hopkins University Press, 2006), 108.

65. Marvin Schwartz, *Tyson: From Farm to Market* (Fayetteville: University of Arkansas Press, 1991), 123.

66. Fornari, "The Big Change," 250.

67. Richard H. Day, "The Economics of Technological Change and the Demise of the Sharecropper," *American Economic Review* 57 (June 1967): 434.

68. Fornari, "The Big Change," 251.

69. Day, "Economics," 428.

70. Fornari, "The Big Change," 251.

71. Day, "Economics," 442.

72. Ralph D. Christy, "The Afro-American, Farming, and Rural Society," in *Social Science Agricultural Agendas and Strategies*, ed. G. Johnson and J. Bonnen (East Lansing: Michigan State University Press, 1991), III-105.

73. Bruce L. Gardner, *American Agriculture in the Twentieth Century: How It Flourished and What It Cost* (Cambridge, MA: Harvard University Press, 2002), 95.

74. Hartwig, "New Varieties."

75. Ibid.

76. "Dr. Julian's Work May Halt Divorce," *Afro-American*, 2 July 1949, 3.

77. "Cheap Sex Hormone Result of 'Accident,'" *Washington Afro-American*, 2 October 1951, 5.

78. Percy L. Julian, Edwin W. Meyer, and Helen Printy, "Sterols VI: 16-Methyltestosterone," *Journal of the American Chemical Society* 70 (November 1948): 3872.

79. Roy Gibbons, "Science Gives Synthetic Key to New Drug," *Chicago Daily Tribune*, 30 September 1949, 1.

80. "Slave's Grandson Made 'Chicagoan of the Year,'" *New York Times*, 18 January 1950, 18; and "Dr. Percy L. Julian Wins 'Chicagoan of the Year' Award," *Afro-American*, 28 January 1950, 12. He was Chicagoan of the Year for 1949, but the dinner was held in January 1950.

81. Produced by National Foam Systems, its official name was Aer-O-Foam. Soyinfo Center, "History of the Glidden Company's Soya Products/Chemurgy Division, a Special Exhibit—The History of Soy Pioneers Around the World—Unpublished Manuscript by William Shurtleff and Akiko Aoyagi," last modified 2004, www.soyinfo center.com/HSS/glidden.php.

82. Max Tishler, "Percy L. Julian, the Scientist," *The Chemist* 42 (March 1965): 109.

83. Ibid., 108

84. "Cheap Sex Hormone Result of 'Accident,'"; Percy L. Julian, Edwin W. Meyer, and Norman C. Krause, "Recovery of Sterols," US Patent 2218971, 22 October 1940 (filed 6 April 1939); and Percy L. Julian and John Wayne Cole, "Process for Recovering Sterols," US Patent 2273045, 17 February 1942 (filed 8 July 1940).

85. John W. Greiner and Glen A. Fevig, "Countercurrent Extraction of Steroids," US Patent 2839544, 17 June 1958 (filed 4 September 1956), 1–2.

86. Tishler, "Percy L. Julian," 110.

87. Emanuel Hershberg and Abraham Kutner, "Isolation of Stigmasterol," US Patent 2520143, 29 August 1950 (filed 27 October 1947), 1; and Percy L. Julian, William J. Karpel, and Jack W. Armstrong, "Oxidation of Soya Sitosteryl Acetate Dibromide," US Patent 2464236, 15 March 1949 (filed 8 May 1946).

88. Percy L. Julian, John Wayne Cole, Arthur Magnani, and Harold E. Conde, "Procedure for the Preparation of Progesterone," US Patent 2433848, 6 January 1948 (filed 10 February 1944), 1.

89. Soyinfo Center, "History of the Glidden Company's Soya Products"; and Tishler, "Percy L. Julian," 110.

90. Soyinfo Center, "History of the Glidden Company's Soya Products."

91. There was also a lively market within the United States of estrogens extracted from horse urine. Norman Applezweig, *Steroid Drugs* (New York: McGraw-Hill, 1962), 23.

92. "Battle of the Sexes: Negro Scientist Key in New Suit," *Chicago Defender*, 12 January 1946, 1; Warren Hall, "Millions in Hormones 1: German Cartel Forces Exorbitant

Prices," *American Weekly*, 12 January 1947, 2–3; and Warren Hall, "Hormones for Millions," *American Weekly*, 11 November 1947, 9.

93. Bernhard Witkop, *Percy Lavon Julian, 1899–1975: A Biographical Memoir*, Biographical Memoirs, vol. 52 (Washington, DC: National Academy Press, 1980), 21.

94. "Improved Use for New Drug on Arthritics Told," *Chicago Daily Tribune*, 28 January 1950, A8; and Applezweig, *Steroid Drugs*, 26.

95. NOVA, "Transcripts: Forgotten Genius. PBS Airdate: February 6, 2007," last modified 2007, www.pbs.org/wgbh/nova/transcripts/3402_julian.html; William L. Laurence, "Rare Cortisone F Made of Soya Bean," *New York Times*, 22 April 1950, 17.

96. John A. Hogg, "Steroids, the Steroid Community, and Upjohn in Perspective: A Profile of Innovation," *Steroids* 57 (December 1992): 601.

97. Applezweig, *Steroid Drugs*, 23–25; Ray F. Dawson, "Diosgenin Production in North America: A Brief History," *HortTechnology* 1 (October/December 1991): 24.

98. Applezweig, *Steroid Drugs*, 26.

99. Sydney B. Self, "Cortisone War," *Wall Street Journal*, 25 November 1953, 1. The story noted that Glidden would continue to make sex hormones, presumably also from Mexican diosgenin, but it seems that the company was eager to get out of the hormone business altogether. See NOVA, "Forgotten Genius."

100. NOVA, "Forgotten Genius"; Soyinfo Center, "History of the Glidden Company's Soya Products"; and Applezweig, *Steroid Drugs*, 30.

101. Applezweig, *Steroid Drugs*, 23–25; Ray F. Dawson, "Diosgenin Production in North America: A Brief History," *HortTechnology* 1 (October/December 1991): 24.

102. Applezweig, *Steroid Drugs*, 32.

103. Hogg, "Steroids, the Steroid Community, and Upjohn," 602–603; Greiner and Fevig, "Countercurrent"; and Applezweig, *Steroid Drugs*, 32.

104. Dawson, "Diosgenin," 24, 26.

105. Jane Hidgon, *An Evidence Based Approach to Dietary Phytochemicals* (New York: Thieme Medical Publishers, 2007), 175–176.

Chapter 7. Thriving in the Shade

1. Norman C. Miller, *The Great Salad Oil Swindle* (New York: Coward McCann, 1965), 142, 157.

2. Ibid., 179.

3. Ibid., 13–21.

4. Ibid., 23. Although De Angelis's Spain deal coincided with Honeymead's shipments, they seem to have been separate deals; Honeymead shipped its oil through the Gulf of Mexico, while Allied used the New York–based Isbrandtsen Line. "Mankato Firm Shipping Soybean Oil to Spain," *Winona* [MN] *Daily News*, 30 December 1957, 3.

5. Miller, *Oil Swindle*, 24. By this time, the USDA was highly distrustful of De Angelis; he supplied the oil as a subcontractor.

6. James P. Houck, Mary E. Ryan and Abraham Subotnik, *Soybeans and Their Products: Markets, Models, and Policy* (Minneapolis: University of Minnesota Press, 1972), 42.

7. "Board of Trade Is Host to Educators," *Cedar Rapids* [Iowa] *Gazette*, 9 September 1955, 2; and "Board of Trade Will Tell Educators How Market Helps Public," *Chicago Daily Tribune*, 2 September 1951, A7.

8. Dwayne Andreas, "Commodity Markets and the Processor," speech, Chicago Board of Trade Commodity Markets Symposium, Union League Club, Chicago, September 1955, E. J. Kahn Papers, Box 14, Subject File: Andreas, Dwayne, Articles and Speeches, New York Public Library Manuscripts and Archives Division, New York, 1.

9. Another variant of the name among Mennonites is Andresen, suggesting some distant kinship between the Andreas family and August Andresen, the Minnesota leader of the congressional butter bloc.

10. E. J. Kahn Jr., *Supermarketer to the World: The Story of Dwayne Andreas, CEO of Archer Daniels Midland* (New York: Warner Books, 1991), 59–61.

11. Alan L. Olmstead and Paul W. Rhode, *Creating Abundance: Biological Innovation and American Agricultural Development* (New York: Cambridge University Press, 2008), 276; and Frank B. Morrison, *Feeds and Feeding: A Handbook for the Student and Stockman*, 22nd ed., unabridged (Ithaca: Morrison Publishing Company, 1956), 544.

12. Kahn, *Supermarketer to the World*, 62.

13. Lew P. Reeve Jr., "Dwayne Andreas Today: Long Way from Early Feed Business in Lisbon and C.R.," *Cedar Rapids Gazette*, 1 November 1964, 22A. Why the name of an alcoholic beverage struck the Mennonites' fancy is not entirely clear.

14. Kahn, *Supermarketer to the World*, 61, 71–74.

15. Reeve, "Dwayne Andreas Today," 22A; and Louis F. Langhurst, "Solvent Extraction Processes," in *Soybeans and Soybean Products*, vol. 2, ed. Klare S. Markley, Fats and Oils: A Series of Monographs (New York: Interscience Publishers Ltd., 1951), 563.

16. Kahn, *Supermarketer to the World*, 72, 78.

17. Ibid., 71; and Wayne G. Broehl Jr., *Cargill: Trading the World's Grain* (Hanover, NH: University Press of New England, 1992), 665, 687.

18. "If you call it an art, and I think it is," Andreas would later comment in an aside to Cargill trainees. Dwayne Andreas, "The Vegetable Oil Industry and Its Outlook for the Future," 217, speech and discussion, Cargill training session, 7 March 1946, E. J. Kahn Papers, Box 14, Subject File: Andreas, Dwayne, Articles and Speeches, New York Public Library Manuscripts and Archives Division, New York.

19. Henry Crosby Emery, "Futures in the Grain Market," *Economic Journal* 9 (March 1899): 49; for another instance of comprehension before Holbrook, see G. Wright Hoffman, "The Hedging of Grain," *Annals of the American Academy of Political and Social Science* 155 (May 1931): 7–22.

20. Andreas, "Commodity Markets," 2–4.

21. Andreas, "Vegetable Oil Industry," 218; "Futures Trade in Soybean Oil Begins Monday," *Chicago Daily Tribune*, 13 July 1950, A9; and "Board of Trade Starts Dealing in Soybean Meal," *Chicago Daily Tribune*, 30 August 1951, C5.

22. Andreas, "Commodity Markets," 4–5.

23. Ibid., 5–9.

24. Ibid., 6.

25. Kahn, *Supermarketer to the World*, 132.

26. Broehl, *Cargill*, 709–710, 762–763; and Kahn, *Supermarketer to the World*, 80.

27. "Sale of Surplus to Russ Barred," *Wisconsin State Journal*, 11 February 1954, 12.

28. Kahn, *Supermarketer to the World*, 83–84.

29. Ibid., 106–107.

30. Ibid., 60.

31. Ibid., 90.

32. Carl Solberg, *Hubert Humphrey: A Biography* (New York: W. W. Norton, 1984), 166.

33. Dan Morgan, *Merchants of Grain* (New York: Viking, 1979), 101–102, 124.

34. Ray A. Goldberg, *Agribusiness Coordination: A Systems Approach to the Wheat, Soybean, and Florida Orange Economies* (Boston: Graduate School of Business Administration, Harvard University, 1968), 124–125; and Morgan, *Merchants*, 125–128.

35. "Roach in Spain for Soybeans," *Waterloo* [Iowa] *Daily Courier*, 5 December 1956, 30; Milt Nelson, "Agriculture's Foreign Trade Promotion," *Cedar Rapids Gazette*, 2 June 1962, 10B; and Stewart Haas, "Bean Gains Favor on Mediterranean," *Waterloo* [Iowa] *Sunday Courier*, 16 February 1963, 25.

36. "Mankato Firm Shipping Soybean Oil to Spain," *Winona* [Minnesota] *Daily News*, 30 December 1957, 3.

37. Solberg, *Hubert Humphrey*, 231–232.

38. "Parade of Political Figures on Restrum at GTA Meet," *Austin* [Minnesota] *Herald*, 17 November 1965, 11.

39. Solberg, *Hubert Humphrey*, 232–233.

40. Ibid., 295; and Kahn, *Supermarketer to the World*, 116.

41. "Archer-Daniels-Midland Names Daniels Chairman and Andreas President," *Wall Street Journal*, 5 February 1968, 16; "Archer-Daniels Holders Approve Acquisition of First Interoceanic," *Wall Street Journal*, 7 November 1969, 26; "Archer-Daniels Designates D. O. Andreas Top Officer," *Wall Street Journal*, 10 November 1970, 26.; and Kahn, *Supermarketer to the World*, 71, 75.

42. James P. Houck, Mary E. Ryan, and Abraham Subotnik, *Soybeans and Their Products: Markets, Models, and Policy* (Minneapolis: University of Minnesota Press, 1972), 46.

43. Earl C. Hedlund, *The Transportation Economics of the Soybean Processing Industry* (Urbana: University of Illinois Press, 1952), 182.

44. Kahn, *Supermarketer to the World*, 133.

45. Kenneth J. Carpenter, *Protein and Energy: A Study of Changing Ideas in Nutrition* (New York: Cambridge University Press, 1994), 160.

46. Ibid., 147.

47. Ibid., 158.

48. Ritchie Calder, *Common Sense about a Starving World* (New York: Macmillan, 1962), 131–32.

49. Carpenter, *Protein and Energy*, 163–168, 175–177.

50. Ibid., 168–175.

51. Soyinfo Center, "Worthington Foods: Work with Soyfoods—A Special Exhibit—The History of Soy Pioneers around the World—Unpublished Manuscript by William Shurtleff and Akiko Aoyagi," last modified 2004, www.soyinfocenter.com/HSS/worthington_foods.php.

52. Ibid.

53. Soyinfo Center, "Henry Ford and His Employees: Work with Soy—A Special Exhibit—The History of Soy Pioneers around the World—Unpublished Manuscript by William Shurtleff and Akiko Aoyagi," last modified 2004, www.soyinfocenter.com/HSS/henry_ford_and_employees.php.

54. William T. Atkinson, "Meat-Like Protein Food Product," US Patent 3488770, 6 January 1970 (filed 7 March 1969, a continuation-in-part of applications filed on 17 August 1966 and 21 May 1964, subsequently abandoned), 1–2.

55. The name is somewhat confusing, as spun edible protein was also often classed as "textured."

56. Clyde Farnsworth, "Versatile Soya Food Star of Cologne Fair," *Chicago Tribune*, 2 October 1967, C7.

57. John A. Prestbo, "Meatless 'Meats': Several Firms Develop Soybean-based Copies of Beef, Pork, Chicken," *Wall Street Journal*, 2 October 1969, 1.

58. "Suspense Film and Food," [Twin Falls, Idaho] *Times-News*, 22 April 1973, 21.

59. US Department of Agriculture, Farm Cooperative Service, *Edible Soy Protein: Operational Aspects of Producing and Marketing*, FCS Research Report 33 (Washington, DC: US Government Printing Office, January 1976), 42, 46.

60. Barry Wilson, "Soya Meat on the Threshold of a Boom," *Agra Europe* (January 1977): M/3–M/8.

61. Shurtleff and Aoyagi, "Worthington Foods."

62. Shurtleff and Aoyagi, "Ford and His Employees."

63. T. J. Mounts, W. J. Wolf, and W. H. Martinez, "Processing and Utilization," in *Soybeans: Improvement, Production, and Uses*, 2nd ed., ed. J. R. Wilcox (Madison, WI: American Society of Agronomy, 1987), 824.

64. F. T. Orthoefer, "Processing and Utilization," in *Soybean Physiology, Agronomy and Utilization*, ed. A. Geoffrey Norman (New York: Academic Press, 1978), 423.

65. USDA, *Edible Soy Protein*, 50.

66. Harry Snyder and T. W. Kwon, *Soybean Utilization* (New York: Van Nostrand Reinhold Company, 1987), 321.

67. Mounts, Wolf, and Martinez, "Processing and Utilization," 242.

68. Diane Swiss, *Introducing Sammy Soy Bean* (Amherst: University of Massachusetts Cooperative Extension Service, ca. 1975).

69. James Trager, *Amber Waves of Grain* (New York: Arthur Fields Books, 1973), 2.

70. Martha M. Hamilton, *The Great American Grain Robbery (and Other Stories)* (Washington, DC: Agribusiness Accountability Project, 1972), 93.

71. Trager, *Amber Waves*, 86.

72. Kazuhisa Oki, *U.S. Food Export Controls Policy: Three Cases from 1973 to 1981*, USJP Occasional Paper 08–13 (Cambridge, MA: Harvard University Program on U.S.–Japan Relations, 2008), 5.

73. Trager, *Amber Waves*, 60.

74. Keith Smith and Wipada Huyser, "World Distribution and Significance of Soybeans," in *Soybeans: Improvement, Production, and Uses*, 2nd ed. (Madison, WI: American Society of Agronomy, 1987), 12.

75. Trager, *Amber Waves*, 59.

76. Smith and Huyser, "World Distribution," 12.

77. Trager, *Amber Waves*, 134.

78. Wayne G. Broehl Jr., *Cargill: Going Global* (Hanover, NH: University Press of New England, 1998), 243; and Oki, *U.S. Food Export Controls*, 9.

79. Bruce L. Gardner, *American Agriculture in the Twentieth Century: How It Flourished and What It Cost* (Cambridge, MA: Harvard University Press, 2002), 151.

80. Oki, *U.S. Food Export Controls*, 9.

81. John Jones, "Freeze, Embargo Create Commodities Turmoil," *Los Angeles Times*, 2 July 1973, B9.

82. "Japanese Upset by Soybean Curbs," *New York Times*, 7 July 1973, 27.

83. "The Soybean Embargo," *Washington Post*, 2 July 1973, A22.

84. Marquis Childs, "The Mismanaged Soybean Embargo," *Washington Post*, 10 July 1973, A19.

85. Kahn, *Supermarketer to the World*, 182–183; and "Humphrey Contributor Gave $25,000 Linked to Break-in Suspect," *Washington Star-News*, 25 August 1973.

Chapter 8. Rising into View

1. Stephen [Gaskin] and The Farm, *Hey Beatnik! This Is The Farm Book* (Summertown, TN: Book Publishing Co., 1974), no page.

2. Stephen [Gaskin], *The Caravan* (New York: Random House, 1972), n.p.

3. Timothy Miller, *The 60s Communes: Hippies and Beyond* (Syracuse: Syracuse University Press, 1999), 17–18.

4. Rick Fields, *How the Swans Came to the Lake: A Narrative History of Buddhism in America,* 3rd ed., revised and updated (Boston, MA: Shambala Publications, 1992), 225–230.

5. Stephen [Gaskin], *Monday Night Class* (Santa Rosa, CA: Book Farm, 1971), n.p.

6. Gaskin, *Caravan,* n.p.

7. Ibid., n.p.

8. Soyinfo Center, "The Soyfoods Movement: A Special Exhibit—The History of Soy Pioneers around the World—Unpublished Manuscript by William Shurtleff and Akiko Aoyagi," last modified 2004, www.soyinfocenter.com/HSS/soyfoods_movement _worldwide1.php.

9. Gaskin, *Caravan,* n.p.

10. Rupert Fike, ed., *Voices from The Farm* (Summertown, TN: Book Publishing Company, 1998), 13.

11. Ibid., 11; and Gaskin, *Hey Beatnik!,* n.p.

12. Gaskin, *Hey Beatnik!,* n.p.

13. Fike, *Voices,* ix; and Alice Alexander, "A Commune's Last Stand in the Tennessee Hill Country," *Washington Post,* 20 May 1979, H1.

14. Gaskin, *Hey Beatnik!,* n.p.

15. "The Plowboy Interview: Stephen Gaskin and The Farm," *Mother Earth News,* May/June 1977, 14–18, www.motherearthnews.com/nature-community/stephen-gas kin-zmaz77mjzbon.aspx.

16. Gaskin, *Hey Beatnik!,* n.p.

17. Soyinfo Center, "Soyfoods Movement."

18. William Shurtleff and Akiko Aoyagi, *The Book of Tempeh: The Delicious, Cholesterol-Free Protein,* 2nd ed. (New York: Harper Colophon Books, 1985), 147.

19. Soyinfo Center, "Soyfoods Movement"; and Shurtleff and Aoyagi, *Book of Tempeh,* 151.

20. *Farm Foods: Products Catalogue* (Summertown, TN: The Farm, 1978), Alphabetical Files, SFM-Farm, Soyinfo Center, Lafayette, CA.

21. Gaskin, *Hey Beatnik!,* n.p.

22. William Shurtleff and Akiko Aoyagi, *History of Soybeans and Soyfoods in Mexico and Central America (1877–2009): Extensively Annotated Bibliography and Sourcebook* (Lafayette, CA: Soyinfo Center, 2009), 86; and "Plowboy Interview: Gaskin."

23. Fike, *Voices,* 74.

24. Ibid., 74–76.

25. Ibid., 76; and Darryl Jordan and Suzie Jenkins, *Plenty Agricultural Program,* as presented to UNICEF Guatemala (Summertown, TN: Plenty, 1980), 29 (held in Alphabetical Files, SFM-Farm, Soyinfo Center, Lafayette, CA).

26. Shurtleff and Aoyagi, *History of Soyfoods in Mexico,* 84; and Jordan and Jenkins, *Plenty,* 6–8.

27. Plenty International, *Soy Demonstration Program: Introducing Soy Foods in the*

Third World, a Step By Step Guide for Demonstrating Soymilk and Tofu Preparation (Summertown, TN: Plenty International, ca. 1980), Alphabetical Files, SFM-Farm, Soyinfo Center, Lafayette, CA; and Jordan and Jenkins, *Plenty*, 28.

28. Shurtleff and Aoyagi, *History of Soyfoods in Mexico*, 138; Jordan and Jenkins, *Plenty*, 28; *Soy Demonstration Program*; and Fike, *Voices*, 79.

29. Fike, *Voices*, 80.

30. Ibid., 79–80.

31. Ibid., 146, 157.

32. Paul Ehrlich, "Introduction," in Harrison, *Make Room*, n.p.

33. Frances Moore Lappé, *Diet for a Small Planet* (New York: Friends of the Earth/ Ballantine, 1971), 4.

34. Frances Moore Lappé, *Diet for a Small Planet: Revised Edition* (New York: Ballantine, 1975), 354.

35. "Health Food Center Sponsors Open House," *Chicago Defender*, 4 June 1966, 21; Dave Potter, "Gregory Starts Eating Again After 54 Days," *Chicago Daily Defender*, 10 January 1968, 3.

36. William Roy Shurtleff and Lawton Lothrop Shurtleff, *The Shurtleff and Lawton Families: Geneology and History*, 2nd ed. (Lafayette, CA: Pine Hill Press, 2005). Lawton passed away in April 2012 at age ninety-seven.

37. Ibid., 234; and Bill Shurtleff, *A Peace Corps Year with Nigerians*, ed. Hans Brinkmann (Frankfurt am Main: Verlag Moritz Diesterweg, 1966), no page ["Introduction"]. It is not clear whether he completed his engineering degree before the Peace Corps, but he was apparently qualified to teach physics.

38. Shurtleff, *A Peace Corps Year*, 64–66.

39. David Harris, *Dreams Die Hard* (New York: St. Martin's/Marek, 1982), 183–184; and Stewart Burns, *Social Movements of the 1960s: Searching for Democracy* (Boston: Twayne Publishers, 1990), 95.

40. William Shurtleff and Akiko Aoyagi, *History of Erewhon—Natural Foods Pioneer in the United States: Extensively Annotated Bibliography and Sourcebook* (Lafayette, CA: Soyinfo Center, 2011), 265.

41. Ibid.

42. Soyinfo Center, "George Ohsawa, the Macrobiotics Movement: A Special Exhibit—The History of Soy Pioneers around the World—Unpublished Manuscript by William Shurtleff and Akiko Aoyagi," last modified 2004, www.soyinfocenter.com /HSS/george_ohsawa_macrobiotics_soyfoods1.php.

43. "The Plowboy Interview: Bill Shurtleff and Akiko Aoyagi," *Mother Earth News*, March/April 1977, 8–18, www.motherearthnews.com/real-food/akiko-aoyagi-zmaz 77mazbon.aspx.

44. Ibid.; and William Shurtleff and Akiko Aoyagi, *The Book of Tofu: Protein Source of the Future . . . Now!* Vol. 1 (Berkeley: Ten Speed Press, 1983), 9.

45. "The Plowboy Interview: Shurtleff."

46. Shurtleff and Aoyagi, *Book of Tofu*, 10.

47. Ibid., 271–273.

48. Ibid., 11.

49. Ibid., passim.

50. Shurtleff and Aoyagi, *History of Tofu*, 5; and Lorna J. Sass, "A Couple on a Tofu Mission in the West," *New York Times*, 24 September 1980, C3.

51. Shurtleff and Aoyagi, *History of Erewhon*, 118–120.

52. Shurtleff and Aoyagi, *History of Tofu*, 5.

53. "Plowboy Interview: Shurtleff."

54. Ibid.

55. William Shurtleff and Akiko Aoyagi, *Tofu and Soymilk Production: The Book of Tofu*, vol. 2. *A Craft and Technical Manual*, 2nd ed. (Lafayette, CA: Soyfoods Center, 1984), 35–36.

56. Ibid., 55.

57. Ibid., 55.

58. Ibid., 63, 68.

59. Ibid., 13; and Shurtleff and Shurtleff, *The Shurtleff and Lawton Families*, 196.

60. Shurtleff and Aoyagi, *History of Tofu*, 6.

61. Ibid., 6.

62. Ibid., 6; and William Shurtleff and Akiko Aoyagi, *The Soyfoods Industry and Market: Directory and Databook*, 5th ed. (Lafayette, CA: Soyfoods Center, 1985), 48. By 1981, according to Shurtleff's later accounting, there were 173 US tofu makers, Asian and non-Asian. Ibid., 52.

63. Sass, "Couple on a Tofu Mission."

64. Lorna J. Sass, "Soy Foods: Versatile, Cheap and on the Rise," *New York Times*, 12 August 1981, C1.

65. Soyinfo Center, "Soyfoods Movement."

66. Ibid.

67. Tsuru Yamauchi, interview by Michiko Kodama, in *Uchinanchu: A History of Okinawans in Hawaii*, ed. Marie Hara, trans. Sandra Iha and Robin Fukijawa (Honolulu: Ethnic Studies Oral History Project, Ethnic Studies Program, University of Hawaii, 1981), 496–503.

68. Soyinfo Center, "History of Tofu: A Chapter from the Unpublished Manuscript, History of Soybeans and Soyfoods: 1100 b.c. to the 1980s by William Shurtleff and Akiko Aoyagi," last modified 2007, www.soyinfocenter.com/HSS/tofu1.php.

69. Before that, they had been used variously for shucked oysters, ice cream, other deli goods, and goldfish sold at carnivals. Jennifer 8. Lee, *The Fortune Cookie Chronicles: Adventures in the World of Chinese Food* (New York: Twelve, 2008), 140.

70. Soyinfo Center, "Chronology of Tofu Worldwide: 965 A.D. to 1929 by William Shurtleff and Akiko Aoyagi," last modified 2001, www.soyinfocenter.com/chronologies_of_soyfoods-tofu.php.

71. "Tofu Is Good, Good for You," *Ada* [Oklahoma] *Evening News* [AP], 25 June 1968, 3.

72. Shurtleff and Aoyagi, *History of Erewhon* (Lafayette, CA: Soyinfo Center, 2011), 120.

73. Douglas Bauer, "Prince of the Pit," *New York Times*, 25 April 1976, 200.

74. Bob Tamarkin, *The New Gatsbys: Fortunes and Misfortunes of Commodity Traders* (New York: William Morrow and Company, 1985), 56.

75. Bauer, "Prince of the Pit."

76. Ibid.

77. Thomas Petzinger, "Speculator Richard Dennis Moves Markets and Makes Millions in Commodity Trades," *Wall Street Journal*, 8 November 1983, 37.

78. Laurie Cohen, "A Rare Trip: Trading Pit to Think Tank," *Chicago Tribune*, 31 July 1983, S5; and Stanley Angrist, "Winning Commodity Traders May Be Made, Not Born: A Turtle Race Worth Watching," *Wall Street Journal*, 5 September 1989, C1.

79. On the downfall of Cook Industries, see Dan Morgan, *Merchants of Grain* (New York: Viking, 1979), 330–341.

80. William Hieronymous, "Commodities: Brazil May Be Stuck with Surplus of Soybeans; Receipts Outlook Cut," *Wall Street Journal*, 22 July 1977, 18.

81. "Mitsui and Co. Acquires Eight Grain Elevators from Cook Industries," *Wall Street Journal*, 7 June 1978.

82. The Hunts, meanwhile, engaged in a three-year legal battle before agreeing in an out-of-court settlement to pay a half-million-dollar fine and to stay out of soybean futures for three years. In 1980, they attempted a corner of the silver market instead, leading to a bust of the silver market that nearly brought the rest of the commodity markets down in its wake. Tamarkin, *The New Gatsbys*, 192–194.

83. Bashir Aslam Qasmi, "An Analysis of the 1980 US Trade Embargo on Exports of Soybeans and Soybean Products to the Soviet Union: A Spatial Price Equilibrium Approach," PhD diss., Iowa State University, 1986, Retrospective Theses and Dissertations (Paper 8110), 149; and Robert Paarlberg, "Lessons of the Grain Embargo," *Foreign Affairs* 59 (1980): 154.

84. US Department of Agriculture, Economic Research Service, *Soybeans and Peanuts: Background for 1990 Farm Legislation*, by Brad Chowder et al., Agriculture Information Bulletin No. 592 (Washington, DC: US Government Printing Office, 1990), 2.

Chapter 9. Cresting the Peak

1. Charles Babcock, "Add the Relish, Stir up an Embarrassment," *Washington Post*, 7 January 1982, A21; and "Tofu and Turkey," *New York Times*, 26 November 1981, A26.

2. Ward Sinclair, "Q: When Is Ketchup a Vegetable? A: When Tofu Is Meat." *Washington Post*, 9 September 1981, A7.

3. Ellen Goodman, "Reagan's Nouvelle Cuisine for Kids," *Washington Post*, 15 September 1981, A23.

4. "Letters to the Editor: Down with Ketchup, up with Tofu," *Washington Post*, 20 September 1981, C6.

5. "Tofu and Turkey."

6. Martha Wagner, "Forget Meatballs, America; It's Time for Tofu," *Chicago Tribune*, 9 June 1983, G7H.

7. "Government Wants More Soy in Schools," *New York Times*, 24 December 1999, A14.

8. Patricia Leigh Brown, "Health Food Fails Test at School in Berkeley," *New York Times*, 13 October 2002, 22; and Vivian S. Toy, "From 'Yuck' to 'Mmmmmm,'" *New York Times*, 19 October 2003, LI1.

9. "Some Students Have Beef with Soy School Lunches," *Washington Post*, 1 April 2000, I2.

10. Soyinfo Center, "The Soyfoods Movement, Part 2: A Special Exhibit—The History of Soy Pioneers around the World—Unpublished Manuscript by William Shurtleff and Akiko Aoyagi," last modified 2004, www.soyinfocenter.com/HSS/soyfoods _movement_worldwide2.php.

11. William Shurtleff, "Soycrafters Conference: The Birthing of a New Industry: The Honeymoon Stage Is Over," *Soycraft*, Winter 1980, 17–18.

12. "Roundtable: 'I Believe in the Gas-Station on Every Corner Tofu Shop Myth,'" *Soycraft*, Winter 1980, 60–62.

13. Richard Leviton, "Effective Soyfoods Marketing," *Soyfoods*, Summer 1980, 47.

14. William Shurtleff and Akiko Aoyagi, *History of Tofu and Tofu Products (965 C.E.– 2013): Extensively Annotated Bibliography and Sourcebook* (Lafayette, CA: Soyinfo Center, 2013), 1613; and William Shurtleff and Akiko Aoyagi, *Soyfoods Industry and Market: Directory and Databook*, 5th ed. (Lafayette, CA: Soyfoods Center, 1985), 51.

15. Shurtleff and Aoyagi, *Tofu and Tofu Products*, 1613.

16. Karen Dukess, "Tofu, Tofu Everywhere," *New York Times*, 2 August 1981, F17.

17. Lorna J. Sass, "Soy Foods: Versatile, Cheap and on the Rise," *New York Times*, 12 August 1981, C1.

18. Shurtleff and Aoyagi, *Tofu and Tofu Products*, 1613.

19. "Roundtable: 'Tofu Shop Myth,'" 62.

20. Leviton's Laughing Grasshopper Tofu Shop arguably bucked the trend to become the New England Soy Dairy.

21. Leviton, "Effective Soyfoods Marketing," 48; and Soyinfo Center, "The Soyfoods Movement, Part 2."

22. Sass, "Soy Foods"; and Soyinfo Center, "The Soyfoods Movement, Part 2."

23. Margaret Sheridan, "Soul's Menu Soy Inventive," *Chicago Tribune*, 7 February 1986, N-A30.

24. Joseph Fucini and Suzy Fucini, *Experience, Inc.: Men and Women Who Founded Famous Companies after the Age of 40* (New York: Free Press, 1987), 68; Sass, "Soy Foods"; Dukess, "Tofu, Tofu," F17; and Shurtleff and Aoyagi, *Tofu and Tofu Products*, 1507.

25. William Shurtleff and Akiko Aoyagi, *Tofutti and Other Soy Ice Creams: The Non-Dairy Frozen Dessert Industry and Market* (Lafayette, CA: Soyfoods Center, 1985), 15–30.

26. Fucini and Fucini, *Experience, Inc.*, 70; and Jerry Jacubovics, "David Mintz: King of Tofu," *Management Review* 75 (December 1986): 13.

27. Shurtleff and Aoyagi, *Tofu and Tofu Products*, 2104.

28. Trish Hall, "Tofu Products May Be in, but Its Fans Wonder if There's Tofu in the Products," *New York Times*, 27 February 1985, 34; and Deborah Leigh Wood, "Nothing Timid in Frozen Tofu's Calorie Count," *Chicago Tribune*, 13 June 1985, G2.

29. Shurtleff and Aoyagi, *Tofu and Tofu Products*, 2665–2666, 2530.

30. Karen Gillingham, "Americanization of a Soy Food," *Los Angeles Times*, 7 June 1984, L1.

31. Shurtleff and Aoyagi, *Tofu and Tofu Products*, 3839.

32. "Tofu Provides an Alternative Meat at Mealtime" [Ad], *Los Angeles Times*, 30 April 1987, I30.

33. Morinaga Nutritional Foods, Inc., "New Products/Convenience Foods: Packaging Breakthrough Extends Life of Tofu" [Special Advertising Supplement], *Los Angeles Times*, 26 June 1986, L35; and Morinaga Nutritional Foods, Inc., "New Products/Convenience Foods: Tofu Maker Celebrating First Year in United States" [Special Advertising Supplement], *Los Angeles Times*, 31 July 1986, I38.

34. Shurtleff and Aoyagi, *Tofu and Tofu Products*, 2519, 2538, 2549.

35. Ibid., 2011, 2489.

36. Ibid., 2877.

37. Shurtleff and Aoyagi, *Soyfoods Industry and Market*, 54; and Shurtleff and Aoyagi, *Tofu and Tofu Products*, 2489

38. Magaly Olivero, "Milking the Soybean for Cha-Cha Cherry," *New York Times*, 9 August 1987, CN23.

39. Mark Messina and Stephen Barnes, "The Role of Soy Products in Reducing the Risk of Cancer," *Journal of the National Cancer Institute* 83 (17 April 1991): 544; Mark Messina, Virginia Messina, and Kenneth D. R. Setchell, *The Simple Soybean and Your Health* (New York: Avery Publishing Group, 1994), xi.

40. Barbara Harland and Donald Oberleas, "Phytate in Foods," *World Review of Nutrition and Dietetics* 52 (1987): 239.

41. Camila Warnick, "The Secret of Soybeans," *Cincinnati Post*, 10 March 1997, 1B.

42. "Time Running out on Cheetahs," *Chicago Tribune*, 23 November 1986, E3.

43. Messina, Messina, and Setchell, *The Simple Soybean*, 72.

44. Messina and Barnes, "The Role of Soy Products," 542.

45. Messina, Messina, and Setchell, *The Simple Soybean*, xi.

46. "Second Annual Soyfoods Symposium Proceedings—Mark J. Messina," last modified 1997, fearn.pair.com/rstevens/symposium97/messina.html.

47. Messina, Messina, and Setchell, *The Simple Soybean*, epigraph.

48. "History of the American Dietetic Association's Vegetarian Position Papers, Part Five: 1997 (Virginia Messina and Kenneth I. Burke)," last modified 1997, letthemeatmeat .com/post/24878934186/1997.

49. Connie LaBarr, "Report of the First International Symposium on the Role of Soy in Preventing and Treating Chronic Disease," *Topics in Clinical Nutrition* 10 (January/March 1994): 86–90.

50. Messina and Barnes, "The Role of Soy Products," 542.

51. "Use of Soy Products Are Traced to Fewer Menopausal Symptoms," *Chicago Tribune*, 18 May 1992, 7.

52. Elizabeth Siegel Watkins, *The Estrogen Elixir: A History of Hormone Replacement in America* (Baltimore: Johns Hopkins University Press, 1997), 223, 240.

53. Jane Brody, "Personal Health: Diet May Be One Reason Complaints about Menopause Are Rare in Asia," *New York Times*, 27 August 1997, C8.

54. Nadia Koutzen, "To the Editor: Soy Milk, Anyone?" *New York Times*, 27 March 1997, A28.

55. Lisa Belkin, "Dairy Items for Those Who Can't Digest Milk," *New York Times*, 15 August 1984, C1.

56. Nicholas J. Gonzalez, "Milk: White Poison for Young Blacks," *New York Amsterdam News*, 5 February 1977, A1.

57. William Shurtleff and Akiko Aoyagi, *Soymilk Industry and Market* (Lafayette, CA: Soyfoods Center, 1984), 36.

58. Ibid., 36.

59. William Shurtleff and Akiko Aoyagi, *History of Soymilk and Other Non-Dairy Milks (1226–2013): Extensively Annotated Bibliography and Sourcebook* (Lafayette, CA: Soyinfo Center, 2013), 9.

60. Soyfoods Association of North America (SANA), "Sales by Product Type, 1996–2011," last modified 2011, www.soyfoods.org/wp-content/uploads/SANA-sales-data -1996-2011-for-web.pdf.

61. In 2002, Dean would acquire the rest of WhiteWave; see Shurtleff and Aoyagi, *History of Soymilk*, 9–10.

62. Shurtleff and Aoyagi, *Soymilk Industry*, 36; John O'Neil, "Use of Soy for Babies Is Focus of Debate," *New York Times*, 3 August 1999, F7.

63. SANA, "Sales."

64. Jane L. Levere, "Advertising: Campaigns for Supplements for That Midlife Event Content That Mother Nature Knows Best," *New York Times*, 18 August 1998, D5.

65. Sally Squires, "FDA to Allow Claims That Soy Products Help Cut Heart Disease Risk," *New York Times*, 21 October 1999, A15.

66. Mark Messina and John W. Erdman, "Third International Symposium on the Role of Soy in Preventing and Treating Chronic Disease: Introduction," *Journal of Nutrition* 130 (2000): 653S.

67. Wendy Lin, "Breakthrough: Soy That Tastes Good!" *Washington Post,* 8 February 2000, 19.

68. Daniel Charles, *Lords of the Harvest: Biotech, Big Money, and the Future of Food* (Cambridge, MA: Perseus Publishing, 2001).

69. Ibid., 61.

70. Ibid., 74.

71. Ibid., 69.

72. Wayne A. Parrot and Thomas E. Clemente, "Transgenic Soybean," in *Soybeans: Improvement, Production, and Uses,* 3rd ed. (Madison, WI: American Society of Agronomy, 2004), 281.

73. Ibid., 281; and Charles, *Lords of the Harvest,* 81–82.

74. Parrot and Clemente, "Transgenic Soybean," 276.

75. Charles, *Lords of the Harvest,* 81.

76. Ibid., 151.

77. Ibid., 120.

78. Ibid., 113.

79. Jack Ralph Kloppenburg Jr., *First the Seed: The Political Economy of Plant Biotechnology* (Cambridge, UK: Cambridge University Press, 1988; 2nd ed. Madison: University of Wisconsin Press, 2004), 243.

80. The first patent-like certificates were issued in 1973. "Protection Is Given to Seed Plants," *New York Times,* 28 April 1973, 41.

81. Kloppenburg Jr., *First the Seed,* 153.

82. Fae Holin and Kate Fisher, "Cream of the Crop: Here Are 2001's Top New Soybean Varieties," *Corn and Soybean Digest* (November 2000): 33–34.

83. Paul Barrett, "High-Court Battle Sprouts from Clash between Farmers and the Seed Industry," *Wall Street Journal,* 23 May 1994, B1.

84. *Asgrow Seed Co. v. Winterboer* (92-2038), 513 U.S. 179 (1995).

85. *Diamond v. Chakrabarty,* 447 U.S. 303 (1980).

86. Charles, *Lords of the Harvest,* 152–153.

87. Parrot and Clemente, "Transgenic Soybean," 266. By 2001, in fact, herbicide-tolerant soybeans were planted on 68 percent of soybean acreage. USDA Economic Research Service, "Adoption of Genetically Engineered Crops in the U.S.: Recent Trends in GE Adoption," last updated 2016, www.ers.usda.gov/data-products/adoption-of-genetically-engineered-crops-in-the-us/recent-trends-in-ge-adoption.aspx.

88. Syl Marking, "Roundup Ready Trait Dominates New Varieties," *Corn and Soybean Digest,* December 1998, 22.

89. US Department of Agriculture, Economic Research Service, *Soybeans and Peanuts: Background for 1990 Farm Legislation,* by Brad Chowder et al., Agriculture Infor-

mation Bulletin No. 592 (Washington, DC: US Government Printing Office, 1990), 10.

90. Scott Kilman, "U.S. Farmers Expect to Boost Planting," *Wall Street Journal*, 1 April 1998, A2.

91. Environmental Working Group, "Farm Subsidy Database: Soybean Subsidies in the United States Totaled 31.8 Billion from 1995–2014," last updated 2017, farm.ewg .org/progdetail.php?fips=00000&progcode=soybean.

92. Scott McMurray, "Marketplace: Environment: No-Till Farms Supplant Furrowed Fields, Cutting Erosion but Spreading Herbicides," *Wall Street Journal*, 8 July 1993, B1; and Charles, *Lords of the Harvest*, 62.

93. Parrot and Clemente, "Transgenic Soybean," 270.

94. Stephen G. Rogers, "Biotechnology and the Soybean," *American Journal of Clinical Nutrition* 68 (suppl.) (1998): 1330S–1332S.

95. "Seven Engineered Foods Declared Safe by FDA: Some Scientists Question Biotech Standard," *Washington Post*, 3 November 1994, A11.

96. Marc Lappé, "Tasting Technology: The Agricultural Revolution in Genetically Engineered Plants," *Gastronomica* 1 (Winter 2001): 25.

97. Parrot and Clemente, "Transgenic Soybean," 268.

98. Ibid., 269.

99. Ibid., 270–272.

100. William Drozkiak, "Germany in Furor over a U.S. Food," *Washington Post*, 7 November 1996, A48.

101. Charles, *Lords of the Harvest*, 257.

102. John Schwartz, "Six Farmers in Class Action vs. Monsanto," *Washington Post*, 15 December 1999, E1.

103. Scott Kilman, "Biotech Scare Sweeps Europe, and Companies Wonder if U.S. Is Next," *Wall Street Journal*, 7 October 1999, A1.

Epilogue: Here to Stay?

1. Robert Falkner, "The Global Biotech Food Fight: Why the United States Got It So Wrong," *Brown Journal of World Affairs* 14 (Fall/Winter 2007): 104–105.

2. Robert Blair and Joe Regenstein, *Genetic Modification and Food Quality: A Down to Earth Analysis* (Chichester, UK: John Wiley & Sons, 2015), 254.

3. "US Consumers Concerned about Safety of GM Foods," *The Organic and Non-GMO Report*, last modified 2007, non-gmoreport.com/articles/jan07/GM_food_safety.php.

4. Ibid.

5. *Public and Scientists' Views on Science and Society* (Washington, DC: Pew Research Center, 2015), 6.

6. Ten percent felt that GM foods were actively "better for health." Cary Funk and Brian Kennedy, *The New Food Fights: U.S. Public Divides Over Food Science* (Washington, DC: Pew Research Center, 2016), 3.

7. There are some voices urging a rapprochement between genetic engineering and organic farming. See Pamela C. Ronald and Raoul W. Adamchak, *Tomorrow's Table: Organic Farming, Genetics, and the Future of Food* (New York: Oxford University Press, 2008).

8. Julia Moskin, "Farmers' Monsanto Lawsuit Dismissed by Federal Judge," *New York Times*, 28 February 2012, B2. The ruling was later affirmed by the US Court of Appeals for the Federal Circuit.

9. "Soybeans and the Spirit of Invention," *New York Times*, 14 May 2013, A24.

10. Blair and Regenstein, *Genetic Modification*, 84; William Neuman, "A Growing Discontent: Rapid Rise in Seed Prices Draws Government Scrutiny," *New York Times*, 12 March 2010, B1; and Georgina Gustin, "Justice Department Ends Monsanto Antitrust Probe," *St. Louis Post-Dispatch*, 19 November 2012.

11. Dan Charles, "The Salt: Campbell Soup Switches Sides in the GMO Labeling Fight," last modified 8 January 2016, www.npr.org/sections/thesalt/2016/01/08/4624 22610/campbell-soup-switches-sides-in-the-gmo-labeling-fight.

12. Marion Desquilbet and David S. Bullock, "Who Pays the Costs of Non-GMO Segregation and Identity Preservation?" *American Journal of Agricultural Economics* 91 (August 2009): 656–672.

13. W. D. McBride and Catherine Greene, "The Profitability of Organic Soybean Production," *Renewable Agriculture and Food Systems* 24 (2009): 276. This was nonetheless still a tiny fraction of the 73 million acres of soybeans.

14. Elaine Watson, "Food Navigator: Post Unveils Non-GMO Verified Grape Nuts as Gen Mills Says Goodbye to GMOs in Original Cheerios," posted 17 January 2014, www.foodnavigator-usa.com/Manufacturers/Post-unveils-non-GMO-verified-Grape -Nuts-as-Gen-Mills-says-goodbye-to-GMOs-in-Original-Cheerios.

15. *Public and Scientists' Views*, 6.

16. Blair and Regenstein, *Genetic Modification*, 85–102; and Dan Charles, "The Salt: European Cancer Experts Don't Agree on How Risky Roundup Is," last modified 13 November 2015, www.npr.org/sections/thesalt/2015/11/13/455810235/european-cancer -experts-dont-agree-on-how-risky-roundup-is.

17. Dan Charles, "The Salt: Why Monsanto Thought Weeds Would Never Defeat Roundup," last modified 11 March 2012, www.npr.org/sections/thesalt/2012/03/11/148 290731/why-monsanto-thought-weeds-would-never-defeat-roundup.

18. "Roundup Unready," *New York Times*, 19 February 2003, A24; William Neuman and Andrew Pollack, "Rise of the Superweeds," *New York Times*, 4 May 2010, B1; and Dan Charles, "NPR Morning Edition: Farmers Switch Course in Battle against Weeds," last modified 20 August 2007, www.npr.org/templates/story/story.php?storyId=137 46169.

19. Dan Charles, "NPR The Salt: Arkansas Tries to Stop an Epidemic of Herbicide Damage," 23 June 2017, www.npr.org/sections/thesalt/2017/06/23/534117683/arkansas -tries-to-stop-an-epidemic-of-herbicide-damage.

20. Stephanie Strom, "Misgivings about How Weed Killer Affects Soil," *New York Times*, 20 September 2013, B1.

21. Alfonso Valenzuela and Nora Morgado, "Trans Fatty Isomers in Human Health and in the Food Industry," *Biological Research* 32 (1999): 273–287.

22. Andrew Pollack, "In a Bean, a Boon to Biotech: Move to Ban Trans Fats May Benefit Plant-Gene Modifiers," *New York Times*, 16 November 2013, B1; and Tanya Blasbalg et al., "Changes in Consumption of Omega-3 and Omega-6 Fatty Acids in the United States during the 20th Century," *American Journal of Clinical Nutrition* 93 (2011): 953.

23. Kim Severson and Melanie Warner, "Fat Substitute, Once Praised, Is Pushed out of the Kitchen," *New York Times*, 13 February 2005, 1.

24. Thomas Lueck, "Public Speaks on Plan to Limit Trans Fats, Mostly in Favor," *New York Times*, 31 October 2006, B2; Anemona Hartocollis, "Restaurants Prepare for Big Switch: No Trans Fat," *New York Times*, 21 June 2008, B1; and "Starbucks Cuts Use of Trans Fats," *New York Times*, 3 January 2007, C7.

25. "An Overdue Ban on Trans Fats," *New York Times*, 12 November 2013, A26; and Sabrina Tavernise, "F.D.A. Seeking Near Total Ban on Trans Fats," *New York Times*, 8 November 2013, A1. There are also small amounts of natural trans fats in meat and dairy products, the so-called ruminant trans fats created in the rumens of cattle. These have not been shown to have the health consequences of artificial trans fats.

26. Alexei Barrionuevo, "Kellogg Will Use New Soybean Oil to Cut Fat," *New York Times*, 9 December 2005, C3.

27. Pollack, "In a Bean, a Boon to Biotech," B1.

28. For a full account, see Susan Allport, *The Queen of Fats: Why Omega-3s Were Removed from the Western Diet and What We Can Do to Replace Them* (Berkeley: University of California Press, 2007).

29. Gary Rivlin, "Magical or Overrated? A Food Additive in a Swirl," *New York Times*, 14 January 2007, B1.

30. Blasbalg et al., "Changes in Consumption," 950.

31. Allport, *Queen of Fats*, 117.

32. Parveen Yaquoob, "Book Review: *The Queen of Fats*," *British Journal of Nutrition* 97 (2007): 806.

33. Evangelos Rizos et al., "Association Between Omega-3 Fatty Acid Supplementation and Risk of Major Cardiovascular Disease Events: A Systematic Review and Meta-analysis," *JAMA* 308 (September 2012): 1024–1033.

34. William S. Harris and Gregory C. Shearer, "Omega-6 Fatty Acids and Cardiovascular Disease: Friend or Foe?" *Circulation: Journal of the American Heart Association*, published online 26 August 2014, circ.ahajournals.org/content/early/2014/08/26/CIR CULATIONAHA.114.012534.

35. Kaayla Daniel, *The Whole Soy Story: The Dark Side of America's Favorite Health Food* (Washington, DC: New Trends Publishing, 2005). For Robbins's views of the Weston A. Price Foundation, see John Robbins, "VegSource: Reflections on the Weston A. Price Foundation," last modified 4 November 2009, www.vegsource.com/news/2009/11/reflec tions-on-the-weston-a-price-foundation.html.

36. For a detailed account, see Elizabeth Siegel Watkins, *The Estrogen Elixir: A History of Hormone Replacement in America* (Baltimore: Johns Hopkins University Press, 1997), 264–285.

37. Marion Burros, "Eating Well: Doubts Cloud Rosy News on Soy," *New York Times*, 26 January 2000, F1.

38. Ethan Balk et al., *Effects of Soy on Health Outcomes*, Evidence Report/Technology Assessment Number 126 (Rockville, MD: Agency for Healthcare Research and Quality, 2005).

39. Ibid., 135.

40. Ibid., 119.

41. Daniel, *The Whole Soy Story*, 11. This is one of the places she cites a supposedly ancient Asian nickname for tofu, the "aptly named 'meat without a bone,'" this time with a touch of sexual double entendre.

42. Jim Rutz, "WorldNetDaily (WND): Soy Is Making Kids 'Gay,'" posted 12 December 2006, www.wnd.com/2006/12/39253. Other sites described phytoestrogens as a strategy on the part of plants to feminize, and therefore lower the fertility, of insect pests, though there is little evidence to support this.

43. Mark Messina, "Insights Gained from Twenty Years of Soy Research," *Journal of Nutrition* 140 (2010): 2292S.

44. B. P. Setchell, "Sperm Counts in Semen of Farm Animals, 1932–1995," *International Journal of Andrology* 20 (1997): 209–214.

45. B. L. Strom et al., "Exposure to Soy-based Formula in Infancy and Endocrinological and Reproductive Outcomes in Young Adulthood," *JAMA* (286): 807–814. For a worried overview of recent research, see Deborah Blum, "The Great Soy Formula Experiment," *Undark*, 2 August 2017, undark.org/article/soy-formula-babies-endocrine -disruptor.

46. See, for example, Faith Goldy, "Faith Goldy: Is Soy Feminizing the West?" published 15 June 2015, www.youtube.com/watch?v=mduUbJTdXag.

47. Kate Knibbs, "Lexicon: Why the Far Right Wing Fears Soy," *The Ringer*, 3 November 2017, www.theringer.com/tech/2017/11/3/16598872/alt-right-lingo-soy -boy.

48. Lon White et al., "Brain Aging and Midlife Tofu Consumption," *Journal of the American College of Nutrition* 19 (2000): 242–255.

49. Sandra File et al., "Eating Soya Improves Human Memory," *Psychopharmacology* 157 (2001):430–436; and Messina, "Insights," 2292S–2293S.

50. Kids with Food Allergies: A Division of the Asthma and Allergy Foundation of

America, "Living with Food Allergies: Allergen Avoidance List," last updated 2017, www
.kidswithfoodallergies.org/page/top-food-allergens.aspx.

51. United Soybean Board, "Soyconnection: Estimating Prevalence of Soy Protein Allergy," last modified 2016, www.soyconnection.com/newsletters/soy-connection/health
-nutrition/articles/Estimating-Prevalence-Of-Soy-Protein-Allergy.

52. Christopher Cordle, "Soy Protein Allergy: Incidence and Relative Severity," *Journal of Nutrition* 134 (2004): 1214S.

53. Katherine Vierk et al., "Prevalence of Self-Reported Food Allergy in American
Adults and Use of Food Labels," *Journal of Allergy and Clinical Immunology* 119 (2007):
1504–1510.

54. Cordle, "Soy Protein Allergy," 1215S.

55. T. Foucard and I. Malmheden Yman, "A Study on Severe Food Reactions in
Sweden—Is Soy Protein an Underestimated Cause of Food Anaphylaxis?" *Allergy* 54
(March 1999): 261–265.

56. Camila Domonoske, "DNA Tests Find Subway Chicken Only 50 Percent Meat,
Canadian News Program Reports," last modified 1 March 2017, www.npr.org/sections
/thetwo-way/2017/03/01/517920680/dna-tests-find-subway-chicken-only-50-percent
-meat-canadian-media-reports.

57. Andrew Pollack, "Biotech's Sparse Harvest," *New York Times*, 14 February
2006, C1.

58. Messina, "Insights," 2293S.

59. Soyfoods Association of North America (SANA), "Sales by Product Type, 1996–
2011," last modified 2011, www.soyfoods.org/wp-content/uploads/SANA-sales-data
-1996-2011-for-web.pdf; and SANA, "Soy Products: Sales and Trends," last updated 2014,
www.soyfoods.org/soy-products/sales-and-trends.

60. Lizzie Widdicombe, "The End of Food," *New Yorker*, 12 May 2014, 34.

61. Rosa Labs LLP, "Soylent: What's in Soylent?" last modified 2016, blog.soylent
.com/post/51243920779/whats-in-soylent.

62. See John King, *Reaching for the Sun: How Plants Work* (New York: Cambridge
University Press, 1997), 48–49.

63. Impossible Foods, "Impossible: Frequently Asked Questions," last modified 2016,
www.impossiblefoods.com/faq/.

64. Beyond Meat, "The Beyond Burger," last modified 2017, beyondmeat.com/prod
ucts/view/beyond-burger.

65. Jason Margolis, "NPR All Things Considered: Soy Seats in New Cars: Are
Companies Doing Enough for Environment?" last modified 4 August 2015, www.npr
.org/2015/08/04/429333129/the-soy-car-seat-are-companies-doing-enough-for-the-en
vironment.

66. D. Howard Doane, "Suggested Policies," in *Proceedings: Second Dearborn Conference, May 12, 13, 14* (Dearborn, MI: Farm Chemurgic Council, 1936), 360.

67. William Shurtleff and Akiko Aoyagi, *History of Biodiesel—With Emphasis on Soy*

NOTES TO PAGE 271   331

Biodiesel (1900–2017): Extensively Annotated Bibliography and Sourcebook (Lafayette, CA: Soyinfo Center, 2017), 8.

68. Vaclav Smil, *Two Prime Movers of Globalization: The History and Impact on Diesel Engines and Gas Turbines* (Cambridge, MA: MIT Press, 2010), 221.

69. See Tiziano Gomiero, "Are Biofuels an Effective and Viable Energy Strategy for Industrialized Societies? A Reasoned Overview of Potentials and Limits," *Sustainability* 7 (2015): 8491–8521, for a detailed examination of the sustainability of biofuels.

Select Bibliography

Archival Sources

Cornell University

Clive McCay Papers 1920–1967, Division of Rare and Manuscript Collections, Carl A. Kroch Library, Cornell University, Ithaca, NY.

Loma Linda University

Archives of the E. G. White Estate Branch Office, Loma Linda University, Loma Linda, CA.

Department of Archives and Special Collections, Del E. Webb Memorial Library, Loma Linda University, Loma Linda, CA.

National Agricultural Library

Plant Exploration Collections, No. 325: USDA Forage Crop Investigation Records, Special Collections, National Agricultural Library, Beltsville, MD.

US Department of Agriculture, Bureau of Plant Industry, Foreign Plant Introduction and Forage Crop Investigations. *Agricultural Exploration in Japan, Chosen (Korea), Northeastern China, Taiwan (Formosa), Singapore, Java, Sumatra and Ceylon, by Dorsett, P. H. and Morse, W. J., Agricultural Explorers, 1928–1932.* Plant Exploration Collections, No. 51: Dorsett-Morse Oriental Agricultural Exploration Expedition, Series I: Journals, Special Collections, National Agricultural Library, Beltsville, MD.

National Archives I

Record Group 210, Records of the War Relocation Authority, Records of Relocation Centers, Subject-Classified General Files 1942–1946, Colorado River, Box 106, National Archives, Washington, DC.

Record Group 210, Records of the War Relocation Authority, Records of Relocation Centers, Subject-Classified General Files 1942–1946, Colorado River, Box 114, National Archives, Washington, DC.

Record Group 210, Records of the War Relocation Authority, Washington Office Records, Documentary Files, Semi-Annual Reports, Box 5, National Archives, Washington, DC.

Record Group 210, Records of the War Relocation Authority, Washington Office Records, Washington Document, Box 5, National Archives, Washington, DC.

National Archives II

Record Group 40, General Records of the Department of Commerce, Subgroup: Records of the Office of Technical Services, Series: Industrial Research and Development Division Subject File, 1944–1948, Box 65, National Archives II, College Park, MD.

Record Group 54, Subgroup: Division of Forage Crops and Diseases, Series: Correspondence with State Agricultural Experiment Stations, 1899–1928, Boxes 10–12: Idaho-Illinois to Illinois-Indiana, National Archives II, College Park, MD.

Record Group 54, Subgroup: Division of Forage Crops and Diseases, Series: General Correspondence, 1905–29, Boxes 92–93: Morgan-Morse to Morse-Napier, National Archives II, College Park, MD.

Record Group 59, Textual Records from the Department of State, M329, Roll 183, 893.61321/6a and 893.61321/7, National Archives II, College Park, MD.

Record Group 88, Records of the Food and Drug Administration, Subgroup: Records of the Bureau of Chemistry, 1877–1943, Series: World War I Project File, 1917–19, National Archives II, College Park, MD.

New York Public Library

E. J. Kahn Papers, Box 14, Subject File: Andreas, Dwayne, Articles and Speeches, New York Public Library Manuscripts and Archives Division, New York.

University of California, Berkeley

Camouflage Net Factory, Reels 256–257, *Japanese-American Evacuation and Resettlement Records, 1930–1974 (bulk 1942–1946)*, BANC MSS 67/14 c, Bancroft Library, University of California, Berkeley.

"Community Government Closing Report," 1945, Topaz Final Reports, Folder 9 of 15, Reels 14–17, *Records of the War Relocation Authority, 1942–1946: Field Basic Documentation*, BANC FILM 1932, Bancroft Library, University of California, Berkeley.

Lawson, Grace. "The Dietary Department," 15 August 1945, Gila River Final Reports, Folder 22 of 31, Reels 40–43, *Records of the War Relocation Authority, 1942–1946: Field Basic Documentation*, BANC FILM 1932, Bancroft Library, University of California, Berkeley.

Martin, Hoyt. "Industry: Final Report, Historical," 1 May 1945, Gila River Final Reports, Folder 29 of 31, Reels 40–43, *Records of the War Relocation Authority, 1942–1946: Field Basic Documentation*, BANC FILM 1932, Bancroft Library, University of California, Berkeley.

University of Illinois

William L. Burlison Papers, 1888–1968, Series 8/6/22, University of Illinois Archives, Urbana, IL.

University of Illinois at Chicago

Archives of the Chicago Board of Trade, Daley Library Special Collections, University of Illinois at Chicago.

Searchable Online Archives

Cornell Home Economics Archive (HEARTH), hearth.library.cornell.edu.

Densho Digital Archive. "Camp Newspaper Collections." archive.densho.org/main.aspx.

SOYINFOCENTER. The entire website is a searchable archive unto itself, as are the bibliographies and source books on numerous topics, all in searchable PDF form. www.soyinfocenter.com.

University of California's Calisphere contains many entries on Japanese internment camps. calisphere.org.

USDA Agricultural Research Service. "Germplasm Resource Information Network (GRIN): National Plant Germplasm System (NPGS)." www.ars-grin.gov/npgs.

Books, Chapters, and Articles

Boyer, R. A. "How Soybeans Help Make Ford," 6–9. In *Proceedings, Eighteenth Annual Meeting of the American Soybean Association.* 12–14 September 1938 at Wooster and Columbus, Ohio.

Bradley, Theodore F. "Nonedible Soybean Oil Products," 853–890. In Klare S. Markley, ed., *Soybeans and Soybean Products,* vol. 2. Fats and Oils: A Series of Monographs. New York: Interscience Publishers Ltd., 1951.

Burnett, R. S. "Soybean Protein Industrial Products," 1003–1053. In Klare S. Markley, ed., *Soybeans and Soybean Products,* vol. 2. Fats and Oils: A Series of Monographs. New York: Interscience Publishers Ltd., 1951.

Carriker, Roy R., and Raymond M. Leuthold. *Some Economic Considerations of Soy Protein-Meat Mixtures.* AE-4398. Urbana, IL: Department of Agricultural Economics, University of Illinois at Urbana-Champaign, March 1976.

Cordle, Christopher. "Soy Protein Allergy: Incidence and Relative Severity." *Journal of Nutrition* 134 (2004): 1213S–1219S.

Cowan, J. C. "Key Factors and Recent Advances in the Flavor Stability of Soybean Oil." *Journal of the American Oil Chemists' Society* 43 (July 1966): 300A–302A, 318A.

Crompton, Mabel P. "The Soybean Crop of Illinois." *Journal of Geography* 39 (April 1940): 142–150.

Daniel, Kaayla. *The Whole Soy Story: The Dark Side of America's Favorite Health Food.* Washington, DC: New Trends Publishing, 2005.

Desquilbet, Marion, and David S. Bullock. "Who Pays the Costs of Non-GMO Segregation and Identity Preservation?" *American Journal of Agricultural Economics* 91 (August 2009): 656–672.

Dies, Edward Jerome. *Soybeans: Gold from the Soil.* New York: Macmillan, 1942.

Dutton, H. J. "History of the Development of Soy Oil for Edible Use." *Journal of the American Oil Chemists' Society* 58 (March 1981): 234–236.

Fornari, Harry D. "The Big Change: Cotton to Soybeans." *Agricultural History* 53 (January 1979): 245–253.

Foucard, T., and I. Malmheden Yman. "A Study on Severe Food Reactions in Sweden— Is Soy Protein an Underestimated Cause of Food Anaphylaxis?" *Allergy* 54 (March 1999): 261–265.

Fucini, Joseph, and Suzy Fucini. *Experience, Inc.: Men and Women Who Founded Famous Companies after the Age of 40.* New York: The Free Press, 1987.

Goldberg, Ray A. *Agribusiness Coordination: A Systems Approach to the Wheat, Soybean, and Florida Orange Economies.* Boston: Graduate School of Business Administration, Harvard University, 1968.

Hartwig, Edgar E. "Soybean Varietal Development 1928–1978," 2–10. In *Fifty Years with Soybeans*, a compilation of invited papers presented during the Advisory Board meeting of the National Soybean Crop Improvement Council, Hilton Head, South Carolina, 26–28 August 1979.

———. "Varietal Development," 187–210. In *Soybeans: Improvement, Production, and Uses*, ed. B. E. Caldwell. Madison, WI: American Society of Agronomy, 1973.

Hirahara, Naomi. *Distinguished Asian American Business Leaders.* Westport, CT: Greenwood Press, 2003.

Ho, Ping-Ti. "The Loess and the Origin of Chinese Agriculture." *American Historical Review* 75 (October 1969): 1–36.

Houch, James P. "Domestic Markets," 589–618. In *Soybeans: Improvement, Production, and Uses*, ed. B. E. Caldwell. Madison, WI: American Society of Agronomy, 1973.

Houck, James P., Mary E. Ryan, and Abraham Subotnik. *Soybeans and Their Products: Markets, Models, and Policy.* Minneapolis: University of Minnesota Press, 1972.

Hymowitz, Theodore. "Dorsett-Morse Soybean Collection Trip to East Asia: Fifty Year Retrospective." *Economic Botany* 38 (October–December 1984): 378–388.

———. "Introduction of the Soybean to Illinois." *Economic Botany* 41:1 (1987): 28–32.

———. "Soybeans," 159–162. In *Evolution of Crop Plants*, ed. N. W. Simmonds. New York: Longman, 1976.

Hymowitz, Theodore, and J. R. Harlan. "Introduction of the Soybean to North America by Samuel Bowen in 1765." *Economic Botany* 37 (December 1983): 371–179.

Markley, Klare S., and Warren H. Goss. *Soybean Chemistry and Technology.* Brooklyn, NY: Chemical Publishing Company, 1944.

Mayer, I. D. "Harvesting Soybeans with the Combine," 21–22. In *Proceedings of the American Soybean Association*, vol. 2, 1928, 1929. N.p.: American Soybean Association, 1930.

McBride, W. D., and Catherine Greene. "The Profitability of Organic Soybean Production." *Renewable Agriculture and Food Systems* 24 (2009): 276–284.

Messina, Mark. "Insights Gained from 20 Years of Soy Research." *Journal of Nutrition* 140 (2010): 2289S–2295S.

Mounts, T. J., W. J. Wolf, and W. H. Martinez. "Processing and Utilization," 819–866. In *Soybeans: Improvement, Production, and Uses*, 2nd ed., ed. J. R. Wilcox. Madison, WI: American Society of Agronomy, 1987.

National Academy of Sciences. National Research Council, Division of Biology and Agriculture. *Genetic Vulnerability of Major Crops*. Washington, DC: National Academy of Sciences, 1972.

Oki, Kazuhisa. *U.S. Food Export Controls Policy: Three Cases from 1973 to 1981*. USJP Occasional Paper 08-13. Cambridge, MA: Harvard University Program on US-Japan Relations, 2008.

Orthoefer, F. T. "Processing and Utilization," 219–246. In *Soybean Physiology, Agronomy, and Utilization*, ed. A. Geoffrey Norman. New York: Academic Press, 1978.

Ostrander, W. A. "It's Fun to Remember." *Soybean Digest* 4 (September 1944): 16–17.

Parrot, Wayne A., and Thomas E. Clemente. "Transgenic Soybean," 265–302. In *Soybeans: Improvement, Production, and Uses*, 3rd ed. Madison, WI: American Society of Agronomy, 2004.

Pendleton, P. W., and Edgar E. Hartwig. "Management," 211–238. In *Soybeans: Improvement, Production, and Uses*, ed. B. E. Caldwell, 353–390. Madison, WI: American Society of Agronomy, 1973.

Probst, A. H., and R. W. Judd. "Origin, U.S. History and Development, and World Distribution," 1–16. In *Soybeans: Improvement, Production, and Uses*, ed. B. E. Caldwell. Madison, WI: American Society of Agronomy, 1973.

Ralston, Brian. "Soy Protein Plastics: Material Formulation, Processing, and Properties." PhD diss., University of Wisconsin–Madison, 2008.

Reigel, W. E. "Protecting the American Soybean Market," 49–51. In *Proceedings of the Sixteenth Annual Meeting of the American Soybean Association*. N.p.: American Soybean Association, 1936.

Ross, R. C. "Cost of Growing and Harvesting Soybeans in Illinois," 46–56. In *Proceedings of the American Soybean Association*, vol. 3, 1930. N.p.: American Soybean Association, 1931.

Scott, Walter O. "Cooperative Extension Efforts in Soybeans," 64–67. In *50 Years with Soybeans*, ed. R. W. Judd. Urbana, IL: National Soybean Crop Improvement Council, 1979.

Shaw, Wilfred. "Commercial Prospects of Soybeans," 28–33. In *Proceedings of the American Soybean Association*, vol. 2, 1928, 1929. N.p.: American Soybean Association, 1930.

Shurtleff, William, and Akiko Aoyagi. *The Book of Tempeh: The Delicious, Cholesterol-Free Protein*, 2nd ed. New York: Harper Colophon Books, 1985.

———. *The Book of Tofu: Protein Source of the Future . . . Now!* Vol. 1. Berkeley, CA: Ten Speed Press, 1983.

———. *The Soyfoods Industry and Market: Directory and Databook*, 5th ed. Lafayette, CA: Soyfoods Center, 1985.

———. *Soymilk Industry and Market*. Lafayette, CA: Soyfoods Center, 1984.

Smith, Keith, and Wipada Huyser. "World Distribution and Significance of Soybeans," 1–22. In *Soybeans: Improvement, Production, and Uses*, 2nd ed. Madison, WI: American Society of Agronomy, 1987.

Snyder, Harry, and T. W. Kwon. *Soybean Utilization*. New York: Van Nostrand Reinhold Company, 1987.

Soyfoods Association of North America (SANA). "Sales by Product Type, 1996–2011" [graph]. Last modified 2011. www.soyfoods.org/wp-content/uploads/SANA-sales-data-1996-2011-for-web.pdf.

Ujj, Orsolya. "European and American Views on Genetically Modified Foods." *The New Atlantis* 49 (Spring/Summer 2016): 77–92.

Upchurch, Woody. "Soybean Industry Builds on Foundation Laid by Tar Heel Farmers, Businessmen." [Lumberton, NC] *Robesonian*, 23 December 1967, 5.

US Department of Agriculture, Bureau of Agricultural Economics. *Soybean Production in War and Peace*, by Edwin G. Strand. Washington, DC: Government Printing Office, September 1943.

———. *Soybeans in American Farming*, by Edwin G. Strand. Technical Bulletin No. 966. Washington, DC: Government Printing Office, November 1948.

US Department of Agriculture, Farm Cooperative Service. *Edible Soy Protein: Operational Aspects of Producing and Marketing*. FCS Research Report 33. Washington, DC: Government Printing Office, January 1976.

Vest, Grant, D. F. Weber, and C. Sloger. "Nodulation and Nitrogen Fixation," 353–390. In *Soybeans: Improvement, Production, and Uses*, ed. B. E. Caldwell. Madison, WI: American Society of Agronomy, 1973.

Wand, Frederick A. "Commercial Outlet for Soybeans," 35–36. In *Proceedings of the American Soybean Association*, vol. 2, 1928, 1929. American Soybean Association: 1930.

———. (As F. A. Wand.) "Relation between the Soybean Grower and the Oil Mill," 104–106. In *Proceedings of the American Soybean Association*, vol. 1, 1925, 1926, 1927. N.p.: American Soybean Association, 1928.

Warren, Forest Glen. "Economic Significance of the Futures Market for Soybeans." PhD diss., University of Illinois, 1945.

Willis, Carol. *Form Follows Finance: Skyscrapers and Skylines in New York and Chicago*. New York: Princeton Architectural Press, 1995.

Young, E. C. "The Proper Place for Soybeans in the System of Farming," 19–21. In *Proceedings of the American Soybean Association*, vol. 2, 1928, 1929. N.p.: American Soybean Association, 1930.

Index

Village Enterprises, 205
vitalism, 23, 24
vitamins, 12, 112, 130, 137, 158
Vitasoy, 244

Wahlforss, Eric, 297n86
Wall Street Journal, 99, 174, 193
Wand, Frederick, 76, 77
Wang, Jeffrey, 275n13
Wannamaker, John E., 165
War Department, Japanese internment camps
    and, 139
War Food Administration (WFA), 124, 125,
    131, 132
War Production Board, 123, 124, 125
War Relocation Authority (WRA), 138, 139,
    140, 142, 143
Warren, Earl, 213
Washburn, Kenneth, 128
Washington Post, 198, 229, 230
Washington Sanitarium, 60, 109, 113
Water Cure movement, 23
Watergate scandal, 198–199
WAVES, 136
Webber, Perry, 110
Wedge Food Co-op, 217
Weight Watchers, 235
Wessling, Hannah L., 55
Wesson, Maurice, 81
Western Health Institute, 23
Weston A. Price Foundation, 264
WFA. *See* War Food Administration
"What Is Tempeh?" (Bates), 217
wheat, 1, 42, 100, 187; futures, 102
"When Is Ketchup a Vegetable?" (*Washington
    Post*), 229
"When Tofu Is Meat" (*Washington Post*), 229
White, Ellen, 23, 24–25
Whitehall, Jean, 156
White Wave Foods, 231, 232, 239, 245

Whole Life Times (Medoff), 236
*Whole Soy Story: The Dark Side of America's
    Favorite Health Food, The* (Daniel), 264
Willemse, Jan, 117, 300n159
William O. Goodrich Company, 83
Williams, C. B., 45–46, 47
Williams, Leonard, 165
Wilson, James, 27
Wisconsin Department of Agriculture, 159
"Woman Off to China as Government Agent
    to Study Soy Bean: Dr. Kin Will Make
    Report for United States on the Most
    Useful Food of Her Native Land" (*New
    York Times Magazine*), 56
Women's Health Initiative (WHI), 265
Women's Medical College, 56
Women's Reserve, 136
Woodward, Patricia, 130, 131, 134
Woodworth, C. M., 70, 163
wool, soybean, 105
World Health Organization (WHO), 202, 259
World Trade Organization (WTO), 254, 257
World War I, 5, 45, 60, 70, 91; soybeans and,
    6, 8, 9, 42, 126
World War II, 49, 117, 144, 221; soybeans and,
    6, 8, 9, 10, 121, 126, 145
Worthington Foods, 192, 194
WRA. *See* War Relocation Authority

Yamaguchi, Ben, 141, 143
Yamauchi, Shoan, 144, 221, 237, 275n6
Yamauchi, Shojin, 221
Yamauchi, Shokin, 15
Yamauchi, Tsuru Kamigawa, 15, 22, 29, 144,
    215, 221; tofu and, 16, 17
Yay Soybeans (Bates), 207
Yearbook of Agriculture (USDA), 46
yogurt, 202, 230, 231, 232, 233, 237, 239
yuba, 26, 59, 108, 109
Yum (Madison Foods), 110